MIDORI DAYS

STORY AND ART BY KAZUROU INOUE

MIDORI DAYS
Action Edition
Volume 4

STORY AND ART BY KAZUROU INOUE

Translation/JN Productions
Touch-up Art & Lettering/James Gaubatz
Cover and Interior Design/Izumi Evers
Editor/Joel Enos

Managing Editor/Annette Roman
Director of Production/Noboru Watanabe
Vice President of Publishing/Alvin Lu
Sr. Director of Acquisitions/Rika Inouye
Vice President of Sales and Marketing/Liza Coppola
Publisher/Hyoe Narita

Printed in the U.S.A.

Published by VIZ Media, LLC
P.O. Box 77010
San Francisco, CA 94107

10 9 8 7 6 5 4 3 2 1
First printing, January 2006

www.viz.com
store.viz.com

Story Thus Far

Lonely Seiji Sawamura spends his high school days in quiet agony. He covers it up with a tough guy exterior that earns him a hot-shot reputation as a bully, but still wins him absolutely no points with the ladies.

Enter painfully shy Midori Kasugano. She's admired Seiji from afar for years until one strange day her dream of being a part of him comes true – only it's not exactly what she had hoped for.

While her real body remains in a coma, a smaller version of Midori appears on Seiji's right hand .

Whether he likes it or not, Seiji's not alone anymore. Now he's got a girlfriend who is literally his right-hand gal.

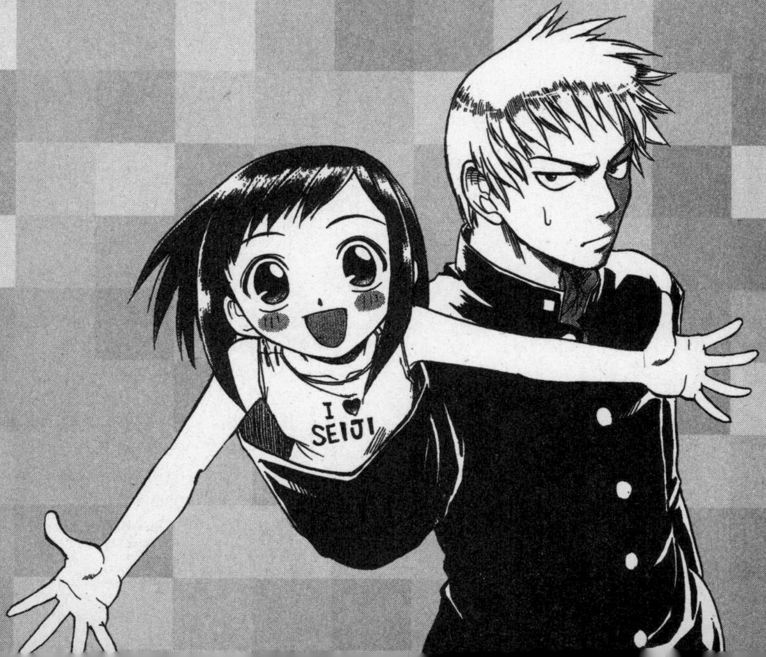
I ♥ SEIJI

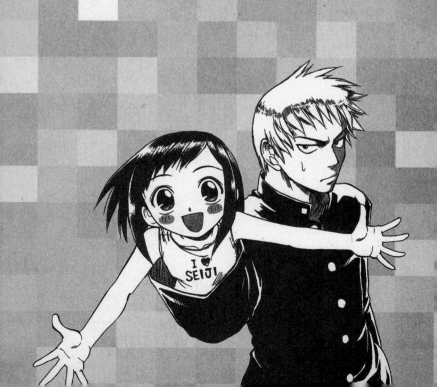

美鳥の日々 Meet The ●●●● Characters

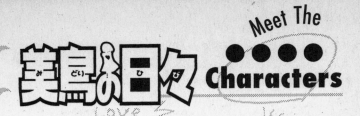

Midori Kasugano

A first-year at Ogura Bashi High School. One day she woke up attached to the right hand of Sawamura, a boy she's had a crush on since middle school. Delighted, she now attends to his every need and showers him with love, whether he wants it or not. Her real body is at home – in a coma.

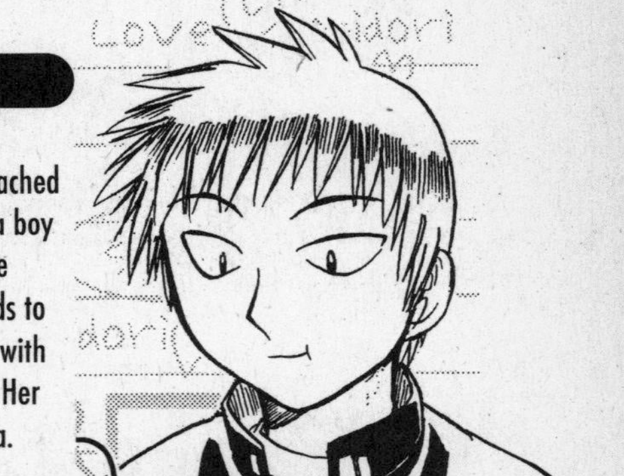

Ayase Takako

She's a tough one. A good girl, naïve and full of spirit, which sometimes is not the best combination, she started out enemies with Sawamura. But after seeing the softer side he tries so hard to hide, she actually kind of likes him. Slowly but surely, she's making her feelings known.

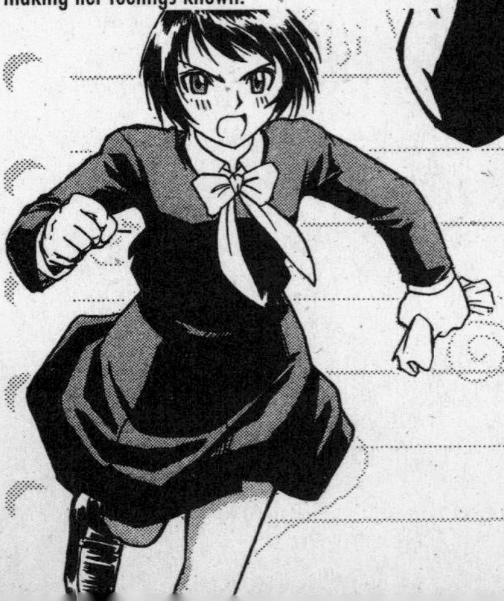

Seiji Sawamura

A second-year at Sakurada Mon High School. His "devil's right hand" is legendary, but his reputation as a bully keeps the girls at bay. Wishing for a girlfriend was one thing; having her appear as a love struck school-girl attached to his right hand is quite another.

Volume. 4

Kota Shingyoji
Midori's best friend in the real world who has a little secret of his own.

Osamu Miyahara
An underclassman who looks up to Sawamura. Only lately, he's been showing himself to be more than just Seiji's number one henchman.

Rin Sawamura
Sawamura's 21-year-old sister. Her demure looks are deceiving. She used to run a gang and is even more of a bully than Seiji.

Shiro Makinoha
Nao's father investigates the paranormal and wants to chop Midori off Seiji's arm so he can study her.

Nao Makinoha
Shiro's spooky daughter is utterly fascinated now that she knows about Midori.

Shuichi Takamizawa
An action-figure freak who is constantly hounding Seiji. He'd love nothing more than his own Midori, which is why Seiji must keep her extra well-hidden from him.

Contents

Volume 4

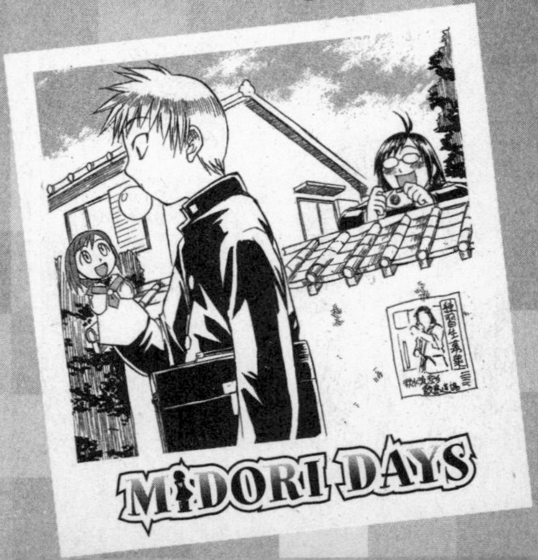

MIDORI DAYS

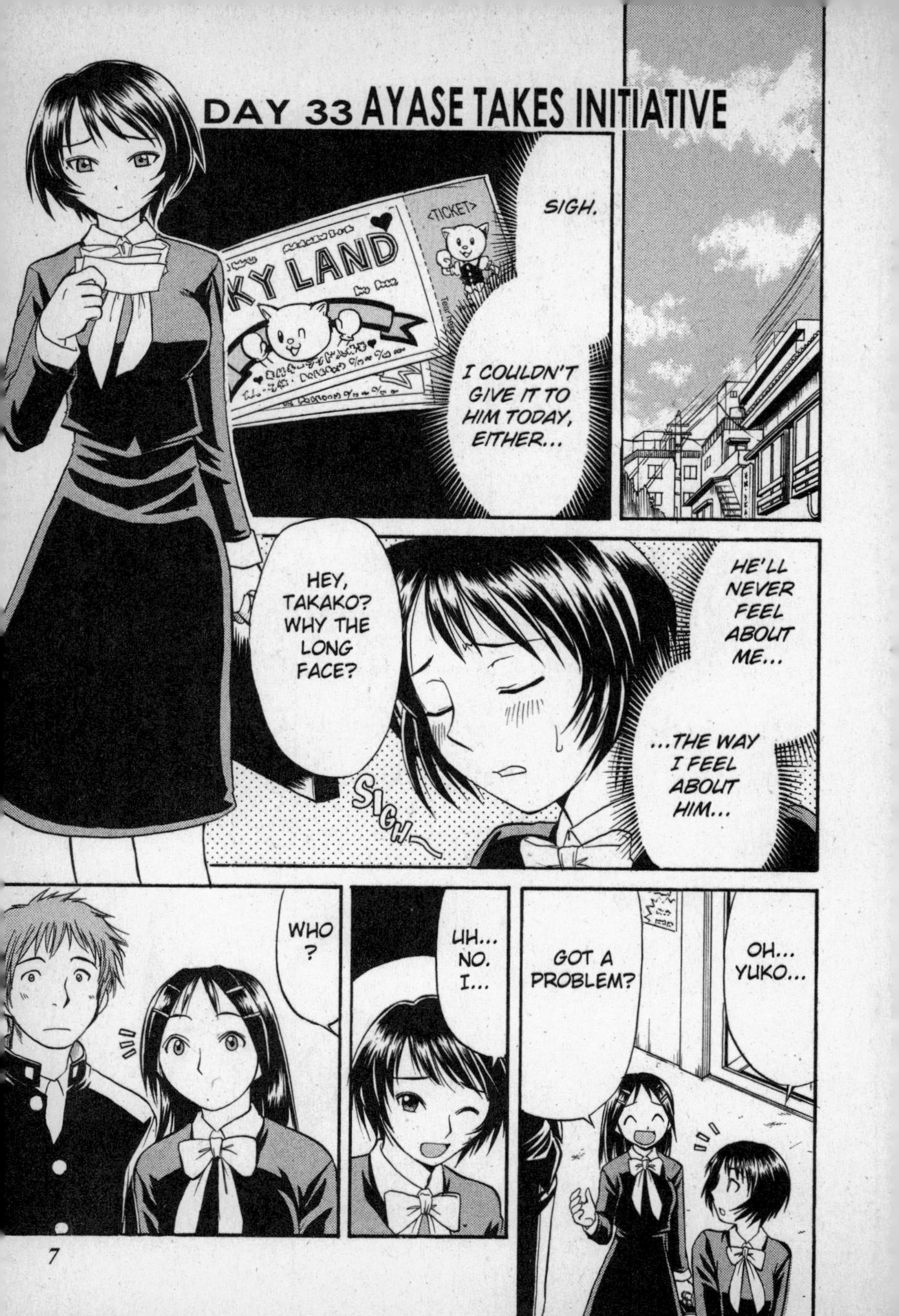
DAY 33 AYASE TAKES INITIATIVE
SIGH.
I COULDN'T GIVE IT TO HIM TODAY, EITHER...
<TICKET>
KY LAND
HE'LL NEVER FEEL ABOUT ME...
...THE WAY I FEEL ABOUT HIM...
SIGH
HEY, TAKAKO? WHY THE LONG FACE?
OH... YUKO...
GOT A PROBLEM?
UH... NO. I...
WHO ?

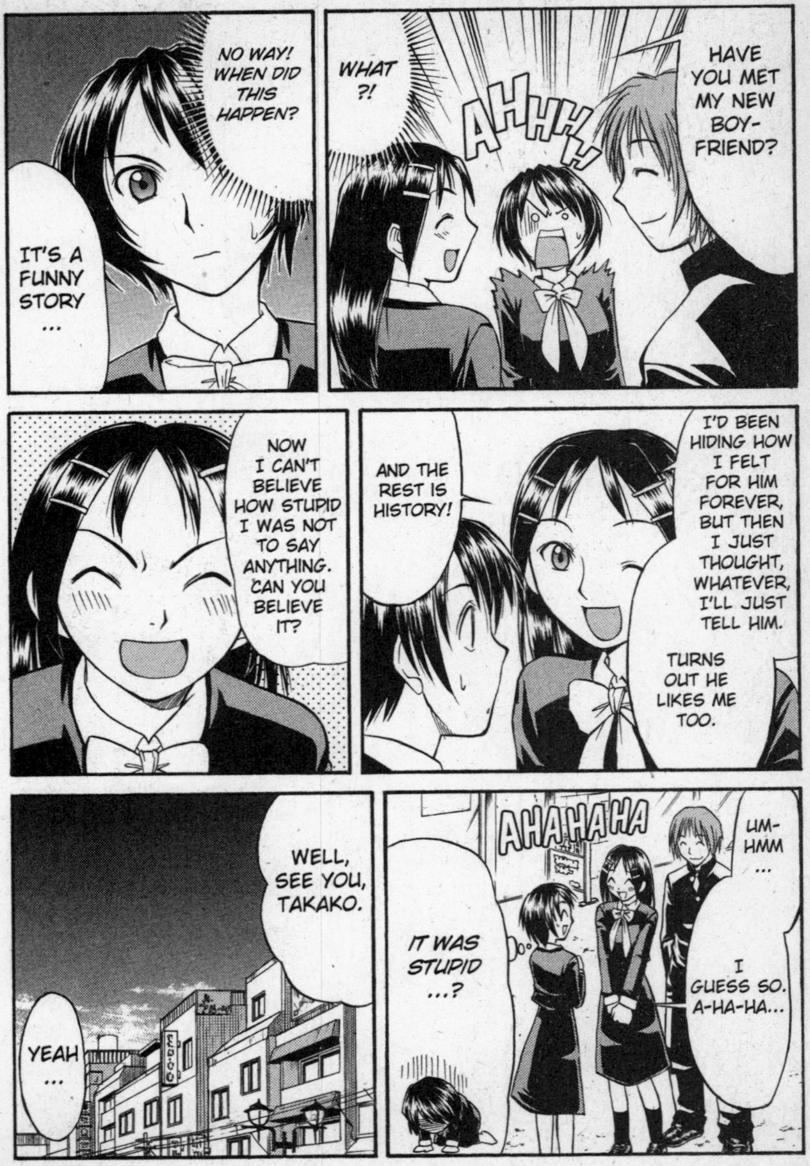
HAVE YOU MET MY NEW BOY-FRIEND?
AHHHH
WHAT ?!
NO WAY! WHEN DID THIS HAPPEN?
IT'S A FUNNY STORY ...
I'D BEEN HIDING HOW I FELT FOR HIM FOREVER, BUT THEN I JUST THOUGHT, WHATEVER, I'LL JUST TELL HIM.
TURNS OUT HE LIKES ME TOO.
AND THE REST IS HISTORY!
NOW I CAN'T BELIEVE HOW STUPID I WAS NOT TO SAY ANYTHING. CAN YOU BELIEVE IT?
UM-HMM ...
AHAHAHA
I GUESS SO. A-HA-HA...
IT WAS STUPID ...?
WELL, SEE YOU, TAKAKO.
YEAH ...

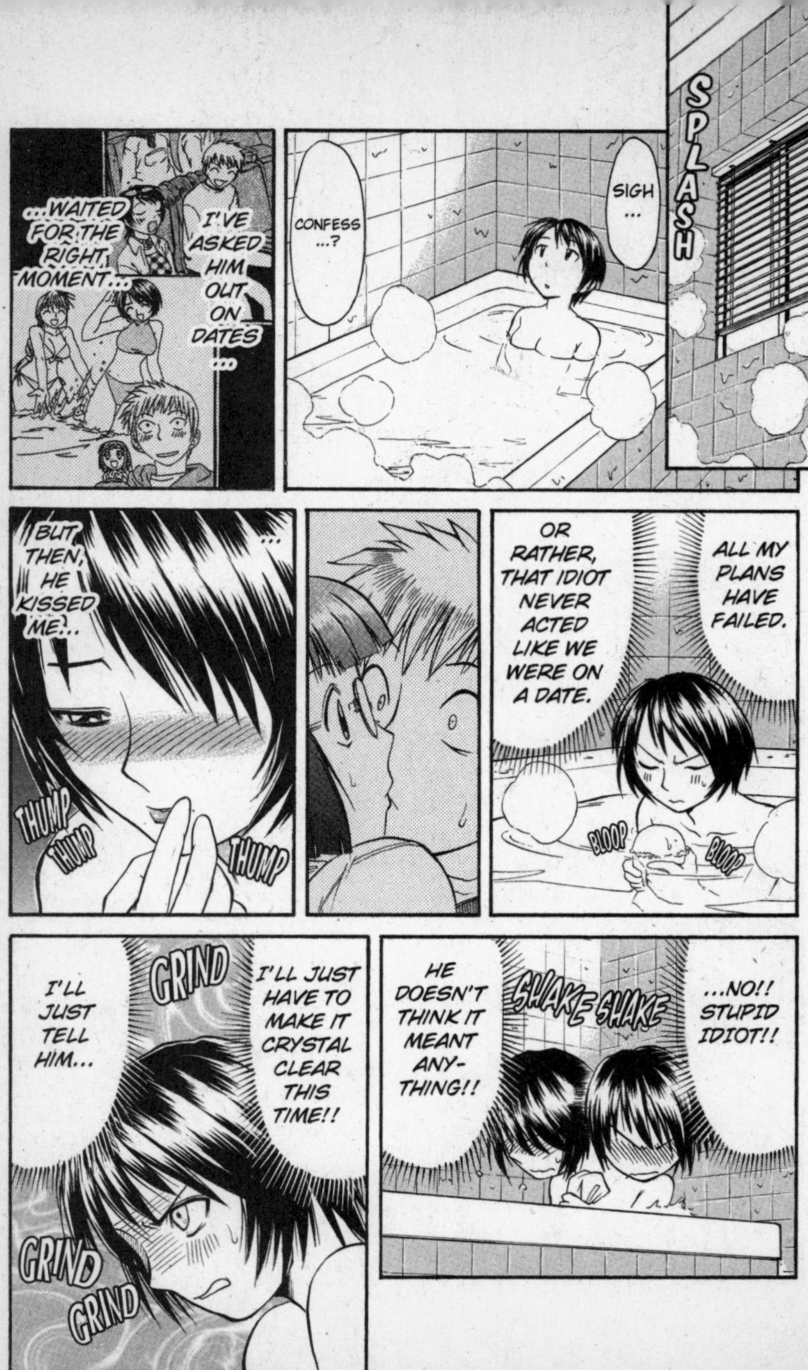
SPLASH
SIGH...
CONFESS...?
I'VE ASKED HIM OUT ON DATES...
...WAITED FOR THE RIGHT MOMENT...
ALL MY PLANS HAVE FAILED.
OR RATHER, THAT IDIOT NEVER ACTED LIKE WE WERE ON A DATE.
BLOOP
BLOOP
...
BUT THEN, HE KISSED ME...
THUMP
THUMP
THUMP
...NO!! STUPID IDIOT!!
SHAKE SHAKE
HE DOESN'T THINK IT MEANT ANYTHING!!
I'LL JUST HAVE TO MAKE IT CRYSTAL CLEAR THIS TIME!!
GRIND
I'LL JUST TELL HIM...
GRIND
GRIND
GRIND

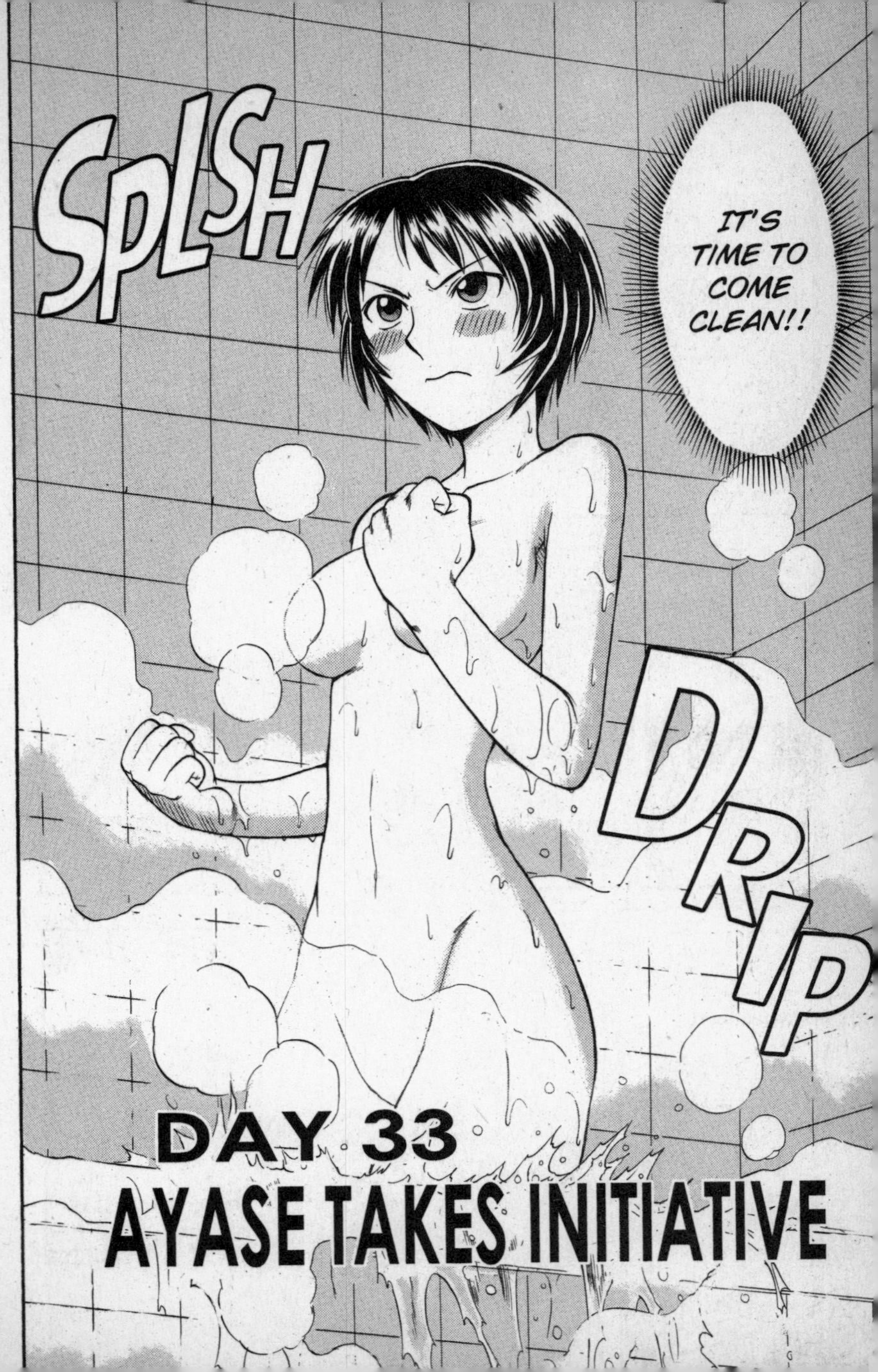
SPLSH
IT'S TIME TO COME CLEAN!!
DRIP
DAY 33
AYASE TAKES INITIATIVE

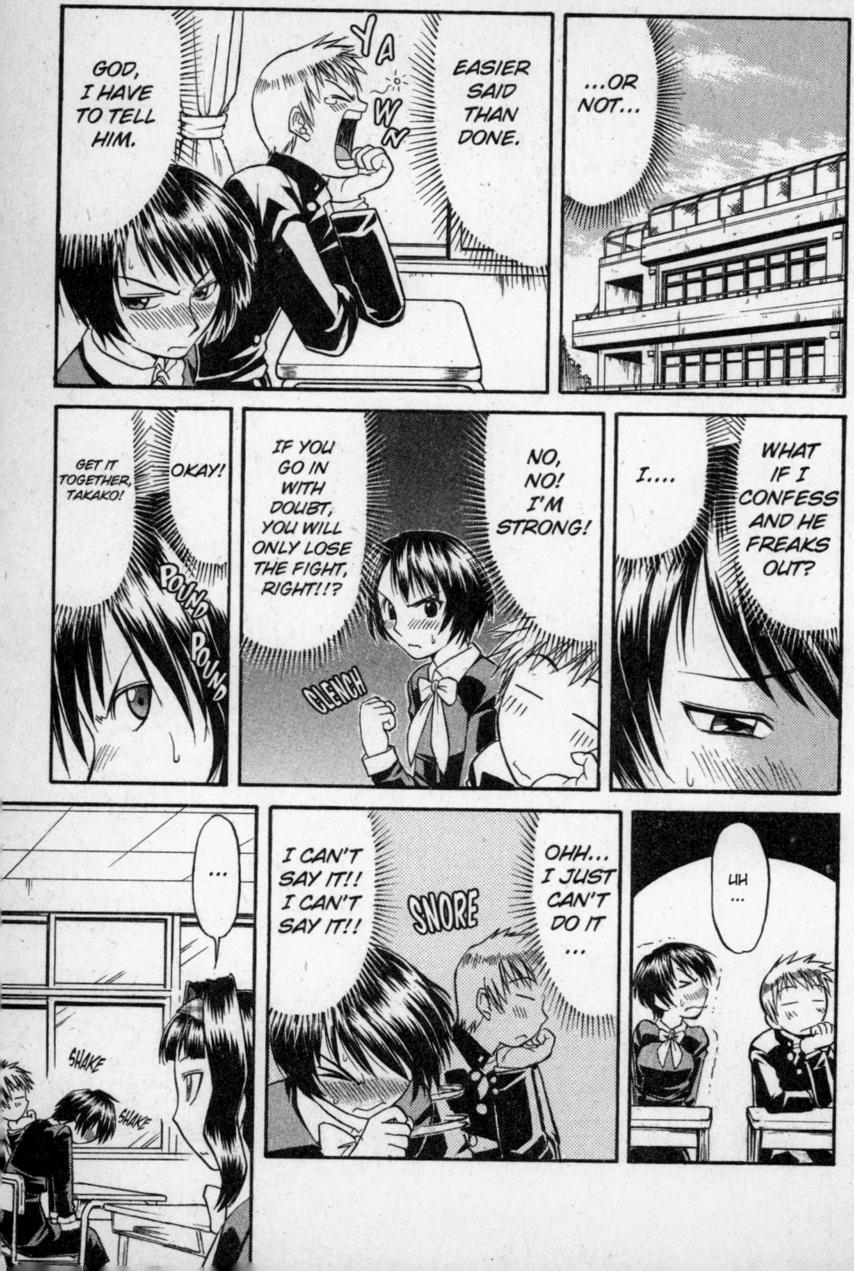
...OR NOT...
EASIER SAID THAN DONE.
YAWN
GOD, I HAVE TO TELL HIM.
WHAT IF I CONFESS AND HE FREAKS OUT?
I....
NO, NO! I'M STRONG!
IF YOU GO IN WITH DOUBT, YOU WILL ONLY LOSE THE FIGHT, RIGHT!!?
CLENCH
OKAY!
GET IT TOGETHER, TAKAKO!
POUND
POUND
UH ...
OHH... I JUST CAN'T DO IT ...
SNORE
I CAN'T SAY IT!! I CAN'T SAY IT!!
...
SHAKE
SHAKE

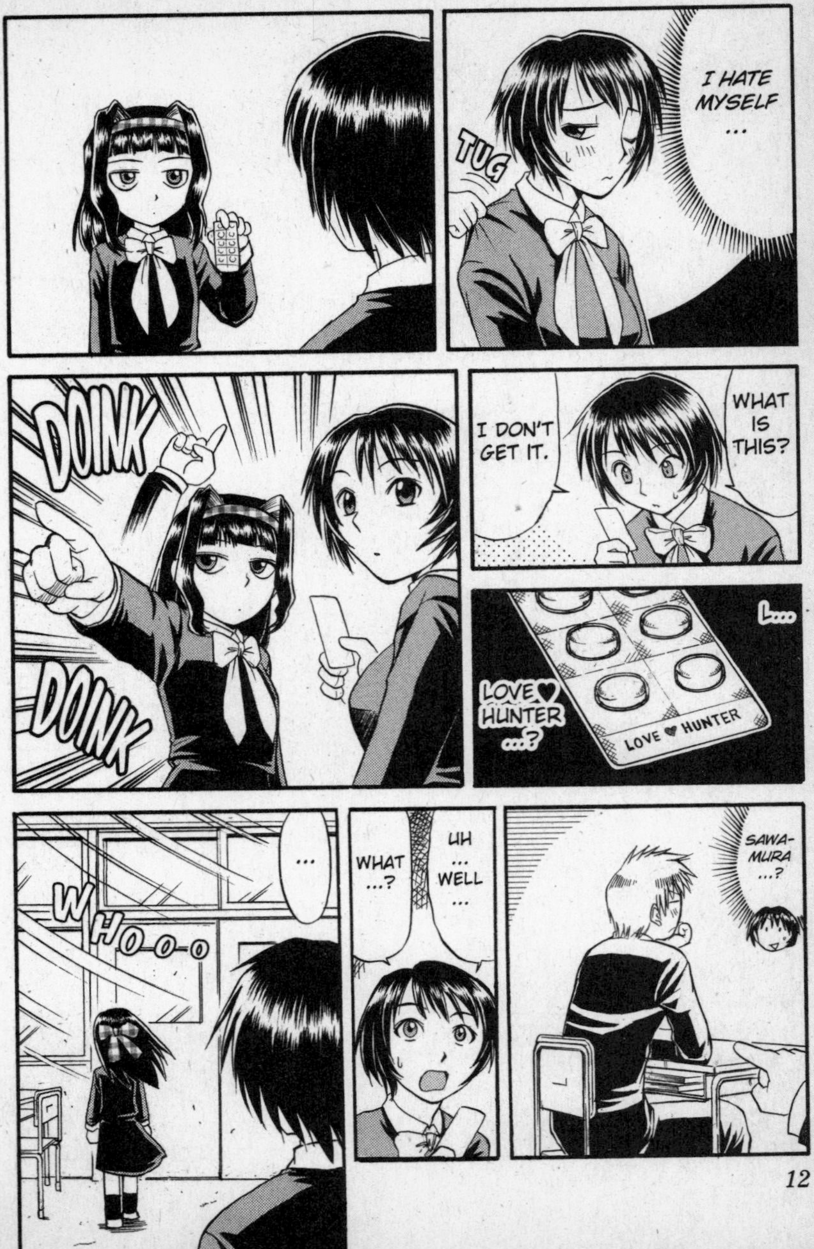
TUG
I HATE MYSELF ...
WHAT IS THIS?
I DON'T GET IT.
L...
LOVE♥ HUNTER ...?
LOVE ♥ HUNTER
DOINK
DOINK
SAWA-MURA ...?
UH ... WELL ...
WHAT ...?
...
WHOOOO

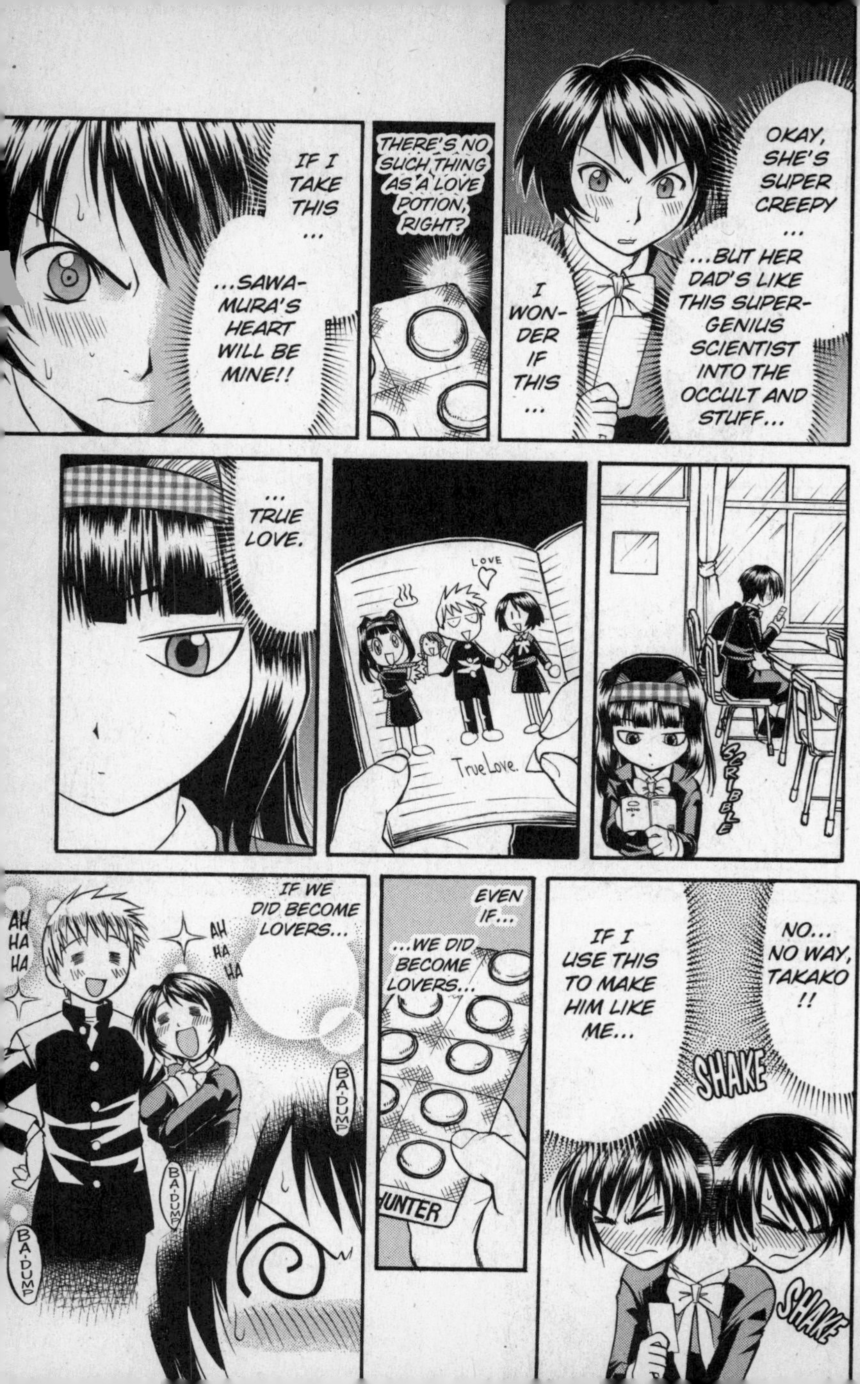
OKAY, SHE'S SUPER CREEPY ...
...BUT HER DAD'S LIKE THIS SUPER-GENIUS SCIENTIST INTO THE OCCULT AND STUFF...
I WONDER IF THIS ...
THERE'S NO SUCH THING AS A LOVE POTION, RIGHT?
IF I TAKE THIS ...
...SAWAMURA'S HEART WILL BE MINE!!
SCRIBBLE
LOVE
True Love.
... TRUE LOVE.
NO... NO WAY, TAKAKO !!
IF I USE THIS TO MAKE HIM LIKE ME...
SHAKE
SHAKE
EVEN IF...
...WE DID BECOME LOVERS...
HUNTER
IF WE DID BECOME LOVERS...
AH HA HA
AH HA HA
BA-DUMP
BA-DUMP
BA-DUMP

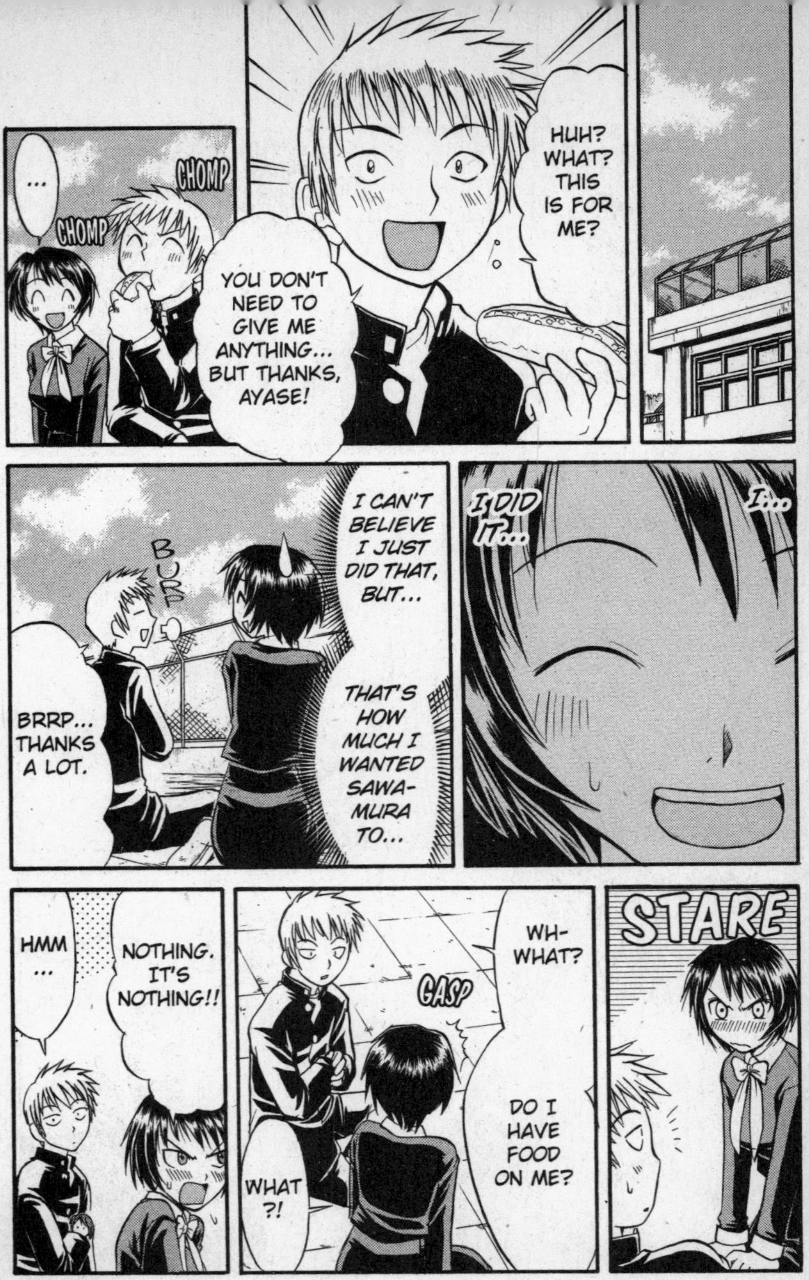
HUH? WHAT? THIS IS FOR ME?
YOU DON'T NEED TO GIVE ME ANYTHING... BUT THANKS, AYASE!
CHOMP
...
CHOMP
I...
I DID IT...
I CAN'T BELIEVE I JUST DID THAT, BUT...
THAT'S HOW MUCH I WANTED SAWAMURA TO...
BURP
BRRP... THANKS A LOT.
STARE
WH-WHAT?
GASP
DO I HAVE FOOD ON ME?
WHAT?!
NOTHING. IT'S NOTHING!!
HMM...

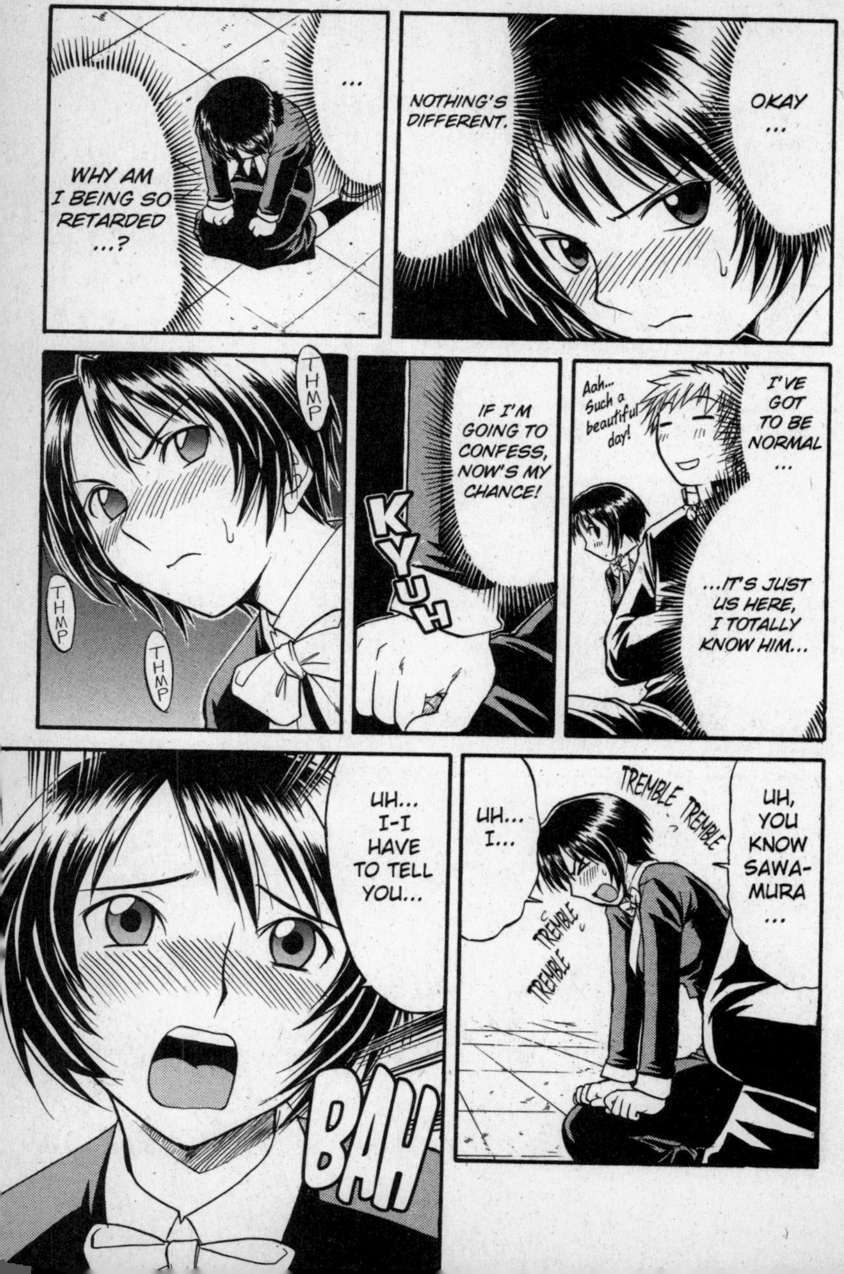
OKAY ...
NOTHING'S DIFFERENT.
...
WHY AM I BEING SO RETARDED ...?
I'VE GOT TO BE NORMAL ...
Aah... Such a beautiful day!
...IT'S JUST US HERE, I TOTALLY KNOW HIM...
IF I'M GOING TO CONFESS, NOW'S MY CHANCE!
KYUH
THMP
THMP
THMP
UH, YOU KNOW SAWAMURA ...
TREMBLE TREMBLE
UH... I...
TREMBLE TREMBLE
UH... I-I HAVE TO TELL YOU...
BAH

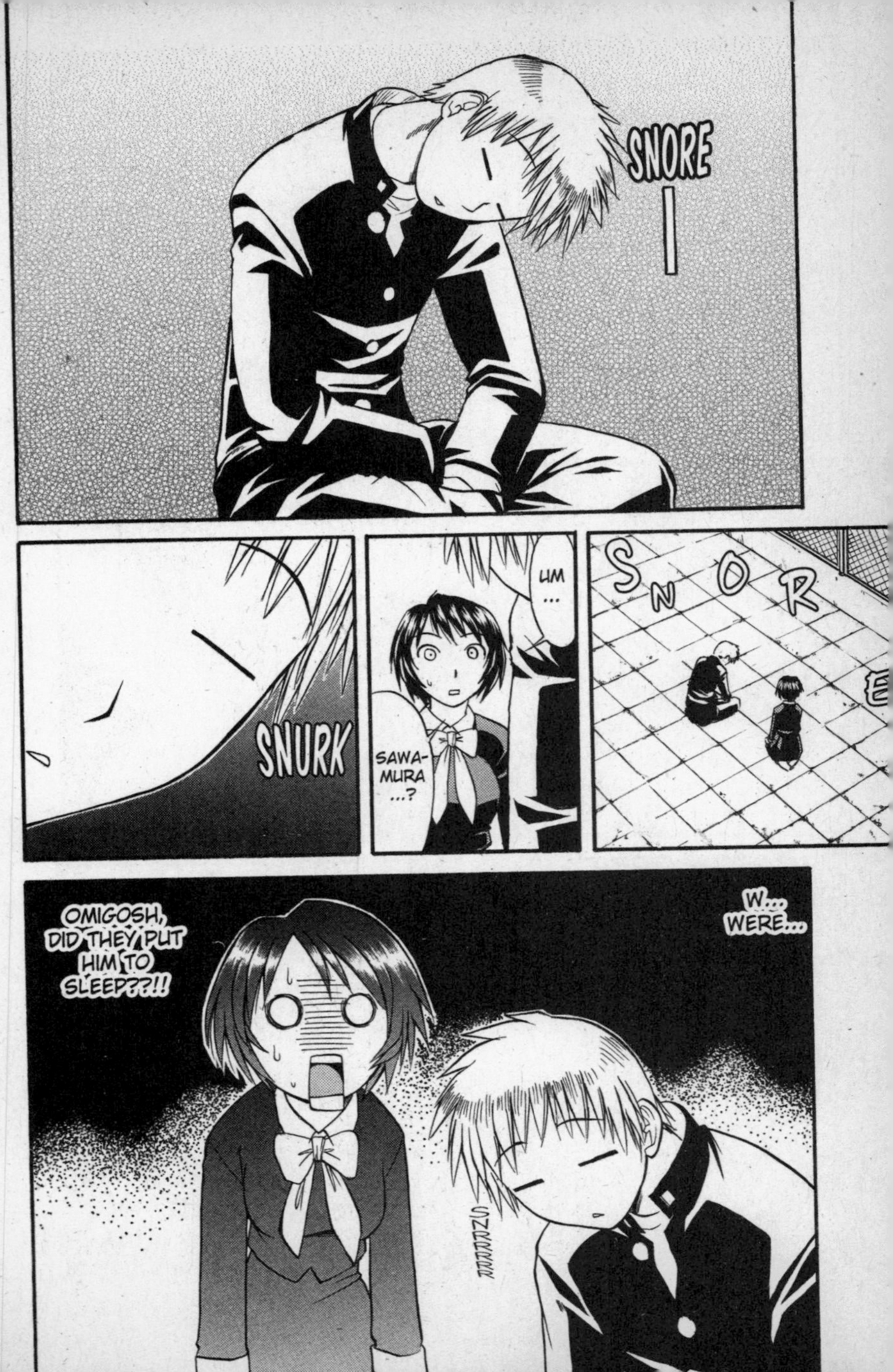
SNORE
SNORE
UM ...
SAWAMURA ...?
SNURK
W... WERE...
OMIGOSH, DID THEY PUT HIM TO SLEEP??!!
SNRRRRR

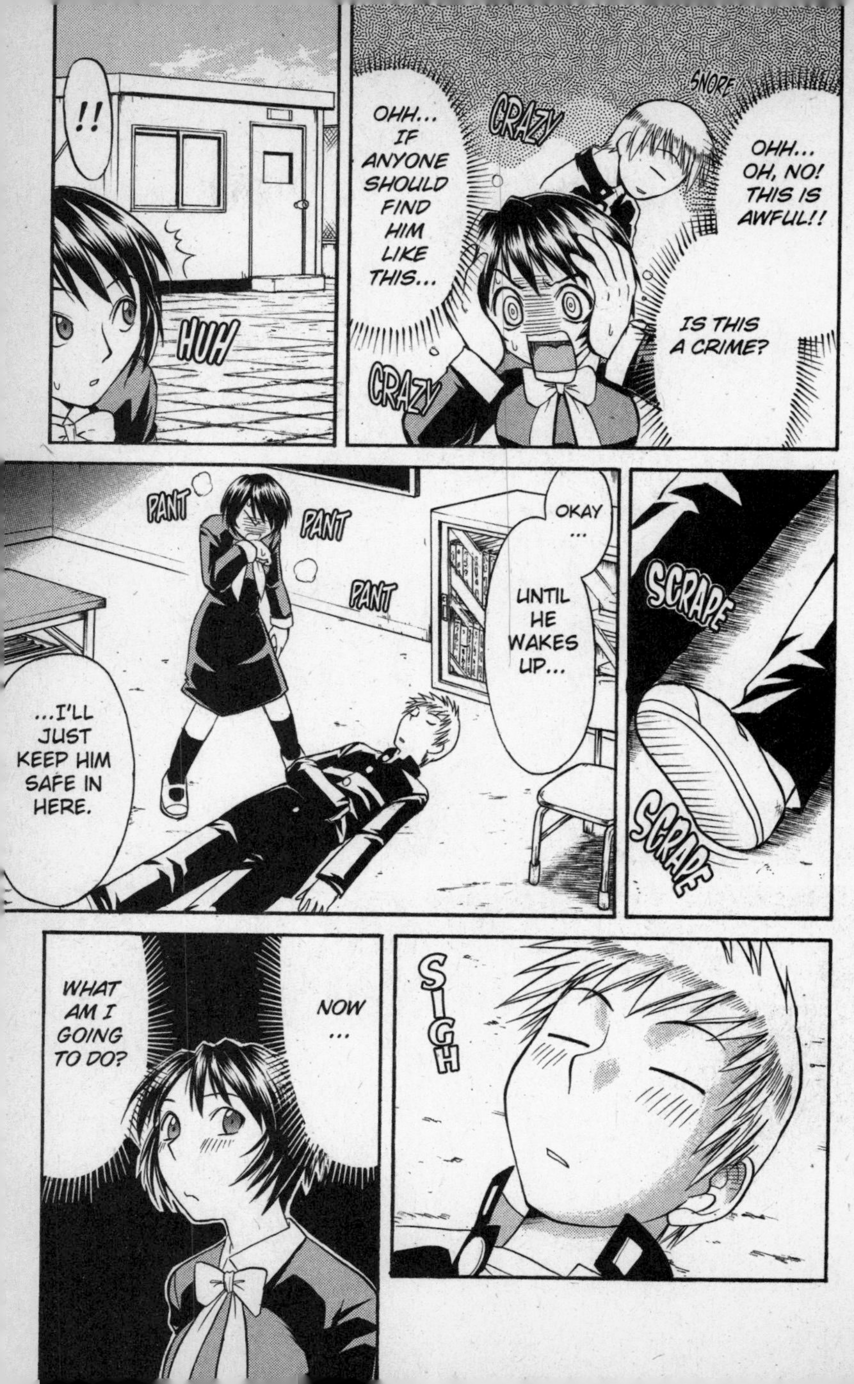
SNORE
OHH... OH, NO! THIS IS AWFUL!!
CRAZY
OHH... IF ANYONE SHOULD FIND HIM LIKE THIS...
IS THIS A CRIME?
CRAZY
!!
HUH
SCRAPE
SCRAPE
OKAY...
UNTIL HE WAKES UP...
PANT
PANT
PANT
...I'LL JUST KEEP HIM SAFE IN HERE.
SIGH
NOW...
WHAT AM I GOING TO DO?

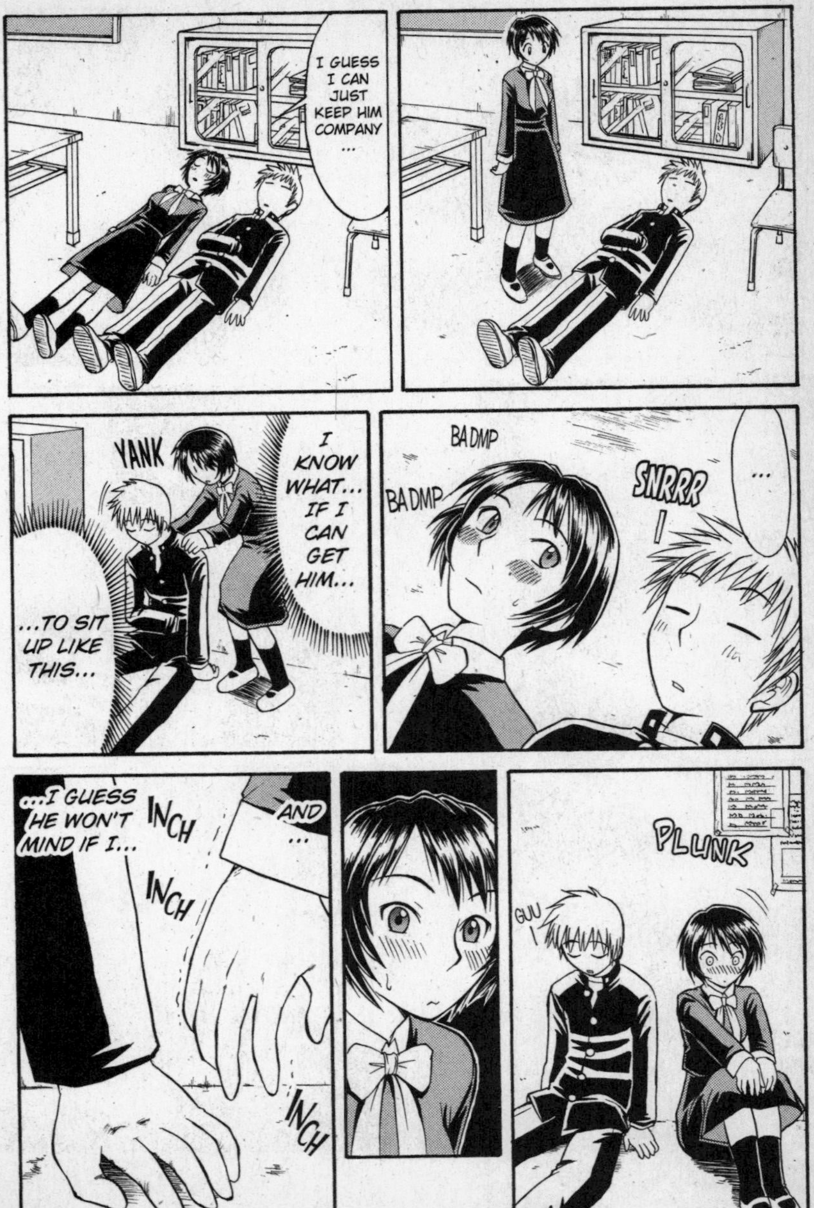
I GUESS I CAN JUST KEEP HIM COMPANY ...
...
SNRRR
BADMP
BADMP
I KNOW WHAT... IF I CAN GET HIM...
YANK
...TO SIT UP LIKE THIS...
PLUNK
GUU
AND ...
...I GUESS HE WON'T MIND IF I...
INCH
INCH
INCH

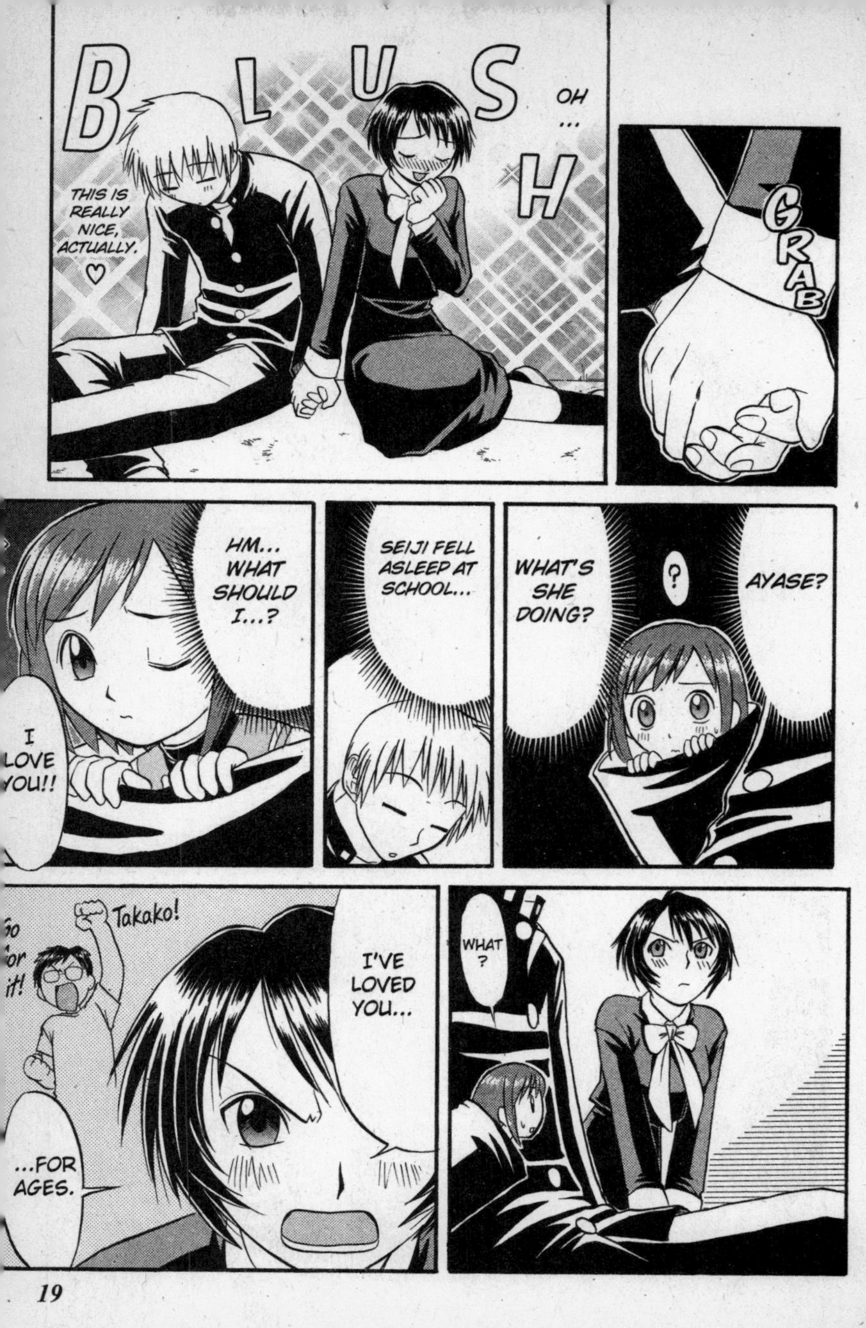
GRAB
OH ...
BLUSH
THIS IS REALLY NICE, ACTUALLY. ♡
AYASE?
?
WHAT'S SHE DOING?
SEIJI FELL ASLEEP AT SCHOOL...
HM... WHAT SHOULD I...?
I LOVE YOU!!
WHAT ?
I'VE LOVED YOU...
Takako!
Go for it!
...FOR AGES.

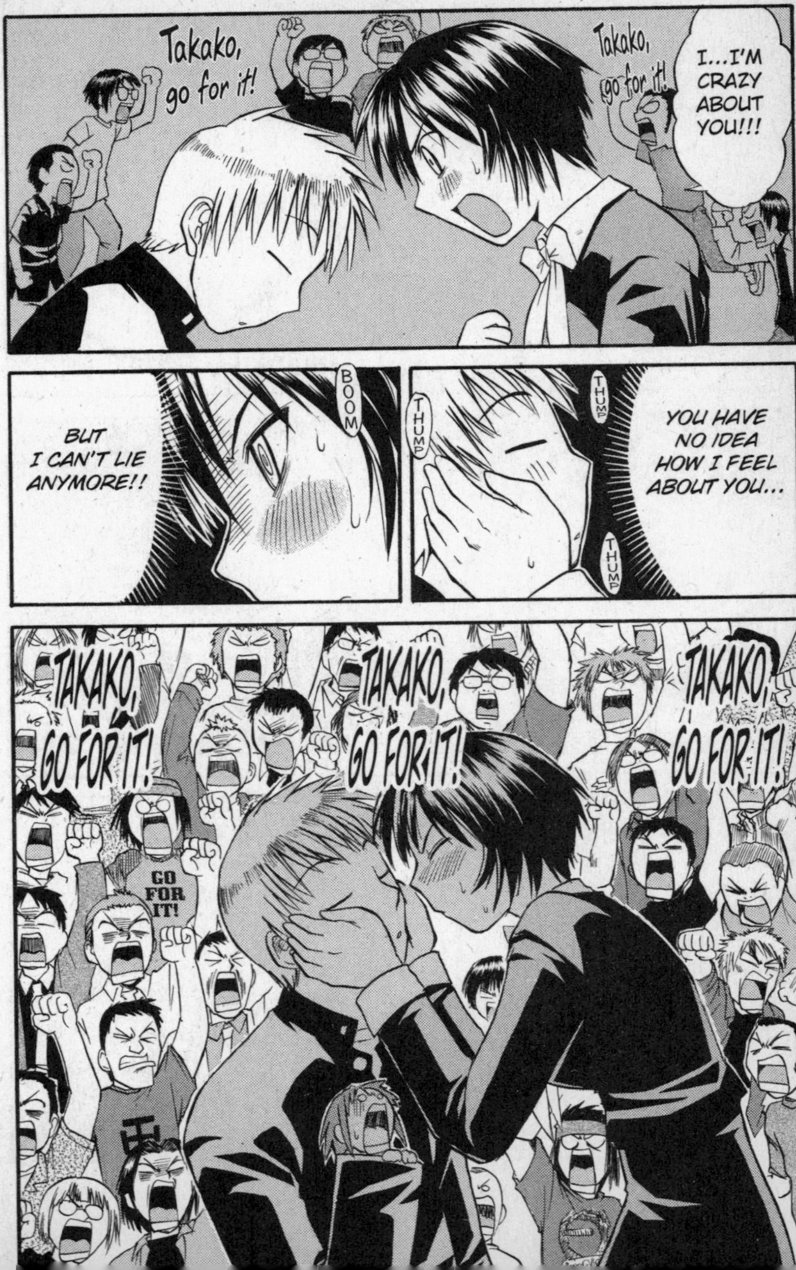
I...I'M CRAZY ABOUT YOU!!!
Takako, go for it!
Takako, go for it!
THUMP
YOU HAVE NO IDEA HOW I FEEL ABOUT YOU...
THUMP
THUMP
BOOM
BUT I CAN'T LIE ANYMORE!!
TAKAKO, GO FOR IT!
TAKAKO, GO FOR IT!
TAKAKO, GO FOR IT!
GO FOR IT!

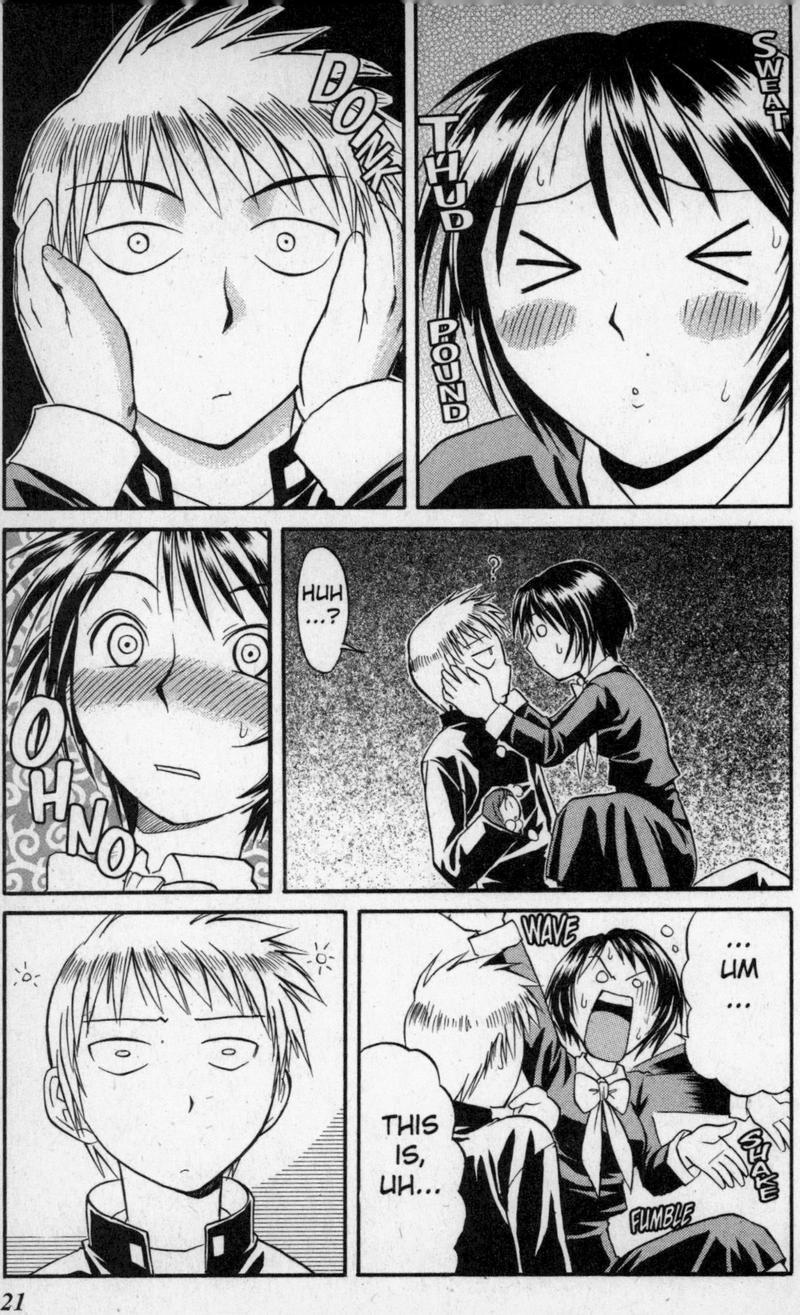
SWEAT
THUD
POUND
DOINK
HUH ...?
?
OH NO
WAVE
... UM ...
THIS IS, UH...
SHAKE
FUMBLE

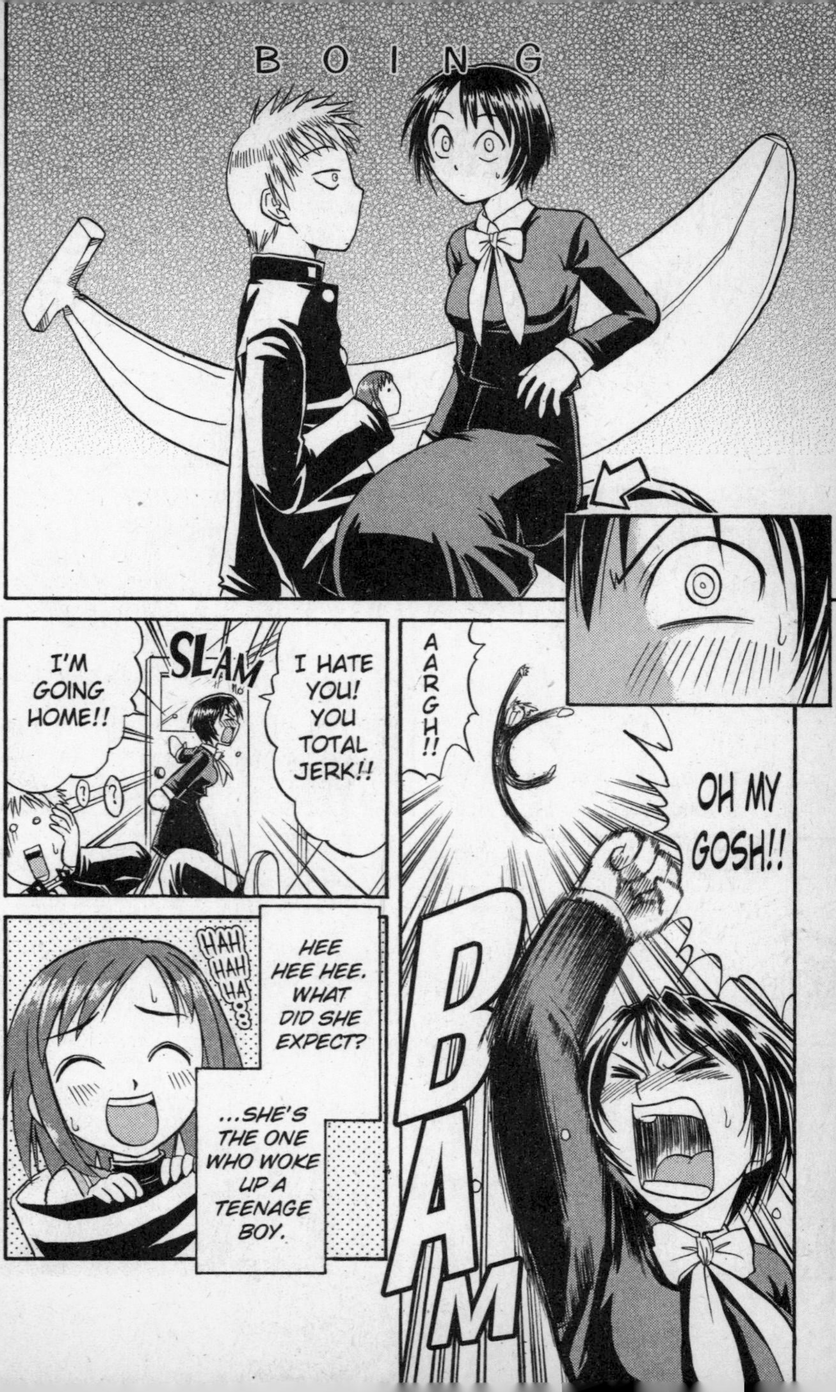
B O I N G
AARGH!!
OH MY GOSH!!
BAM
I HATE YOU! YOU TOTAL JERK!!
SLAM
I'M GOING HOME!!
HEE HEE HEE. WHAT DID SHE EXPECT?
HAH HAH HA
...SHE'S THE ONE WHO WOKE UP A TEENAGE BOY.

DAY 34 REVENGE OF THE PERVERTED DOCTOR

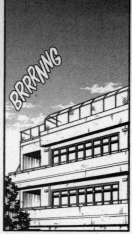

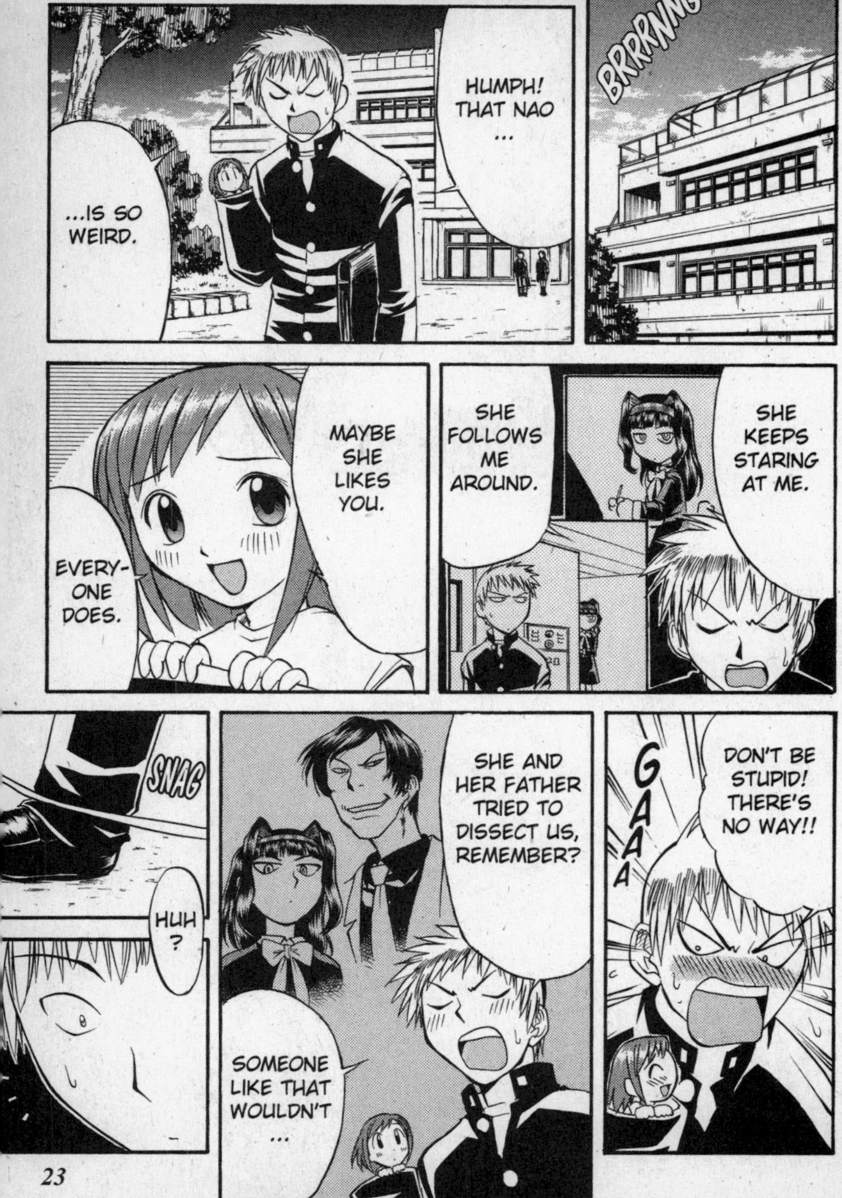
BRRRNNG
HUMPH! THAT NAO ...
...IS SO WEIRD.
SHE KEEPS STARING AT ME.
SHE FOLLOWS ME AROUND.
MAYBE SHE LIKES YOU.
EVERY-ONE DOES.
GAAAA
DON'T BE STUPID! THERE'S NO WAY!!
SHE AND HER FATHER TRIED TO DISSECT US, REMEMBER?
SOMEONE LIKE THAT WOULDN'T ...
SNAG
HUH ?

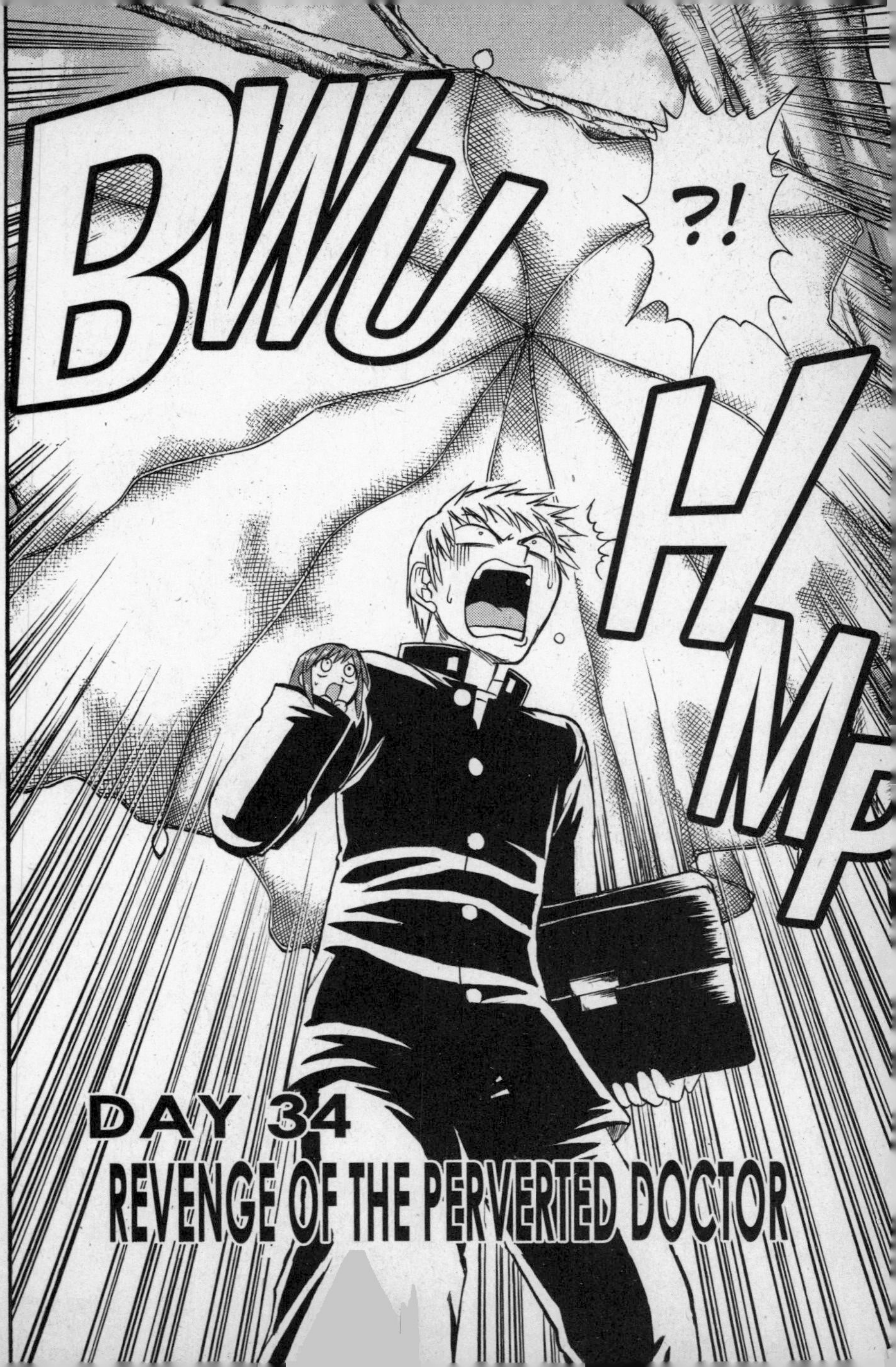
BWUHMP
?!

DAY 34
REVENGE OF THE PERVERTED DOCTOR

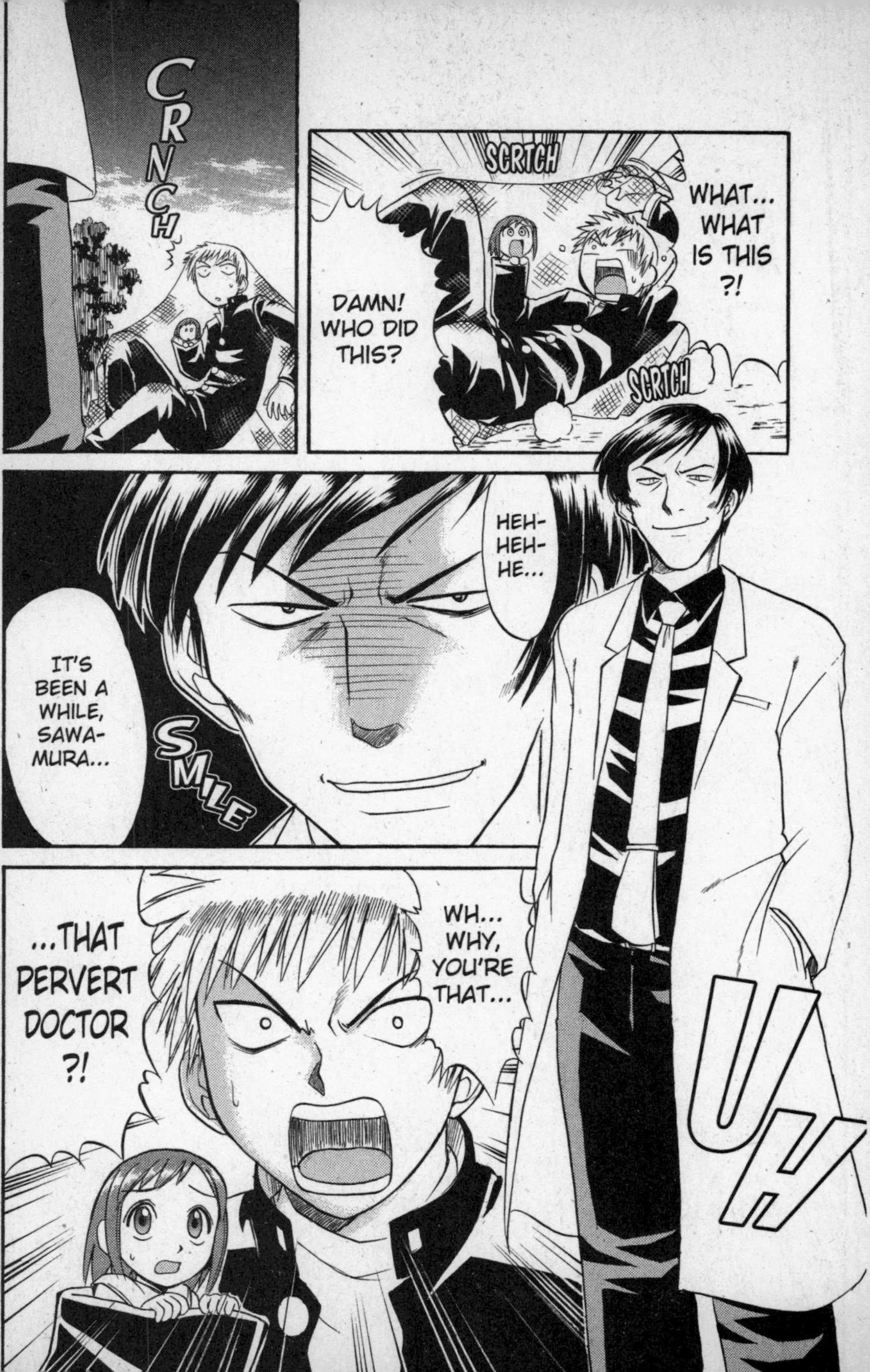
SCRTCH
WHAT... WHAT IS THIS ?!
DAMN! WHO DID THIS?
SCRTCH
CRNCH
HEH-HEH-HE...
IT'S BEEN A WHILE, SAWAMURA...
SMILE
UH
WH... WHY, YOU'RE THAT...
...THAT PERVERT DOCTOR ?!

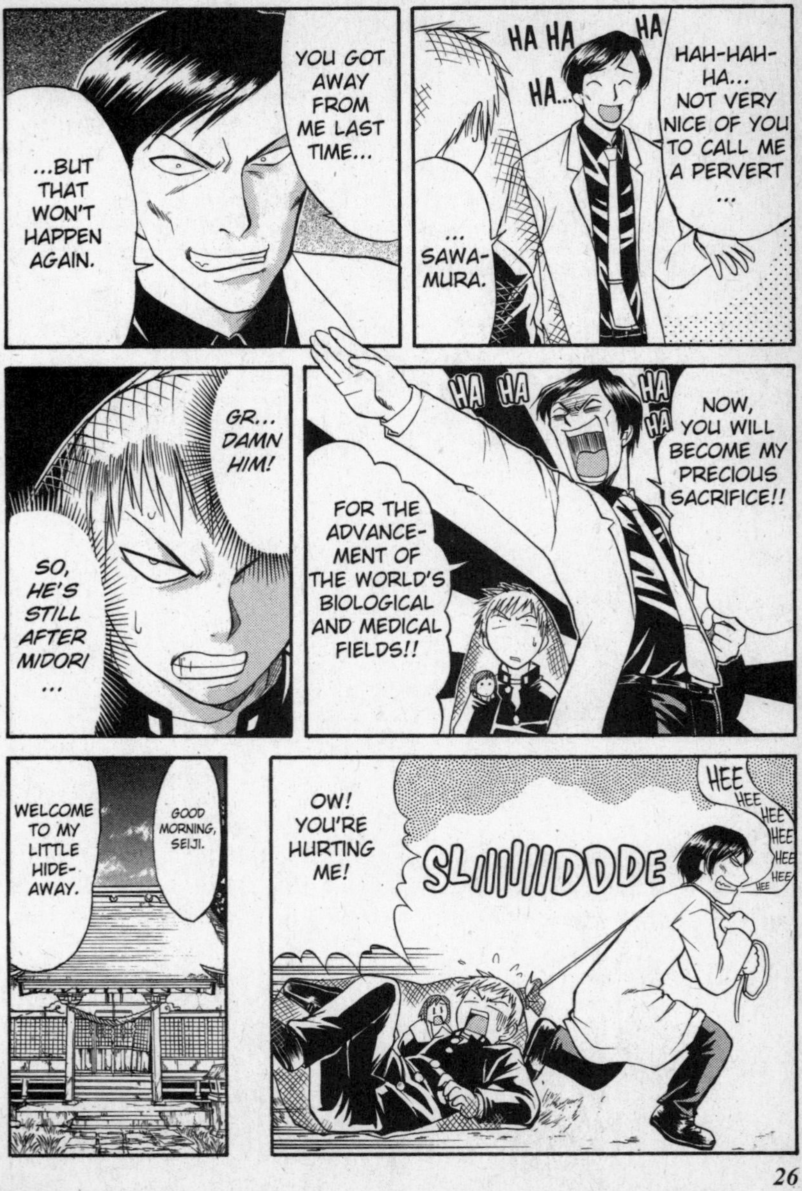
HA HA HA HA...
HAH-HAH-HA... NOT VERY NICE OF YOU TO CALL ME A PERVERT...
...SAWAMURA.
YOU GOT AWAY FROM ME LAST TIME...
...BUT THAT WON'T HAPPEN AGAIN.
HA HA HA HA
NOW, YOU WILL BECOME MY PRECIOUS SACRIFICE!!
FOR THE ADVANCEMENT OF THE WORLD'S BIOLOGICAL AND MEDICAL FIELDS!!
GR... DAMN HIM!
SO, HE'S STILL AFTER MIDORI...
HEE HEE HEE HEE HEE HEE HEE
SLIIIIIIDDDE
OW! YOU'RE HURTING ME!
GOOD MORNING, SEIJI.
WELCOME TO MY LITTLE HIDE-AWAY.

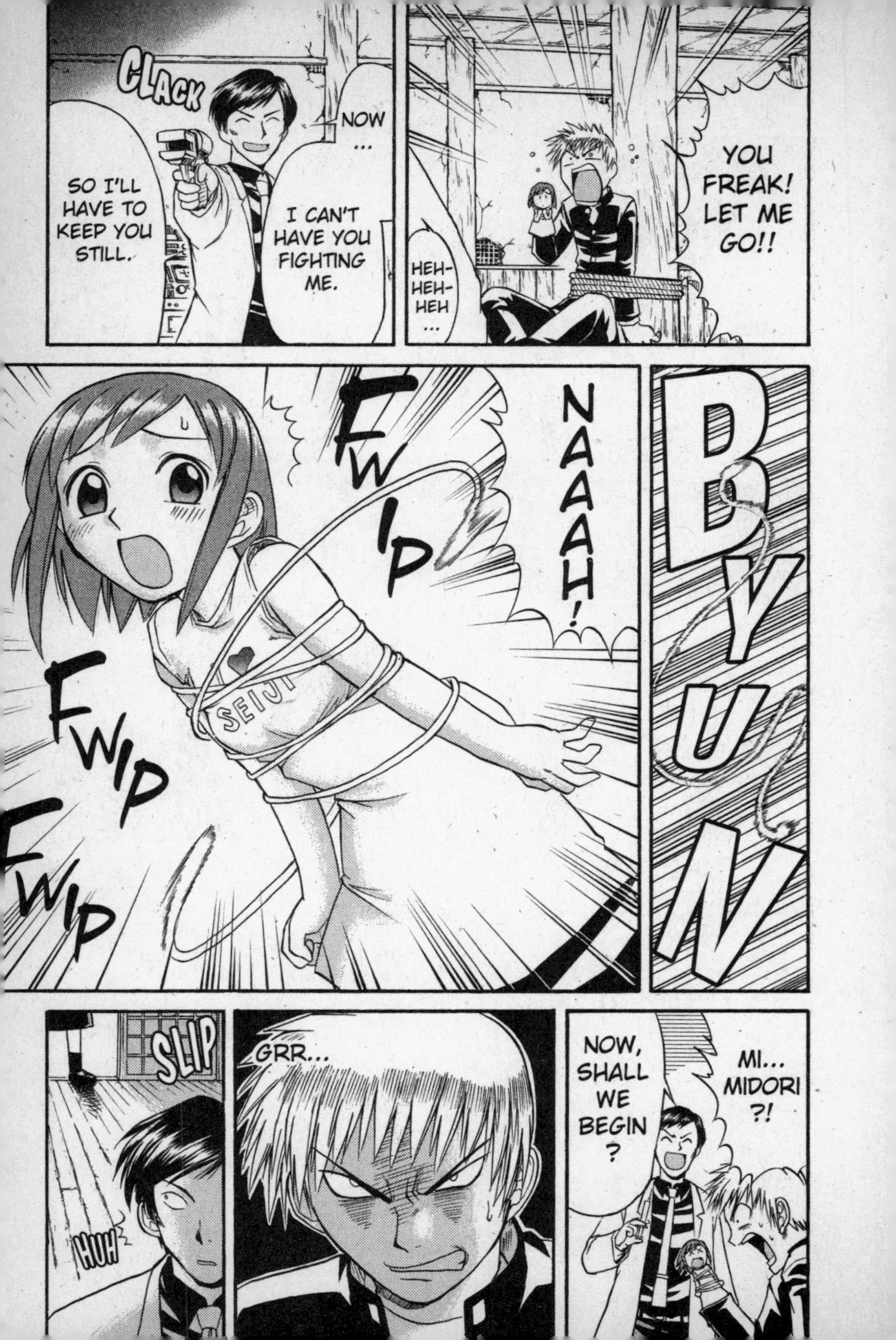
YOU FREAK! LET ME GO!!
HEH-HEH-HEH...
CLACK
NOW...
I CAN'T HAVE YOU FIGHTING ME.
SO I'LL HAVE TO KEEP YOU STILL.
BYUN
NAAAAH!
FWIP
FWIP
FWIP
MI... MIDORI?!
NOW, SHALL WE BEGIN?
GRR...
SLIP
HUH

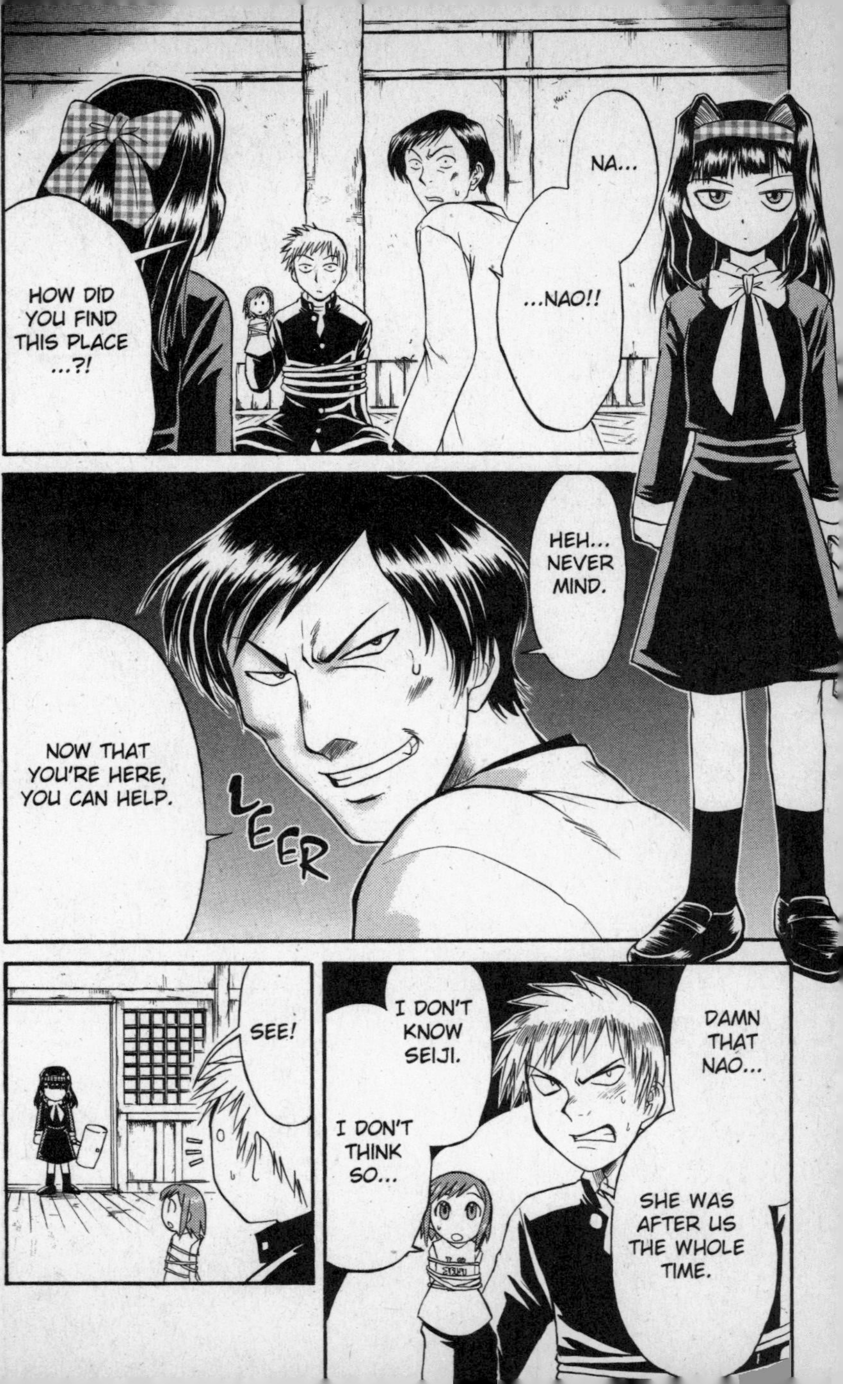
NA...
...NAO!!
HOW DID YOU FIND THIS PLACE ...?!
HEH... NEVER MIND.
NOW THAT YOU'RE HERE, YOU CAN HELP.
LEER
DAMN THAT NAO...
SHE WAS AFTER US THE WHOLE TIME.
I DON'T KNOW SEIJI.
I DON'T THINK SO...
SEE!

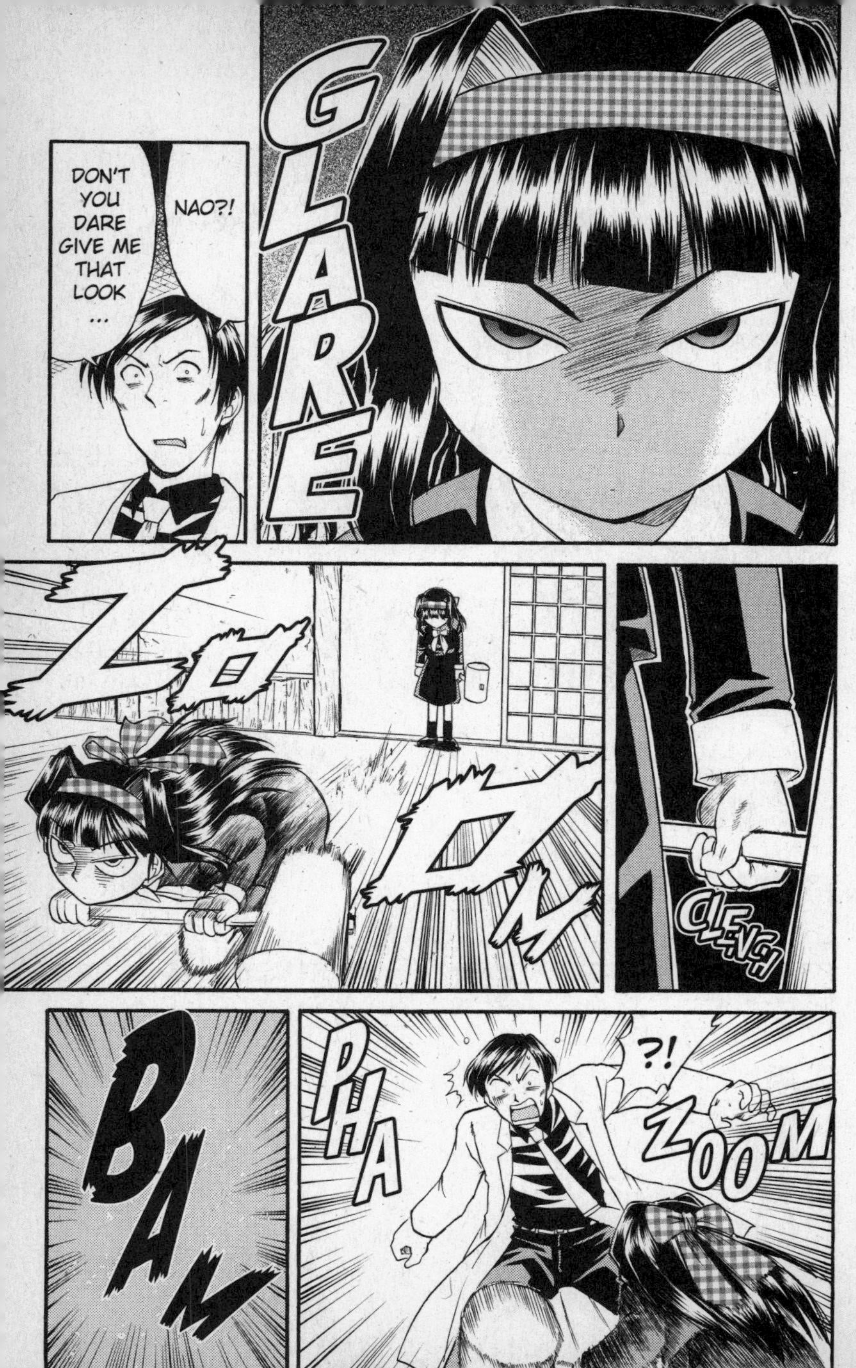
GLARE
NAO?!
DON'T YOU DARE GIVE ME THAT LOOK ...
CLENCH
ZOOM
?!
PHA
ZOOM
BAM

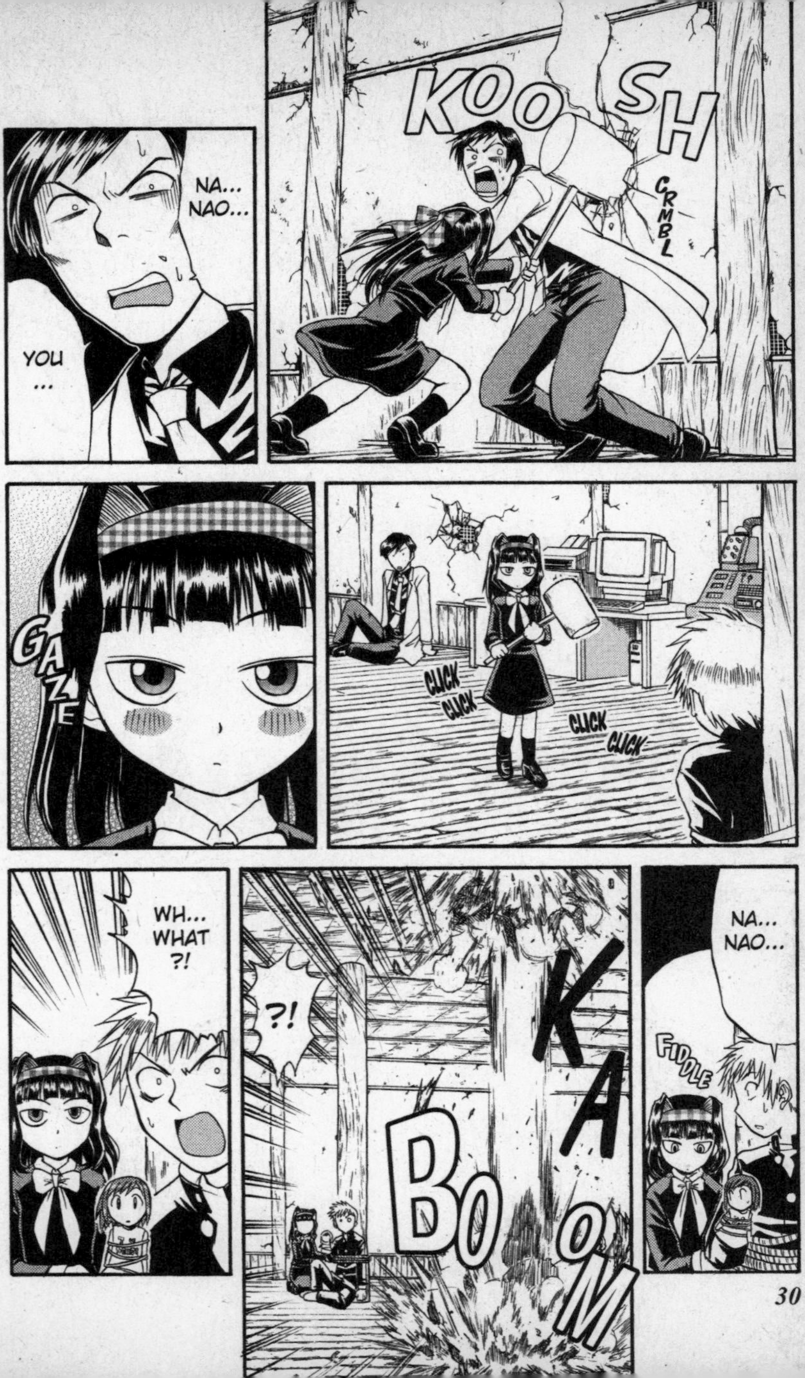

KOOSH
CRMBL
NA... NAO...
YOU ...
CLICK CLICK
CLICK CLICK
GAZE
NA... NAO...
FIDDLE
?!
KABOOM
WH... WHAT ?!

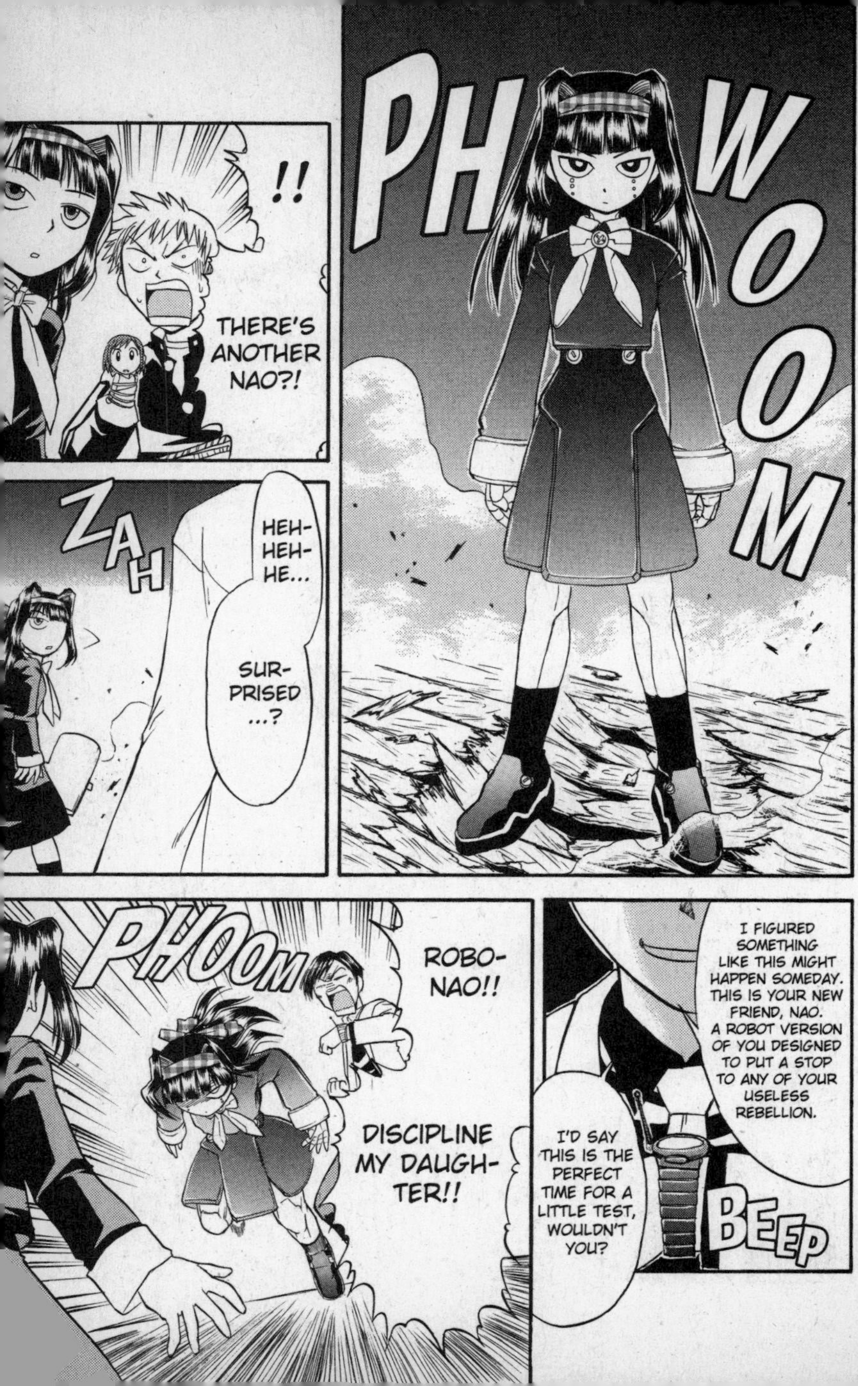
PHWOOM
!!
THERE'S ANOTHER NAO?!
ZAH
HEH-HEH-HE...
SURPRISED...?
I FIGURED SOMETHING LIKE THIS MIGHT HAPPEN SOMEDAY. THIS IS YOUR NEW FRIEND, NAO. A ROBOT VERSION OF YOU DESIGNED TO PUT A STOP TO ANY OF YOUR USELESS REBELLION.
I'D SAY THIS IS THE PERFECT TIME FOR A LITTLE TEST, WOULDN'T YOU?
BEEP
PHOOM
ROBO-NAO!!
DISCIPLINE MY DAUGHTER!!

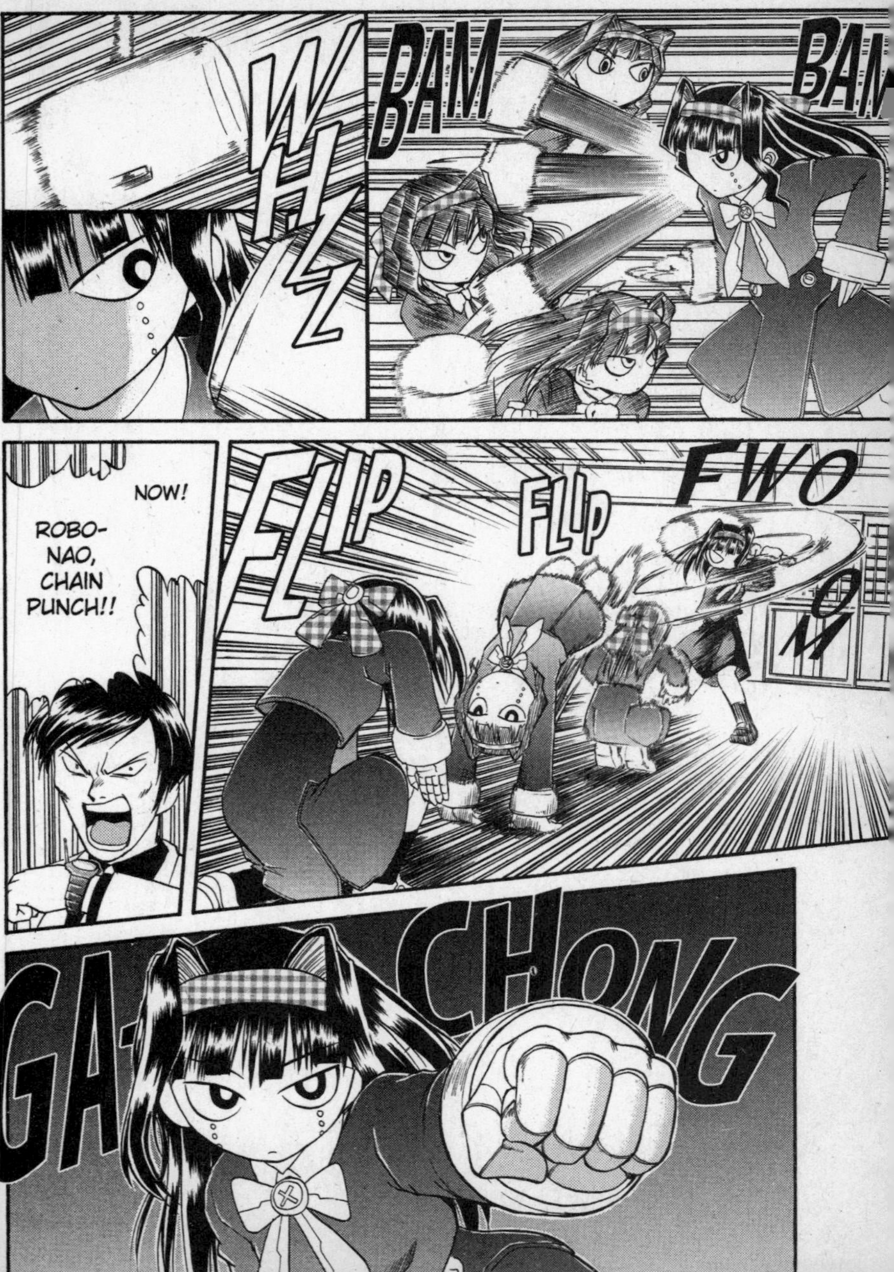
BAM
BAM
WHIZZ
FWOOM
FLIP
FLIP
NOW!
ROBO-NAO, CHAIN PUNCH!!
GA-CHONG

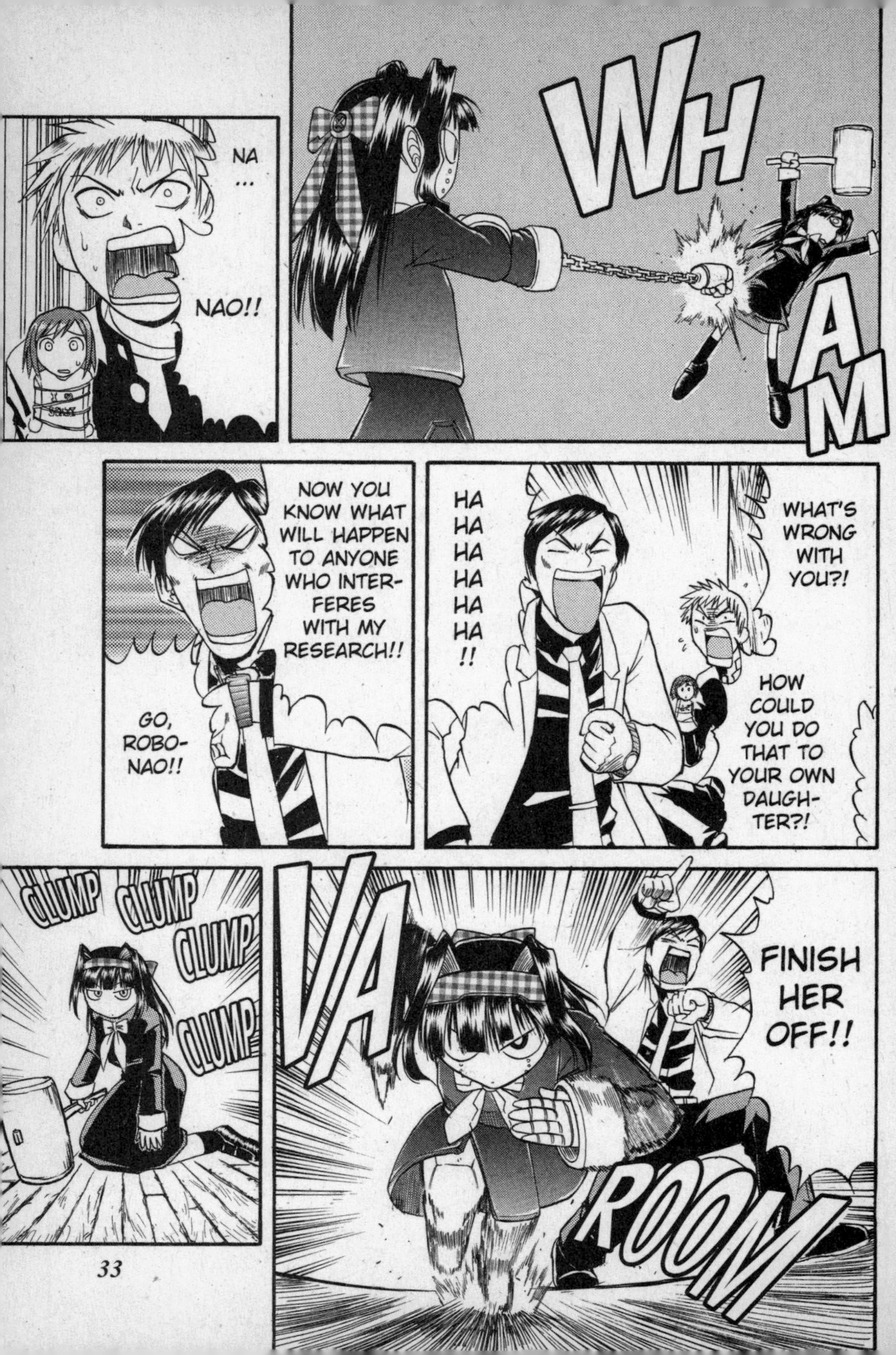
WHAM
NA ...
NAO!!
WHAT'S WRONG WITH YOU?!
HA HA HA HA HA HA HA !!
HOW COULD YOU DO THAT TO YOUR OWN DAUGHTER?!
NOW YOU KNOW WHAT WILL HAPPEN TO ANYONE WHO INTERFERES WITH MY RESEARCH!!
GO, ROBO-NAO!!
FINISH HER OFF!!
VAROOM
CLUMP
CLUMP
CLUMP
CLUMP

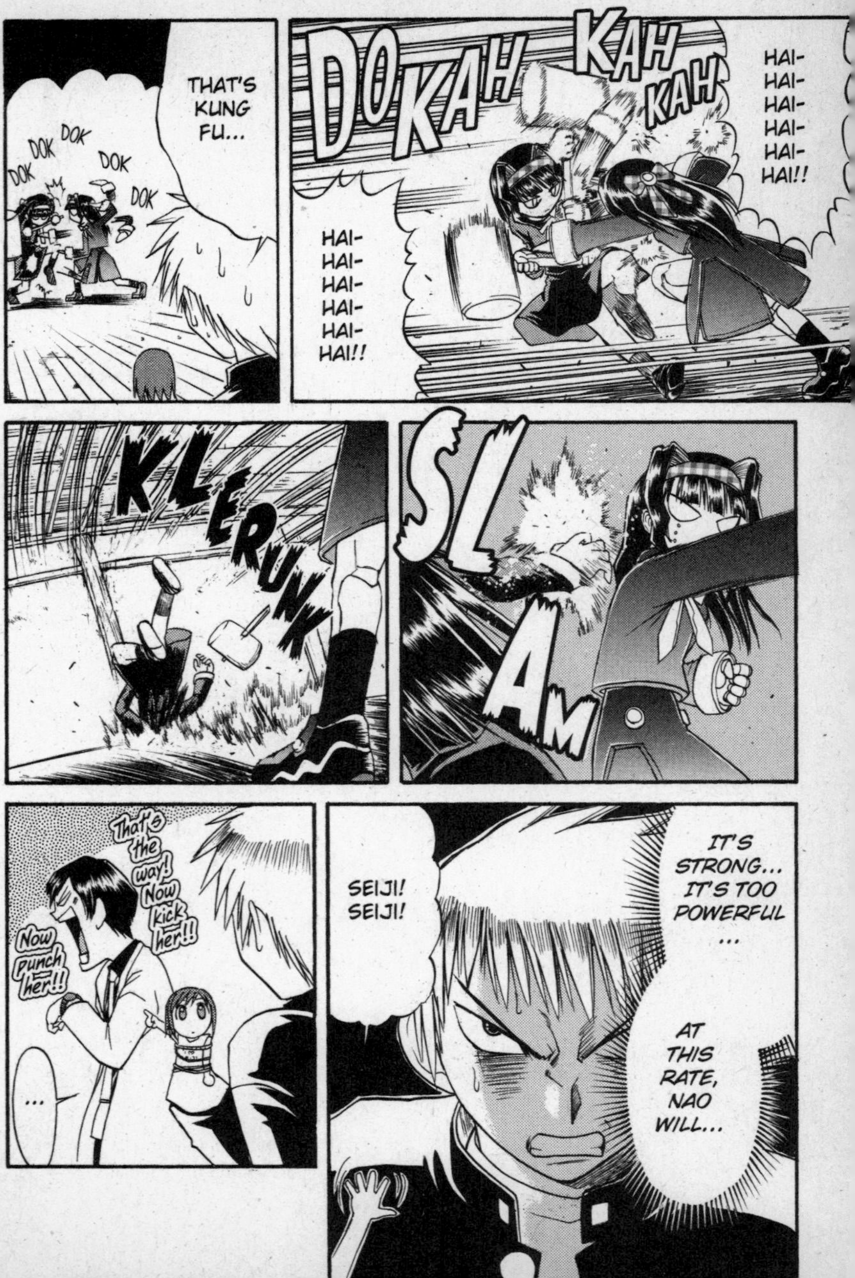
DOKAH
KAH
KAH
HAI-HAI-HAI-HAI-HAI-HAI!!
HAI-HAI-HAI-HAI-HAI-HAI!!
THAT'S KUNG FU...
DOK
DOK
DOK
DOK
DOK
SLAM
KLERUNK
IT'S STRONG... IT'S TOO POWERFUL...
SEIJI! SEIJI!
AT THIS RATE, NAO WILL...
That's the way! Now kick her!!
Now punch her!!
...

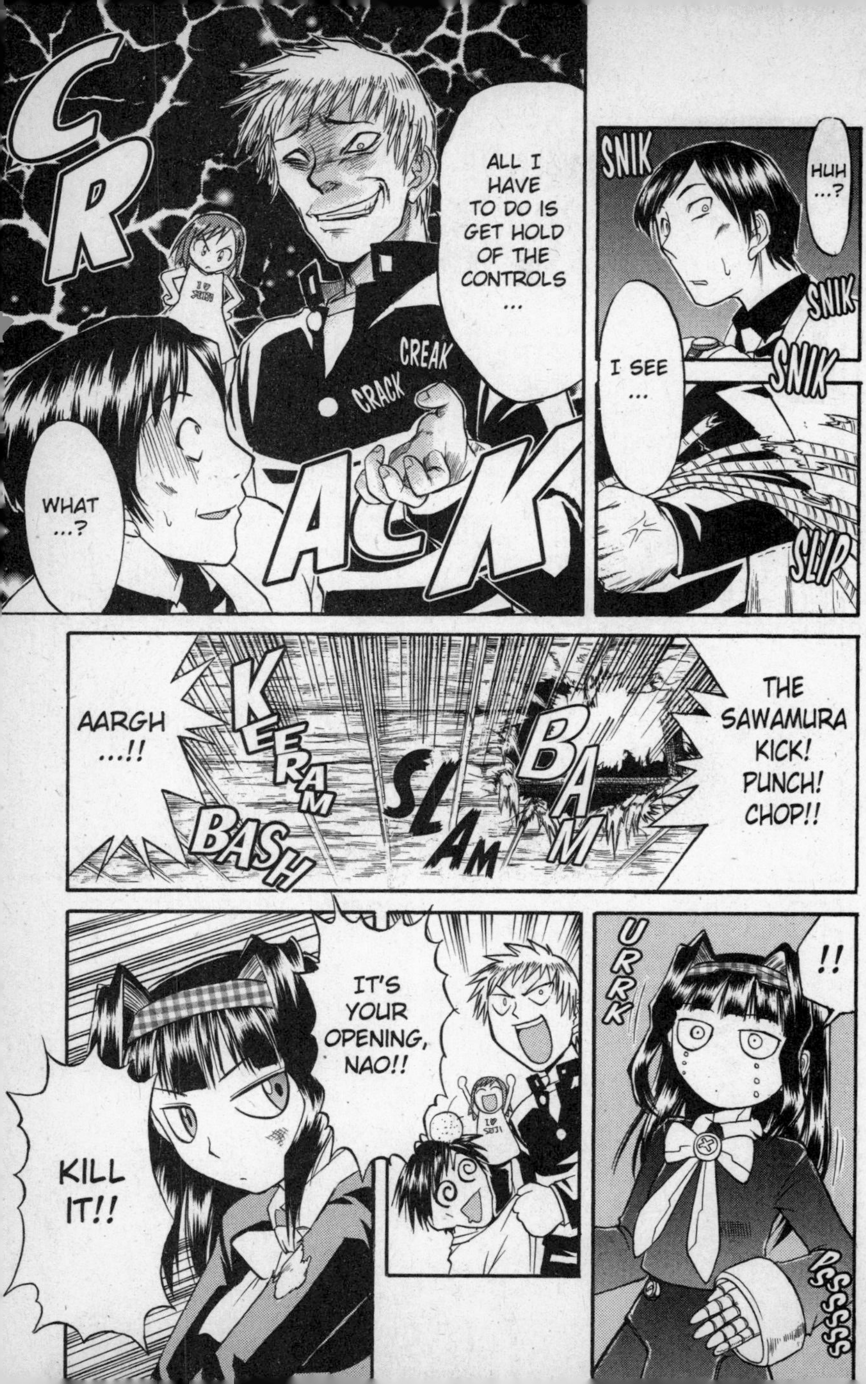

SNIK
HUH ...?
SNIK
I SEE ...
SNIK
SLIP
CRACK
ALL I HAVE TO DO IS GET HOLD OF THE CONTROLS ...
CREAK
CRACK
WHAT ...?
THE SAWAMURA KICK! PUNCH! CHOP!!
BAM
SLAM
KEERAM
BASH
AARGH ...!!
URRK
!!
PSSSSS
IT'S YOUR OPENING, NAO!!
KILL IT!!

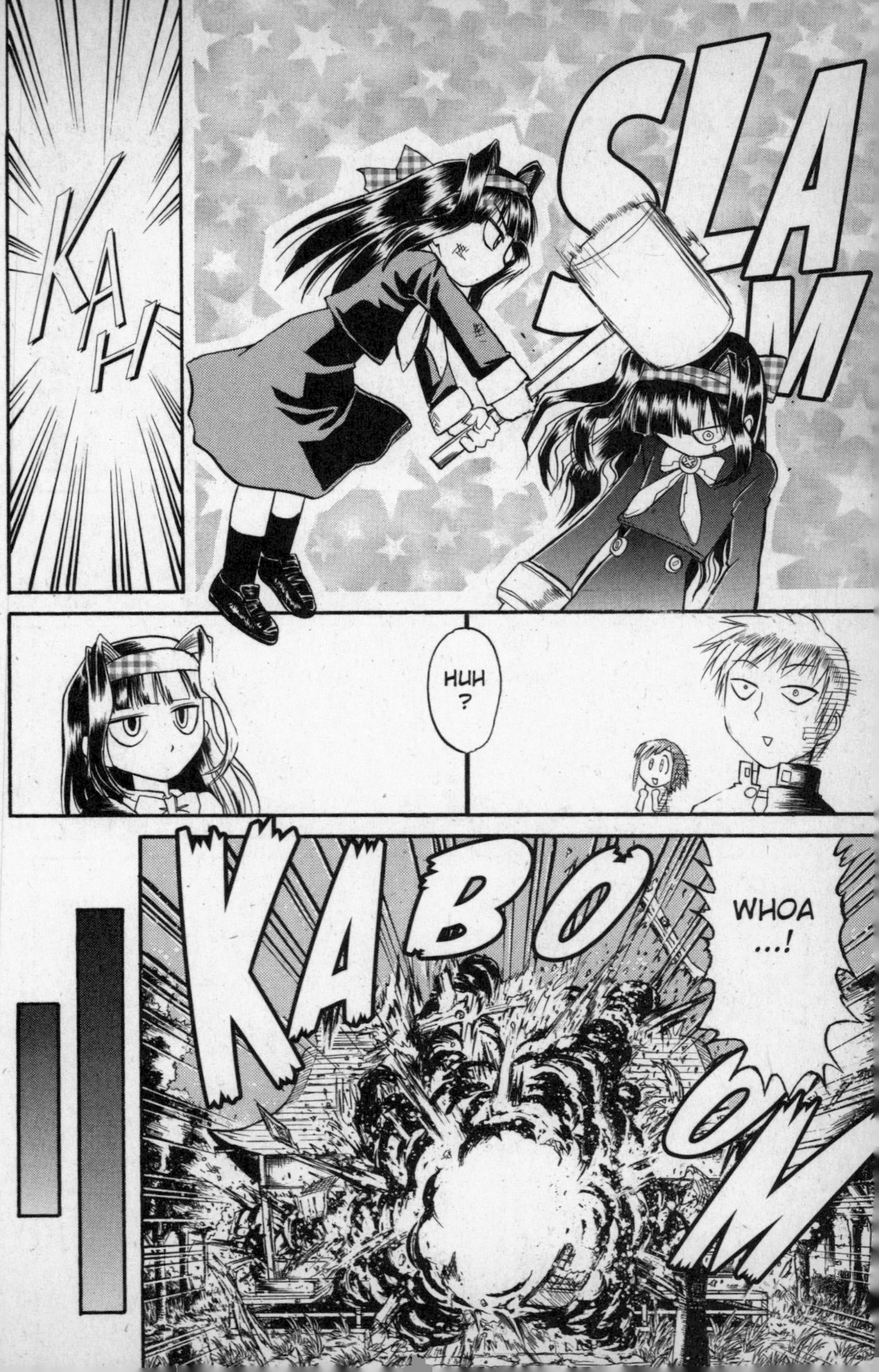
SLAM
KAH
HUH ?
WHOA ...!
KABOOM

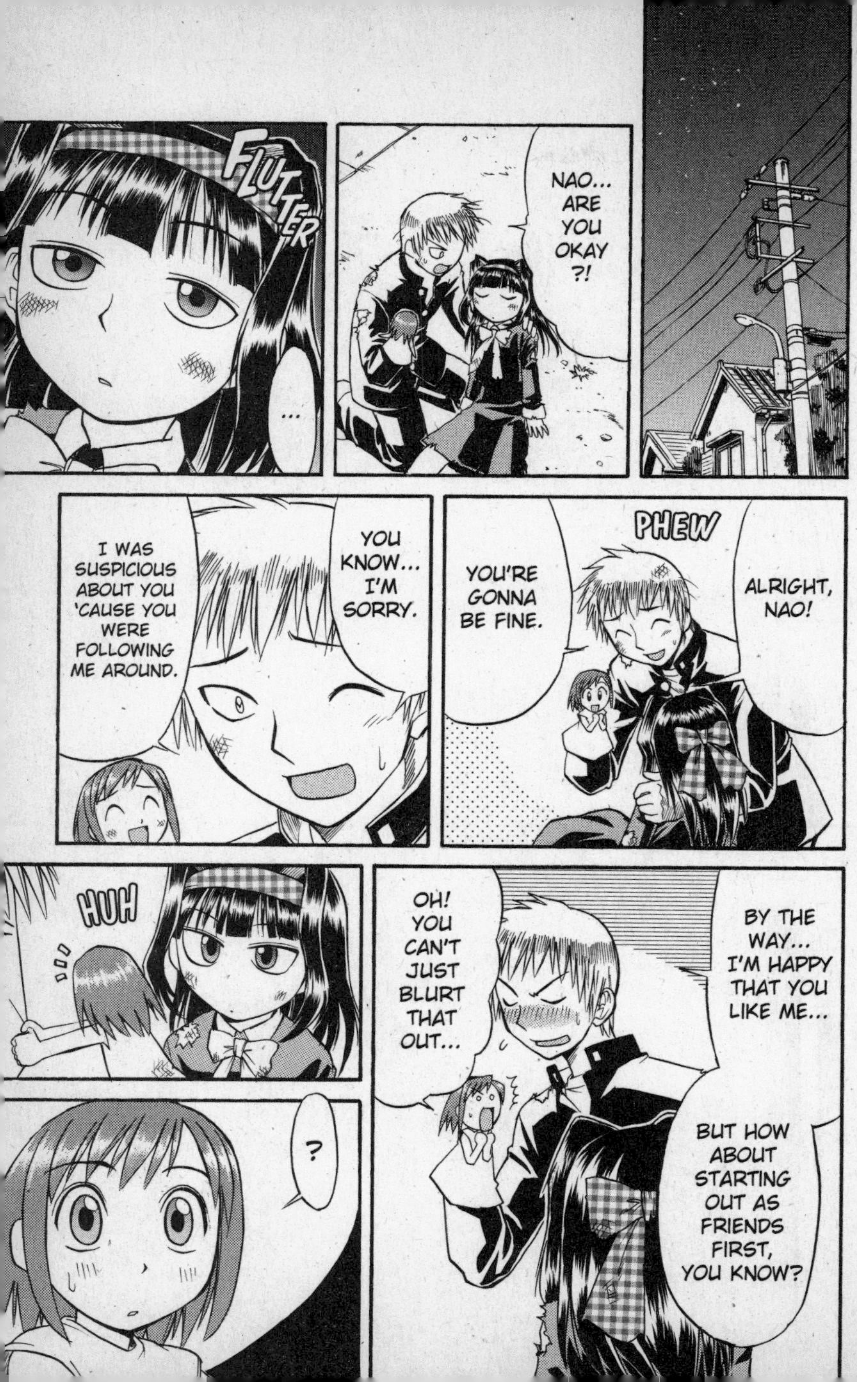
NAO... ARE YOU OKAY ?!
FLUTTER
...
PHEW
ALRIGHT, NAO!
YOU'RE GONNA BE FINE.
YOU KNOW... I'M SORRY.
I WAS SUSPICIOUS ABOUT YOU 'CAUSE YOU WERE FOLLOWING ME AROUND.
BY THE WAY... I'M HAPPY THAT YOU LIKE ME...
OH! YOU CAN'T JUST BLURT THAT OUT...
BUT HOW ABOUT STARTING OUT AS FRIENDS FIRST, YOU KNOW?
HUH
?

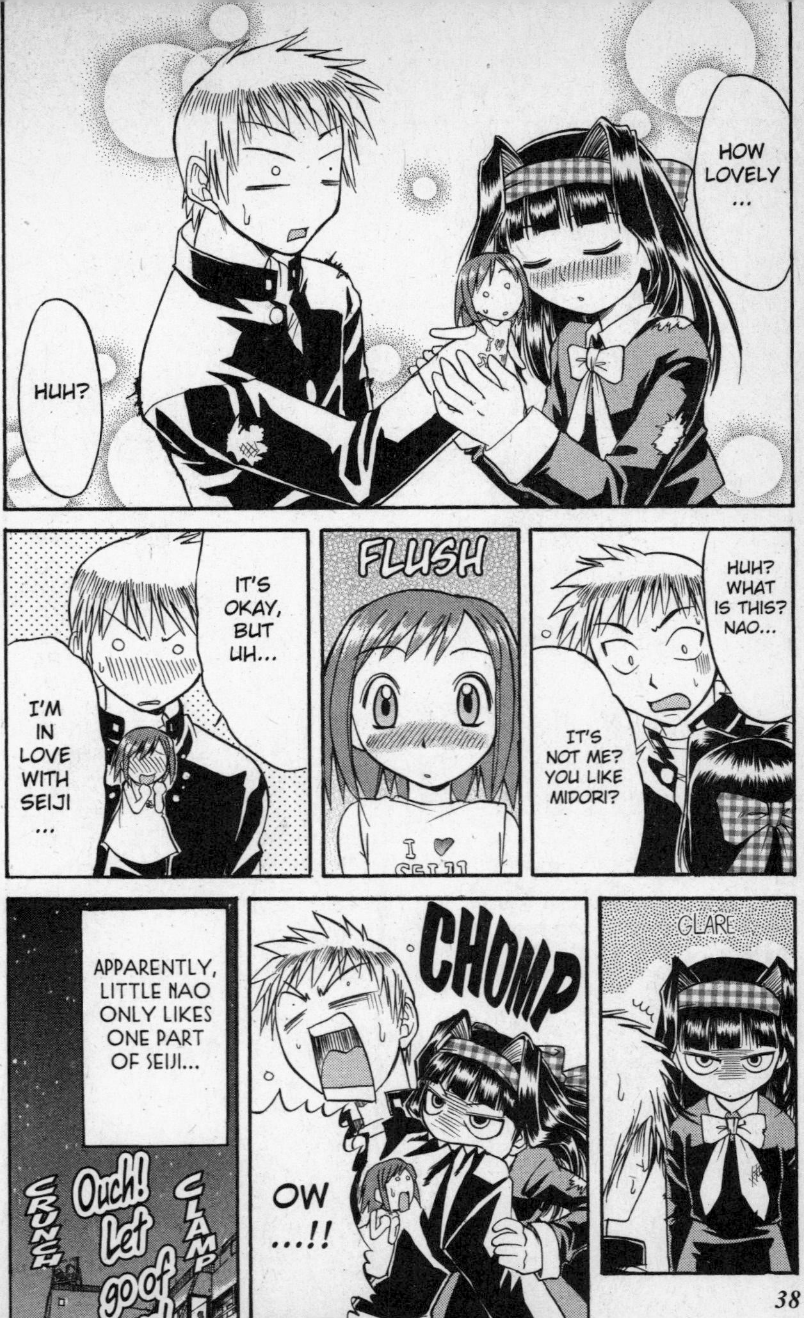
HOW LOVELY ...
HUH?
HUH? WHAT IS THIS? NAO...
IT'S NOT ME? YOU LIKE MIDORI?
FLUSH
I ♥ SEIJI
IT'S OKAY, BUT UH...
I'M IN LOVE WITH SEIJI ...
GLARE
CHOMP
OW ...!!
APPARENTLY, LITTLE NAO ONLY LIKES ONE PART OF SEIJI...
CLAMP
Ouch! Let go of me!
CRUNCH

DAY 35 MY GIRL

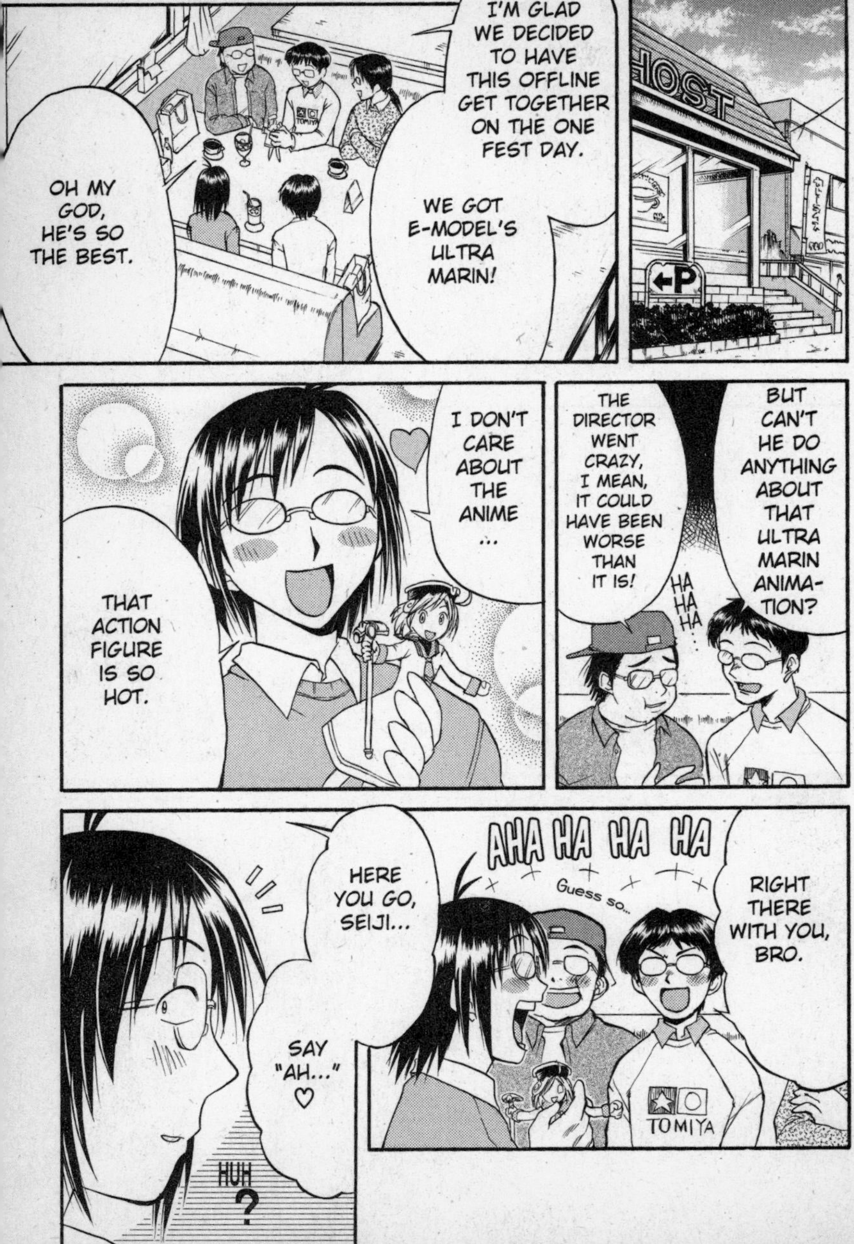

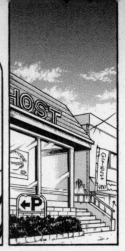

HOST
P
BOY, I'M GLAD WE DECIDED TO HAVE THIS OFFLINE GET TOGETHER ON THE ONE FEST DAY.
WE GOT E-MODEL'S ULTRA MARIN!
OH MY GOD, HE'S SO THE BEST.
BUT CAN'T HE DO ANYTHING ABOUT THAT ULTRA MARIN ANIMATION?
THE DIRECTOR WENT CRAZY, I MEAN, IT COULD HAVE BEEN WORSE THAN IT IS!
HA HA HA...
I DON'T CARE ABOUT THE ANIME ...
THAT ACTION FIGURE IS SO HOT.
AHA HA HA HA
RIGHT THERE WITH YOU, BRO.
Guess so...
TOMIYA
HERE YOU GO, SEIJI...
SAY "AH..." ♡
HUH ?

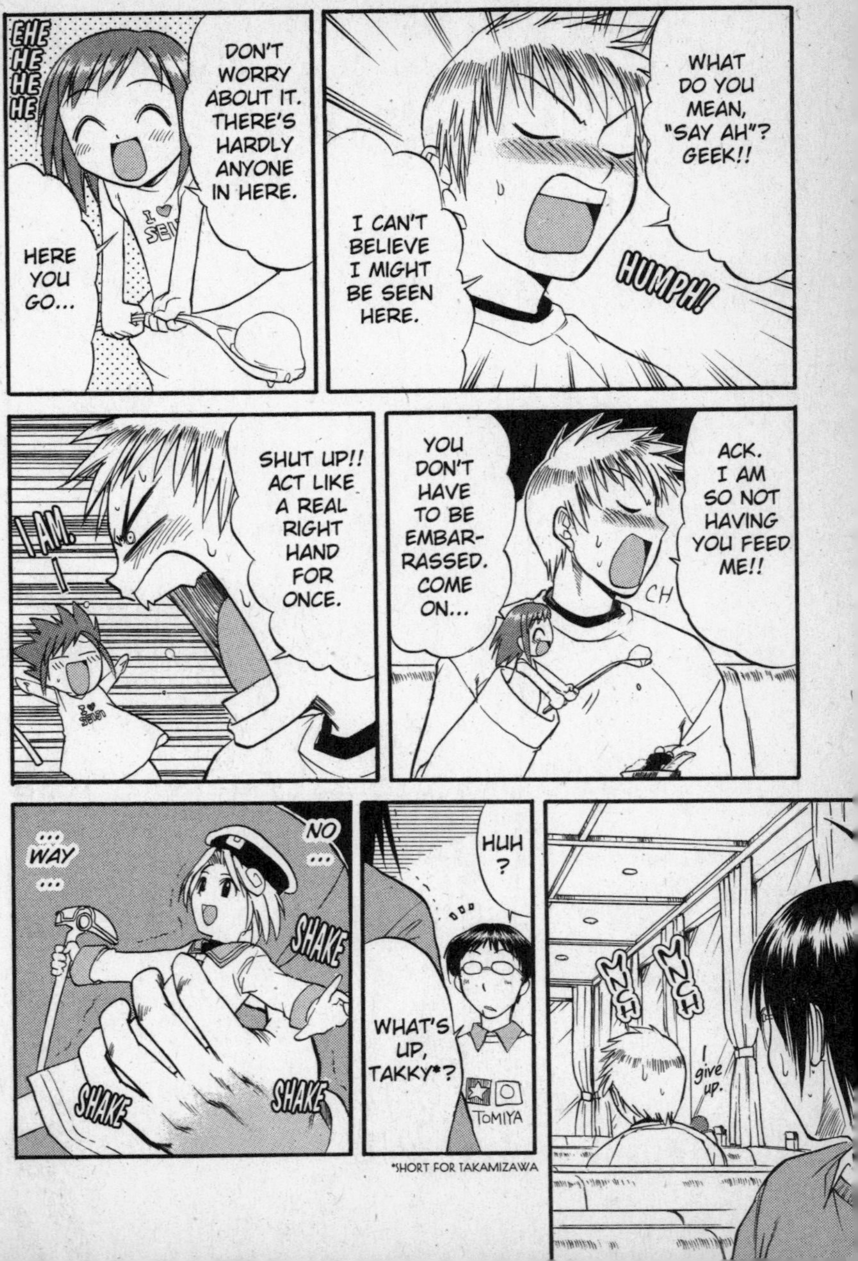
WHAT DO YOU MEAN, "SAY AH"? GEEK!!
HUMPH!
I CAN'T BELIEVE I MIGHT BE SEEN HERE.
EHE HE HE HE
DON'T WORRY ABOUT IT. THERE'S HARDLY ANYONE IN HERE.
HERE YOU GO...
ACK. I AM SO NOT HAVING YOU FEED ME!!
CH
YOU DON'T HAVE TO BE EMBARRASSED. COME ON...
SHUT UP!! ACT LIKE A REAL RIGHT HAND FOR ONCE.
I AM. I
MNCH
MNCH
I give up.
HUH?
WHAT'S UP, TAKKY*?
TOMIYA
NO...
...WAY...
SHAKE
SHAKE
SHAKE

*SHORT FOR TAKAMIZAWA

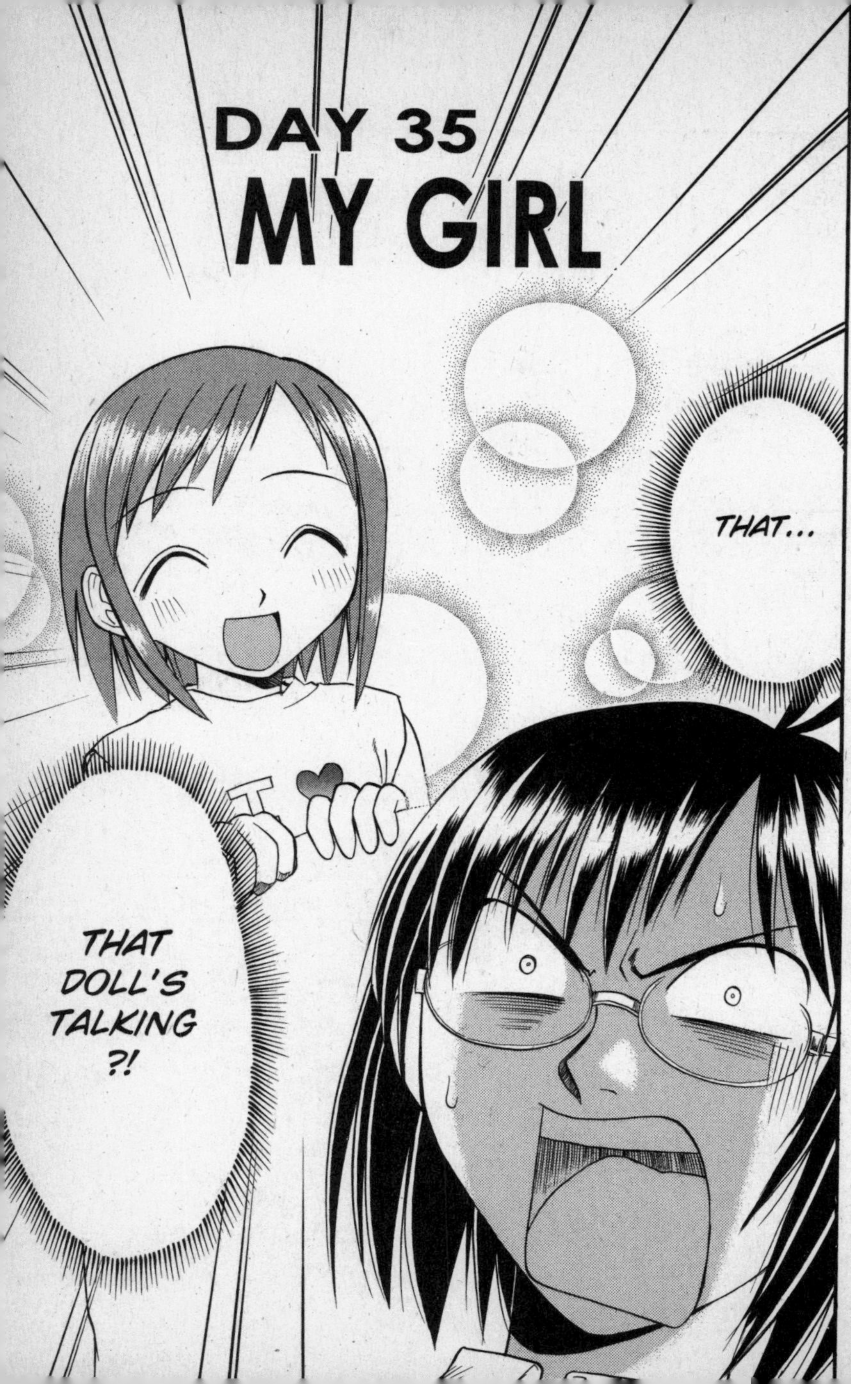
DAY 35
MY GIRL
THAT...
THAT DOLL'S TALKING ?!

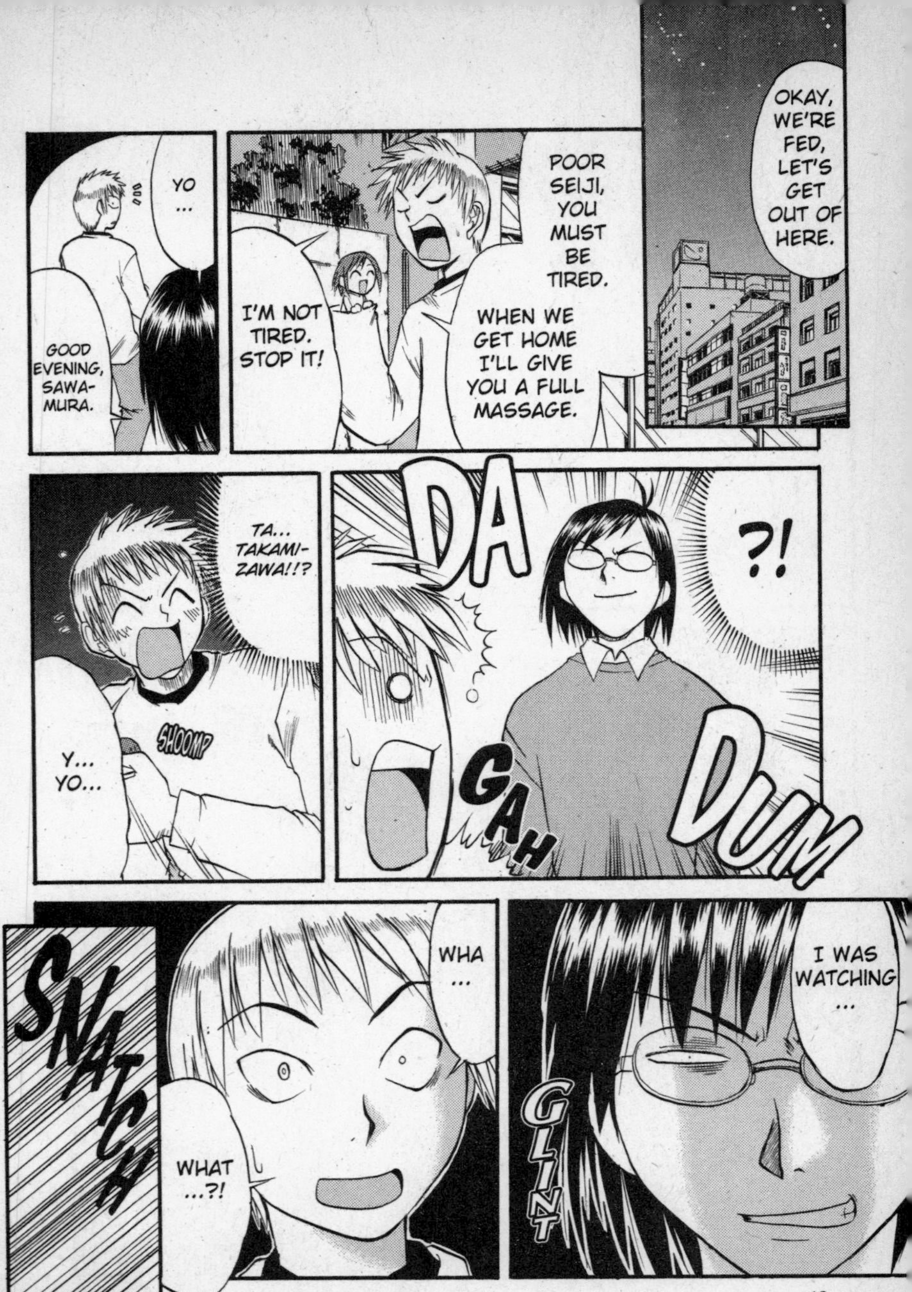
OKAY, WE'RE FED, LET'S GET OUT OF HERE.
POOR SEIJI, YOU MUST BE TIRED.
WHEN WE GET HOME I'LL GIVE YOU A FULL MASSAGE.
I'M NOT TIRED. STOP IT!
YO ...
GOOD EVENING, SAWA-MURA.
DA
?!
GAH
DUM
TA... TAKAMI-ZAWA!!?
SHOOMP
Y... YO...
I WAS WATCHING ...
GLINT
WHA ...
WHAT ...?!
SNATCH

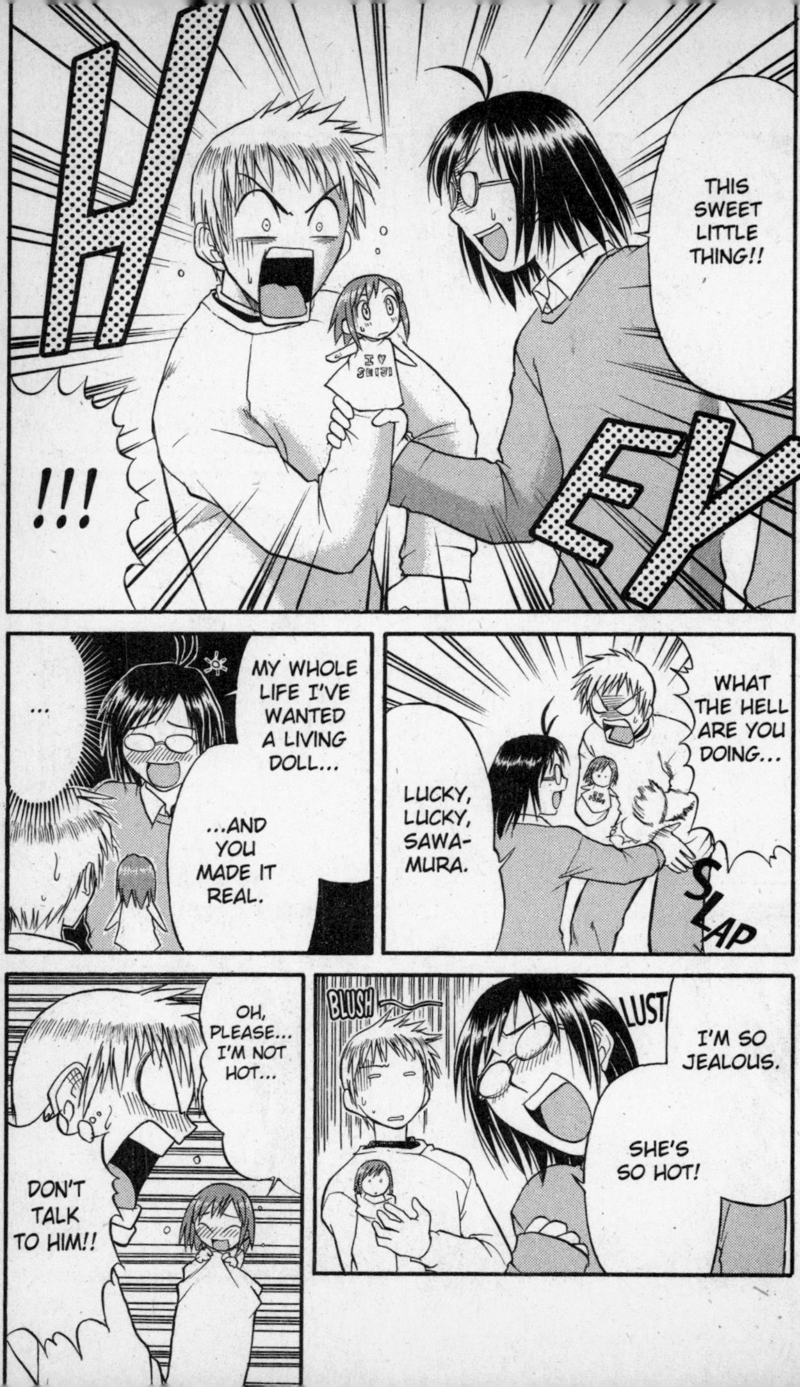
THIS SWEET LITTLE THING!!
HEY
I ♥ SEIJI
!!!
WHAT THE HELL ARE YOU DOING...
LUCKY, LUCKY, SAWAMURA.
SLAP
MY WHOLE LIFE I'VE WANTED A LIVING DOLL...
...AND YOU MADE IT REAL.
...
LUST
I'M SO JEALOUS.
SHE'S SO HOT!
BLUSH
OH, PLEASE... I'M NOT HOT...
DON'T TALK TO HIM!!

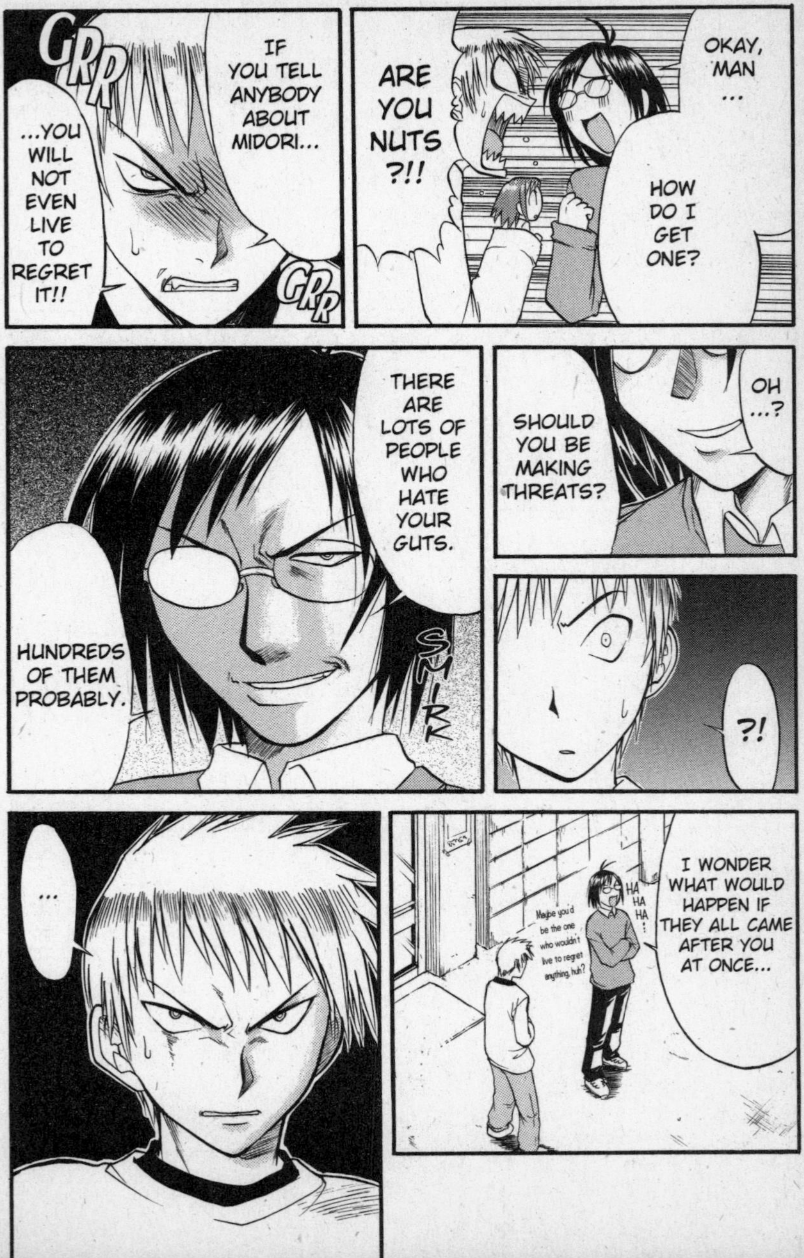
OKAY, MAN ...
HOW DO I GET ONE?
ARE YOU NUTS ?!!
IF YOU TELL ANYBODY ABOUT MIDORI...
GRR
...YOU WILL NOT EVEN LIVE TO REGRET IT!!
GRR
OH ...?
SHOULD YOU BE MAKING THREATS?
?!
THERE ARE LOTS OF PEOPLE WHO HATE YOUR GUTS.
SMIRK
HUNDREDS OF THEM PROBABLY.
I WONDER WHAT WOULD HAPPEN IF THEY ALL CAME AFTER YOU AT ONCE...
HA HA HA!
Maybe you'd be the one who wouldn't live to regret anything, huh?
...

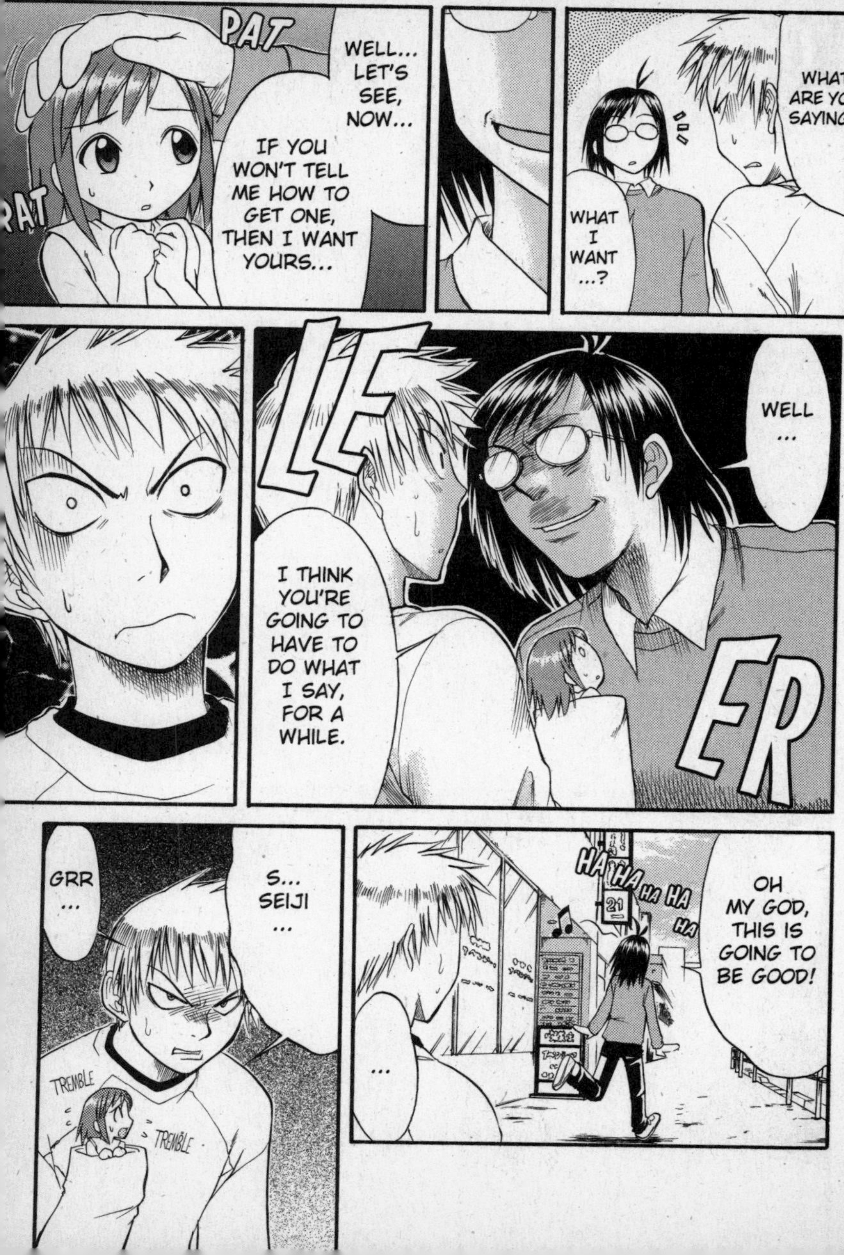
WHAT ARE YOU SAYING?
WHAT I WANT ...?
PAT
WELL... LET'S SEE, NOW...
IF YOU WON'T TELL ME HOW TO GET ONE, THEN I WANT YOURS...
WELL ...
LE
ER
I THINK YOU'RE GOING TO HAVE TO DO WHAT I SAY, FOR A WHILE.
OH MY GOD, THIS IS GOING TO BE GOOD!
HA HA HA HA HA
...
S... SEIJI ...
GRR ...
TREMBLE
TREMBLE

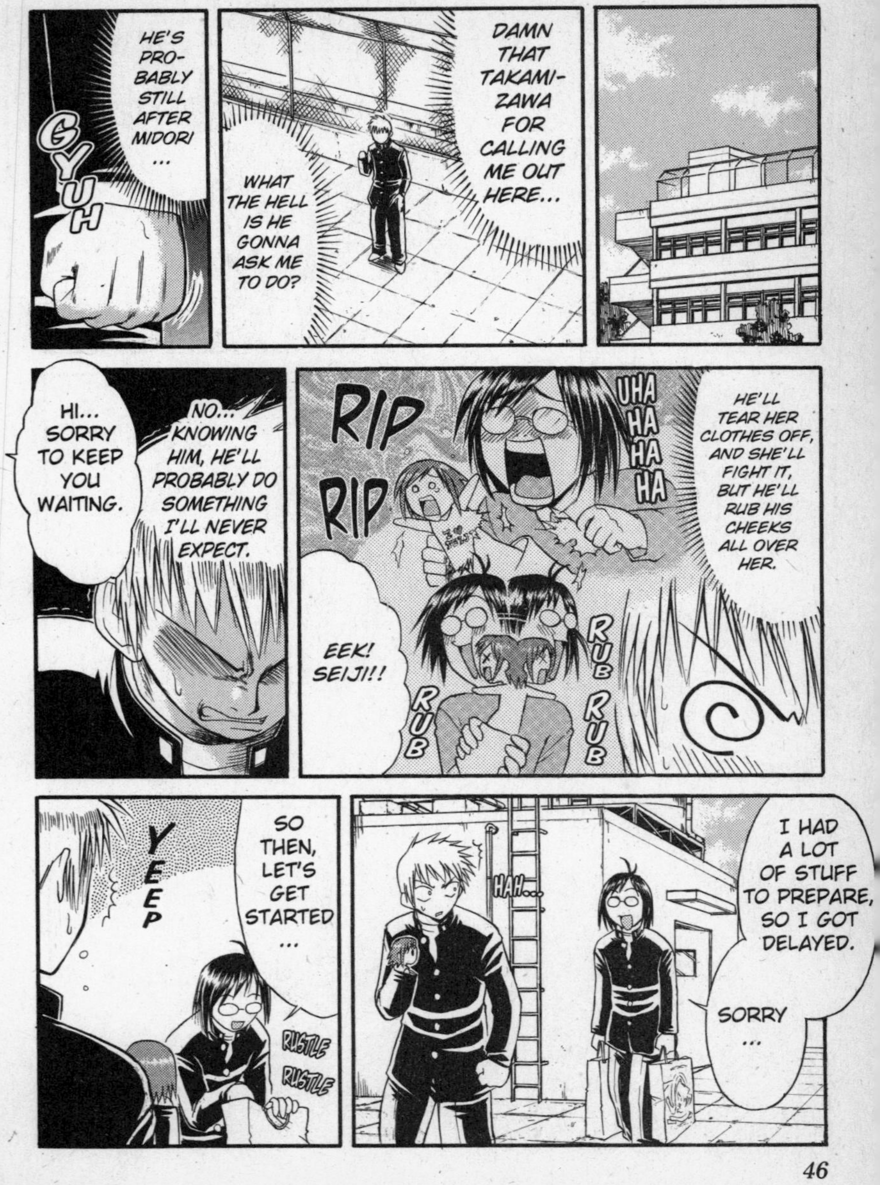
DAMN THAT TAKAMI-ZAWA FOR CALLING ME OUT HERE...
WHAT THE HELL IS HE GONNA ASK ME TO DO?
HE'S PRO-BABLY STILL AFTER MIDORI ...
GYUH
HE'LL TEAR HER CLOTHES OFF, AND SHE'LL FIGHT IT, BUT HE'LL RUB HIS CHEEKS ALL OVER HER.
UHA HA HA HA HA
RIP
RIP
RUB RUB
EEK! SEIJI!!
RUB
RUB
NO... KNOWING HIM, HE'LL PROBABLY DO SOMETHING I'LL NEVER EXPECT.
HI... SORRY TO KEEP YOU WAITING.
I HAD A LOT OF STUFF TO PREPARE, SO I GOT DELAYED.
SORRY ...
HAH...
YEEP
SO THEN, LET'S GET STARTED ...
RUSTLE
RUSTLE

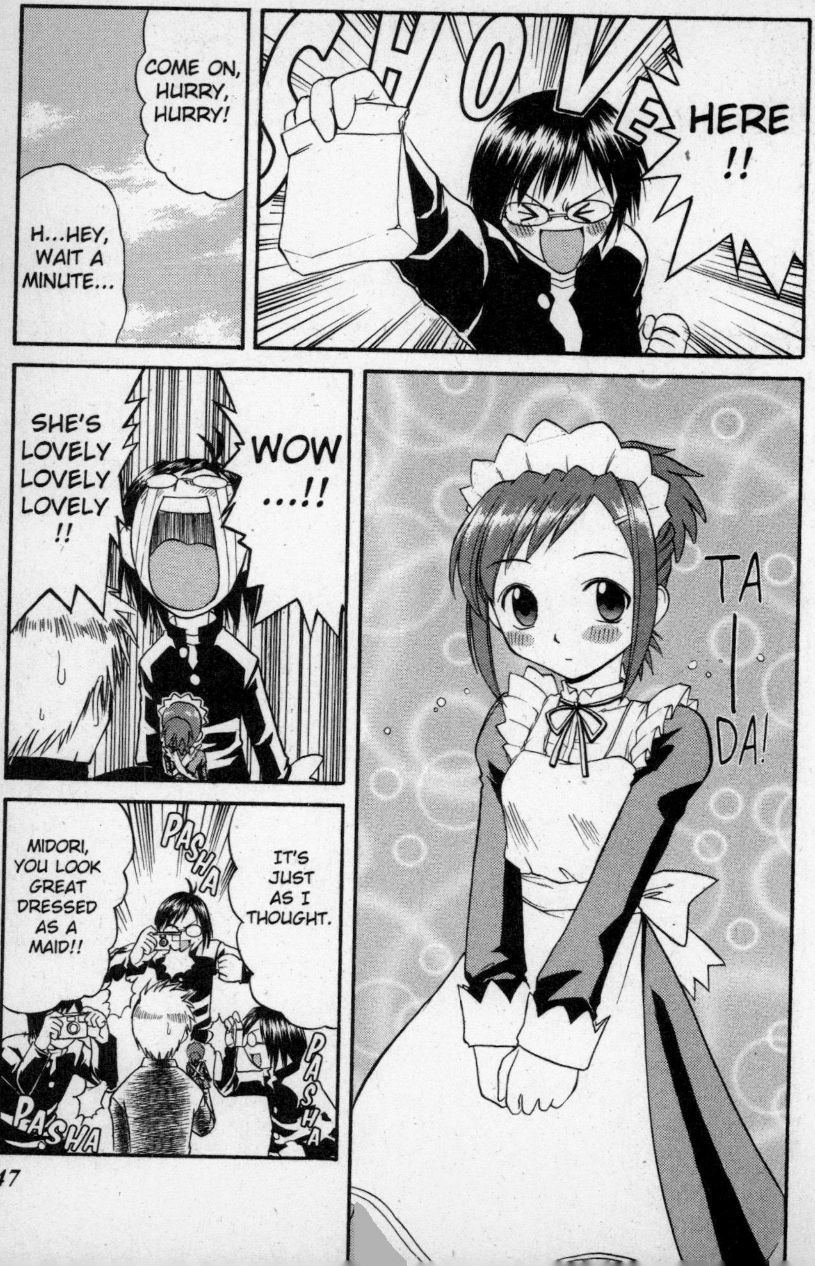
SHOVE
HERE!!
COME ON, HURRY, HURRY!
H...HEY, WAIT A MINUTE...
TA-I-DA!
WOW...!!
SHE'S LOVELY LOVELY LOVELY!!
PASHA
IT'S JUST AS I THOUGHT.
MIDORI, YOU LOOK GREAT DRESSED AS A MAID!!
PASHA
PASHA

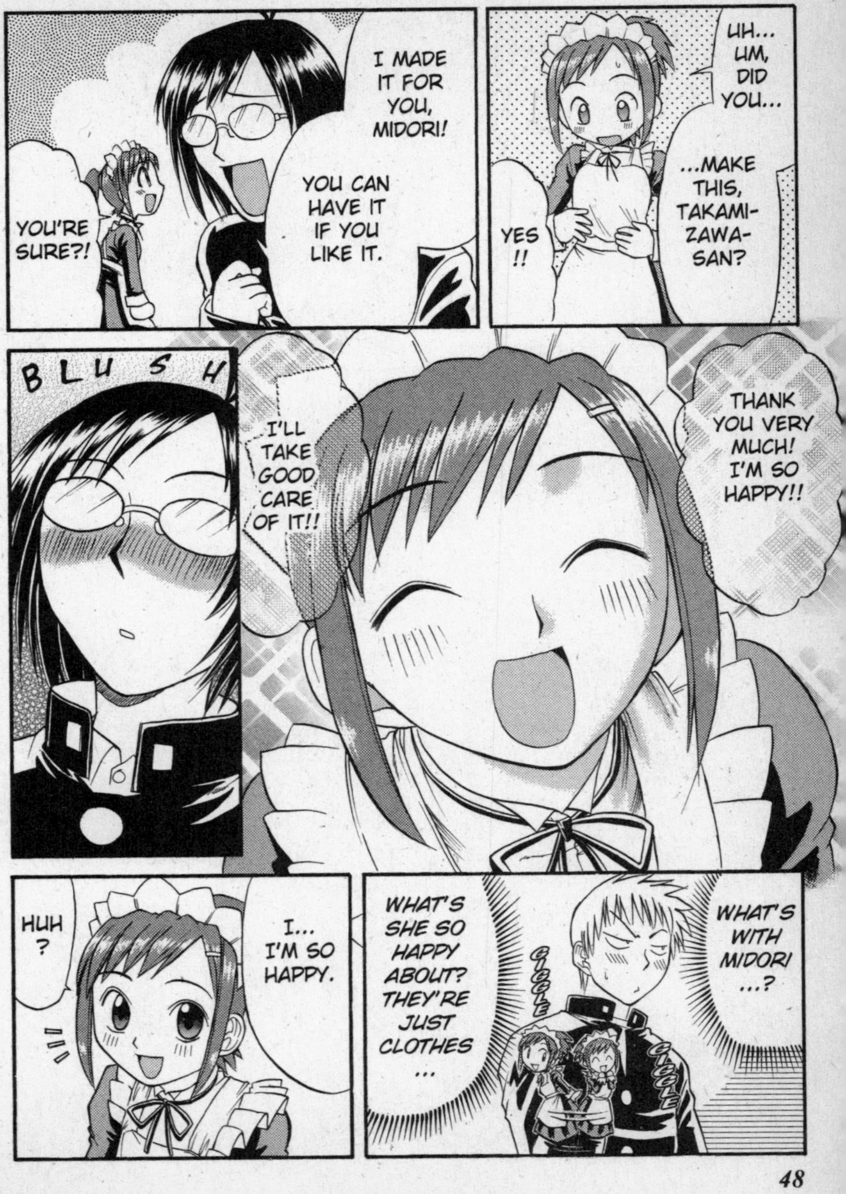
UH... UM, DID YOU...
...MAKE THIS, TAKAMI-ZAWA-SAN?
YES !!
I MADE IT FOR YOU, MIDORI!
YOU CAN HAVE IT IF YOU LIKE IT.
YOU'RE SURE?!
THANK YOU VERY MUCH! I'M SO HAPPY!!
I'LL TAKE GOOD CARE OF IT!!
BLUSH
WHAT'S WITH MIDORI ...?
WHAT'S SHE SO HAPPY ABOUT? THEY'RE JUST CLOTHES ...
GIGGLE
GIGGLE
I... I'M SO HAPPY.
HUH ?

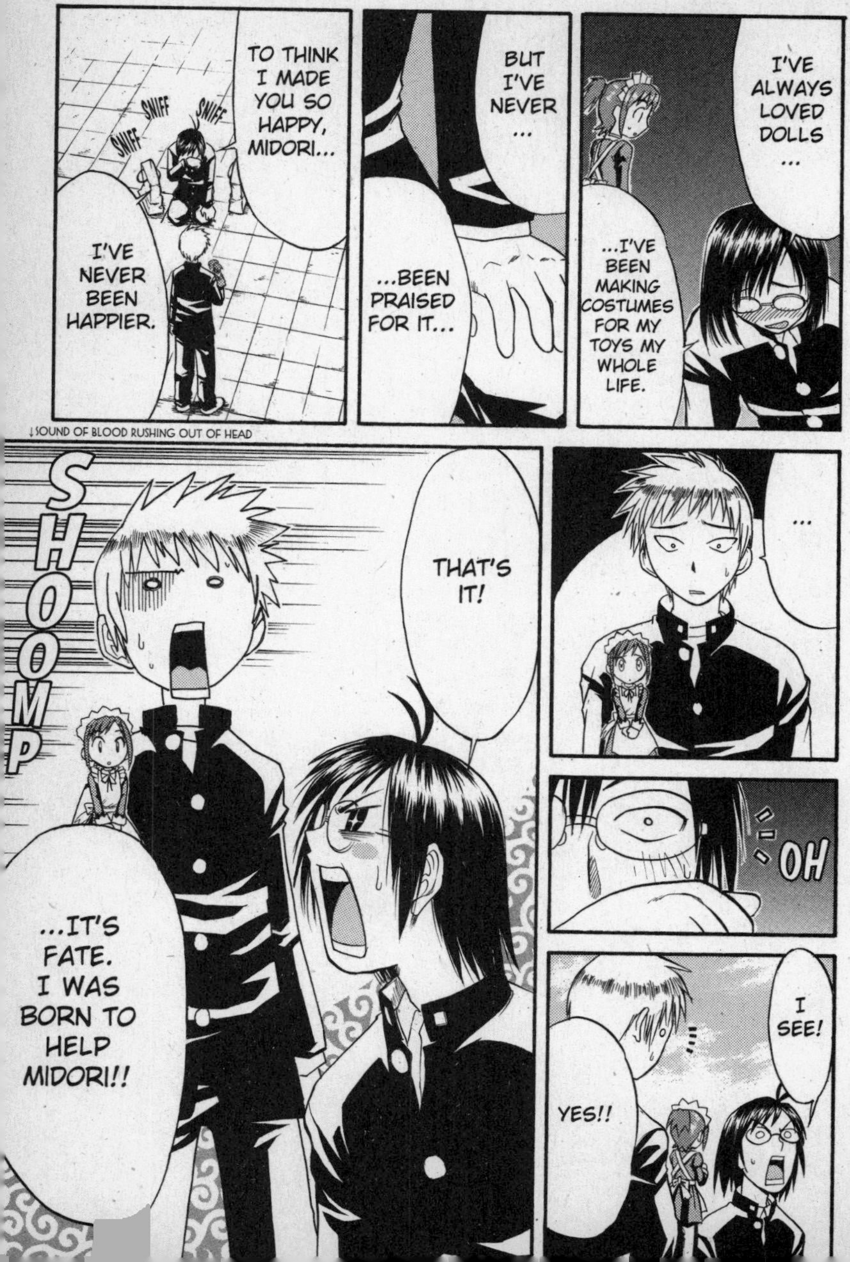
I'VE ALWAYS LOVED DOLLS ...
...I'VE BEEN MAKING COSTUMES FOR MY TOYS MY WHOLE LIFE.
BUT I'VE NEVER ...
...BEEN PRAISED FOR IT...
TO THINK I MADE YOU SO HAPPY, MIDORI...
SNIFF
SNIFF
SNIFF
I'VE NEVER BEEN HAPPIER.
↓SOUND OF BLOOD RUSHING OUT OF HEAD
...
...OH
I SEE!
YES!!
THAT'S IT!
...IT'S FATE. I WAS BORN TO HELP MIDORI!!
SHOOMP

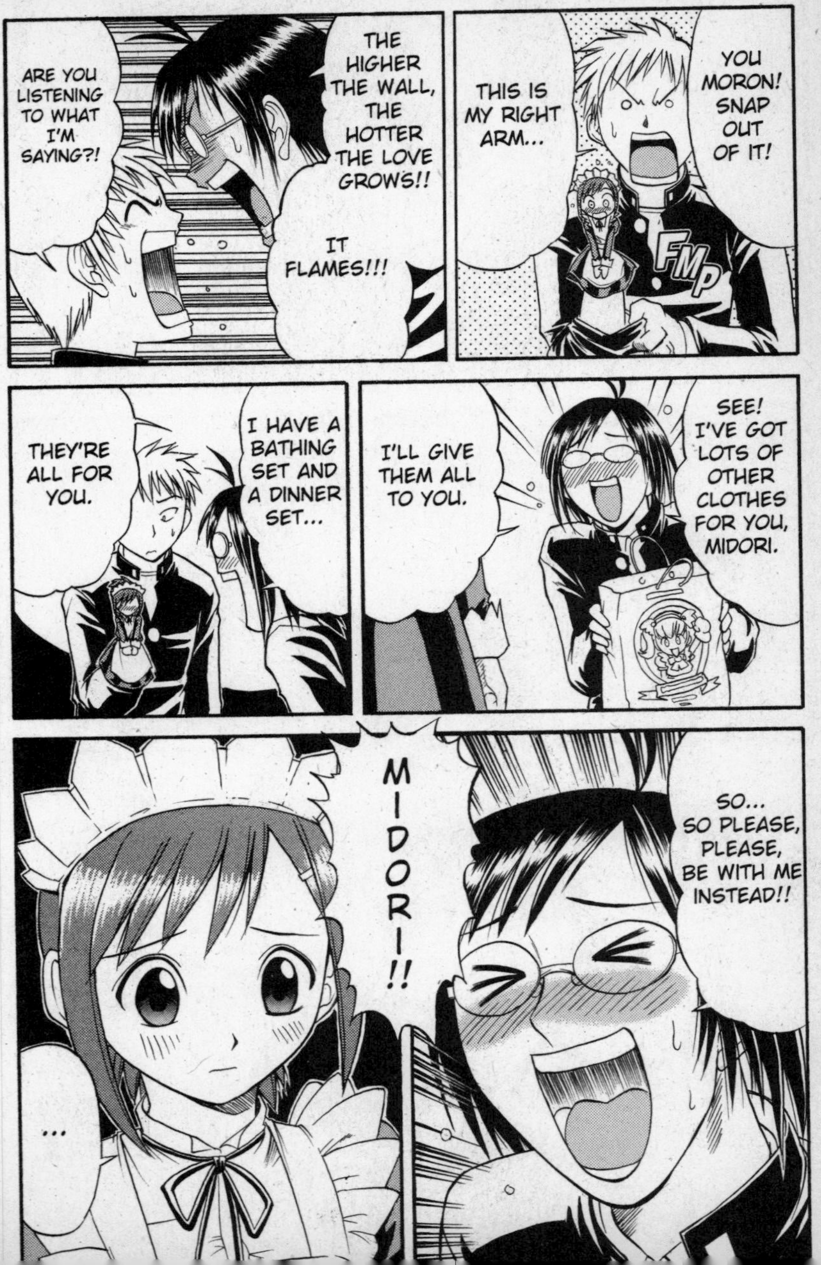
YOU MORON! SNAP OUT OF IT!
THIS IS MY RIGHT ARM...
FMP
THE HIGHER THE WALL, THE HOTTER THE LOVE GROWS!!
IT FLAMES!!!
ARE YOU LISTENING TO WHAT I'M SAYING?!
SEE! I'VE GOT LOTS OF OTHER CLOTHES FOR YOU, MIDORI.
I'LL GIVE THEM ALL TO YOU.
I HAVE A BATHING SET AND A DINNER SET...
THEY'RE ALL FOR YOU.
SO... SO PLEASE, PLEASE, BE WITH ME INSTEAD!!
MIDORI!!
...

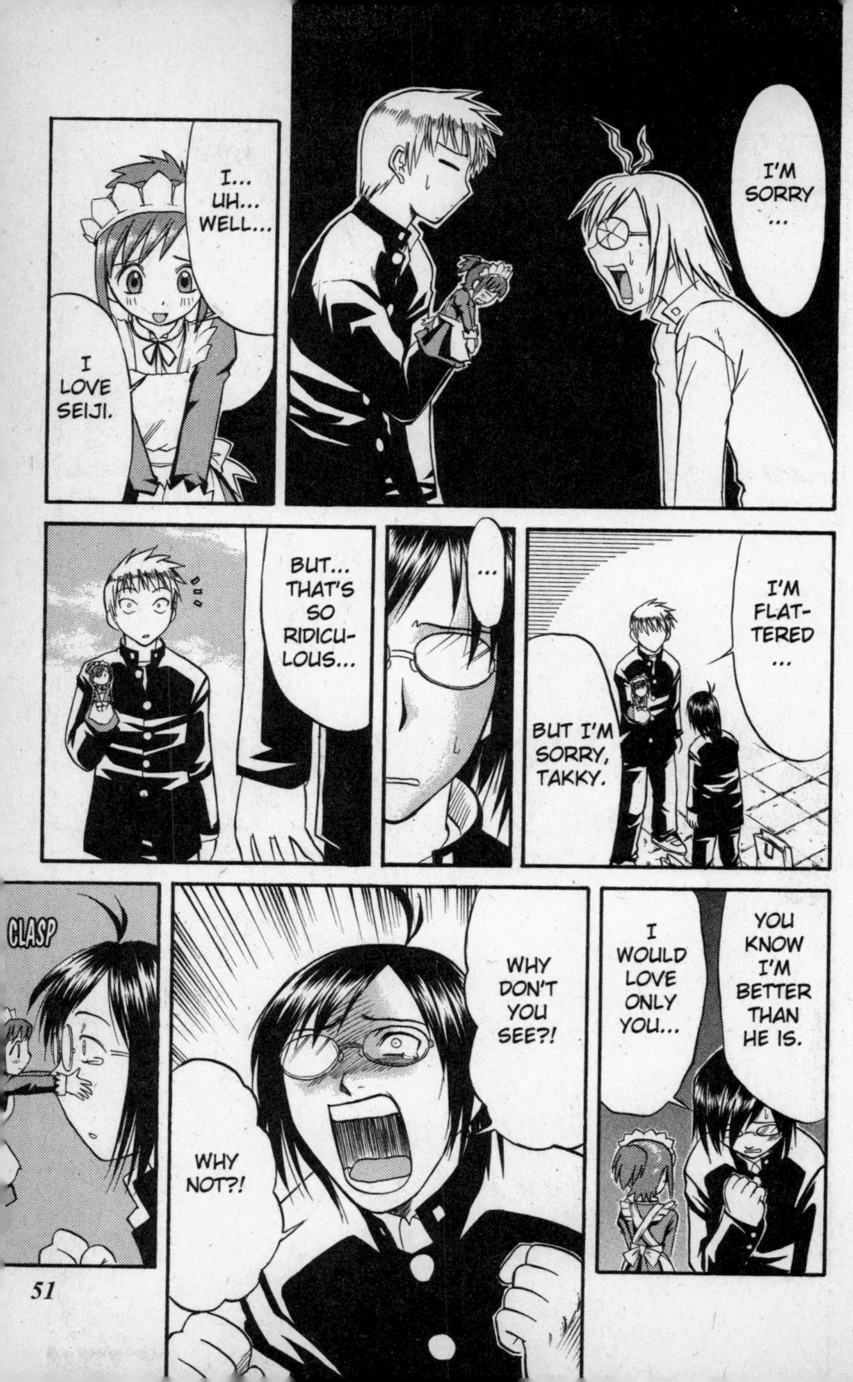

I'M SORRY...
I... UH... WELL...
I LOVE SEIJI.
I'M FLATTERED...
BUT I'M SORRY, TAKKY.
...
BUT... THAT'S SO RIDICULOUS...
YOU KNOW I'M BETTER THAN HE IS.
I WOULD LOVE ONLY YOU...
WHY DON'T YOU SEE?!
WHY NOT?!
CLASP

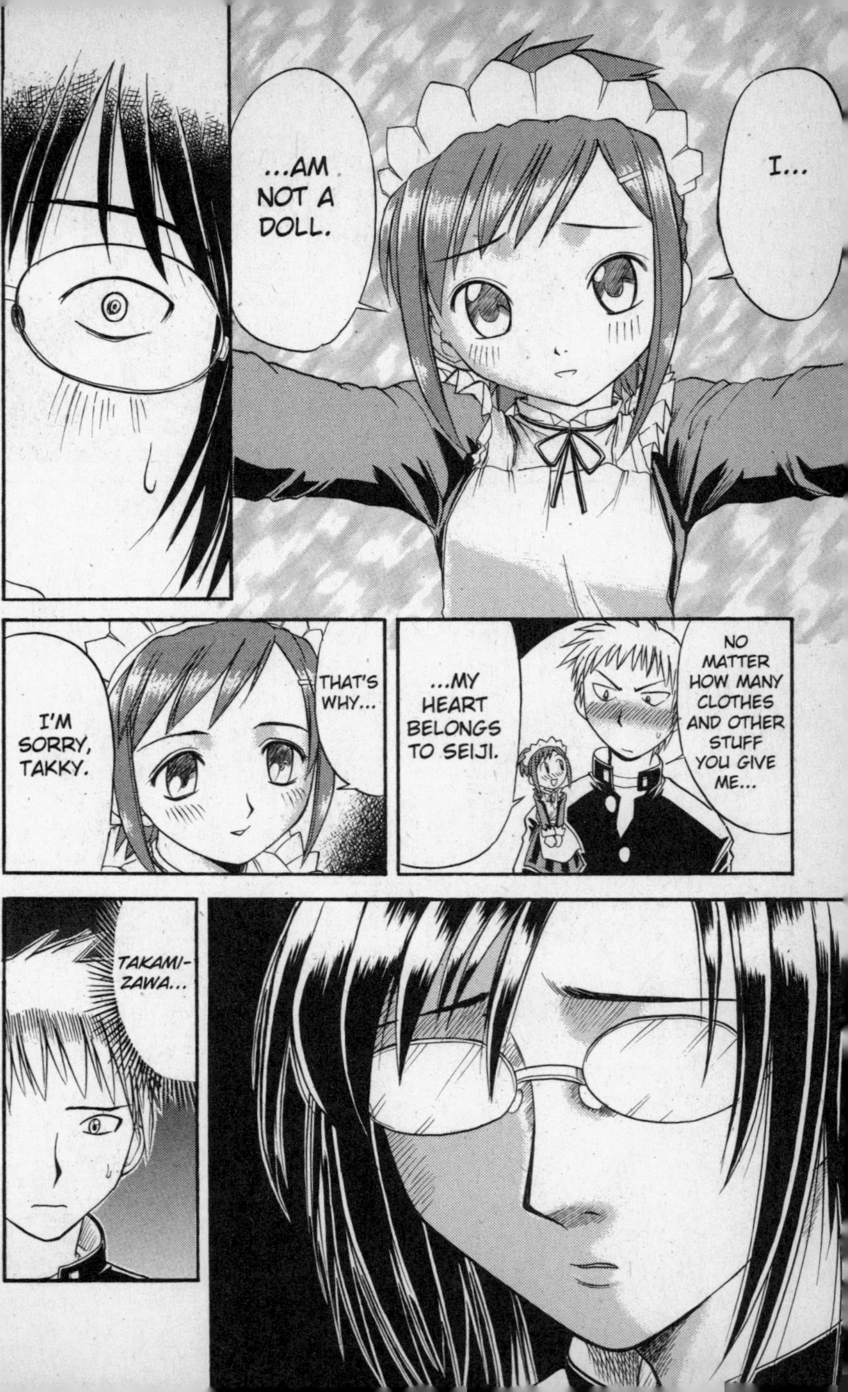
I...
...AM NOT A DOLL.
NO MATTER HOW MANY CLOTHES AND OTHER STUFF YOU GIVE ME...
...MY HEART BELONGS TO SEIJI.
THAT'S WHY...
I'M SORRY, TAKKY.
TAKAMI-ZAWA...

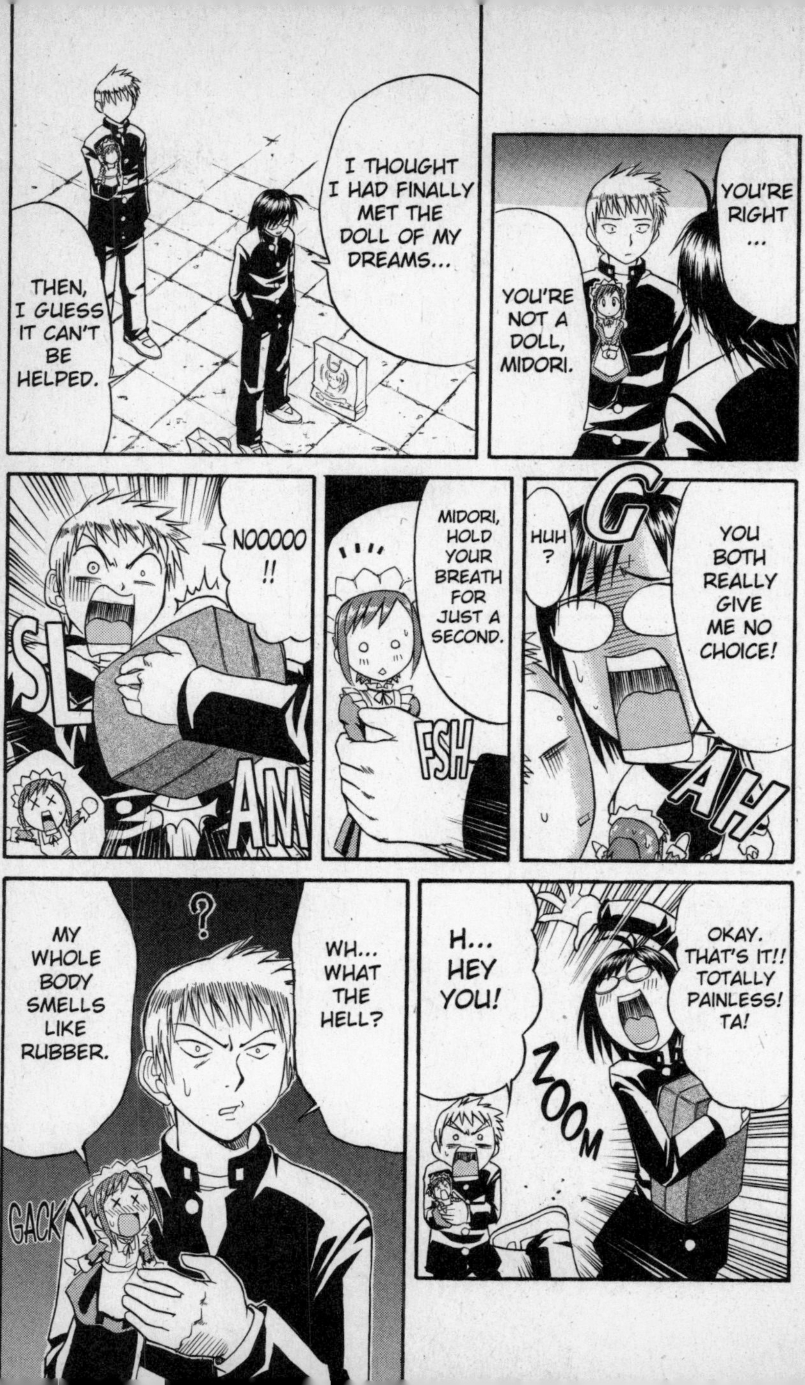
YOU'RE RIGHT ...
YOU'RE NOT A DOLL, MIDORI.
I THOUGHT I HAD FINALLY MET THE DOLL OF MY DREAMS...
THEN, I GUESS IT CAN'T BE HELPED.
YOU BOTH REALLY GIVE ME NO CHOICE!
G
AH
HUH ?
MIDORI, HOLD YOUR BREATH FOR JUST A SECOND.
FSH
NOOOOO !!
SL
AM
OKAY. THAT'S IT!! TOTALLY PAINLESS! TA!
H... HEY YOU!
ZOOM
WH... WHAT THE HELL?
?
MY WHOLE BODY SMELLS LIKE RUBBER.
GACK

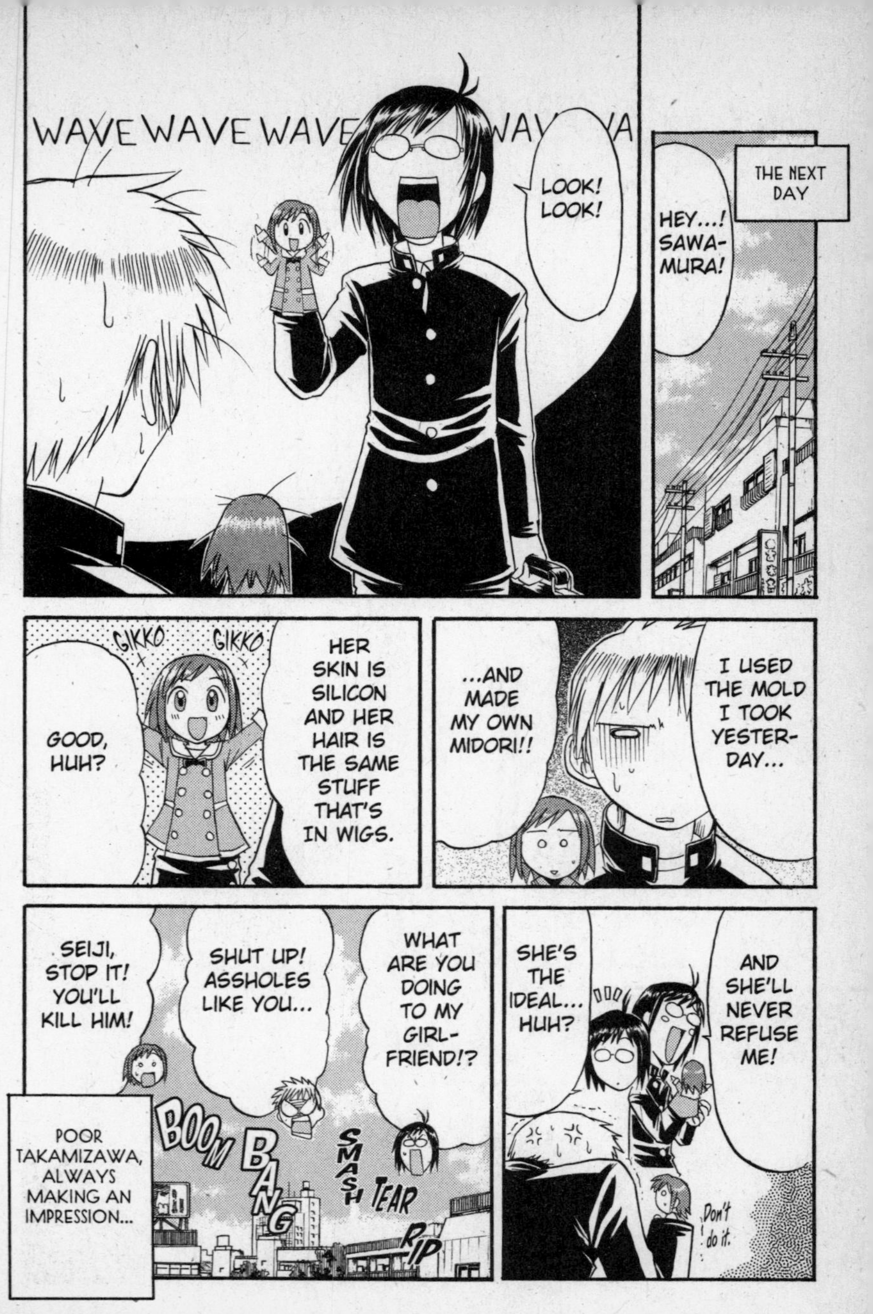
THE NEXT DAY
HEY...! SAWAMURA!
WAVE WAVE WAVE
LOOK! LOOK!
I USED THE MOLD I TOOK YESTERDAY...
...AND MADE MY OWN MIDORI!!
GIKKO GIKKO
HER SKIN IS SILICON AND HER HAIR IS THE SAME STUFF THAT'S IN WIGS.
GOOD, HUH?
AND SHE'LL NEVER REFUSE ME!
SHE'S THE IDEAL... HUH?
Don't do it.
WHAT ARE YOU DOING TO MY GIRLFRIEND!?
SHUT UP! ASSHOLES LIKE YOU...
SEIJI, STOP IT! YOU'LL KILL HIM!
BOOM
BANG
SMASH
TEAR
RIP
POOR TAKAMIZAWA, ALWAYS MAKING AN IMPRESSION...

DAY 36 THE GIRL THAT WASN'T

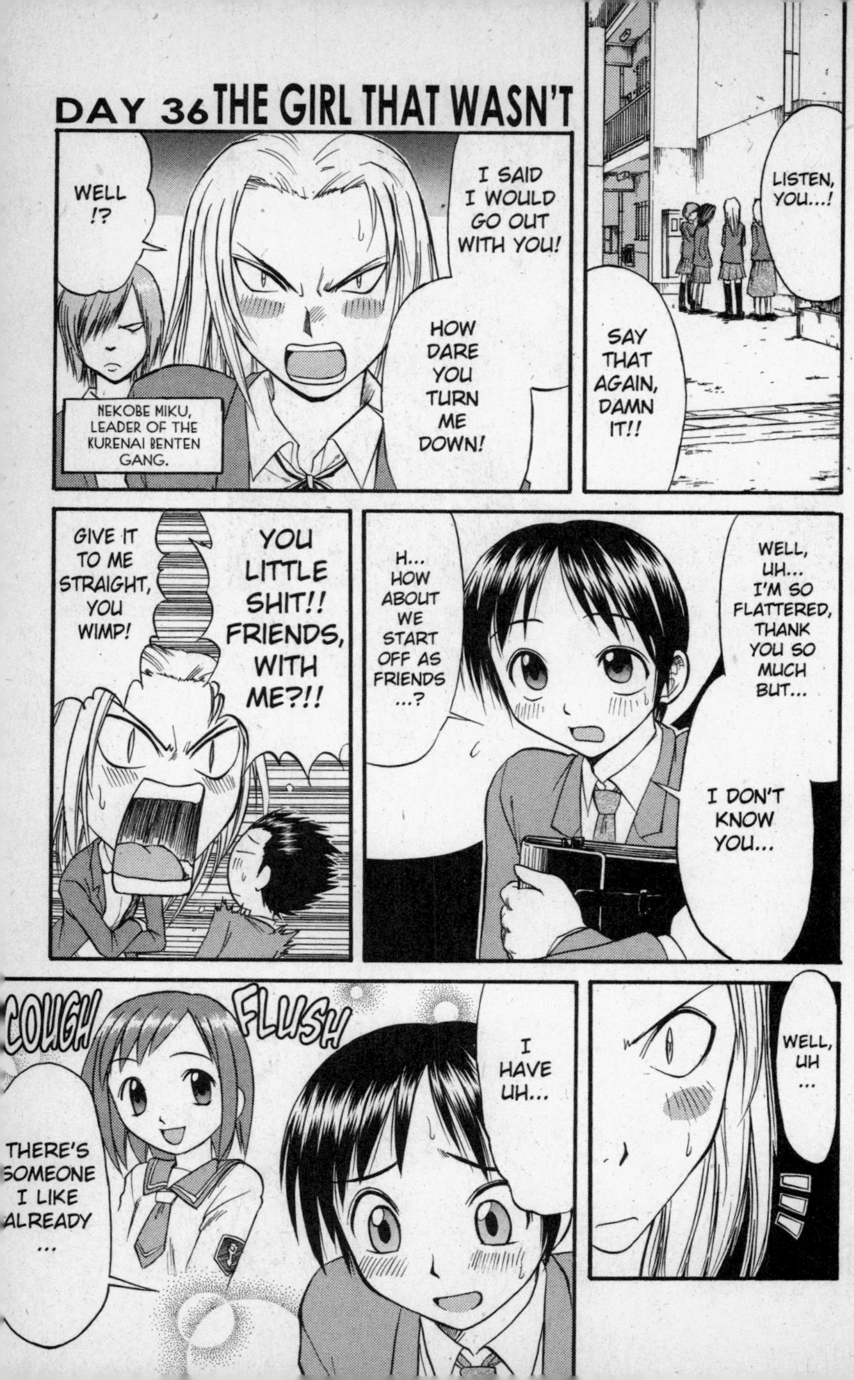

LISTEN, YOU...!
SAY THAT AGAIN, DAMN IT!!
I SAID I WOULD GO OUT WITH YOU!
WELL !?
HOW DARE YOU TURN ME DOWN!
NEKOBE MIKU, LEADER OF THE KURENAI BENTEN GANG.
WELL, UH... I'M SO FLATTERED, THANK YOU SO MUCH BUT...
I DON'T KNOW YOU...
H... HOW ABOUT WE START OFF AS FRIENDS ...?
YOU LITTLE SHIT!! FRIENDS, WITH ME?!!
GIVE IT TO ME STRAIGHT, YOU WIMP!
WELL, UH ...
I HAVE UH...
FLUSH
COUGH
THERE'S SOMEONE I LIKE ALREADY ...

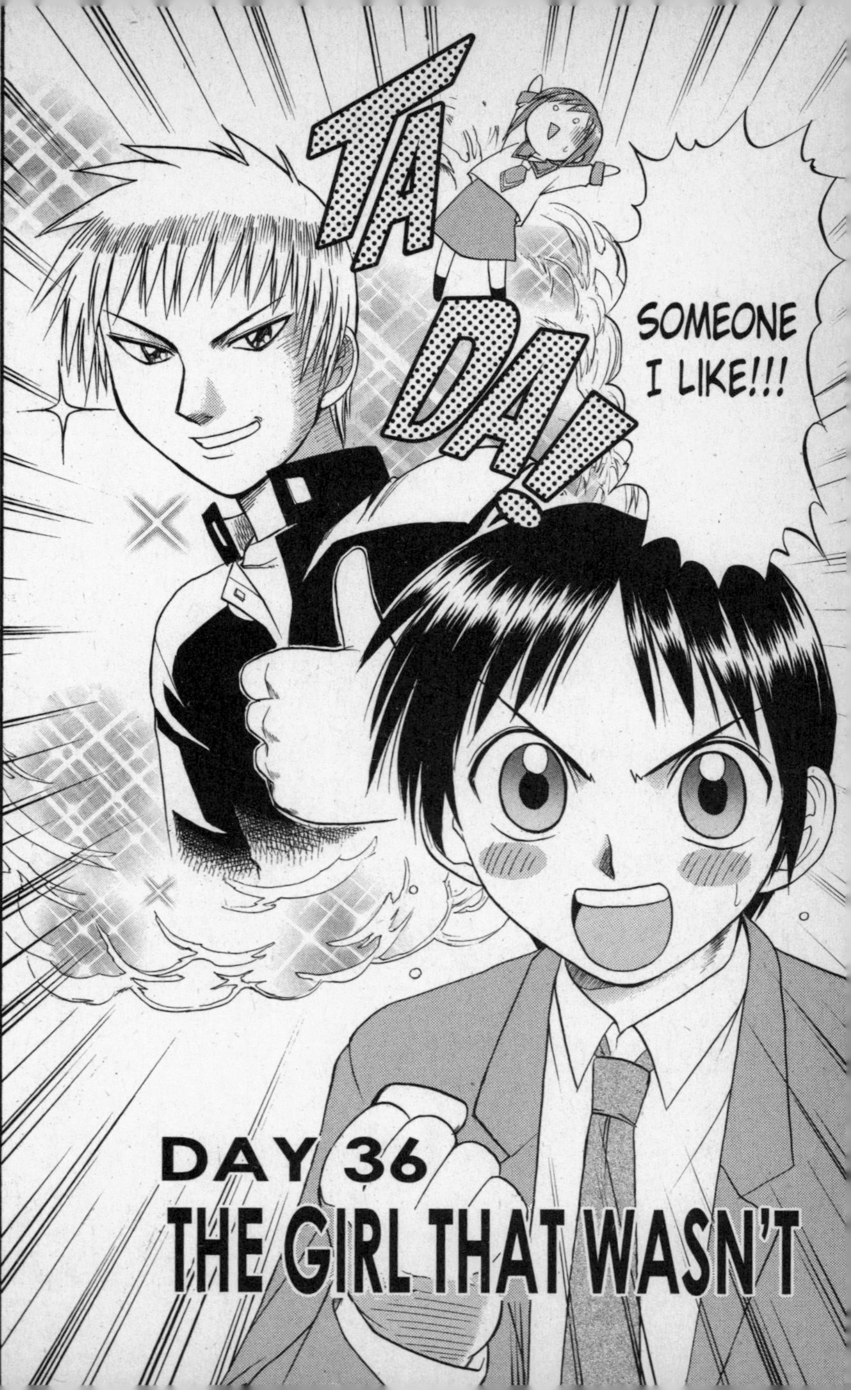
TA DA!
SOMEONE I LIKE!!!
DAY 36
THE GIRL THAT WASN'T

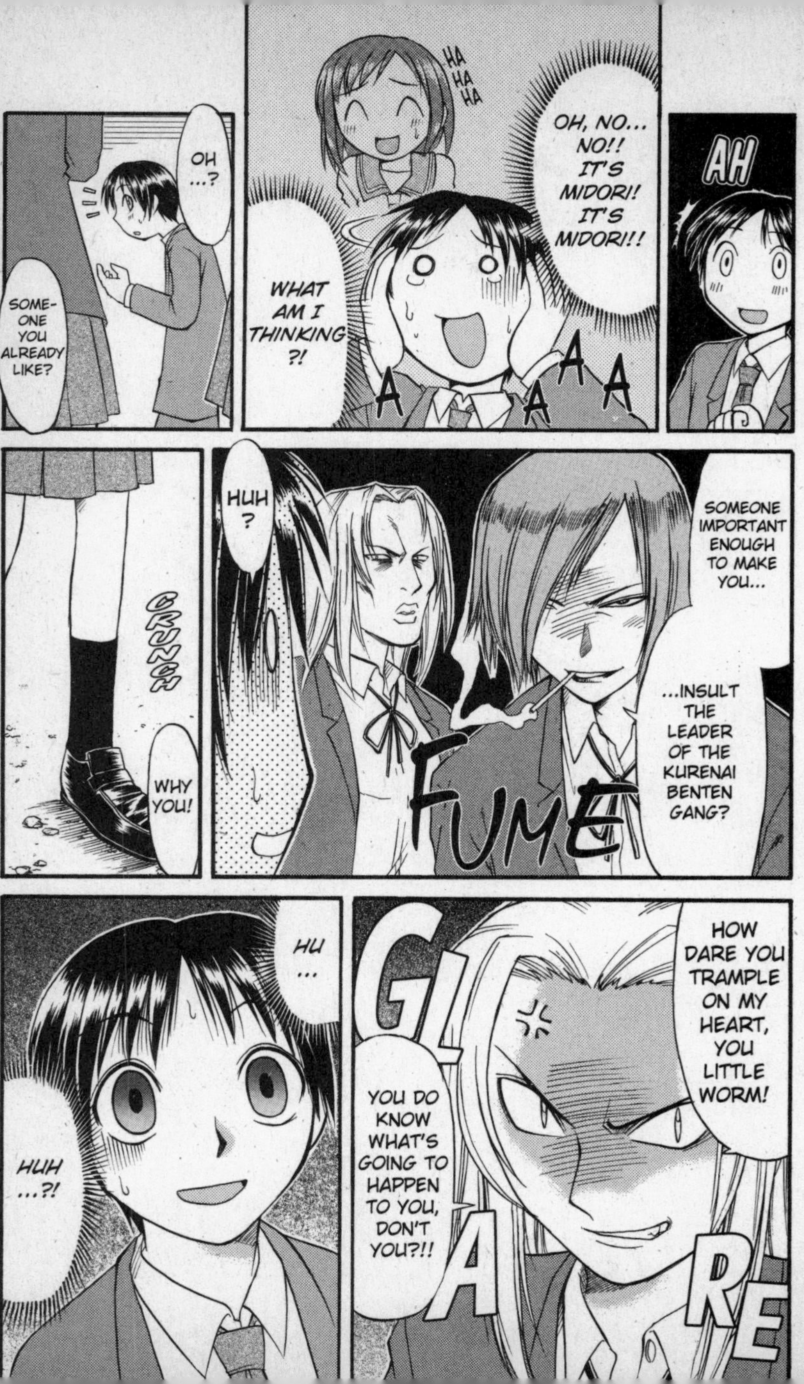
AH
OH, NO... NO!! IT'S MIDORI! IT'S MIDORI!!
HA HA HA
WHAT AM I THINKING ?!
AAAAA
OH ...?
SOME-ONE YOU ALREADY LIKE?
SOMEONE IMPORTANT ENOUGH TO MAKE YOU...
HUH ?
...INSULT THE LEADER OF THE KURENAI BENTEN GANG?
FUME
CRUNCH
WHY YOU!
HOW DARE YOU TRAMPLE ON MY HEART, YOU LITTLE WORM!
GLARE
YOU DO KNOW WHAT'S GOING TO HAPPEN TO YOU, DON'T YOU?!!
HU ...
HUH ...?!

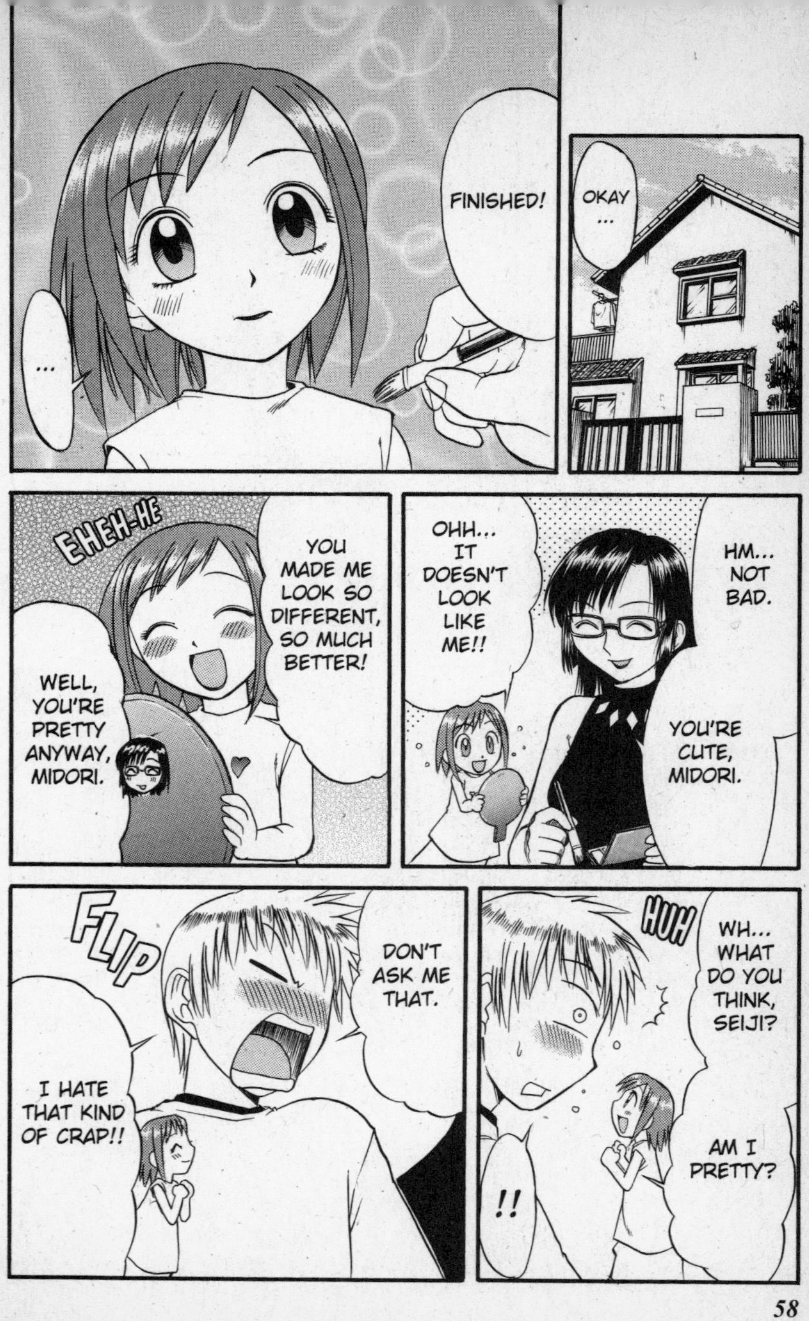
OKAY ...
FINISHED!
...
HM... NOT BAD.
OHH... IT DOESN'T LOOK LIKE ME!!
YOU'RE CUTE, MIDORI.
EHEH-HE
YOU MADE ME LOOK SO DIFFERENT, SO MUCH BETTER!
WELL, YOU'RE PRETTY ANYWAY, MIDORI.
HUH
WH... WHAT DO YOU THINK, SEIJI?
AM I PRETTY?
!!
FLIP
DON'T ASK ME THAT.
I HATE THAT KIND OF CRAP!!

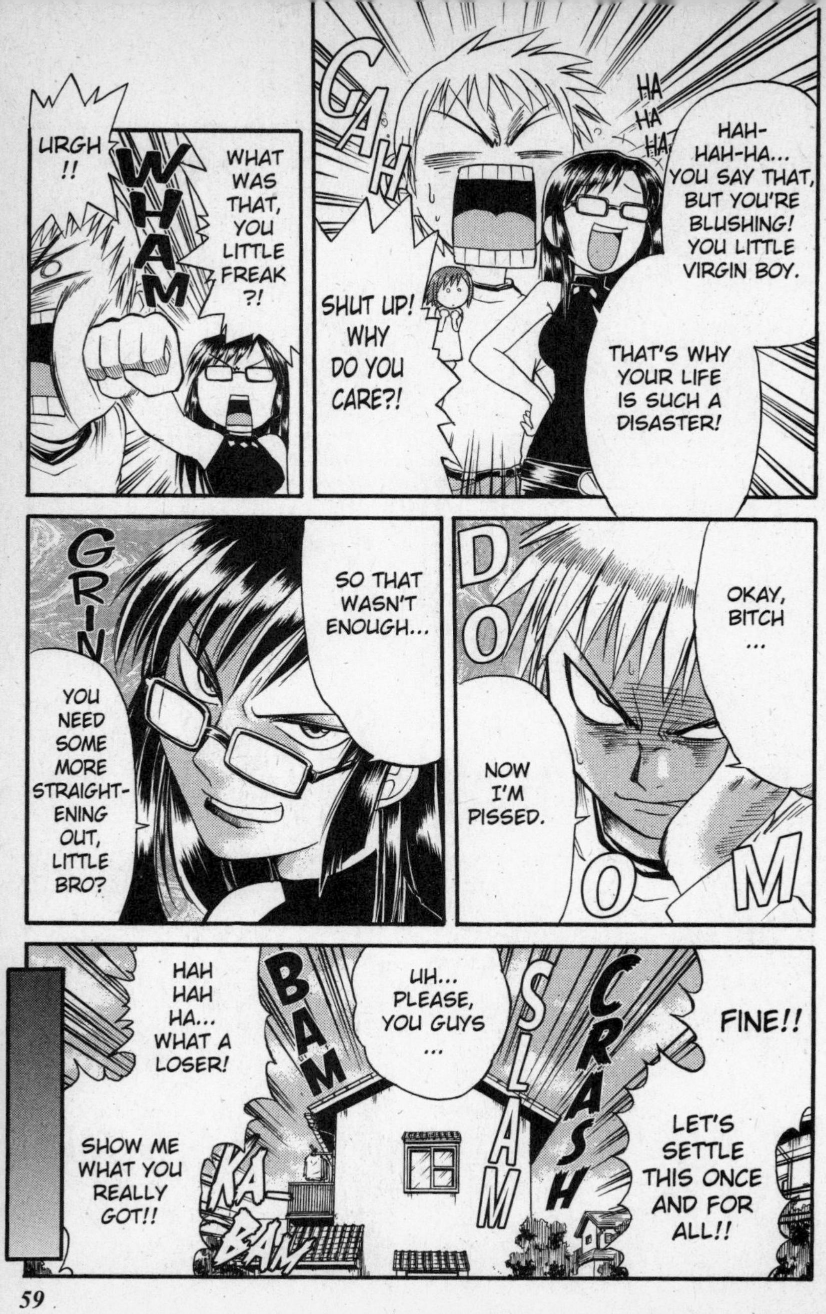
HA HA HA
HAH-HAH-HA... YOU SAY THAT, BUT YOU'RE BLUSHING! YOU LITTLE VIRGIN BOY.
GAH
SHUT UP! WHY DO YOU CARE?!
THAT'S WHY YOUR LIFE IS SUCH A DISASTER!
WHAT WAS THAT, YOU LITTLE FREAK?!
WHAM
URGH!!
OKAY, BITCH...
DOOM
NOW I'M PISSED.
SO THAT WASN'T ENOUGH...
GRIN
YOU NEED SOME MORE STRAIGHT-ENING OUT, LITTLE BRO?
FINE!!
LET'S SETTLE THIS ONCE AND FOR ALL!!
CRASH
SLAM
UH... PLEASE, YOU GUYS...
BAM
HAH HAH HA... WHAT A LOSER!
SHOW ME WHAT YOU REALLY GOT!!
KA BAM

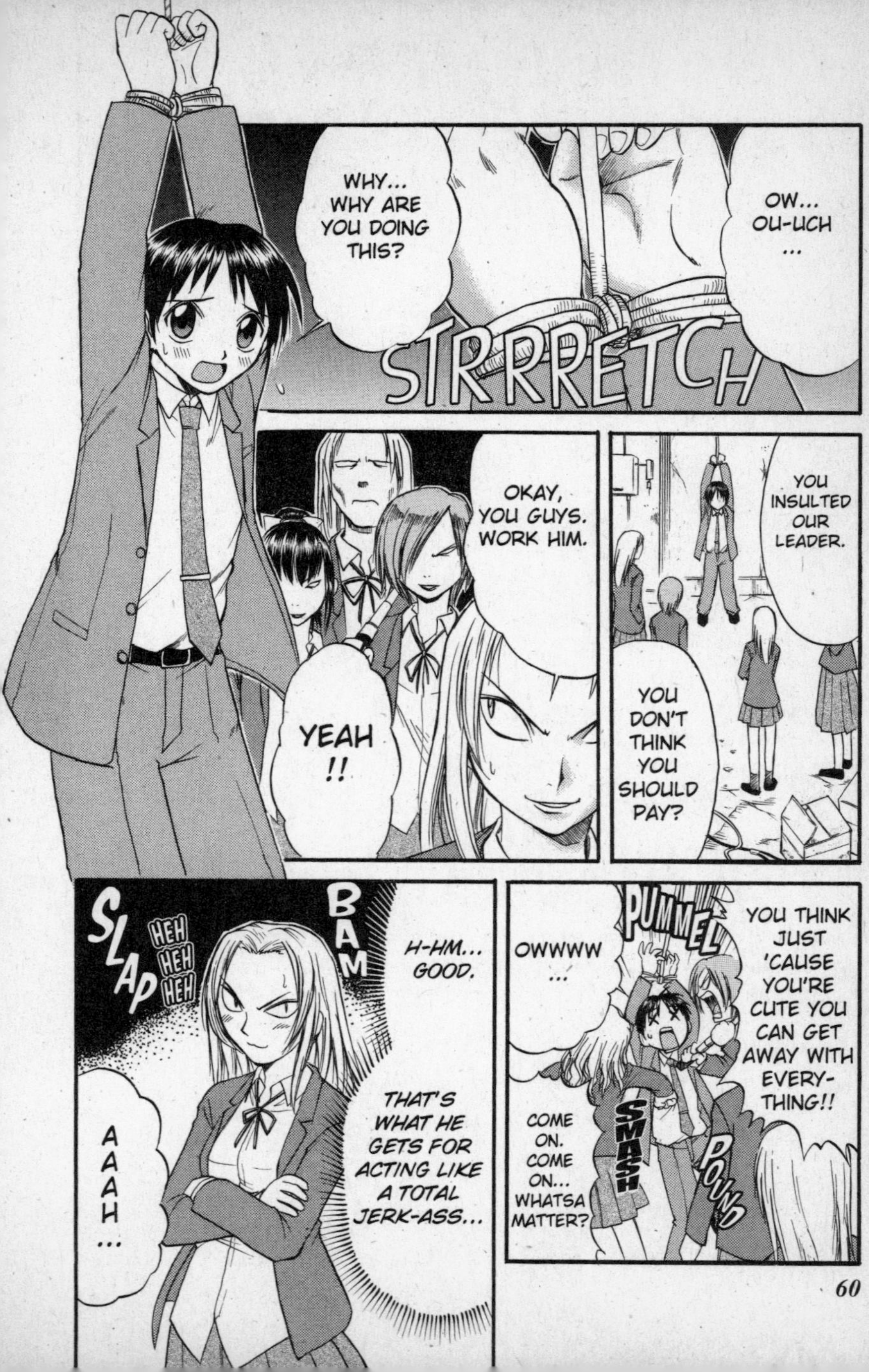
OW... OU-UCH ...
WHY... WHY ARE YOU DOING THIS?
STRRRETCH
YOU INSULTED OUR LEADER.
YOU DON'T THINK YOU SHOULD PAY?
OKAY, YOU GUYS. WORK HIM.
YEAH !!
YOU THINK JUST 'CAUSE YOU'RE CUTE YOU CAN GET AWAY WITH EVERY-THING!!
PUMMEL
OWWWW ...
SMASH
POUND
COME ON. COME ON... WHATSA MATTER?
BAM
H-HM... GOOD.
SLAP
HEH HEH HEH
THAT'S WHAT HE GETS FOR ACTING LIKE A TOTAL JERK-ASS...
AAAAH ...

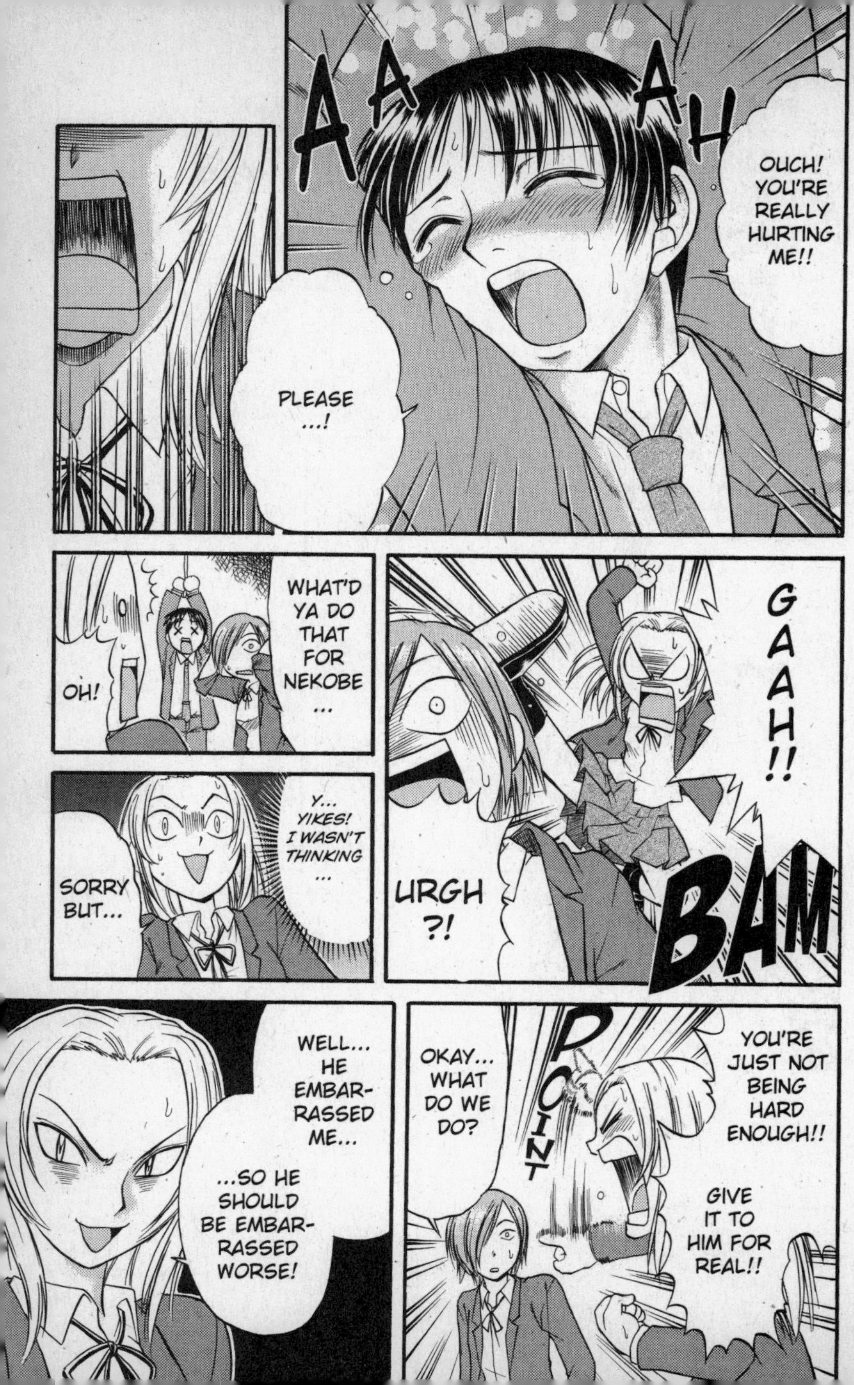
AAAH
OUCH! YOU'RE REALLY HURTING ME!!
PLEASE ...!
GAAH!!
BAM
URGH ?!
WHAT'D YA DO THAT FOR NEKOBE ...
OH!
Y... YIKES! I WASN'T THINKING ...
SORRY BUT...
POINT
YOU'RE JUST NOT BEING HARD ENOUGH!!
GIVE IT TO HIM FOR REAL!!
OKAY... WHAT DO WE DO?
WELL... HE EMBARRASSED ME...
...SO HE SHOULD BE EMBARRASSED WORSE!

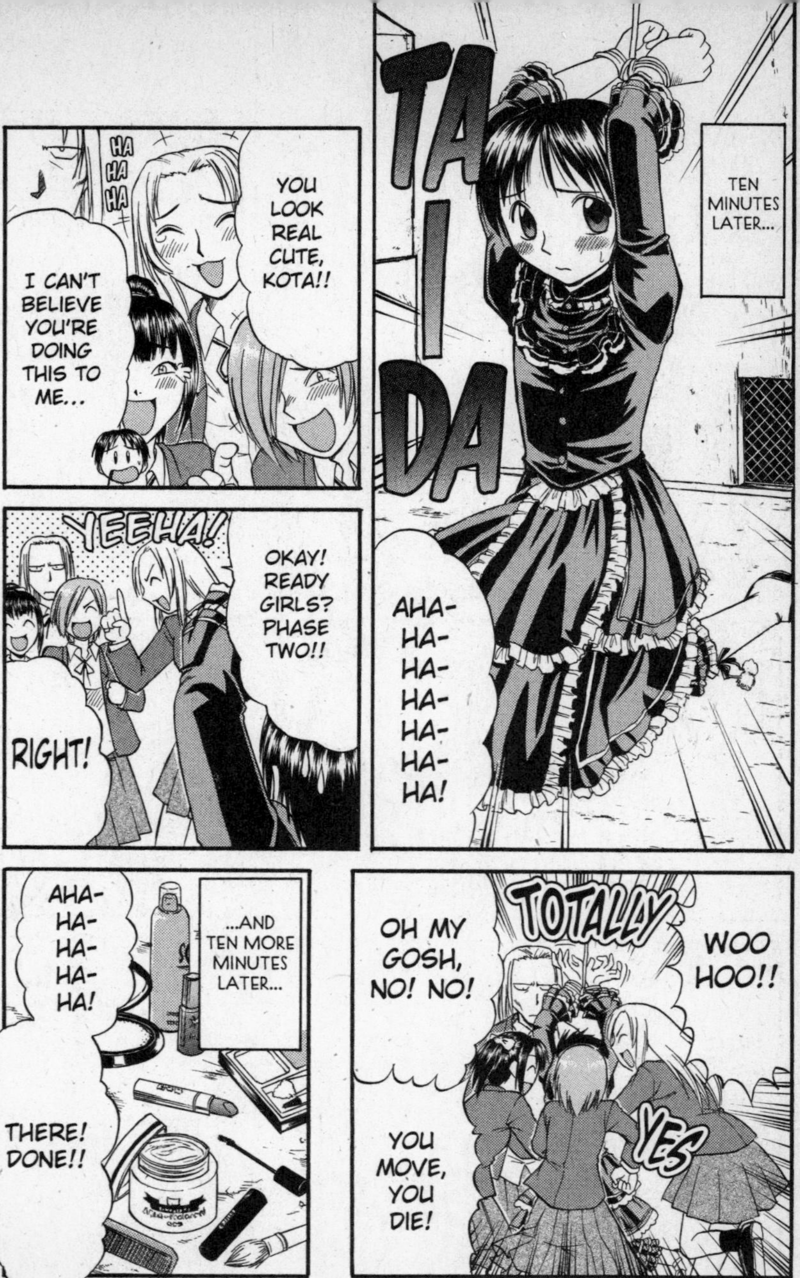
TEN MINUTES LATER...
TA I DA
AHA-HA-HA-HA-HA-HA-HA!
YOU LOOK REAL CUTE, KOTA!!
HA HA HA
I CAN'T BELIEVE YOU'RE DOING THIS TO ME...
YEEHA!
OKAY! READY GIRLS? PHASE TWO!!
RIGHT!
WOO HOO!!
TOTALLY
OH MY GOSH, NO! NO!
YES
YOU MOVE, YOU DIE!
...AND TEN MORE MINUTES LATER...
AHA-HA-HA-HA-HA!
THERE! DONE!!

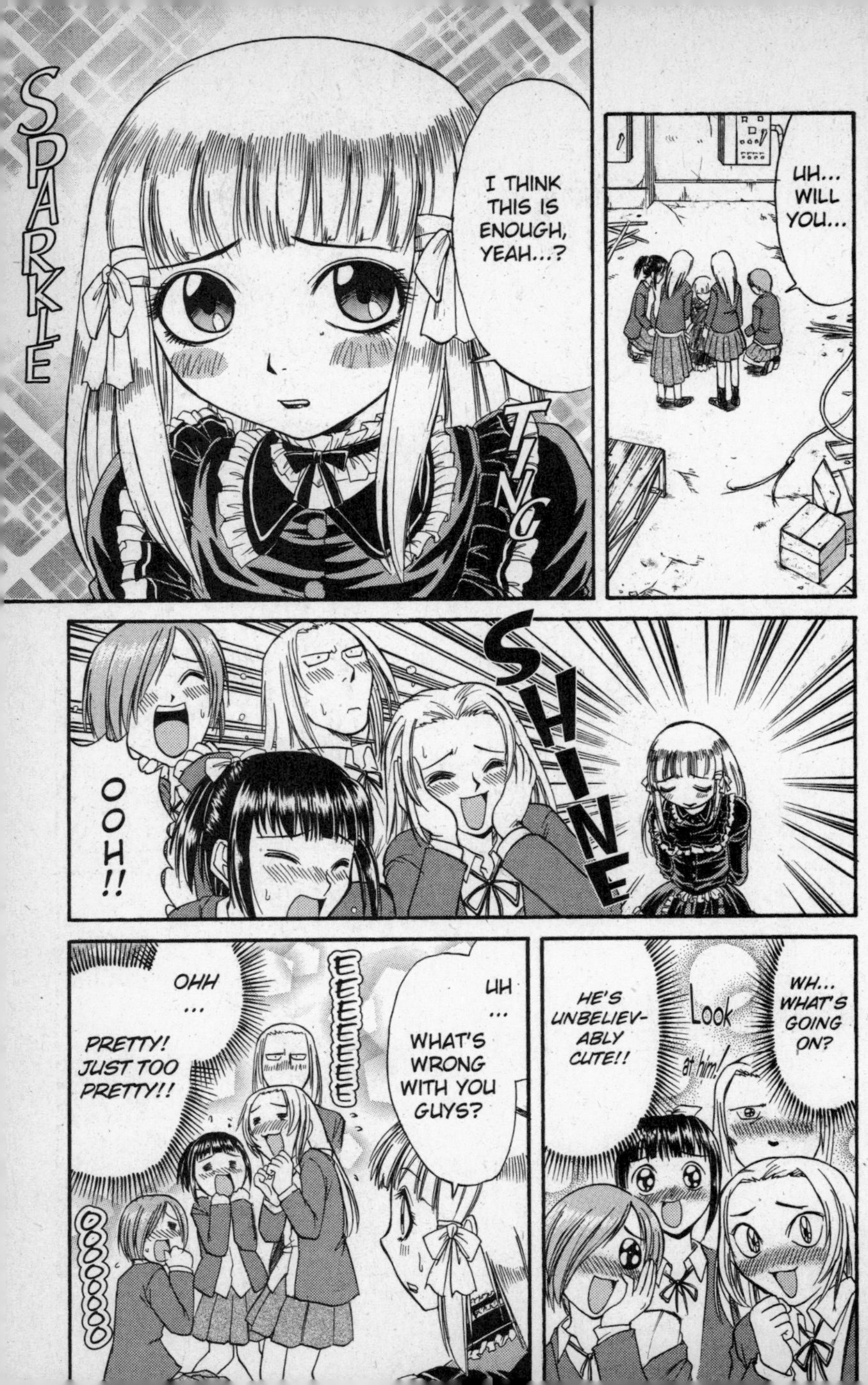
UH... WILL YOU...
SPARKLE
I THINK THIS IS ENOUGH, YEAH...?
TINC
SHINE
OOH!!
WH... WHAT'S GOING ON?
Look at him!
HE'S UNBELIEVABLY CUTE!!
UH ... WHAT'S WRONG WITH YOU GUYS?
EEEEEEEE
OHH ...
PRETTY! JUST TOO PRETTY!!
OOOOOOOO

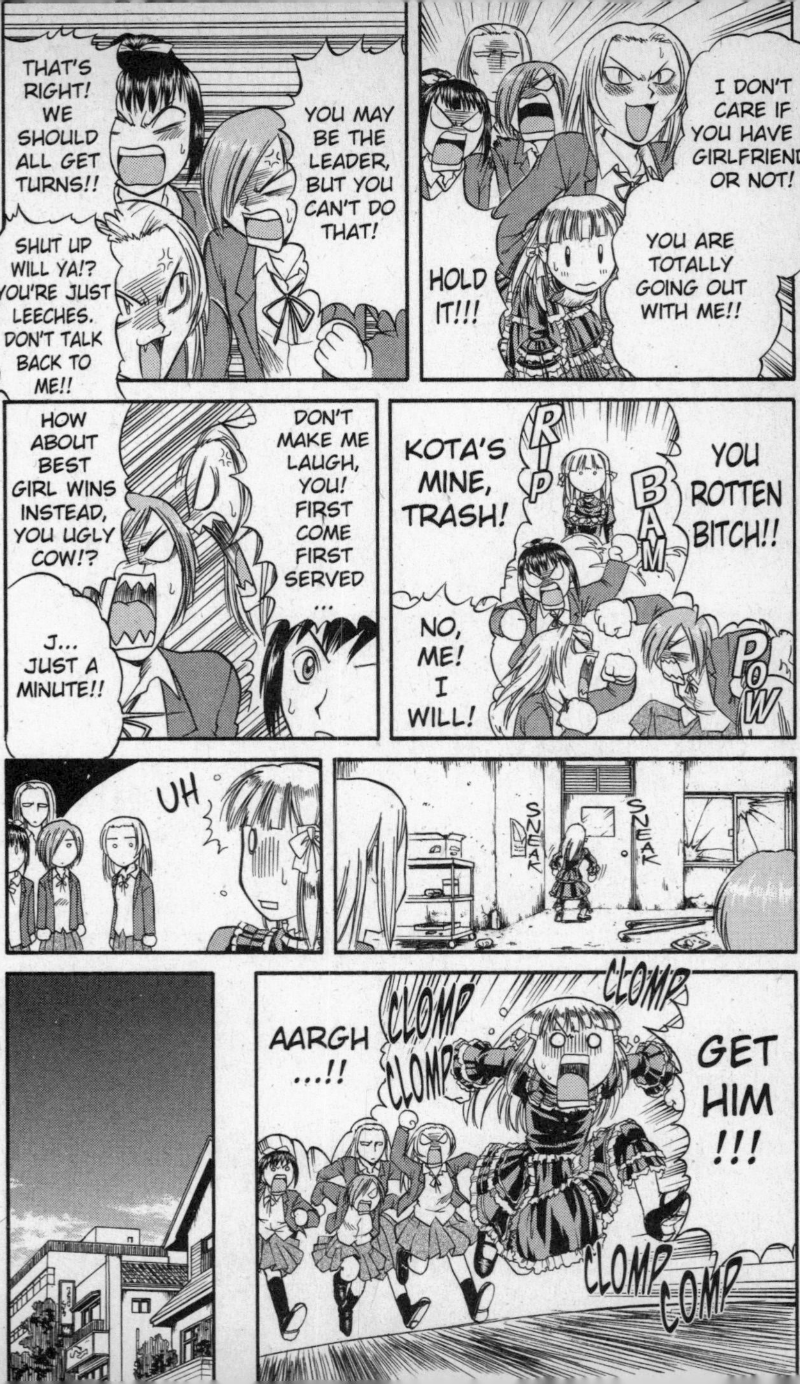
I DON'T CARE IF YOU HAVE A GIRLFRIEND, OR NOT!
YOU ARE TOTALLY GOING OUT WITH ME!!
HOLD IT!!!
YOU MAY BE THE LEADER, BUT YOU CAN'T DO THAT!
THAT'S RIGHT! WE SHOULD ALL GET TURNS!!
SHUT UP WILL YA!? YOU'RE JUST LEECHES. DON'T TALK BACK TO ME!!
YOU ROTTEN BITCH!!
BAM
RIP
KOTA'S MINE, TRASH!
POW
NO, ME! I WILL!
DON'T MAKE ME LAUGH, YOU! FIRST COME FIRST SERVED ...
HOW ABOUT BEST GIRL WINS INSTEAD, YOU UGLY COW!?
J... JUST A MINUTE!!
SNEAK
SNEAK
UH
CLOMP
GET HIM !!!
CLOMP
CLOMP
AARGH ...!!
CLOMP
COMP

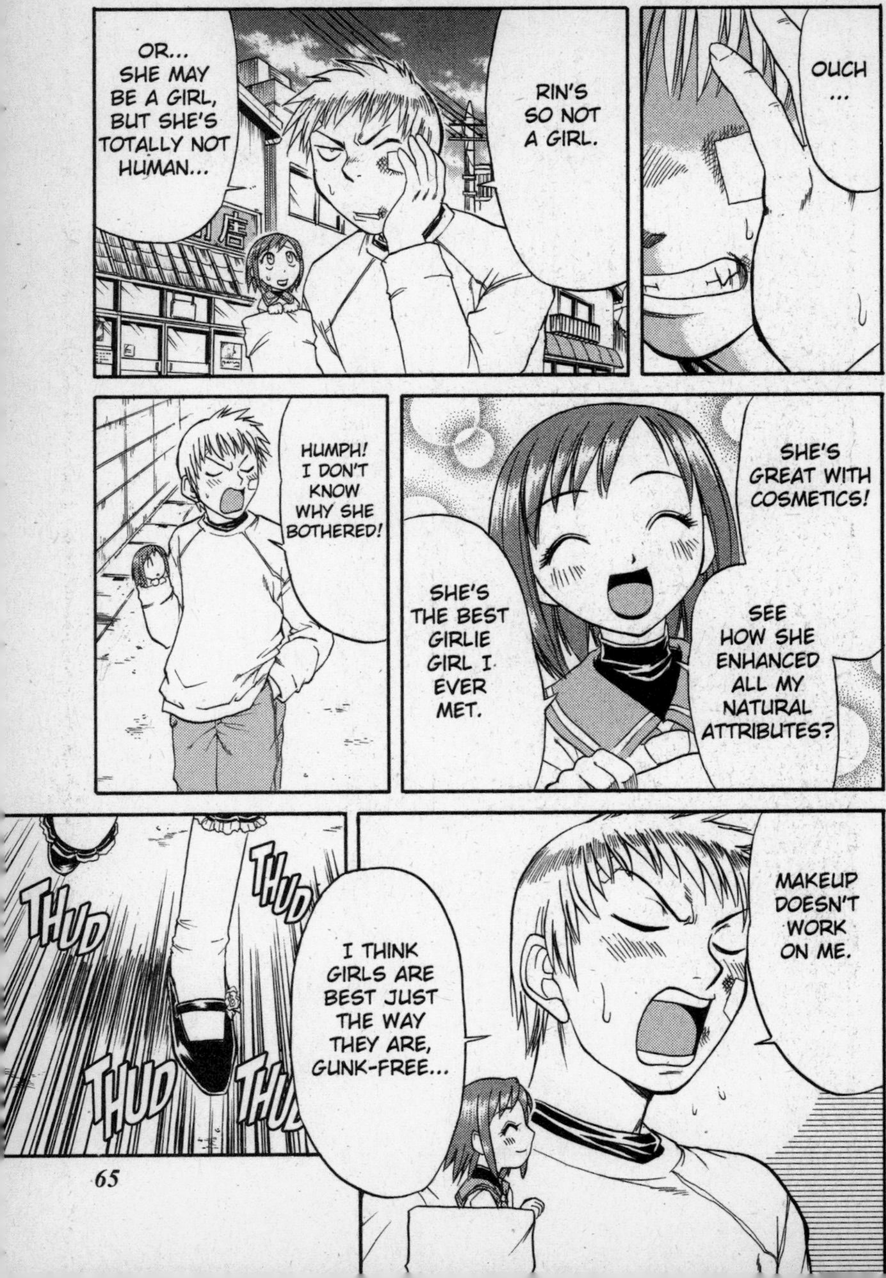
OUCH ...
RIN'S SO NOT A GIRL.
OR... SHE MAY BE A GIRL, BUT SHE'S TOTALLY NOT HUMAN...
SHE'S GREAT WITH COSMETICS!
SEE HOW SHE ENHANCED ALL MY NATURAL ATTRIBUTES?
SHE'S THE BEST GIRLIE GIRL I EVER MET.
HUMPH! I DON'T KNOW WHY SHE BOTHERED!
MAKEUP DOESN'T WORK ON ME.
I THINK GIRLS ARE BEST JUST THE WAY THEY ARE, GUNK-FREE...
THUD
THUD
THUD

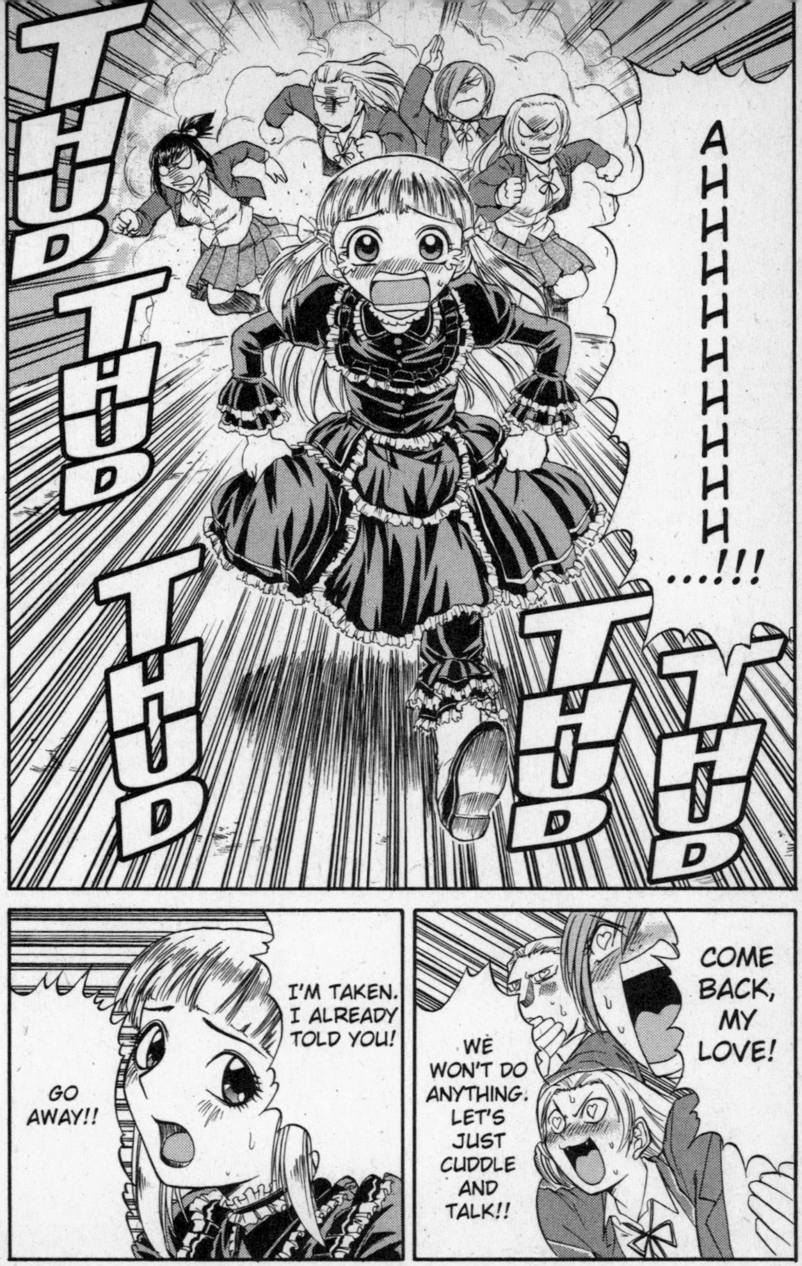
AHHHHHHHHH...!!!
THUD
THUD
THUD
THUD
THUD
COME BACK, MY LOVE!
WE WON'T DO ANYTHING. LET'S JUST CUDDLE AND TALK!!
I'M TAKEN. I ALREADY TOLD YOU!
GO AWAY!!

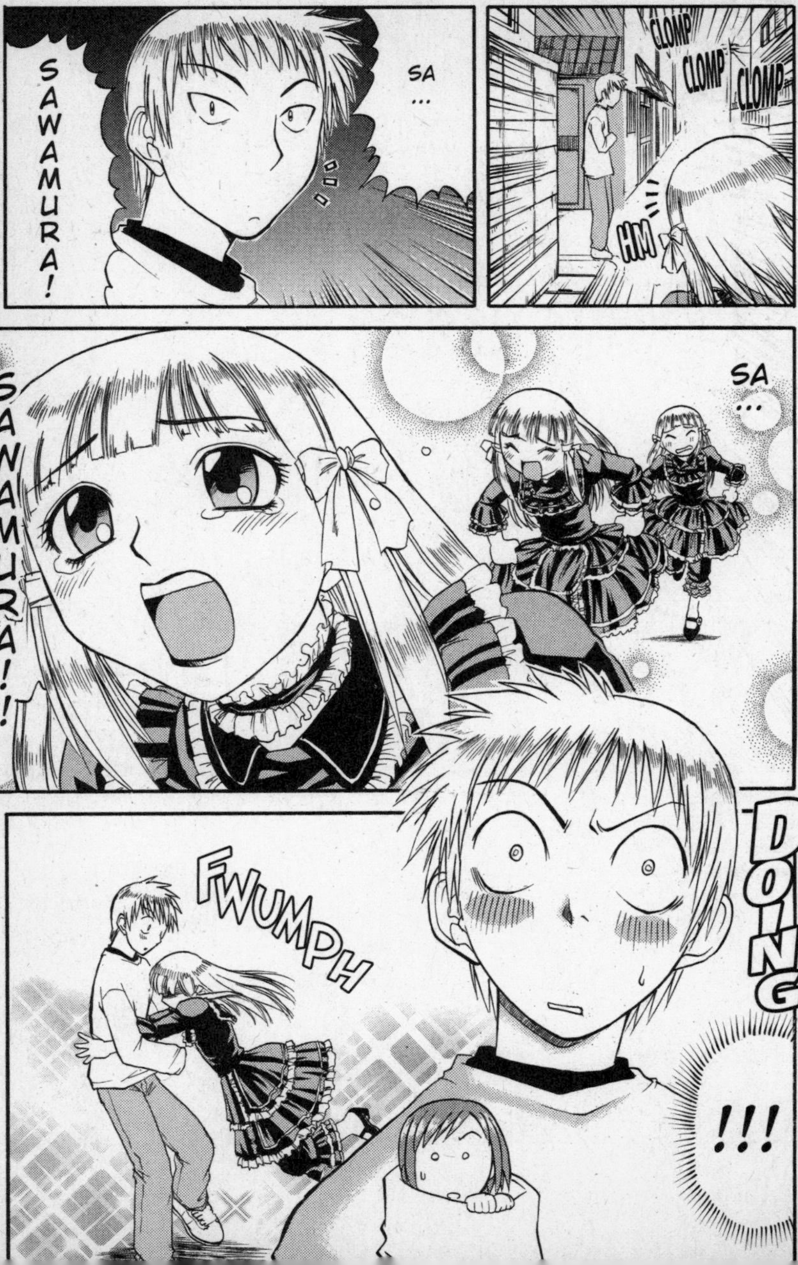
CLOMP
CLOMP
CLOMP
HM
SA ...
SAWAMURA!
SA ...
SAWAMURA!!
DOING
FWUMPH
!!!

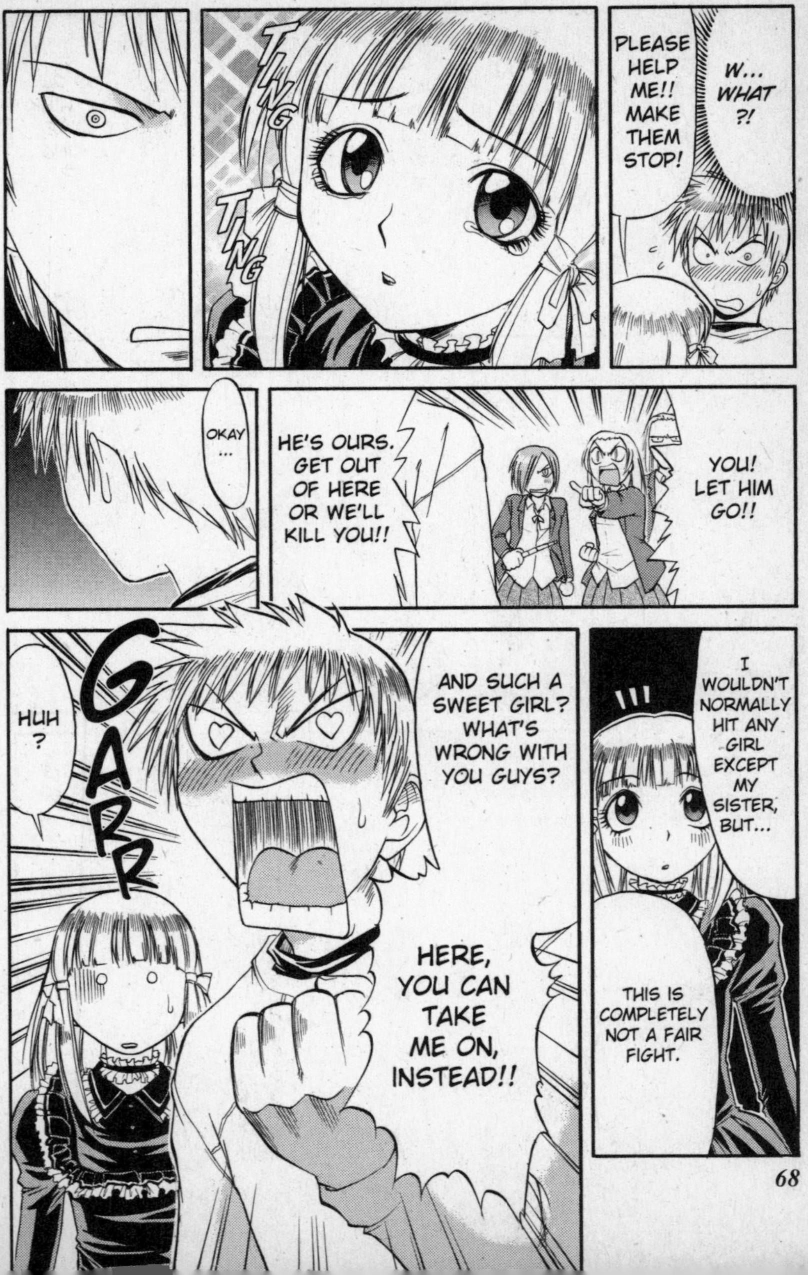
W... WHAT ?!
PLEASE HELP ME!! MAKE THEM STOP!
TING
TING
YOU! LET HIM GO!!
HE'S OURS. GET OUT OF HERE OR WE'LL KILL YOU!!
OKAY ...
I WOULDN'T NORMALLY HIT ANY GIRL EXCEPT MY SISTER, BUT...
!!!
THIS IS COMPLETELY NOT A FAIR FIGHT.
AND SUCH A SWEET GIRL? WHAT'S WRONG WITH YOU GUYS?
GARR
HUH ?
HERE, YOU CAN TAKE ME ON, INSTEAD!!

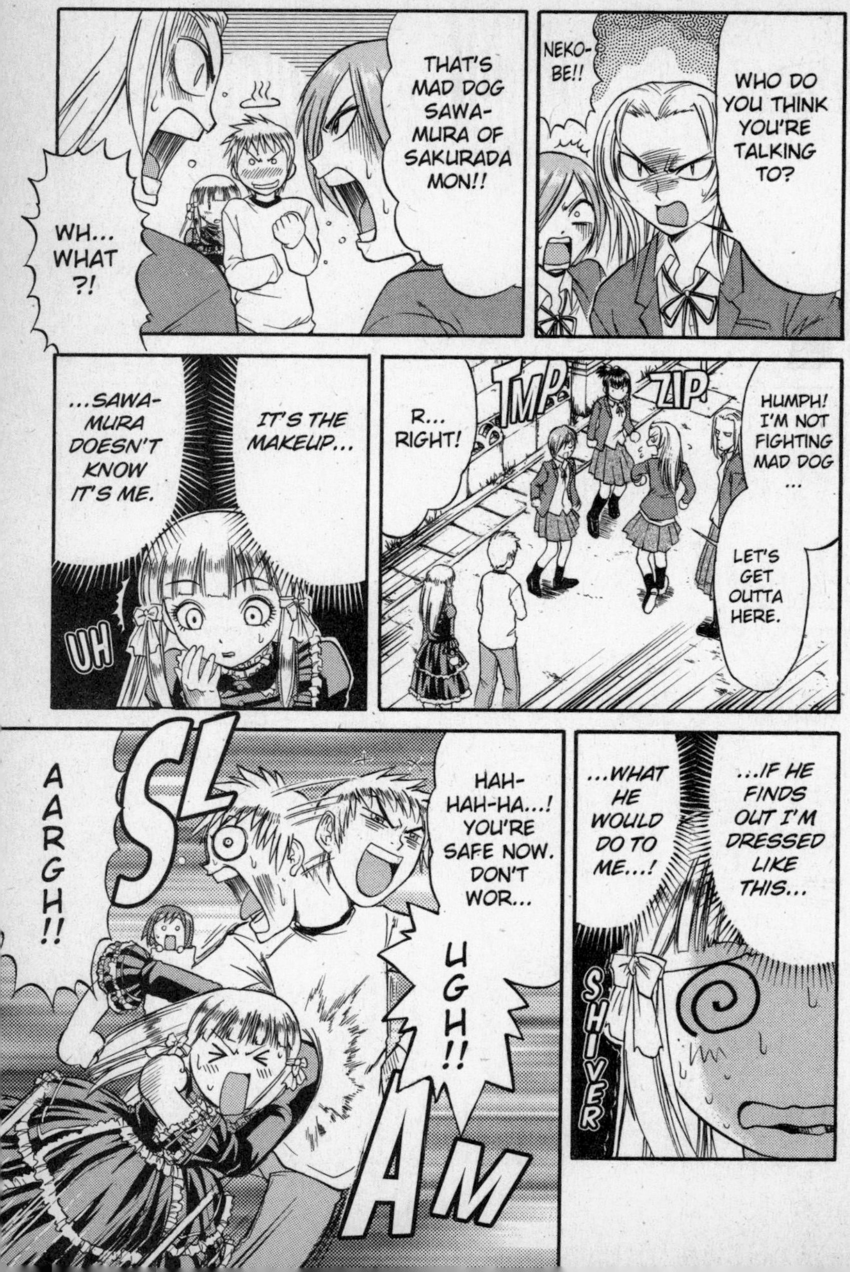
WHO DO YOU THINK YOU'RE TALKING TO?
NEKO-BE!!
THAT'S MAD DOG SAWA-MURA OF SAKURADA MON!!
WH... WHAT ?!
HUMPH! I'M NOT FIGHTING MAD DOG ...
LET'S GET OUTTA HERE.
ZIP
TMP
R... RIGHT!
IT'S THE MAKEUP...
...SAWA-MURA DOESN'T KNOW IT'S ME.
UH
...IF HE FINDS OUT I'M DRESSED LIKE THIS...
...WHAT HE WOULD DO TO ME...!
SHIVER
HAH-HAH-HA...! YOU'RE SAFE NOW. DON'T WOR...
SL
AARGH!!
UGH!!
AM

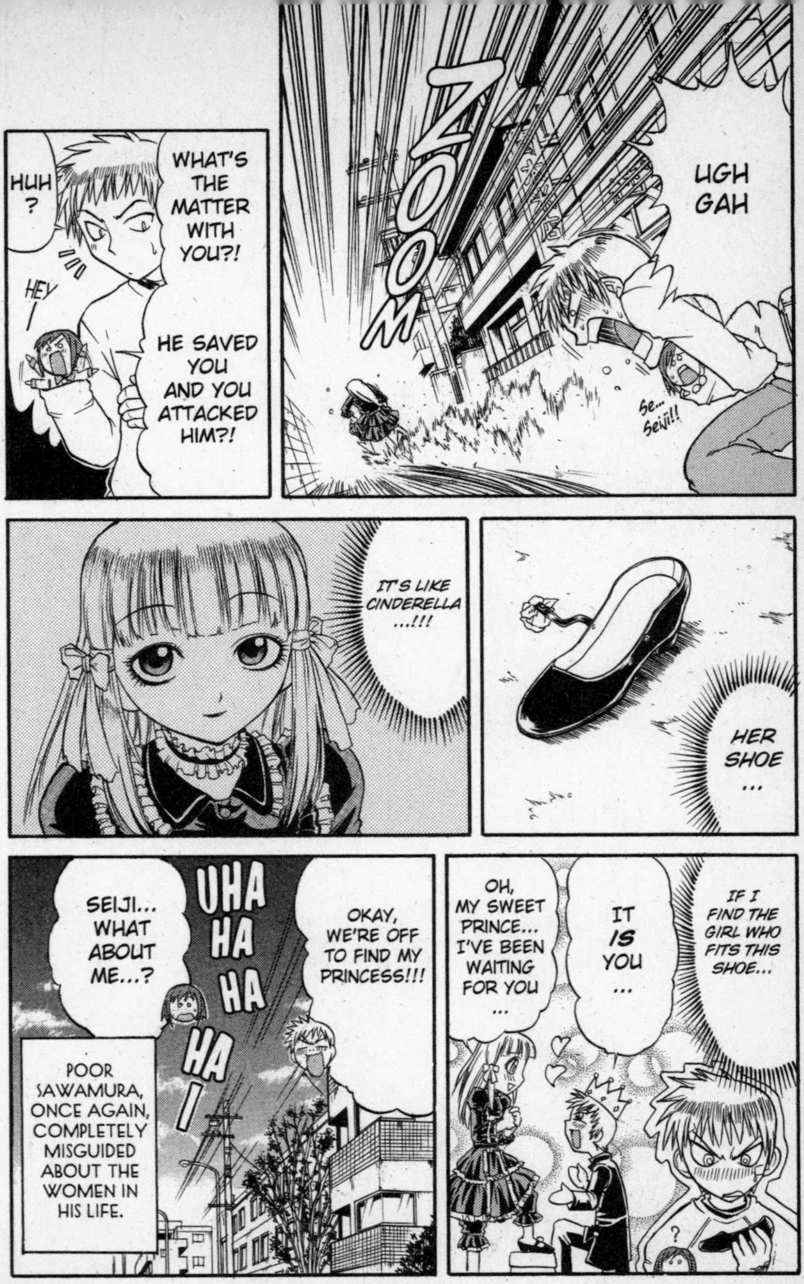
ZOOM
UGH GAH
Se... Seiji!!
WHAT'S THE MATTER WITH YOU?!
HE SAVED YOU AND YOU ATTACKED HIM?!
HUH?
HEY!
HER SHOE...
IT'S LIKE CINDERELLA...!!!
IF I FIND THE GIRL WHO FITS THIS SHOE...
IT IS YOU...
OH, MY SWEET PRINCE... I'VE BEEN WAITING FOR YOU...
OKAY, WE'RE OFF TO FIND MY PRINCESS!!!
UHA HA HA HA!
SEIJI... WHAT ABOUT ME...?
POOR SAWAMURA, ONCE AGAIN, COMPLETELY MISGUIDED ABOUT THE WOMEN IN HIS LIFE.

DAY 37
THE ADVENTURER

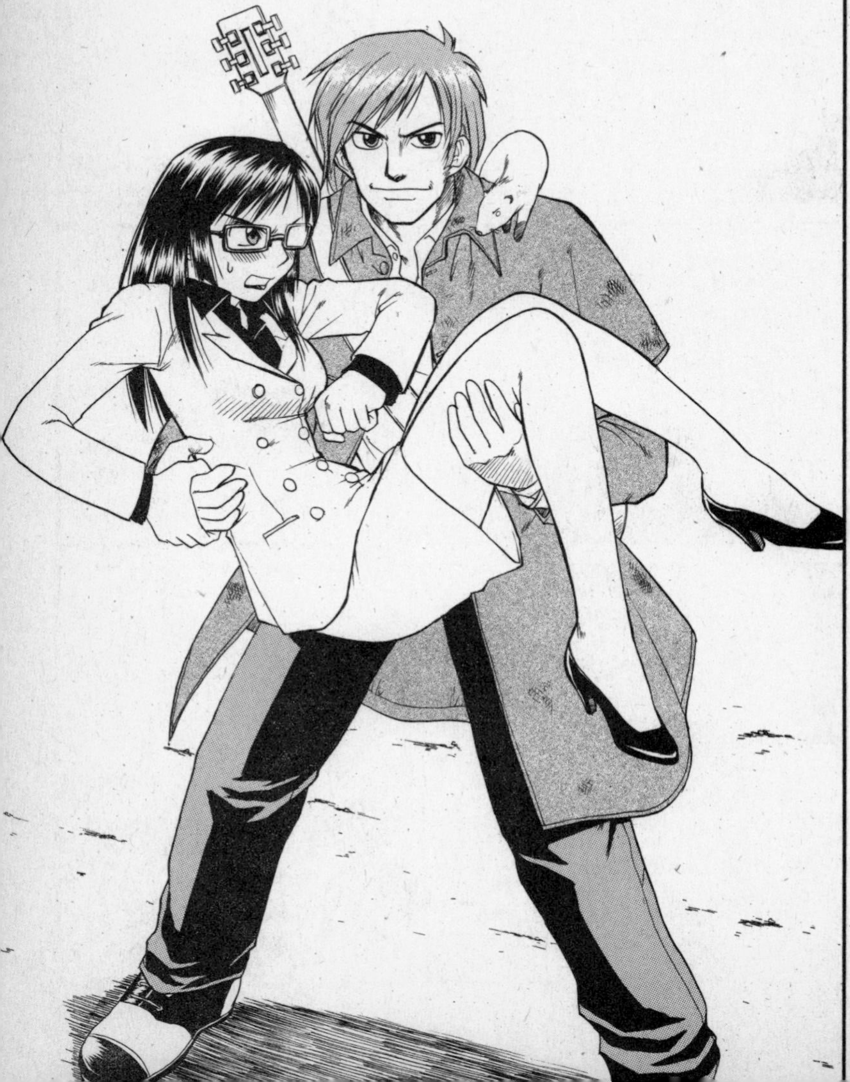

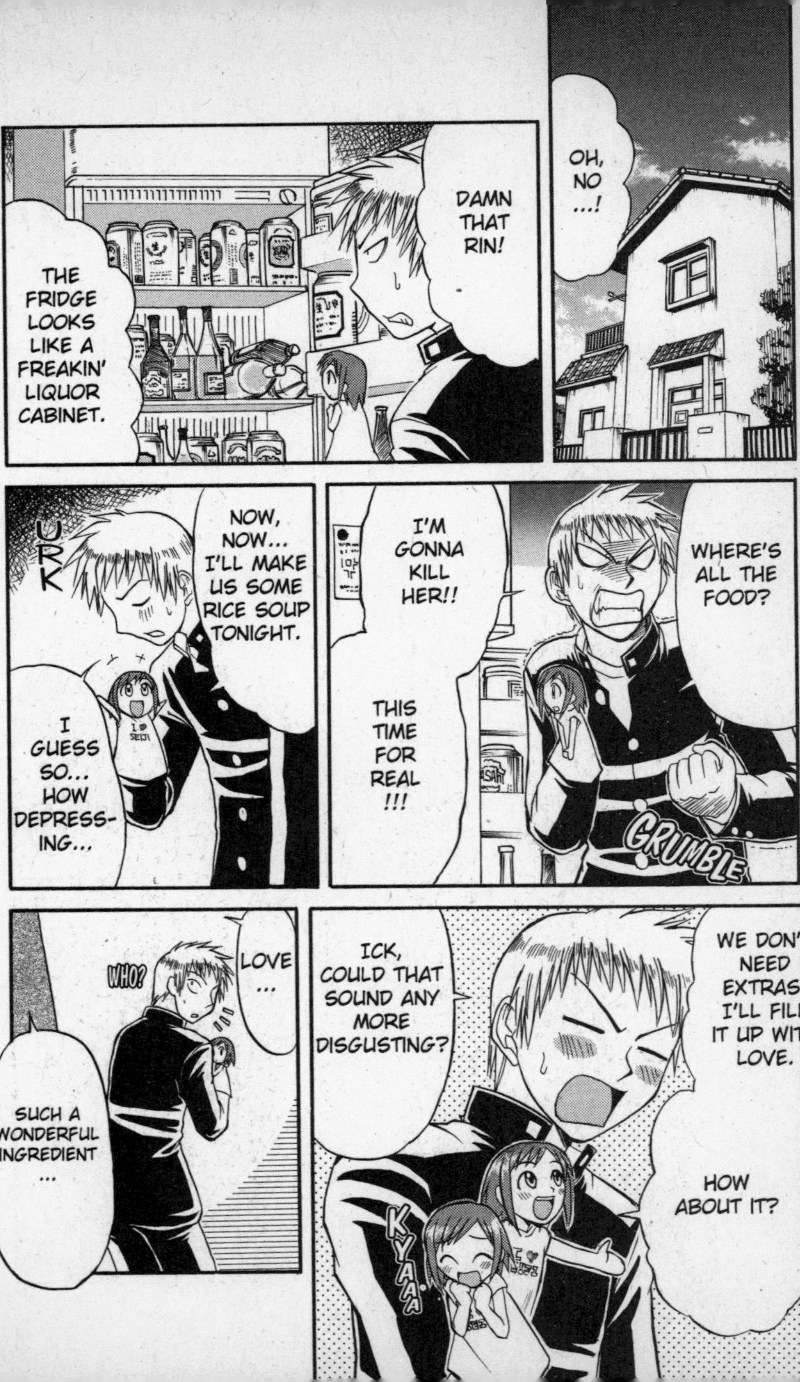
OH, NO ...!
DAMN THAT RIN!
THE FRIDGE LOOKS LIKE A FREAKIN' LIQUOR CABINET.
WHERE'S ALL THE FOOD?
GRUMBLE
I'M GONNA KILL HER!!
THIS TIME FOR REAL !!!
URK
NOW, NOW... I'LL MAKE US SOME RICE SOUP TONIGHT.
I GUESS SO... HOW DEPRESSING...
WE DON'T NEED EXTRAS. I'LL FILL IT UP WITH LOVE.
HOW ABOUT IT?
KYAAA
ICK, COULD THAT SOUND ANY MORE DISGUSTING?
LOVE ...
WHO?
SUCH A WONDERFUL INGREDIENT ...

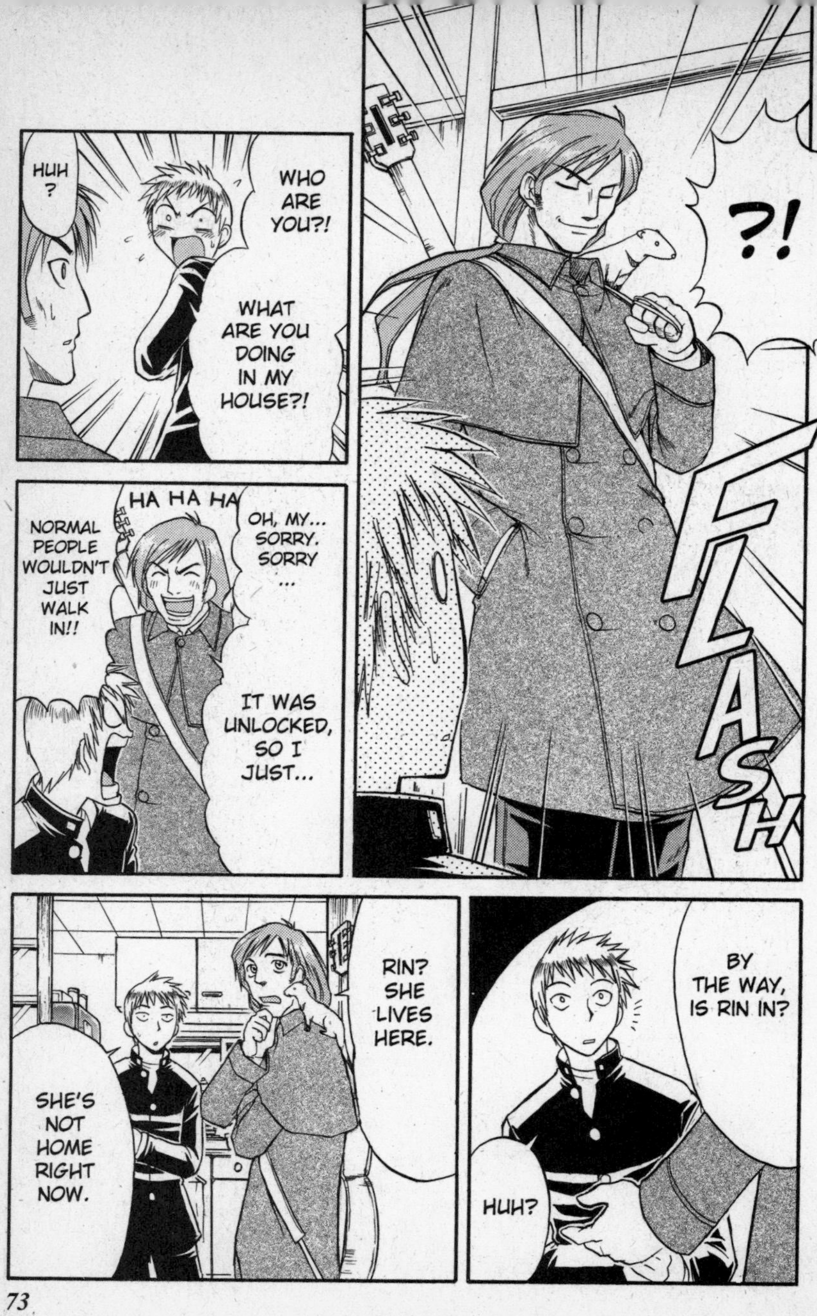
?!
FLASH
WHO ARE YOU?!
HUH?
WHAT ARE YOU DOING IN MY HOUSE?!
OH, MY... SORRY. SORRY ...
HA HA HA
NORMAL PEOPLE WOULDN'T JUST WALK IN!!
IT WAS UNLOCKED, SO I JUST...
BY THE WAY, IS RIN IN?
HUH?
RIN? SHE LIVES HERE.
SHE'S NOT HOME RIGHT NOW.

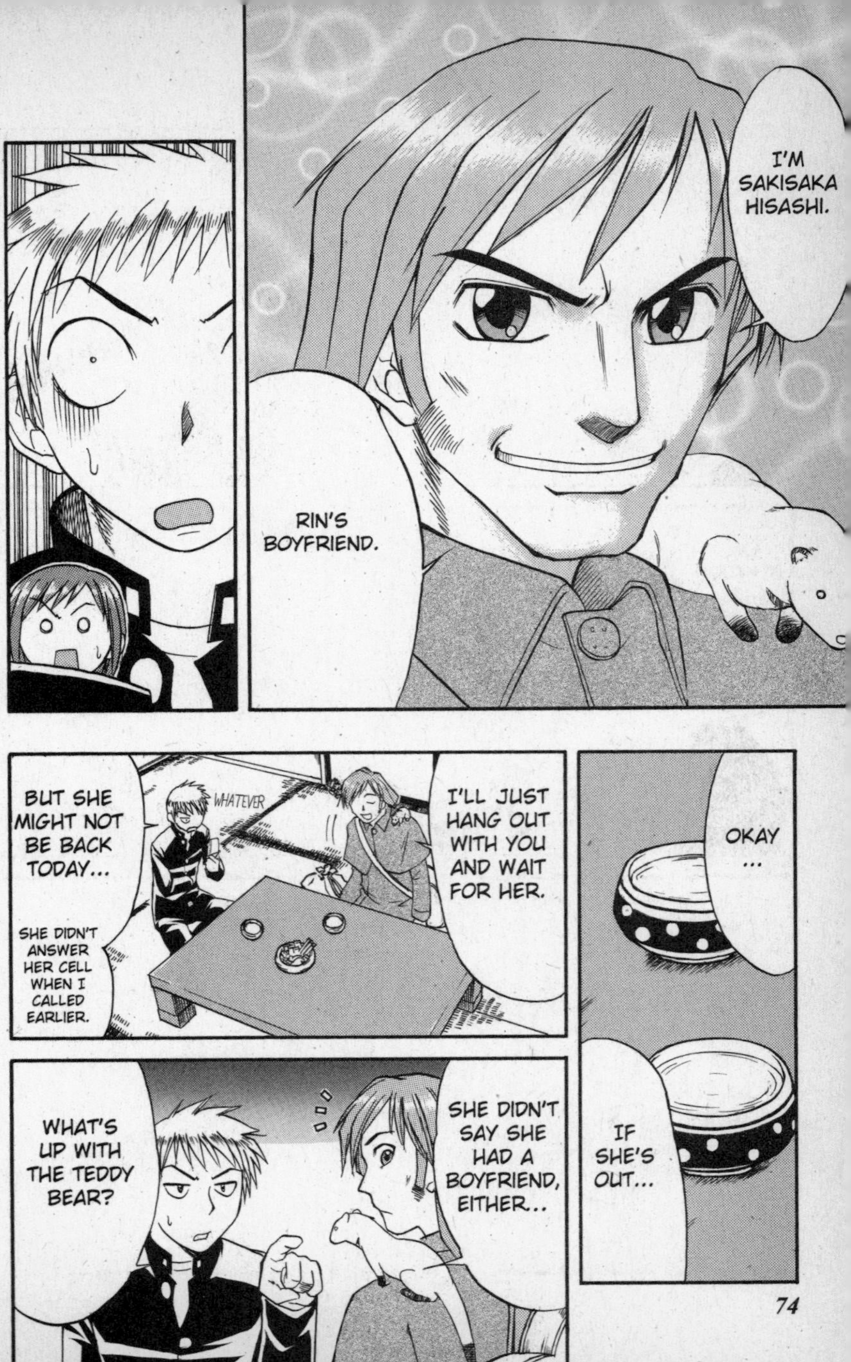
I'M SAKISAKA HISASHI.
RIN'S BOYFRIEND.
OKAY ...
IF SHE'S OUT...
I'LL JUST HANG OUT WITH YOU AND WAIT FOR HER.
BUT SHE MIGHT NOT BE BACK TODAY...
SHE DIDN'T ANSWER HER CELL WHEN I CALLED EARLIER.
WHATEVER
SHE DIDN'T SAY SHE HAD A BOYFRIEND, EITHER...
WHAT'S UP WITH THE TEDDY BEAR?

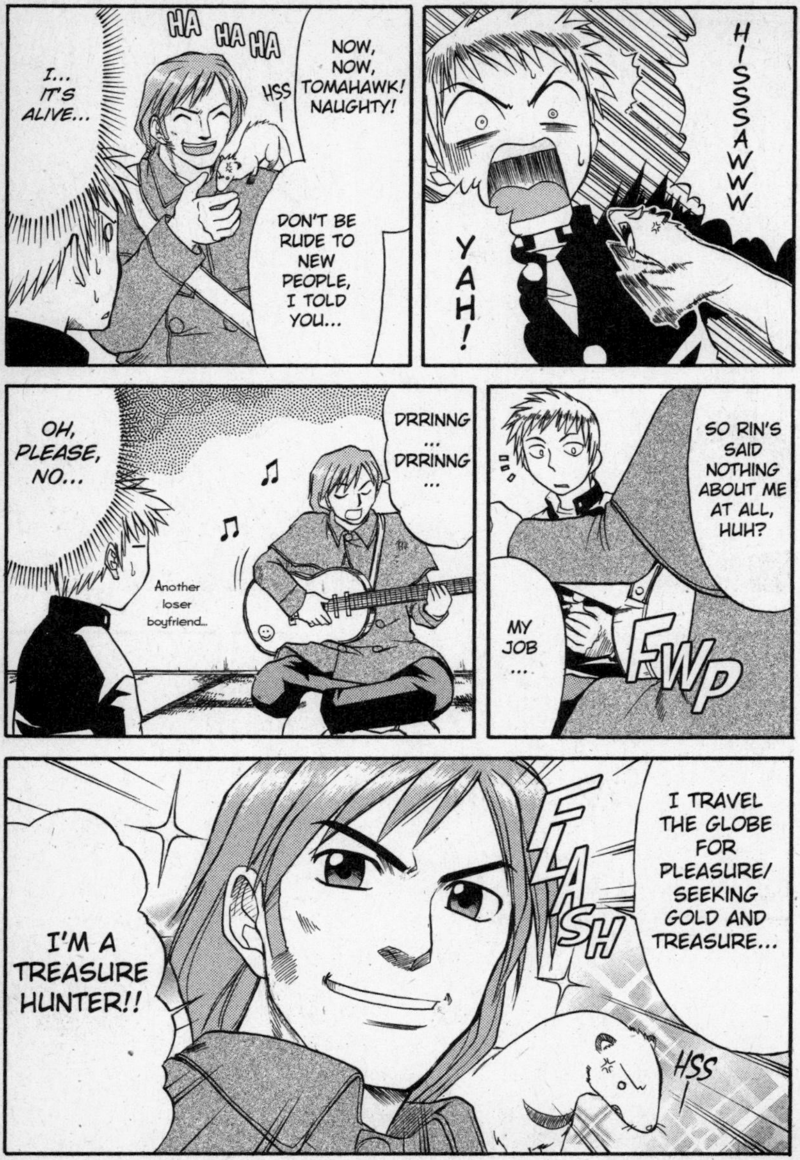
HISSSAWWW
YAH!
NOW, NOW, TOMAHAWK! NAUGHTY!
DON'T BE RUDE TO NEW PEOPLE, I TOLD YOU...
HSS
HA HA HA
I... IT'S ALIVE...
SO RIN'S SAID NOTHING ABOUT ME AT ALL, HUH?
FWP
MY JOB ...
DRRINNG ... DRRINNG ...
OH, PLEASE, NO...
Another loser boyfriend...
I TRAVEL THE GLOBE FOR PLEASURE/ SEEKING GOLD AND TREASURE...
FLASH
HSS
I'M A TREASURE HUNTER!!

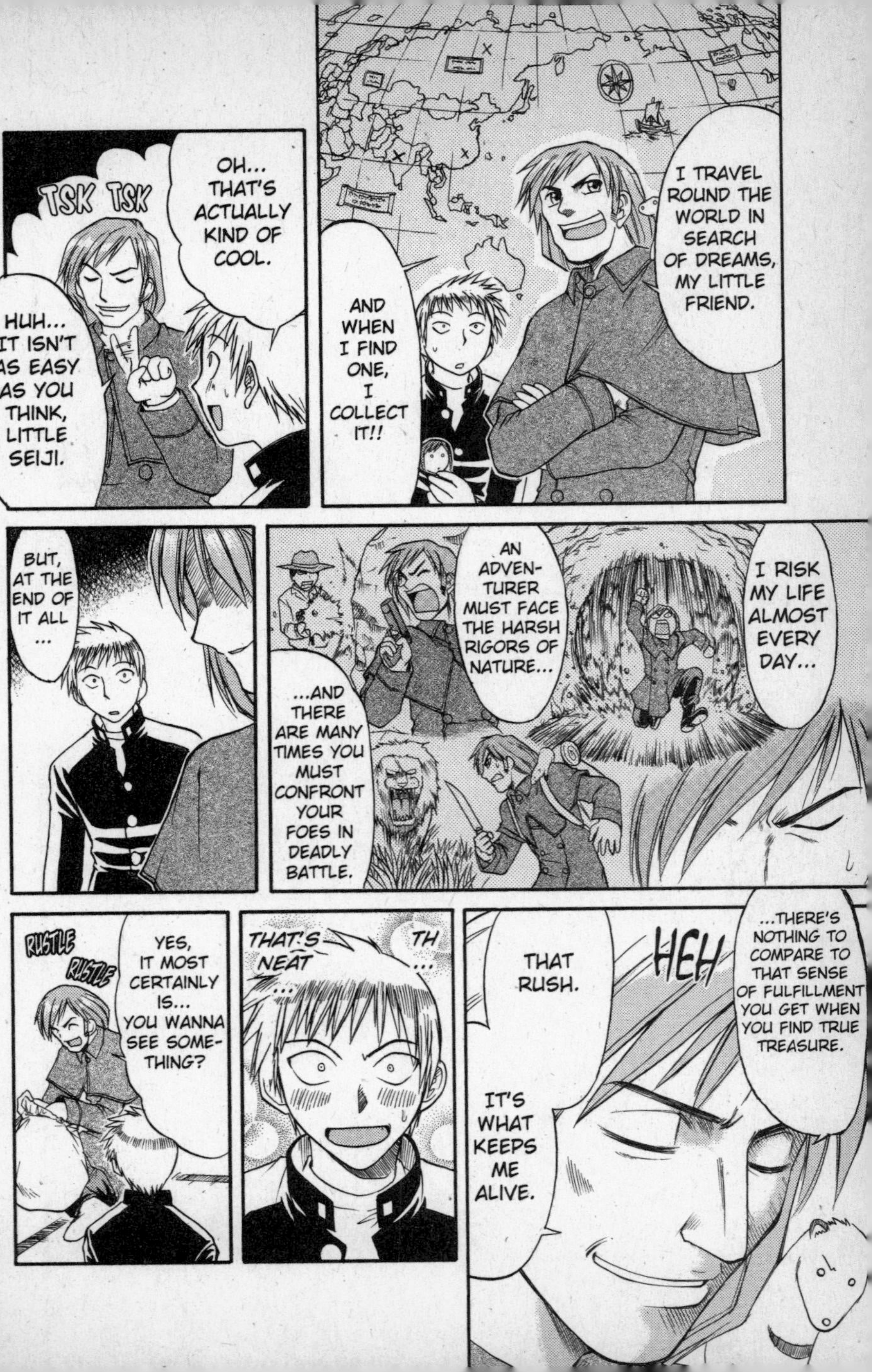
I TRAVEL ROUND THE WORLD IN SEARCH OF DREAMS, MY LITTLE FRIEND.
AND WHEN I FIND ONE, I COLLECT IT!!
OH... THAT'S ACTUALLY KIND OF COOL.
TSK TSK
HUH... IT ISN'T AS EASY AS YOU THINK, LITTLE SEIJI.
I RISK MY LIFE ALMOST EVERY DAY...
AN ADVEN-TURER MUST FACE THE HARSH RIGORS OF NATURE...
...AND THERE ARE MANY TIMES YOU MUST CONFRONT YOUR FOES IN DEADLY BATTLE.
BUT, AT THE END OF IT ALL ...
...THERE'S NOTHING TO COMPARE TO THAT SENSE OF FULFILLMENT YOU GET WHEN YOU FIND TRUE TREASURE.
HEH
THAT RUSH.
IT'S WHAT KEEPS ME ALIVE.
TH...
THAT'S NEAT...
RUSTLE
RUSTLE
YES, IT MOST CERTAINLY IS... YOU WANNA SEE SOME-THING?

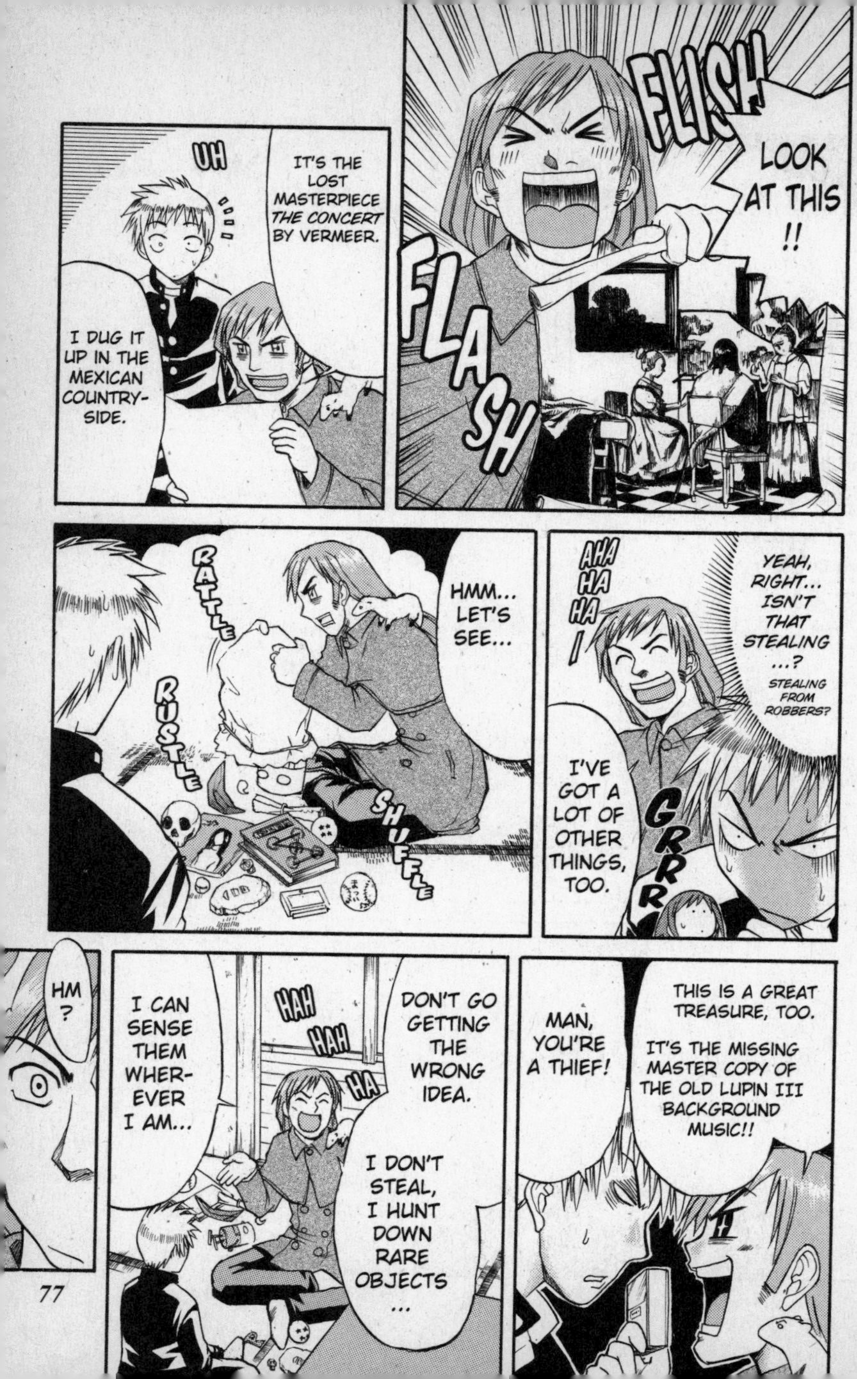
FLISH
LOOK AT THIS !!
FLASH
IT'S THE LOST MASTERPIECE *THE CONCERT* BY VERMEER.
UH
...
I DUG IT UP IN THE MEXICAN COUNTRY-SIDE.
YEAH, RIGHT... ISN'T THAT STEALING ...?
STEALING FROM ROBBERS?
AHAHAHAHA!
I'VE GOT A LOT OF OTHER THINGS, TOO.
GRRR
HMM... LET'S SEE...
RATTLE
RUSTLE
SHUFFLE
THIS IS A GREAT TREASURE, TOO.
IT'S THE MISSING MASTER COPY OF THE OLD LUPIN III BACKGROUND MUSIC!!
MAN, YOU'RE A THIEF!
DON'T GO GETTING THE WRONG IDEA.
HAH
HAH
HA
I DON'T STEAL, I HUNT DOWN RARE OBJECTS ...
I CAN SENSE THEM WHER-EVER I AM...
HM ?

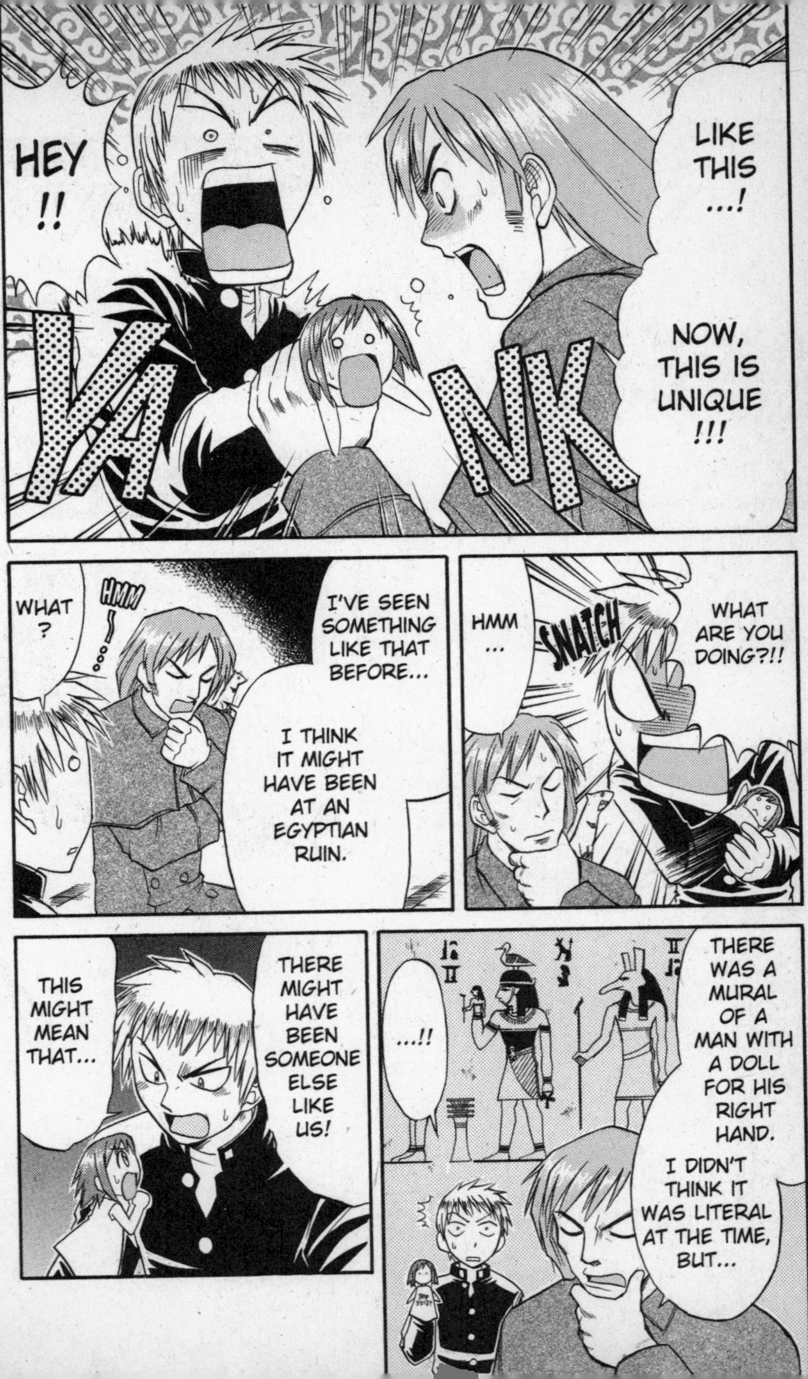
LIKE THIS ...!
NOW, THIS IS UNIQUE !!!
HEY !!
YANK
WHAT ARE YOU DOING?!!
SNATCH
HMM ...
I'VE SEEN SOMETHING LIKE THAT BEFORE...
I THINK IT MIGHT HAVE BEEN AT AN EGYPTIAN RUIN.
HMM
WHAT ?
THERE WAS A MURAL OF A MAN WITH A DOLL FOR HIS RIGHT HAND.
...!!
I DIDN'T THINK IT WAS LITERAL AT THE TIME, BUT...
THERE MIGHT HAVE BEEN SOMEONE ELSE LIKE US!
THIS MIGHT MEAN THAT...

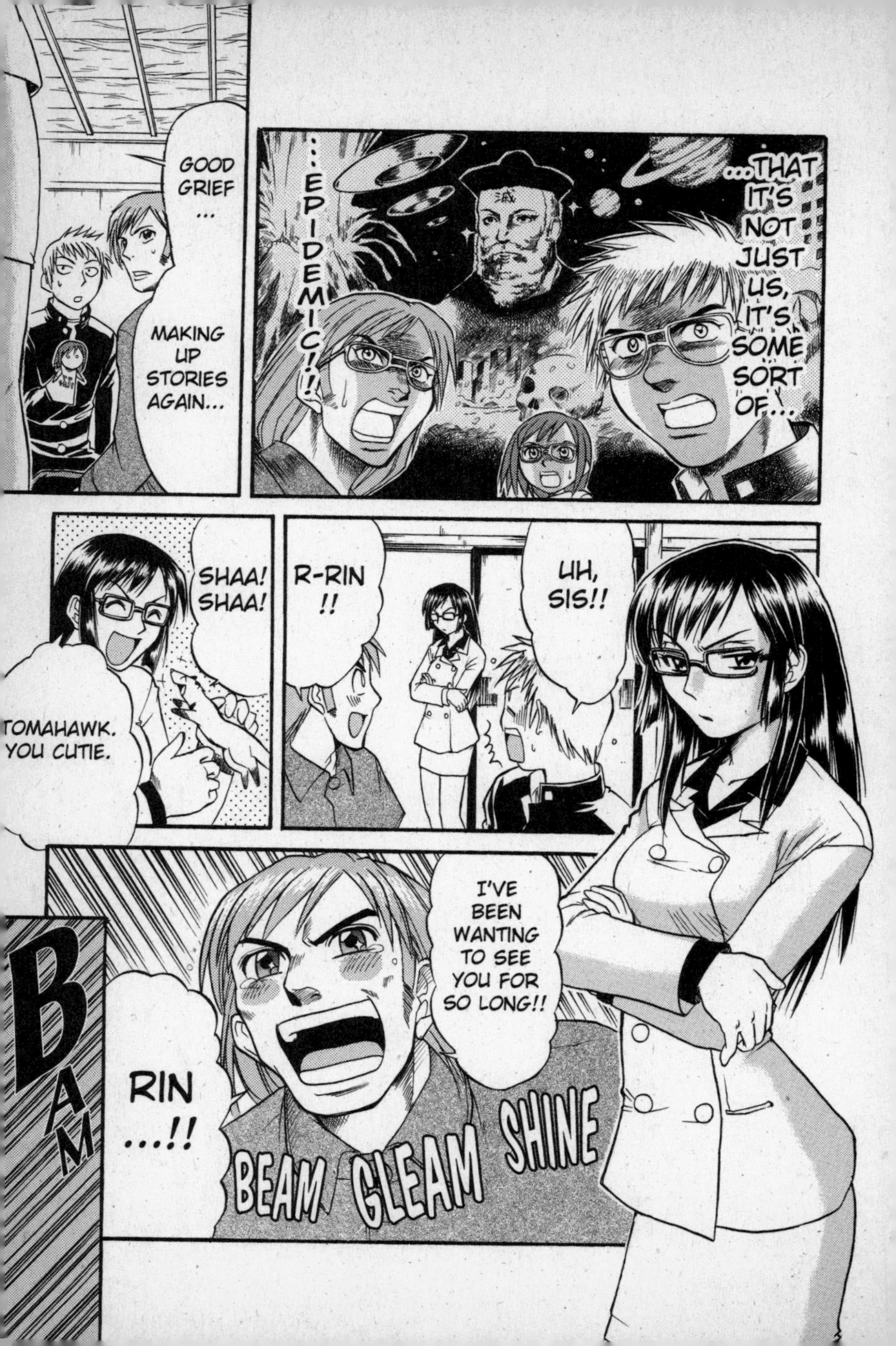
...THAT IT'S NOT JUST US, IT'S SOME SORT OF...
...EPIDEMIC!!
GOOD GRIEF...
MAKING UP STORIES AGAIN...
UH, SIS!!
R-RIN!!
SHAA! SHAA!
TOMAHAWK. YOU CUTIE.
I'VE BEEN WANTING TO SEE YOU FOR SO LONG!!
RIN...!!
BEAM GLEAM SHINE
BAM

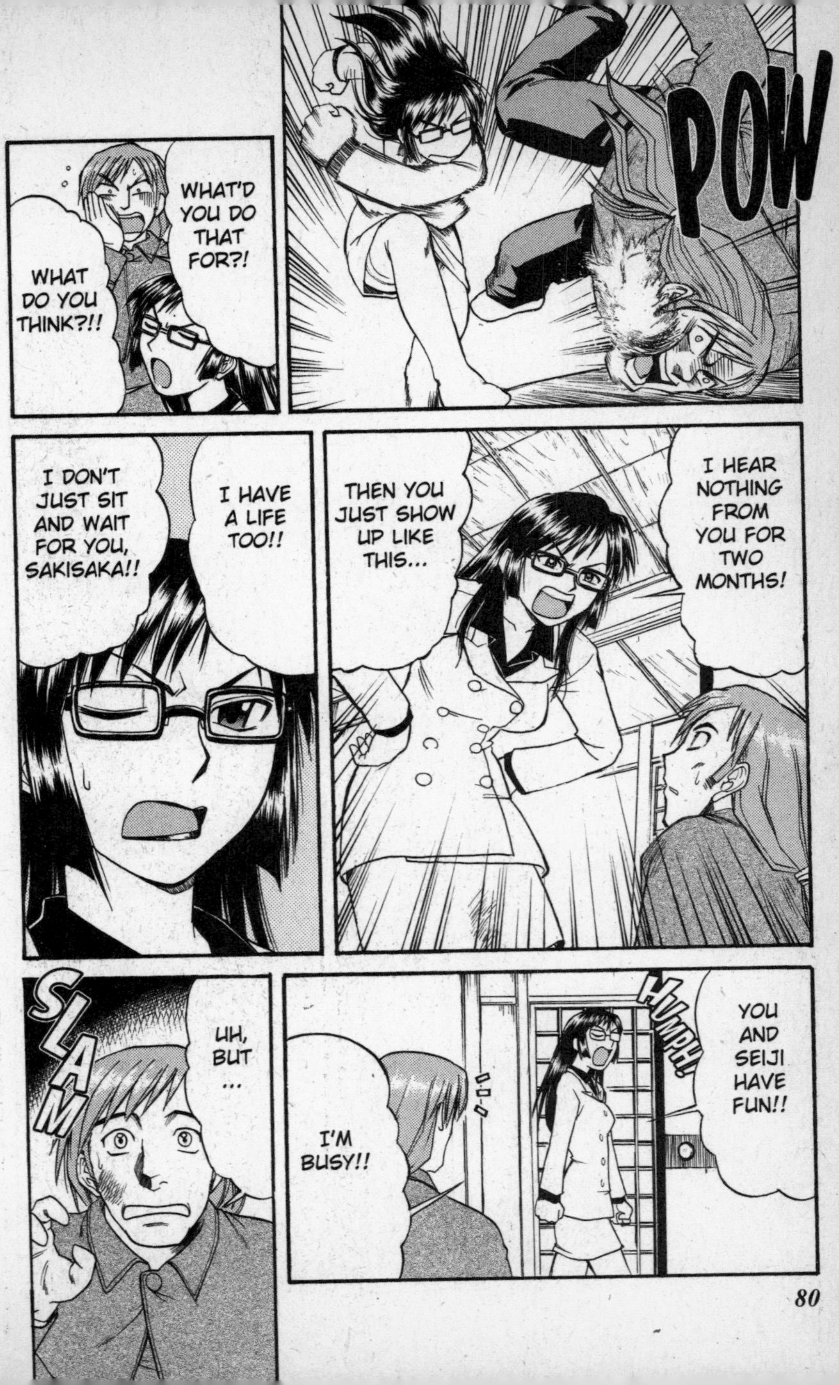
POW
WHAT'D YOU DO THAT FOR?!
WHAT DO YOU THINK?!!
I HEAR NOTHING FROM YOU FOR TWO MONTHS!
THEN YOU JUST SHOW UP LIKE THIS...
I HAVE A LIFE TOO!!
I DON'T JUST SIT AND WAIT FOR YOU, SAKISAKA!!
HUMPH!
YOU AND SEIJI HAVE FUN!!
I'M BUSY!!
SLAM
UH, BUT ...

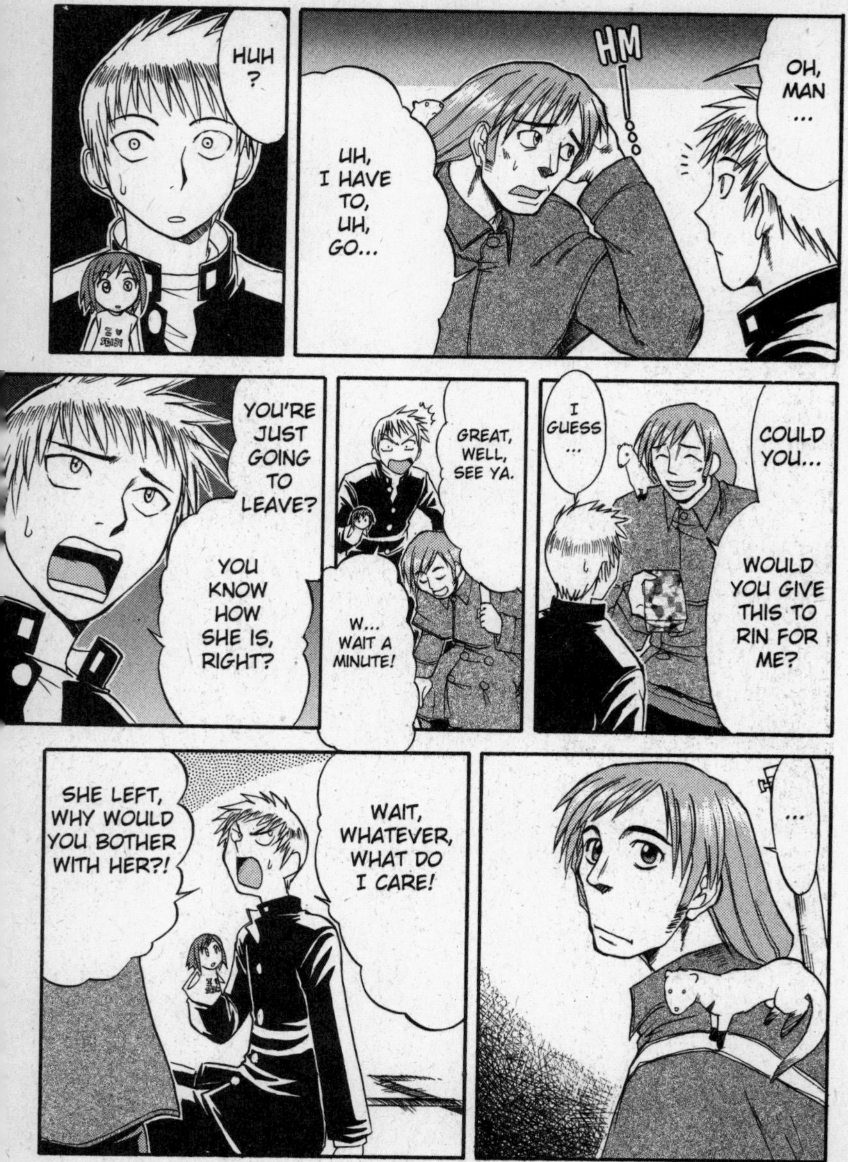
OH, MAN ...
HM
UH, I HAVE TO, UH, GO...
HUH ?
COULD YOU...
WOULD YOU GIVE THIS TO RIN FOR ME?
I GUESS ...
GREAT, WELL, SEE YA.
W... WAIT A MINUTE!
YOU'RE JUST GOING TO LEAVE?
YOU KNOW HOW SHE IS, RIGHT?
...
WAIT, WHATEVER, WHAT DO I CARE!
SHE LEFT, WHY WOULD YOU BOTHER WITH HER?!

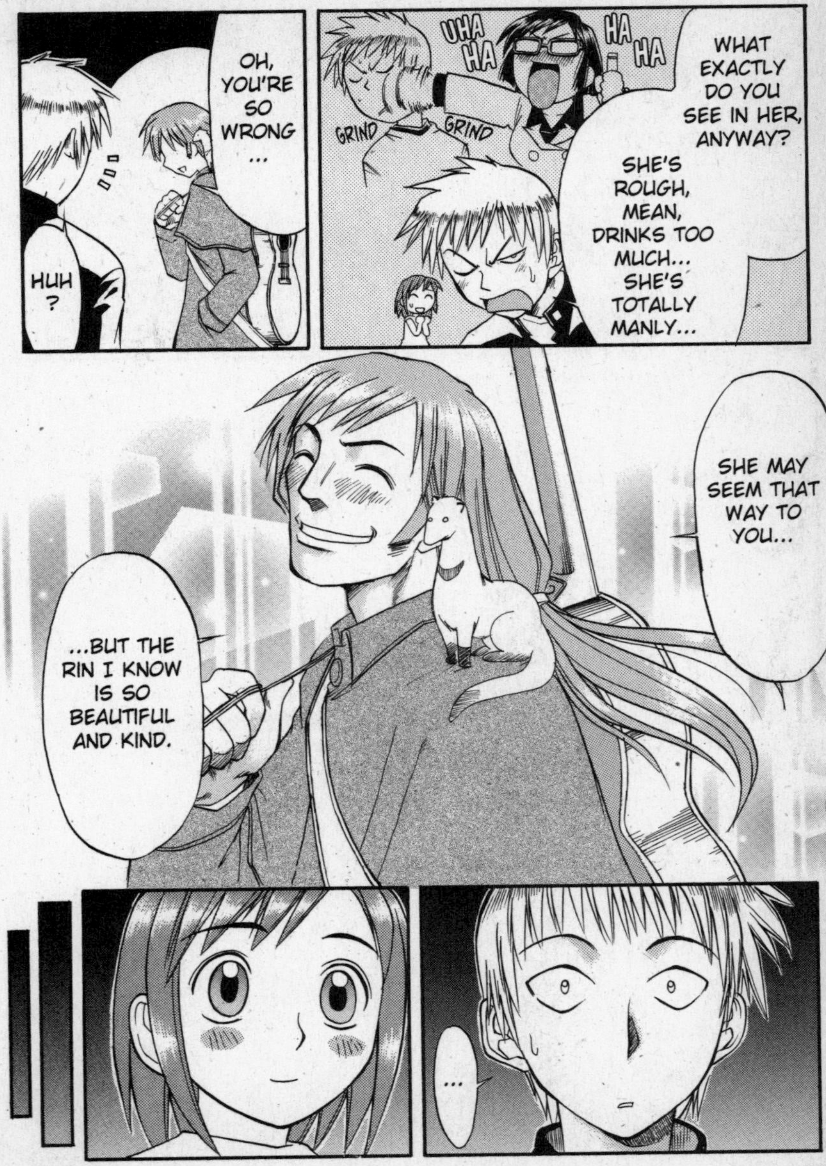
UHA HA
HA HA
WHAT EXACTLY DO YOU SEE IN HER, ANYWAY?
SHE'S ROUGH, MEAN, DRINKS TOO MUCH... SHE'S TOTALLY MANLY...
GRIND
GRIND
OH, YOU'RE SO WRONG ...
HUH ?
SHE MAY SEEM THAT WAY TO YOU...
...BUT THE RIN I KNOW IS SO BEAUTIFUL AND KIND.
...

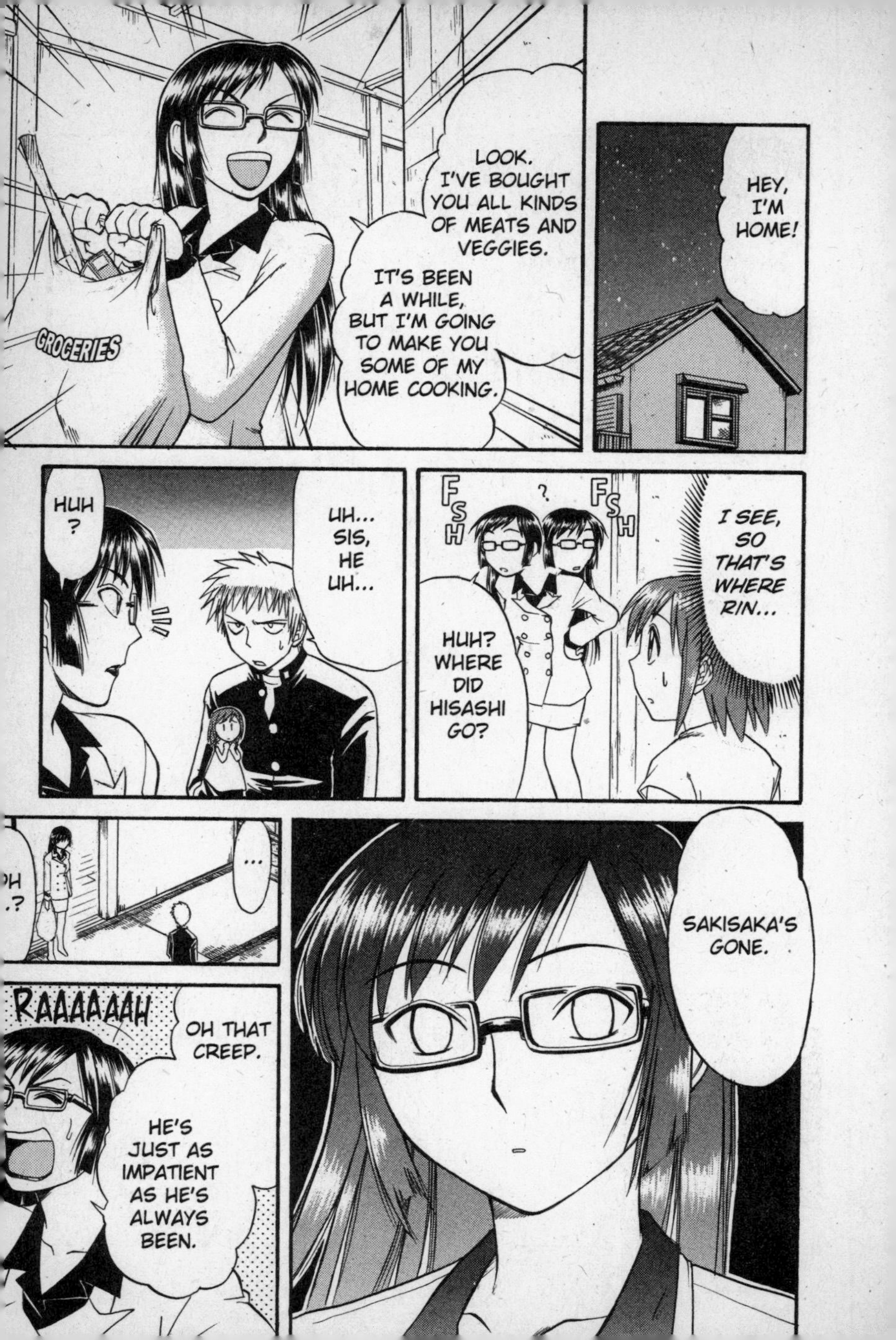
HEY, I'M HOME!
LOOK. I'VE BOUGHT YOU ALL KINDS OF MEATS AND VEGGIES.
IT'S BEEN A WHILE, BUT I'M GOING TO MAKE YOU SOME OF MY HOME COOKING.
GROCERIES
FSH
?
FSH
I SEE, SO THAT'S WHERE RIN...
HUH? WHERE DID HISASHI GO?
UH... SIS, HE UH...
HUH ?
SAKISAKA'S GONE.
...
RAAAAAAH
OH THAT CREEP.
HE'S JUST AS IMPATIENT AS HE'S ALWAYS BEEN.

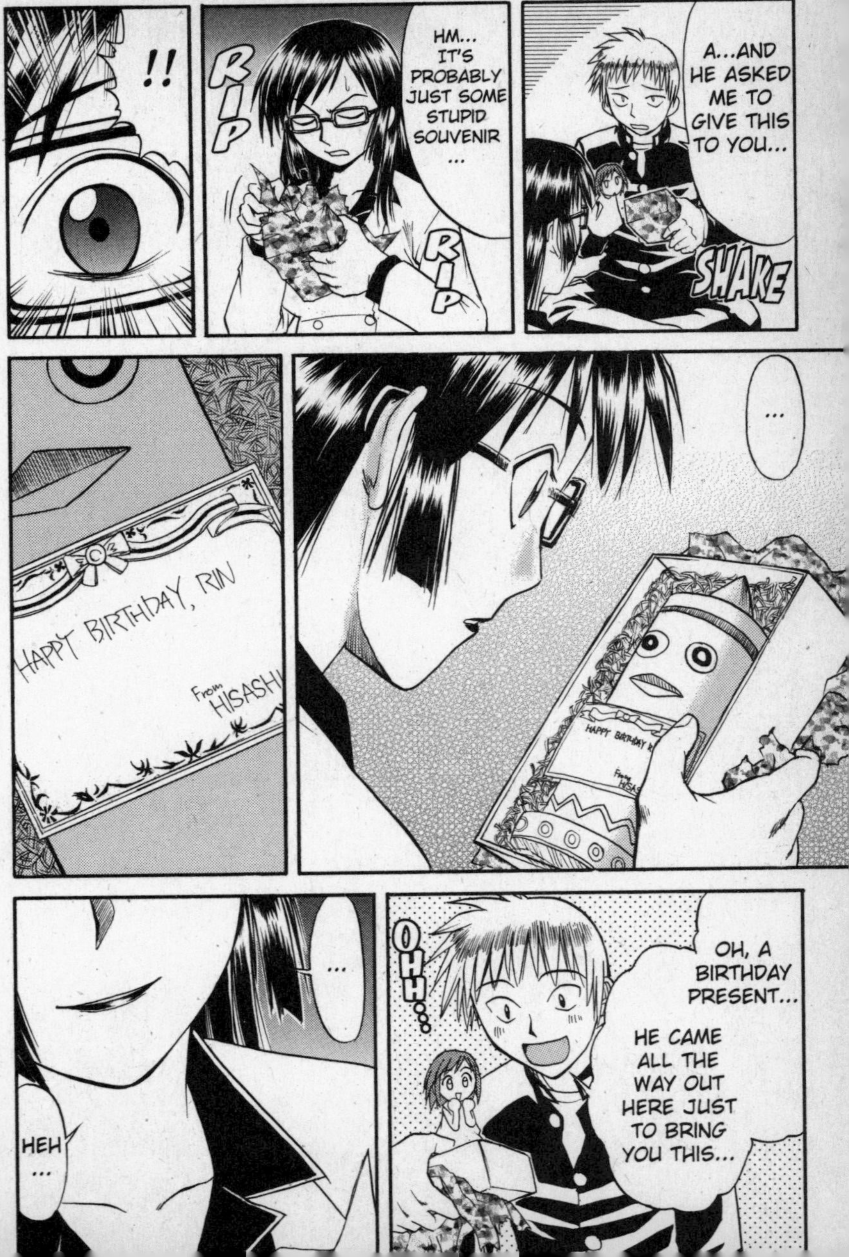
A...AND HE ASKED ME TO GIVE THIS TO YOU...
SHAKE
HM... IT'S PROBABLY JUST SOME STUPID SOUVENIR ...
RIP
RIP
!!
...
HAPPY BIRTHDAY, RIN
From HISASHI
OHH...
OH, A BIRTHDAY PRESENT...
HE CAME ALL THE WAY OUT HERE JUST TO BRING YOU THIS...
...
HEH ...

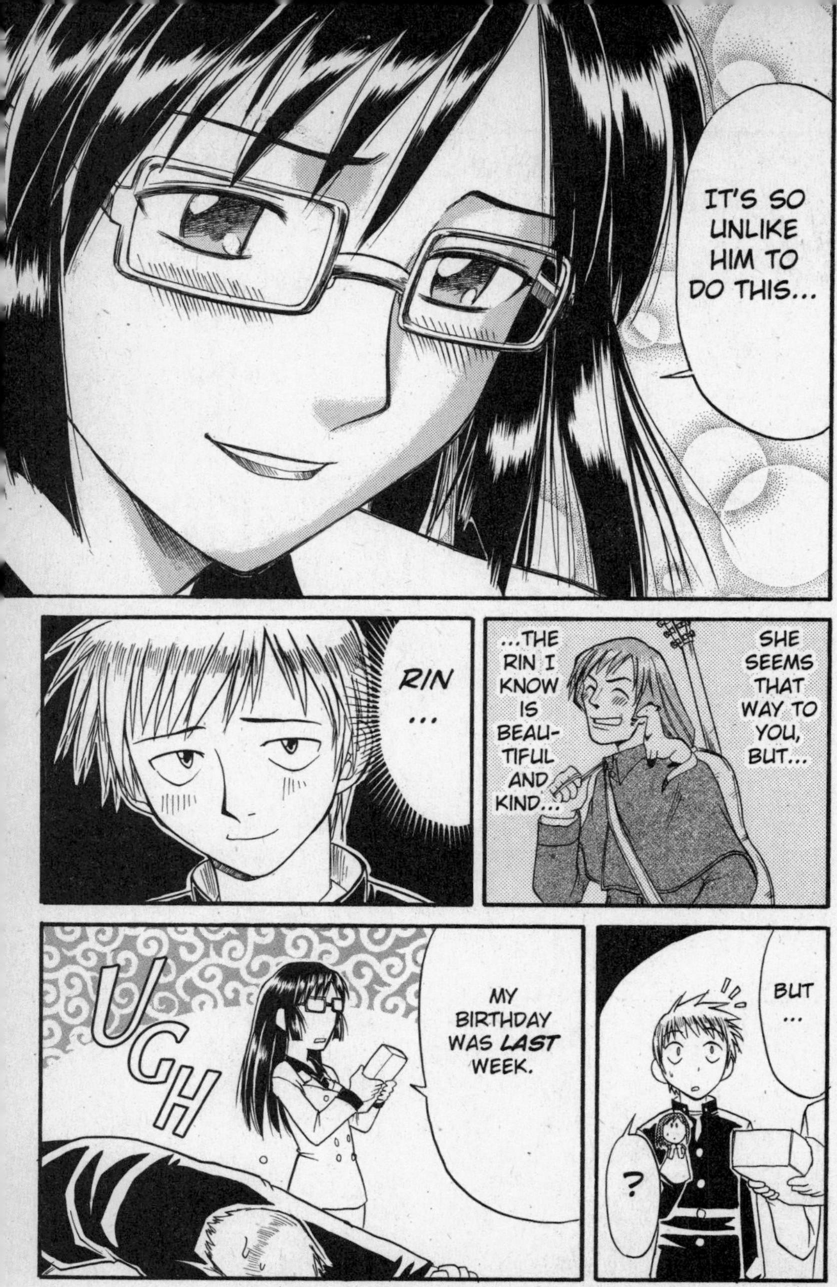
IT'S SO UNLIKE HIM TO DO THIS...
SHE SEEMS THAT WAY TO YOU, BUT...
...THE RIN I KNOW IS BEAU-TIFUL AND KIND...
RIN ...
BUT ...
?
MY BIRTHDAY WAS LAST WEEK.
UGH

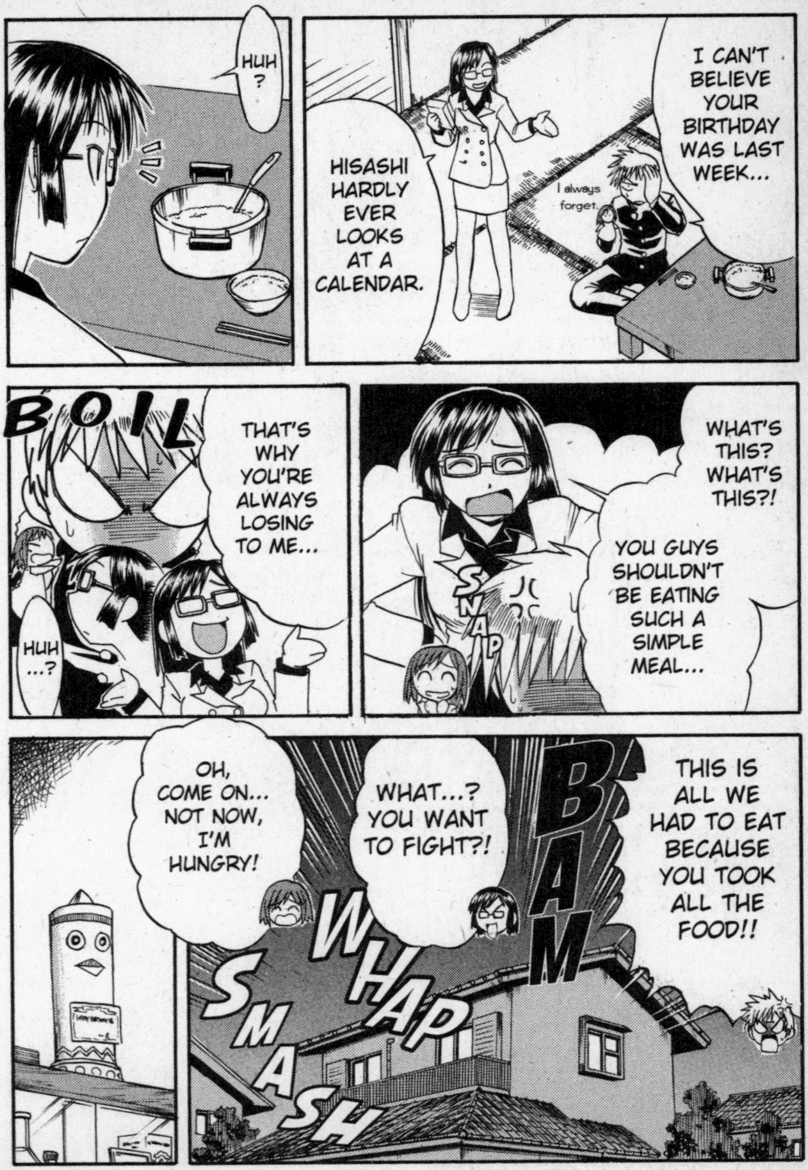
I CAN'T BELIEVE YOUR BIRTHDAY WAS LAST WEEK...
I always forget.
HISASHI HARDLY EVER LOOKS AT A CALENDAR.
HUH ?
WHAT'S THIS? WHAT'S THIS?!
YOU GUYS SHOULDN'T BE EATING SUCH A SIMPLE MEAL...
SNAP
BOIL
THAT'S WHY YOU'RE ALWAYS LOSING TO ME...
HUH ...?
THIS IS ALL WE HAD TO EAT BECAUSE YOU TOOK ALL THE FOOD!!
BAM
WHAT...? YOU WANT TO FIGHT?!
WHAP
SMASH
OH, COME ON... NOT NOW, I'M HUNGRY!

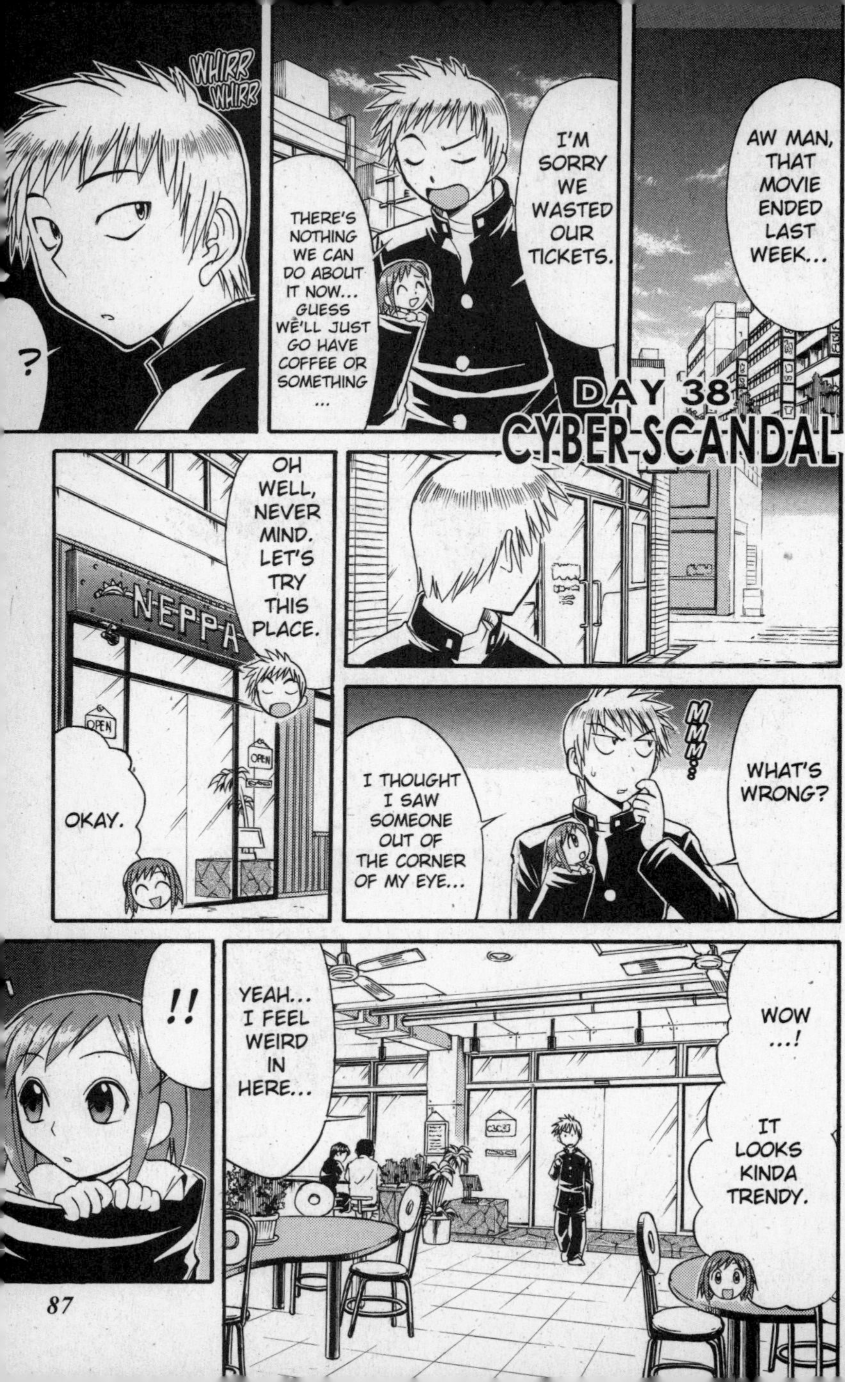
AW MAN, THAT MOVIE ENDED LAST WEEK...
DAY 38
CYBER SCANDAL
I'M SORRY WE WASTED OUR TICKETS.
THERE'S NOTHING WE CAN DO ABOUT IT NOW... GUESS WE'LL JUST GO HAVE COFFEE OR SOMETHING ...
WHIRR WHIRR
?
WHAT'S WRONG?
MMM...
I THOUGHT I SAW SOMEONE OUT OF THE CORNER OF MY EYE...
OH WELL, NEVER MIND. LET'S TRY THIS PLACE.
NEPPA
OPEN
OPEN
OKAY.
WOW ...!
IT LOOKS KINDA TRENDY.
YEAH... I FEEL WEIRD IN HERE...
!!

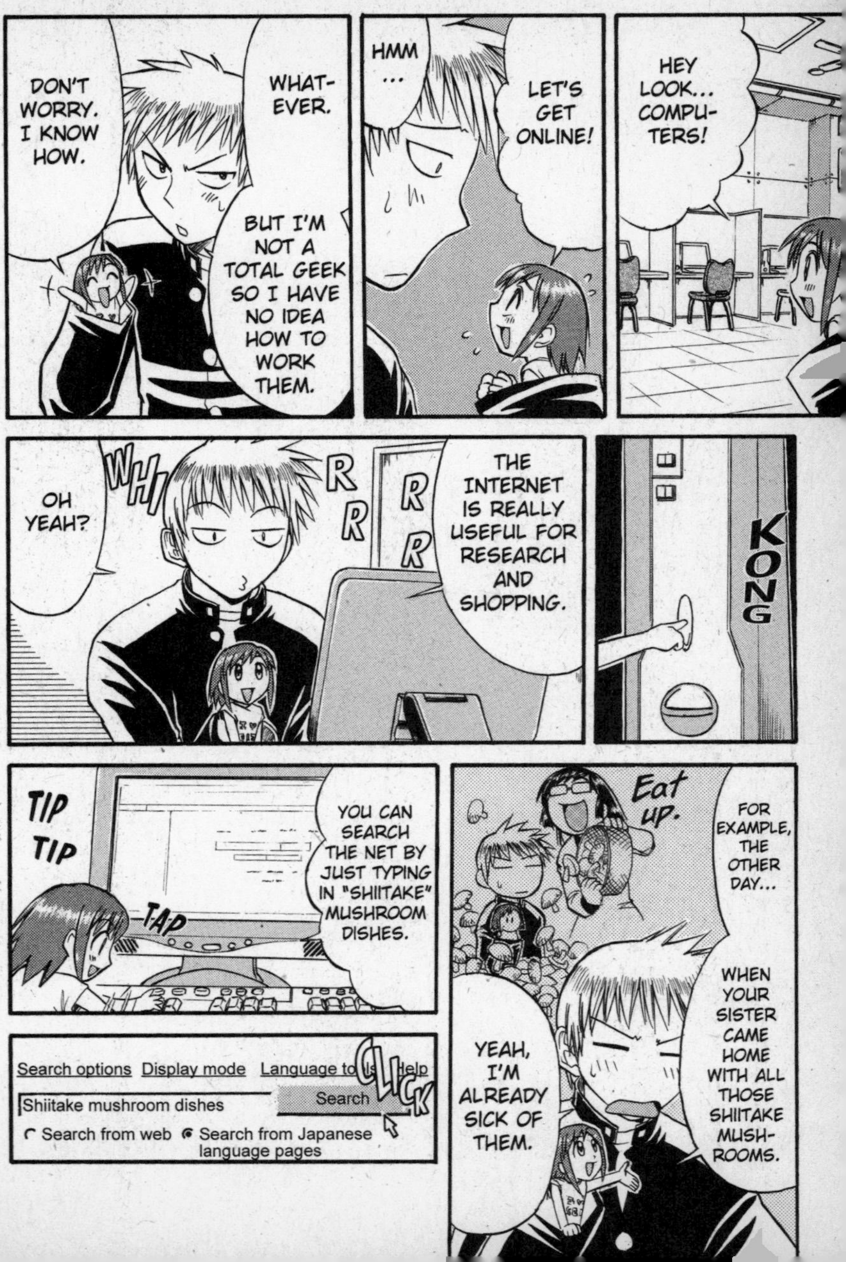
HEY LOOK... COMPUTERS!
LET'S GET ONLINE!
HMM ...
WHATEVER.
BUT I'M NOT A TOTAL GEEK SO I HAVE NO IDEA HOW TO WORK THEM.
DON'T WORRY. I KNOW HOW.
KONG
THE INTERNET IS REALLY USEFUL FOR RESEARCH AND SHOPPING.
WHIRRRR
OH YEAH?
FOR EXAMPLE, THE OTHER DAY...
Eat up.
WHEN YOUR SISTER CAME HOME WITH ALL THOSE SHIITAKE MUSHROOMS.
YEAH, I'M ALREADY SICK OF THEM.
YOU CAN SEARCH THE NET BY JUST TYPING IN "SHIITAKE" MUSHROOM DISHES.
TAP
TIP TIP
Search options Display mode Language tools Help
Shiitake mushroom dishes
Search
CLICK
Search from web
Search from Japanese language pages

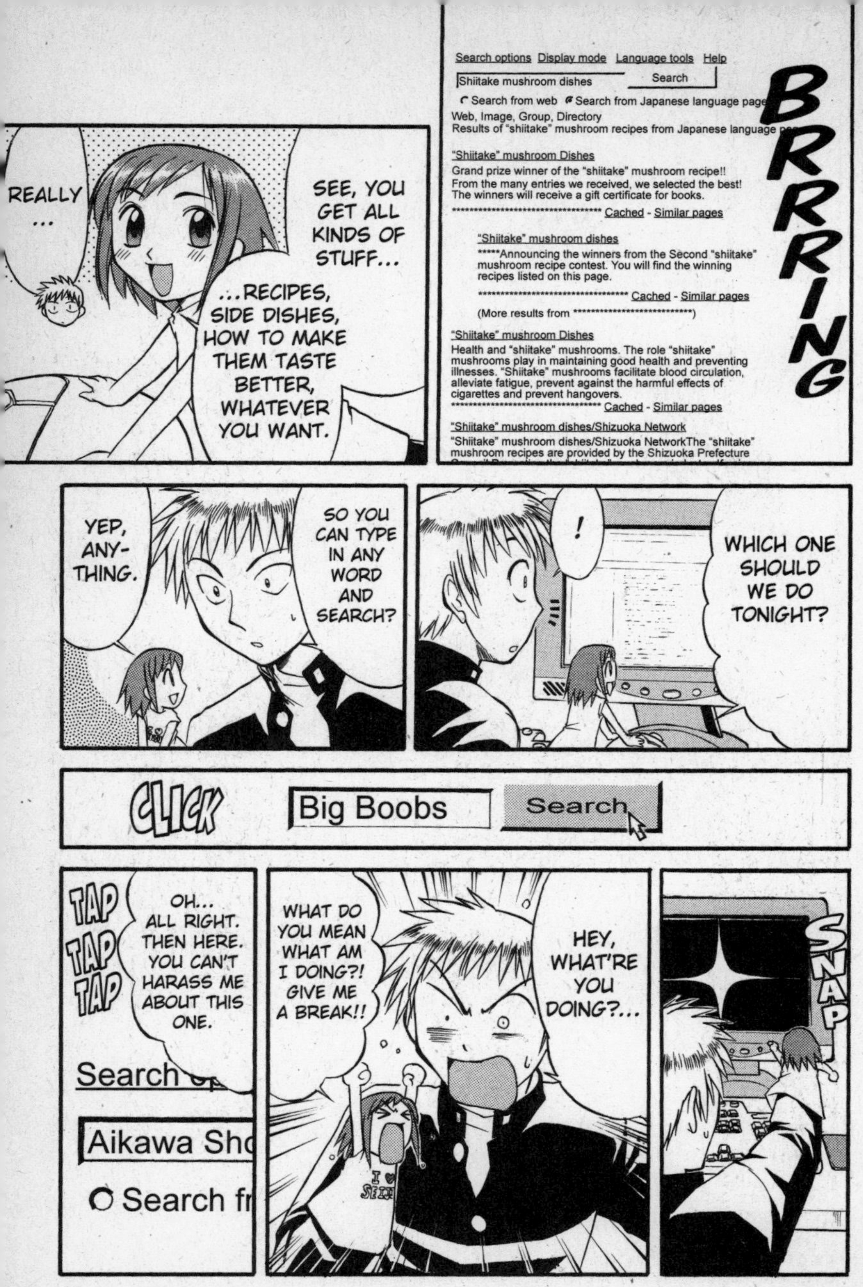

BRRRING
Search options Display mode Language tools Help
Shiitake mushroom dishes Search
Search from web Search from Japanese language page
Web, Image, Group, Directory
Results of "shiitake" mushroom recipes from Japanese language
"Shiitake" mushroom Dishes
Grand prize winner of the "shiitake" mushroom recipe!! From the many entries we received, we selected the best! The winners will receive a gift certificate for books.
********************************** Cached - Similar pages
"Shiitake" mushroom dishes
*****Announcing the winners from the Second "shiitake" mushroom recipe contest. You will find the winning recipes listed on this page.
********************************** Cached - Similar pages
(More results from ****************************)
"Shiitake" mushroom Dishes
Health and "shiitake" mushrooms. The role "shiitake" mushrooms play in maintaining good health and preventing illnesses. "Shiitake" mushrooms facilitate blood circulation, alleviate fatigue, prevent against the harmful effects of cigarettes and prevent hangovers.
********************************** Cached - Similar pages
"Shiitake" mushroom dishes/Shizuoka Network
"Shiitake" mushroom dishes/Shizuoka NetworkThe "shiitake" mushroom recipes are provided by the Shizuoka Prefecture
SEE, YOU GET ALL KINDS OF STUFF...
...RECIPES, SIDE DISHES, HOW TO MAKE THEM TASTE BETTER, WHATEVER YOU WANT.
REALLY ...
WHICH ONE SHOULD WE DO TONIGHT?
!
SO YOU CAN TYPE IN ANY WORD AND SEARCH?
YEP, ANY-THING.
CLICK
Big Boobs
Search
SNAP
HEY, WHAT'RE YOU DOING?...
WHAT DO YOU MEAN WHAT AM I DOING?! GIVE ME A BREAK!!
TAP TAP TAP
OH... ALL RIGHT. THEN HERE. YOU CAN'T HARASS ME ABOUT THIS ONE.
Search op
Aikawa Sho
Search fr

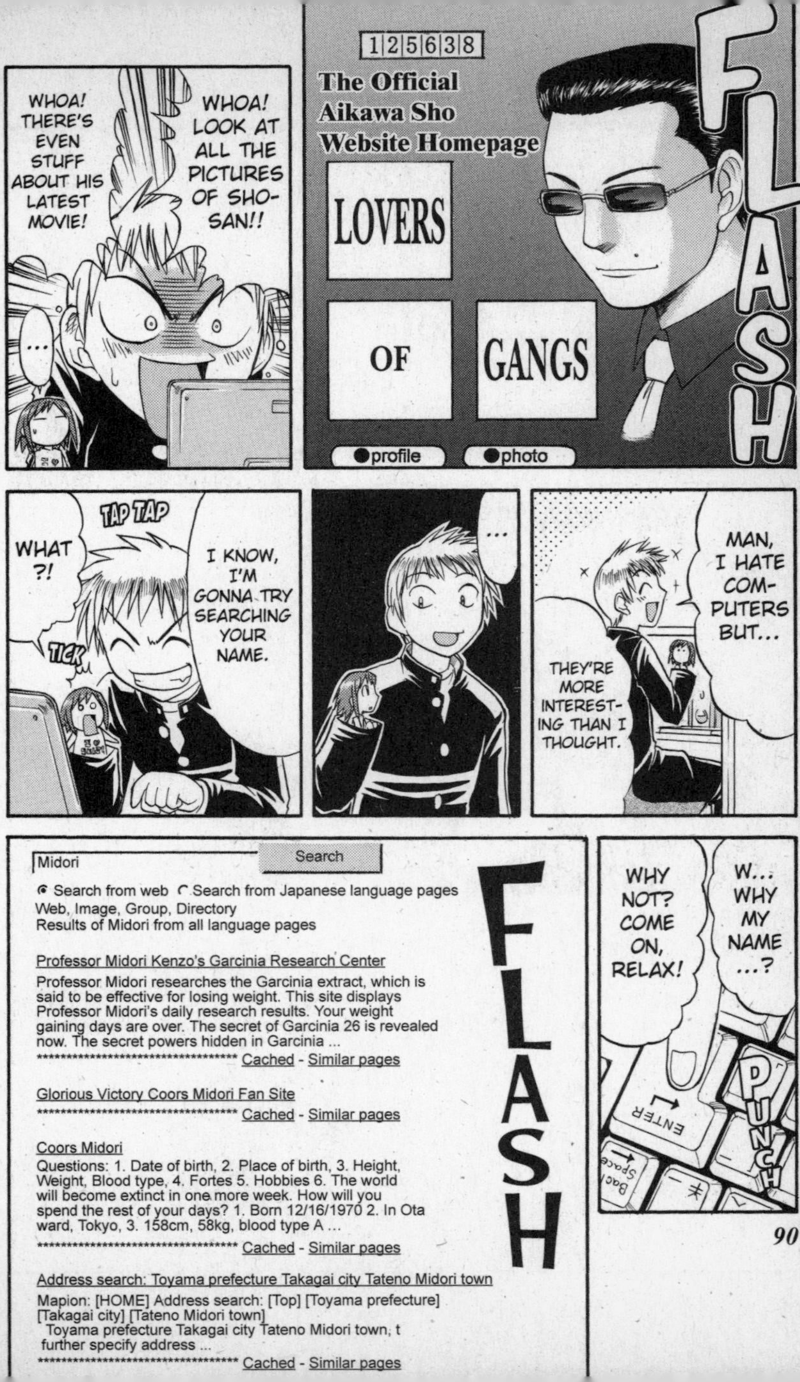
125638
The Official Aikawa Sho Website Homepage
LOVERS
OF
GANGS
profile
photo
FLASH
WHOA! LOOK AT ALL THE PICTURES OF SHO-SAN!!
WHOA! THERE'S EVEN STUFF ABOUT HIS LATEST MOVIE!
...
MAN, I HATE COM-PUTERS BUT...
THEY'RE MORE INTEREST-ING THAN I THOUGHT.
...
I KNOW, I'M GONNA TRY SEARCHING YOUR NAME.
TAP TAP
WHAT ?!
TICK
W... WHY MY NAME ...?
WHY NOT? COME ON, RELAX!
PUNCH
ENTER
Back Space
Midori
Search
Search from web Search from Japanese language pages
Web, Image, Group, Directory
Results of Midori from all language pages
Professor Midori Kenzo's Garcinia Research Center
Professor Midori researches the Garcinia extract, which is said to be effective for losing weight. This site displays Professor Midori's daily research results. Your weight gaining days are over. The secret of Garcinia 26 is revealed now. The secret powers hidden in Garcinia ...
************************************ Cached - Similar pages
Glorious Victory Coors Midori Fan Site
************************************ Cached - Similar pages
Coors Midori
Questions: 1. Date of birth, 2. Place of birth, 3. Height, Weight, Blood type, 4. Fortes 5. Hobbies 6. The world will become extinct in one more week. How will you spend the rest of your days? 1. Born 12/16/1970 2. In Ota ward, Tokyo, 3. 158cm, 58kg, blood type A ...
************************************ Cached - Similar pages
Address search: Toyama prefecture Takagai city Tateno Midori town
Mapion: [HOME] Address search: [Top] [Toyama prefecture] [Takagai city] [Tateno Midori town]
Toyama prefecture Takagai city Tateno Midori town, t further specify address ...
************************************ Cached - Similar pages
FLASH

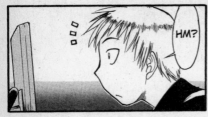

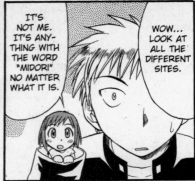

WOW... LOOK AT ALL THE DIFFERENT SITES.
IT'S NOT ME. IT'S ANYTHING WITH THE WORD "MIDORI" NO MATTER WHAT IT IS.
HM?
Internet Idol Midori's Room
WOW, INTERNET IDOL?
THIS SOUNDS COOL. HERE, LET'S LOOK.
!!
IF IT'S X-RATED, THEN I'M TURNING THE COMPUTER OFF, OKAY?!
ALL RIGHT, ALL RIGHT.
THUD
THUD
I WONDER WHAT SHE'LL LOOK LIKE?
SNICKER
AFTER ALL, SHE CALLS HERSELF AN IDOL...
... YOU KNOW ...

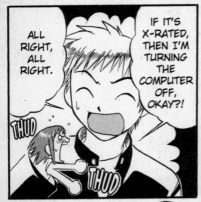

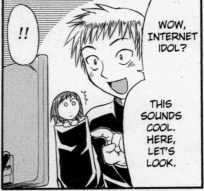

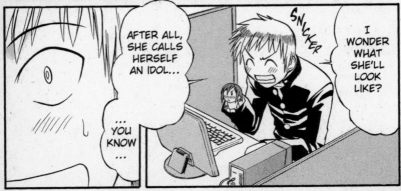

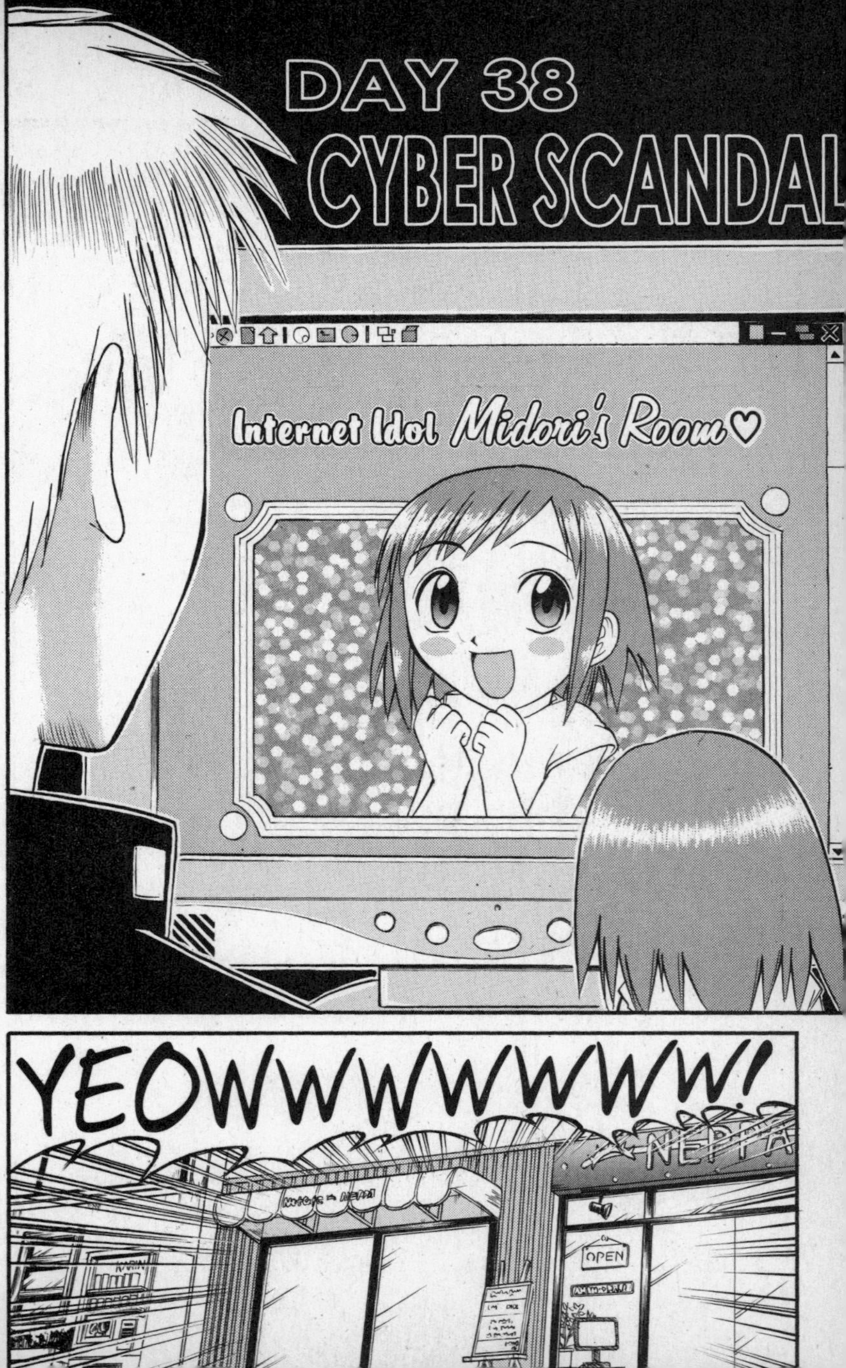
DAY 38
CYBER SCANDAL
Internet Idol Midori's Room♡
YEOWWWWWWW!
NEPPA
OPEN

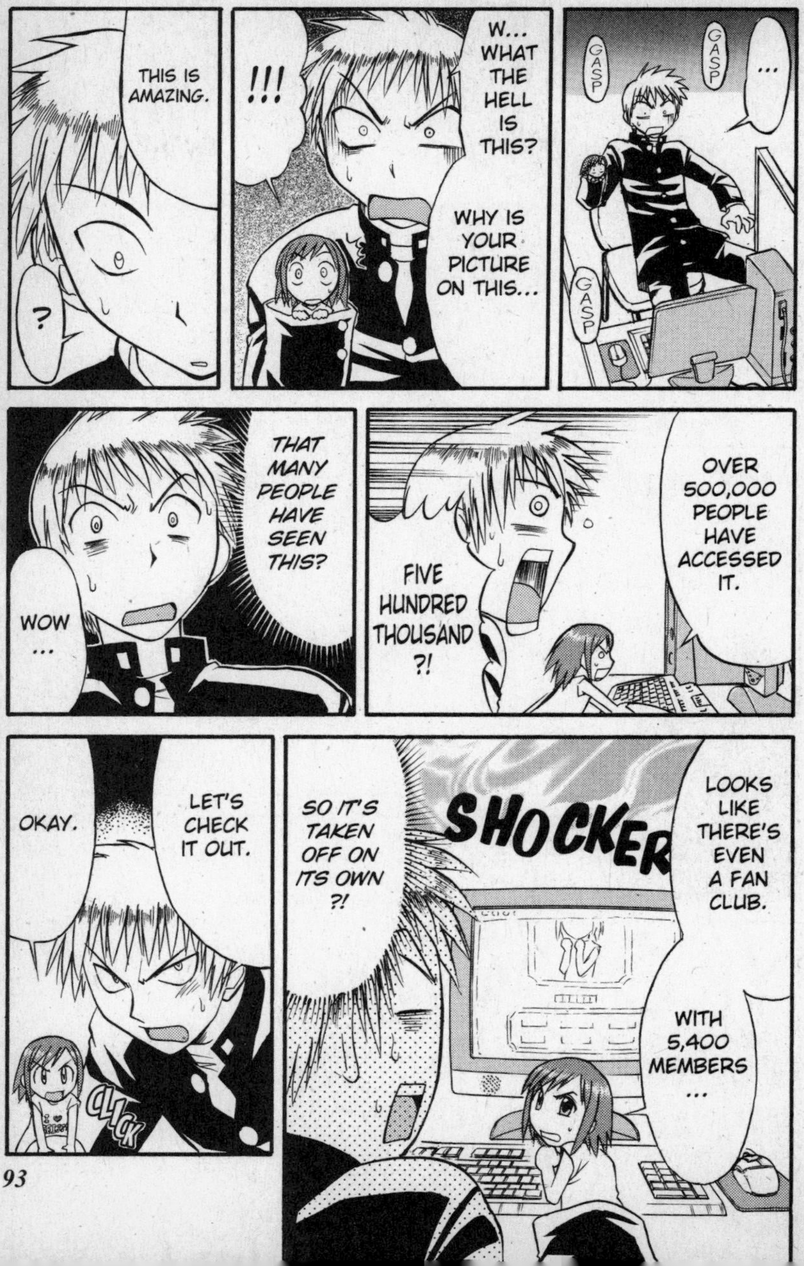
...
GASP
GASP
GASP
W... WHAT THE HELL IS THIS?
WHY IS YOUR PICTURE ON THIS...
!!!
THIS IS AMAZING.
?
OVER 500,000 PEOPLE HAVE ACCESSED IT.
FIVE HUNDRED THOUSAND ?!
THAT MANY PEOPLE HAVE SEEN THIS?
WOW ...
LOOKS LIKE THERE'S EVEN A FAN CLUB.
SHOCKER
SO IT'S TAKEN OFF ON ITS OWN ?!
WITH 5,400 MEMBERS ...
LET'S CHECK IT OUT.
OKAY.
CLICK

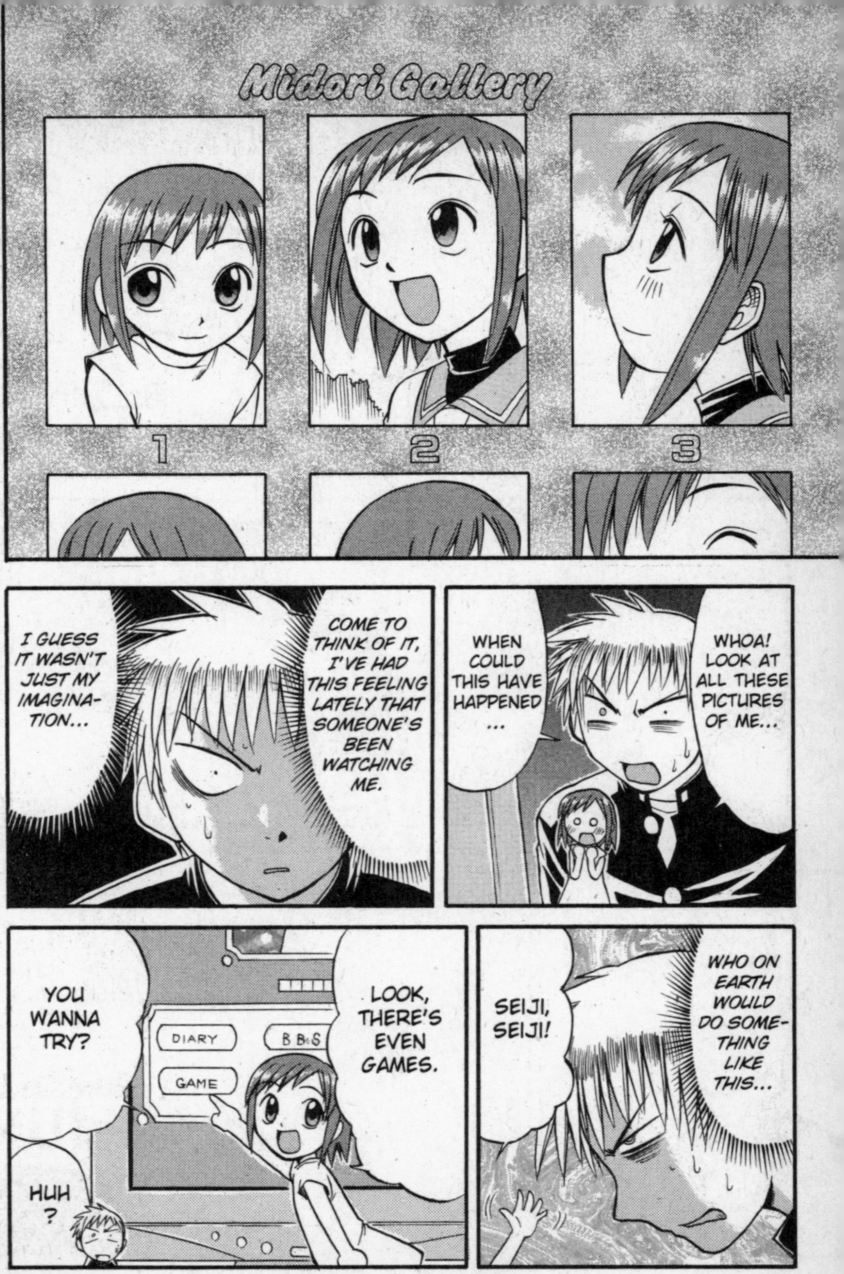
Midori Gallery
1
2
3
WHOA! LOOK AT ALL THESE PICTURES OF ME...
WHEN COULD THIS HAVE HAPPENED ...
COME TO THINK OF IT, I'VE HAD THIS FEELING LATELY THAT SOMEONE'S BEEN WATCHING ME.
I GUESS IT WASN'T JUST MY IMAGINATION...
WHO ON EARTH WOULD DO SOMETHING LIKE THIS...
SEIJI, SEIJI!
DIARY
BBS
GAME
LOOK, THERE'S EVEN GAMES.
YOU WANNA TRY?
HUH ?

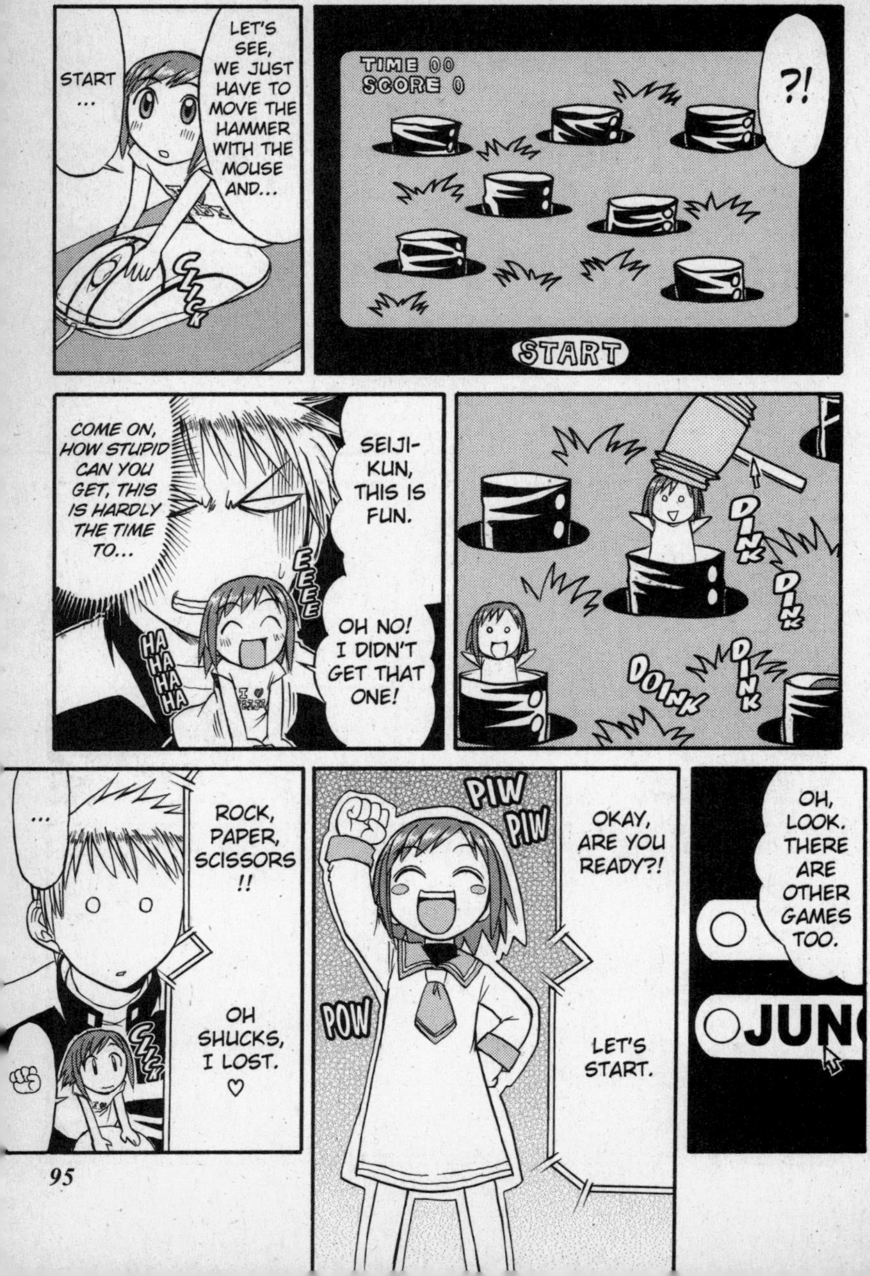
?!
TIME 00
SCORE 0
START
LET'S SEE, WE JUST HAVE TO MOVE THE HAMMER WITH THE MOUSE AND...
START ...
CLICK
DINK
DINK
DOINK
DINK
SEIJI-KUN, THIS IS FUN.
OH NO! I DIDN'T GET THAT ONE!
EEEE
COME ON, HOW STUPID CAN YOU GET, THIS IS HARDLY THE TIME TO...
HAHAHAHAHA
OH, LOOK. THERE ARE OTHER GAMES TOO.
JUN
OKAY, ARE YOU READY?!
PIW PIW
LET'S START.
POW
ROCK, PAPER, SCISSORS!!
...
OH SHUCKS, I LOST. ♡
CLICK

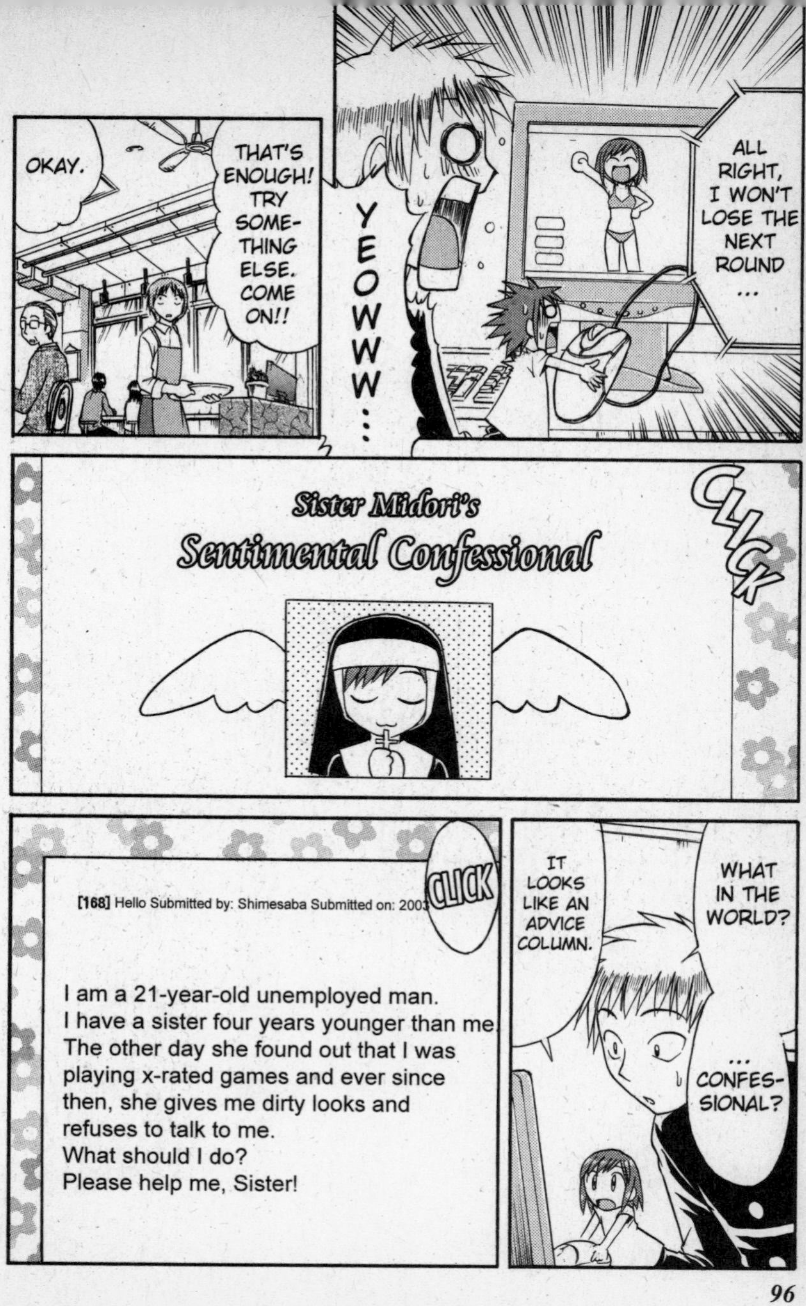
ALL RIGHT, I WON'T LOSE THE NEXT ROUND ...
YEOWWW...
THAT'S ENOUGH! TRY SOME-THING ELSE. COME ON!!
OKAY.
CLICK
Sister Midori's
Sentimental Confessional
WHAT IN THE WORLD?
IT LOOKS LIKE AN ADVICE COLUMN.
... CONFES-SIONAL?
CLICK
[168] Hello Submitted by: Shimesaba Submitted on: 2003
I am a 21-year-old unemployed man.
I have a sister four years younger than me.
The other day she found out that I was playing x-rated games and ever since then, she gives me dirty looks and refuses to talk to me.
What should I do?
Please help me, Sister!

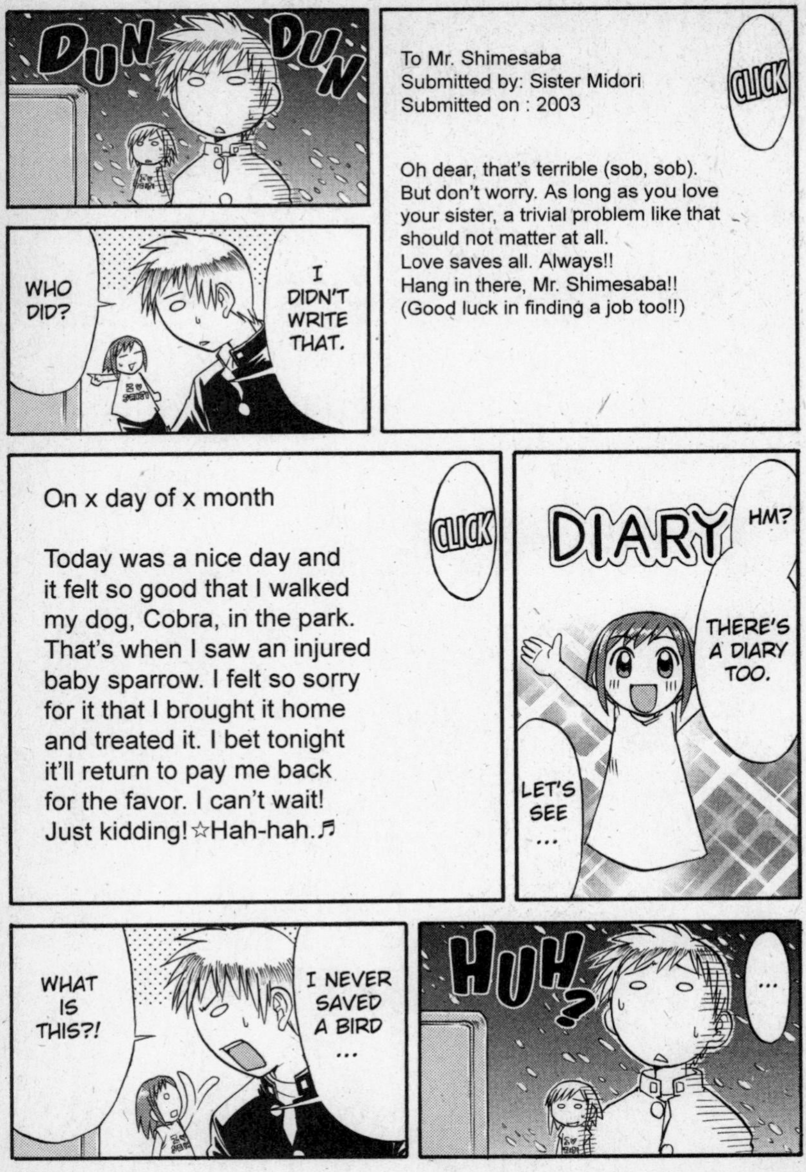

CLICK
To Mr. Shimesaba
Submitted by: Sister Midori
Submitted on : 2003
Oh dear, that's terrible (sob, sob). But don't worry. As long as you love your sister, a trivial problem like that should not matter at all. Love saves all. Always!! Hang in there, Mr. Shimesaba!! (Good luck in finding a job too!!)
DUN DUN
I DIDN'T WRITE THAT.
WHO DID?
DIARY
HM?
THERE'S A DIARY TOO.
LET'S SEE ...
CLICK
On x day of x month
Today was a nice day and it felt so good that I walked my dog, Cobra, in the park. That's when I saw an injured baby sparrow. I felt so sorry for it that I brought it home and treated it. I bet tonight it'll return to pay me back for the favor. I can't wait! Just kidding!☆Hah-hah.♬
HUH?
...
I NEVER SAVED A BIRD ...
WHAT IS THIS?!

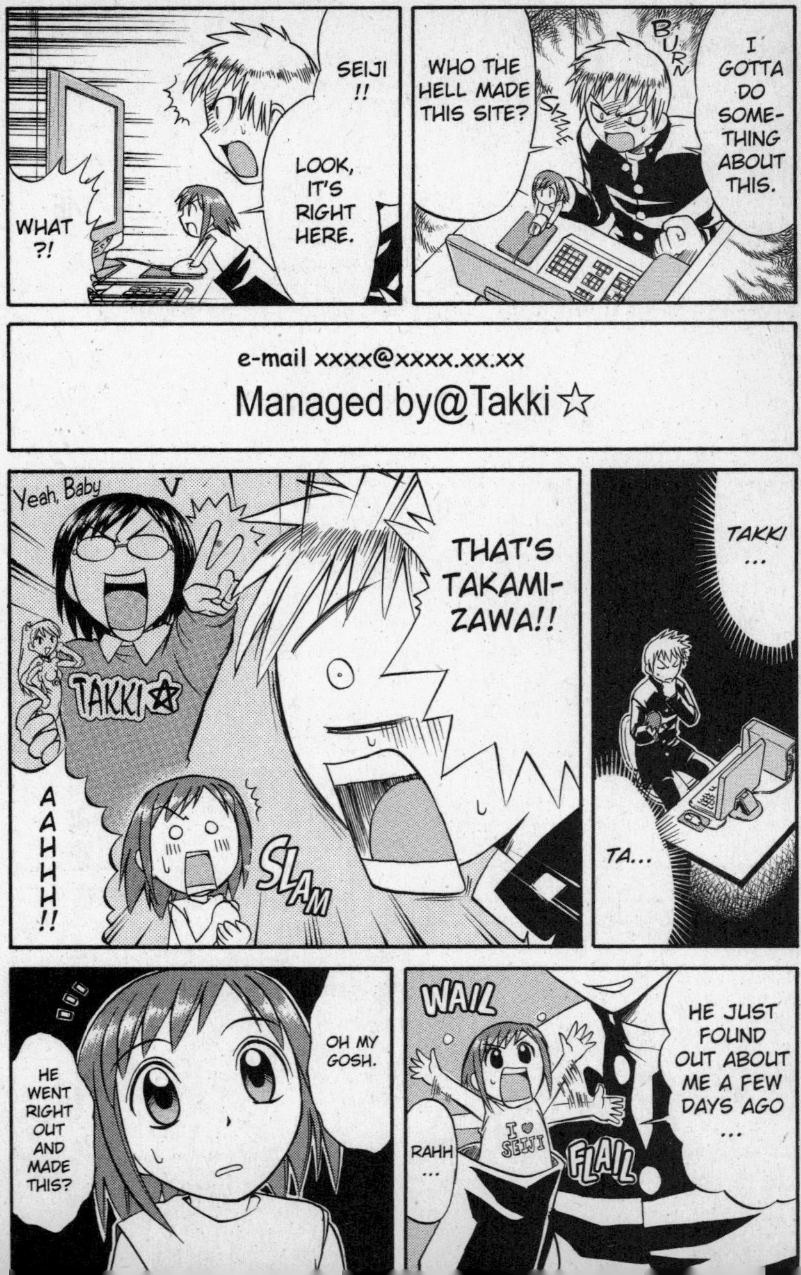

I GOTTA DO SOMETHING ABOUT THIS.
BURN
WHO THE HELL MADE THIS SITE?
SEIJI!!
LOOK, IT'S RIGHT HERE.
WHAT?!
e-mail xxxx@xxxx.xx.xx
Managed by@Takki☆
TAKKI...
TA...
THAT'S TAKAMIZAWA!!
Yeah, Baby
V
TAKKI☆
AAHHH?!!
SLAM
HE JUST FOUND OUT ABOUT ME A FEW DAYS AGO...
WAIL
FLAIL
I ♥ SEIJI
RAHH...
OH MY GOSH.
HE WENT RIGHT OUT AND MADE THIS?

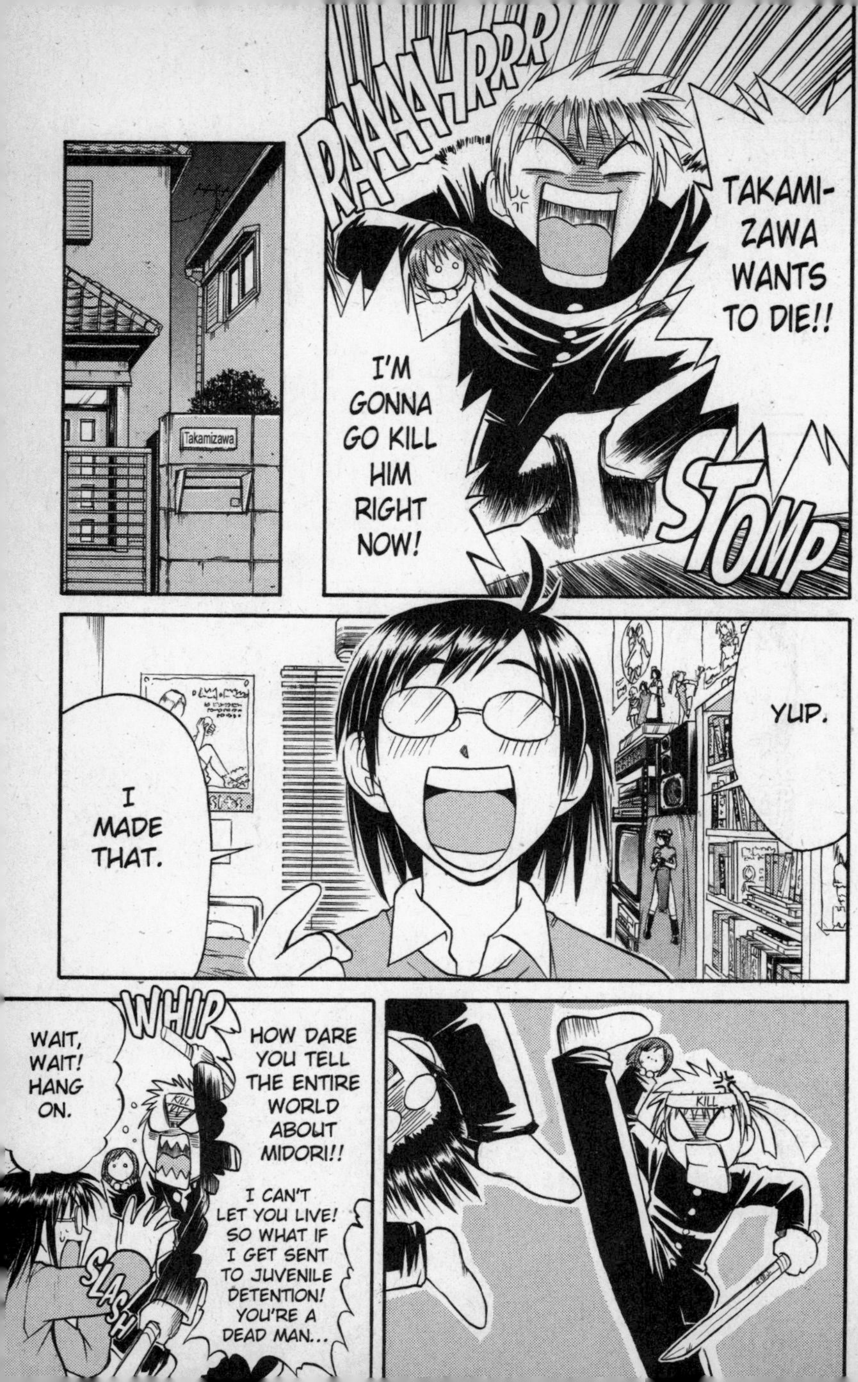
RAAAAHRRR
TAKAMI-ZAWA WANTS TO DIE!!
I'M GONNA GO KILL HIM RIGHT NOW!
STOMP
Takamizawa
YUP.
I MADE THAT.
KILL
KILL
WHIP
HOW DARE YOU TELL THE ENTIRE WORLD ABOUT MIDORI!!
WAIT, WAIT! HANG ON.
I CAN'T LET YOU LIVE! SO WHAT IF I GET SENT TO JUVENILE DETENTION! YOU'RE A DEAD MAN...
SLASH

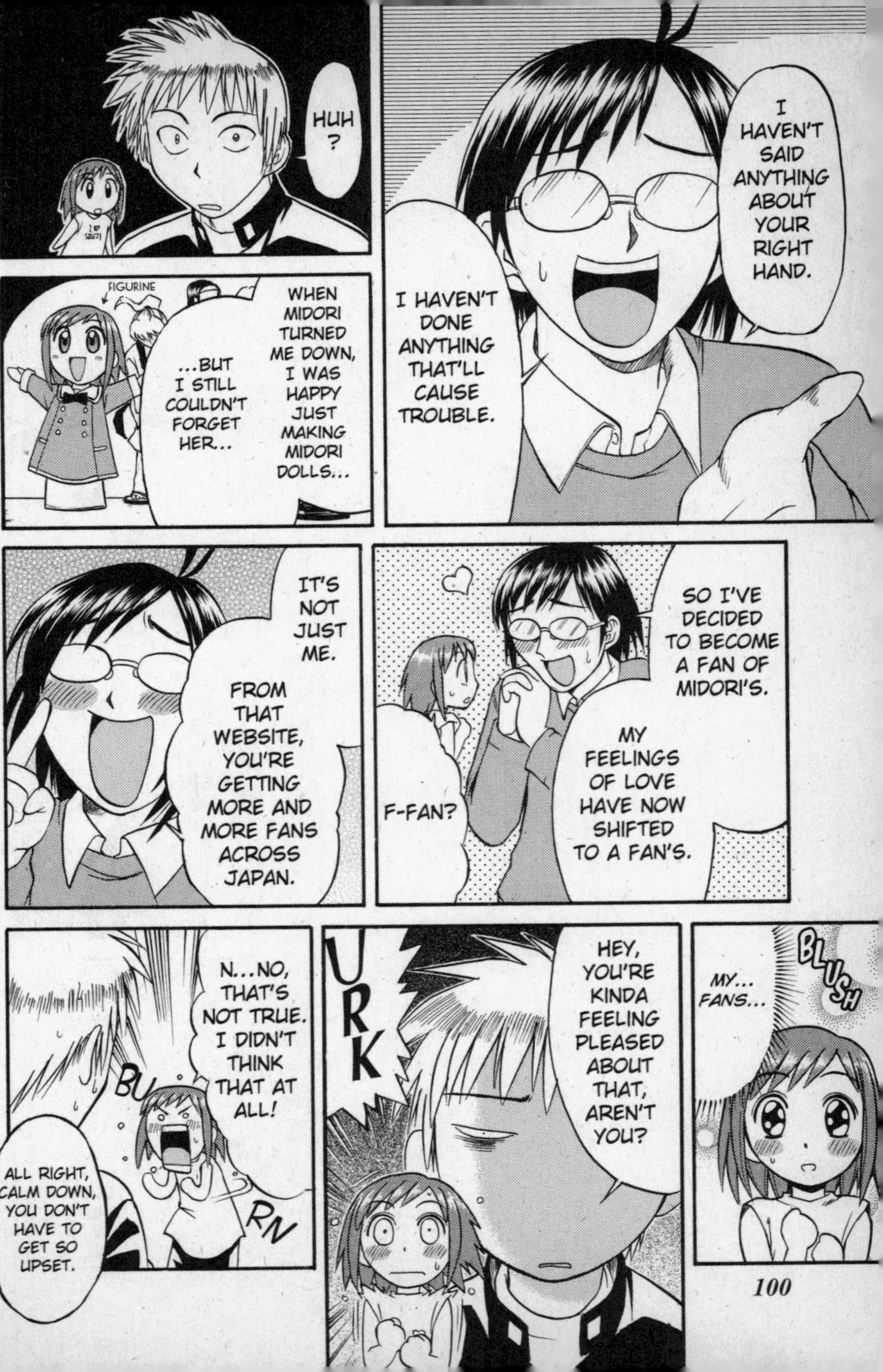
I HAVEN'T SAID ANYTHING ABOUT YOUR RIGHT HAND.
I HAVEN'T DONE ANYTHING THAT'LL CAUSE TROUBLE.
HUH?
WHEN MIDORI TURNED ME DOWN, I WAS HAPPY JUST MAKING MIDORI DOLLS...
...BUT I STILL COULDN'T FORGET HER...
FIGURINE
SO I'VE DECIDED TO BECOME A FAN OF MIDORI'S.
MY FEELINGS OF LOVE HAVE NOW SHIFTED TO A FAN'S.
F-FAN?
IT'S NOT JUST ME.
FROM THAT WEBSITE, YOU'RE GETTING MORE AND MORE FANS ACROSS JAPAN.
BLUSH
MY... FANS...
HEY, YOU'RE KINDA FEELING PLEASED ABOUT THAT, AREN'T YOU?
URK
N...NO, THAT'S NOT TRUE. I DIDN'T THINK THAT AT ALL!
BU
RN
ALL RIGHT, CALM DOWN, YOU DON'T HAVE TO GET SO UPSET.

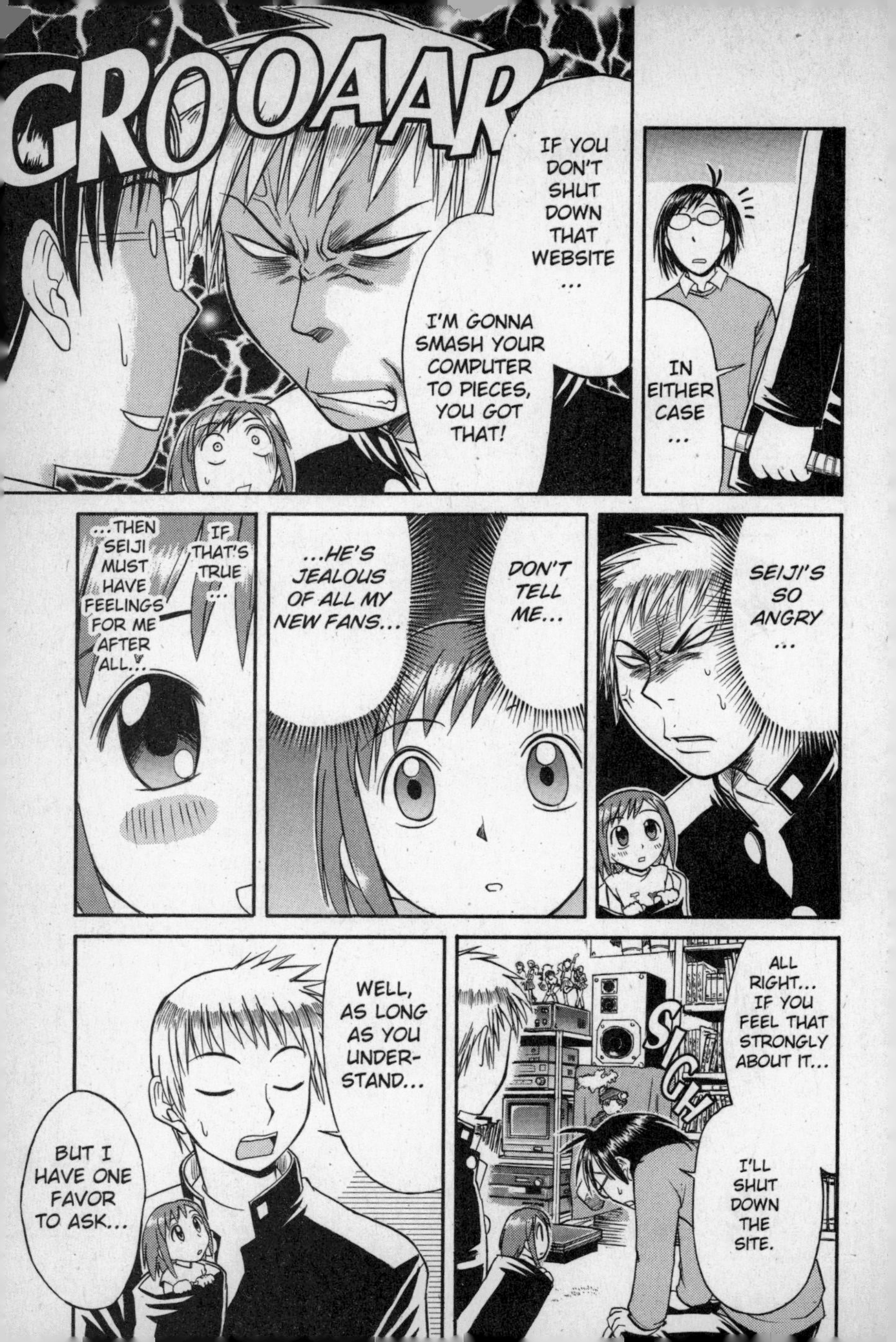
IN EITHER CASE ...
IF YOU DON'T SHUT DOWN THAT WEBSITE ...
I'M GONNA SMASH YOUR COMPUTER TO PIECES, YOU GOT THAT!
GROOAAR
SEIJI'S SO ANGRY ...
DON'T TELL ME...
...HE'S JEALOUS OF ALL MY NEW FANS...
IF THAT'S TRUE ...
...THEN SEIJI MUST HAVE FEELINGS FOR ME AFTER ALL...
ALL RIGHT... IF YOU FEEL THAT STRONGLY ABOUT IT...
SIGH
I'LL SHUT DOWN THE SITE.
WELL, AS LONG AS YOU UNDER-STAND...
BUT I HAVE ONE FAVOR TO ASK...

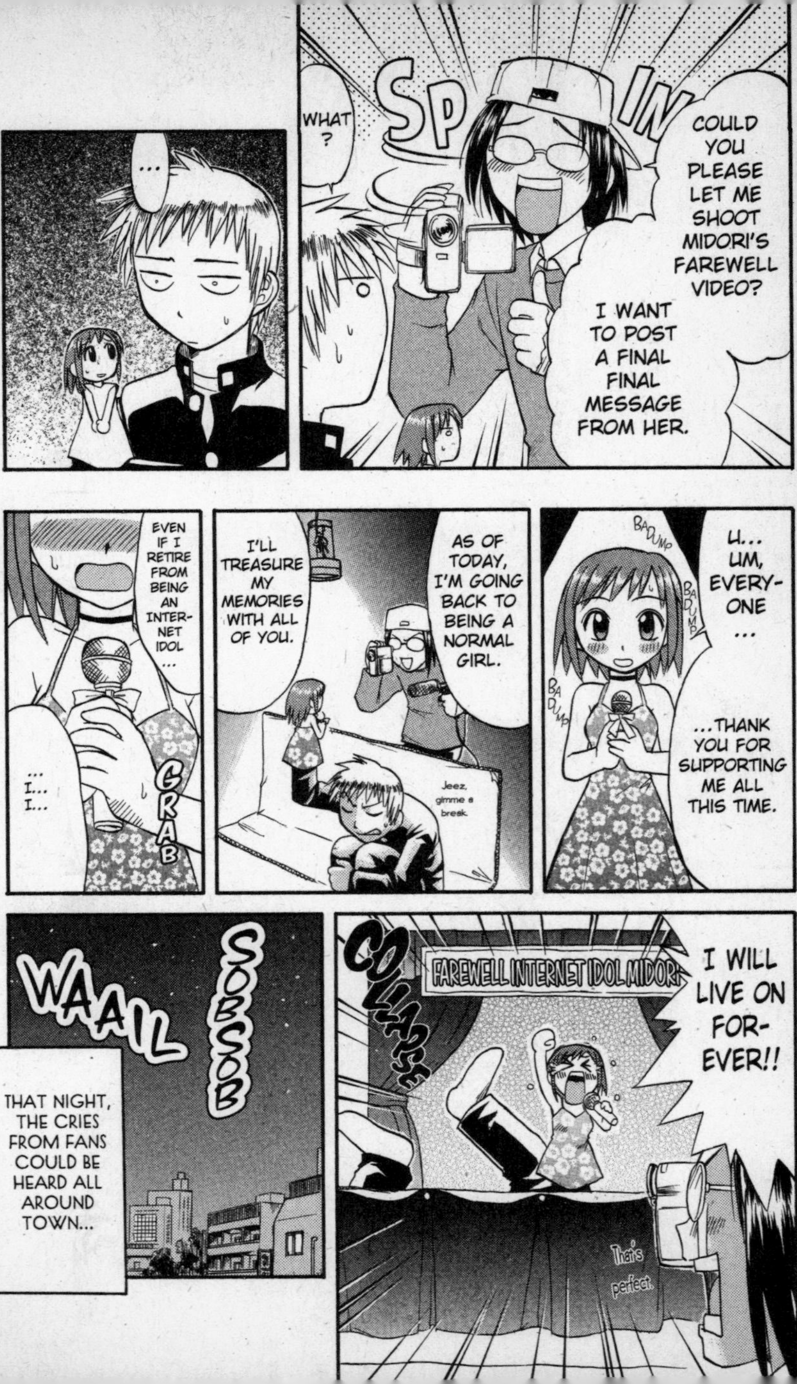
COULD YOU PLEASE LET ME SHOOT MIDORI'S FAREWELL VIDEO?
I WANT TO POST A FINAL FINAL MESSAGE FROM HER.
SPIN
WHAT?
...
BADUMP
U... UM, EVERY-ONE...
BADUMP
BADUMP
...THANK YOU FOR SUPPORTING ME ALL THIS TIME.
AS OF TODAY, I'M GOING BACK TO BEING A NORMAL GIRL.
I'LL TREASURE MY MEMORIES WITH ALL OF YOU.
Jeez, gimme a break.
EVEN IF I RETIRE FROM BEING AN INTER-NET IDOL...
GRAB
...I... I...
I WILL LIVE ON FOR-EVER!!
FAREWELL INTERNET IDOL MIDORI
COLLAPSE
That's perfect.
SOBSOB
WAAAIL
THAT NIGHT, THE CRIES FROM FANS COULD BE HEARD ALL AROUND TOWN...

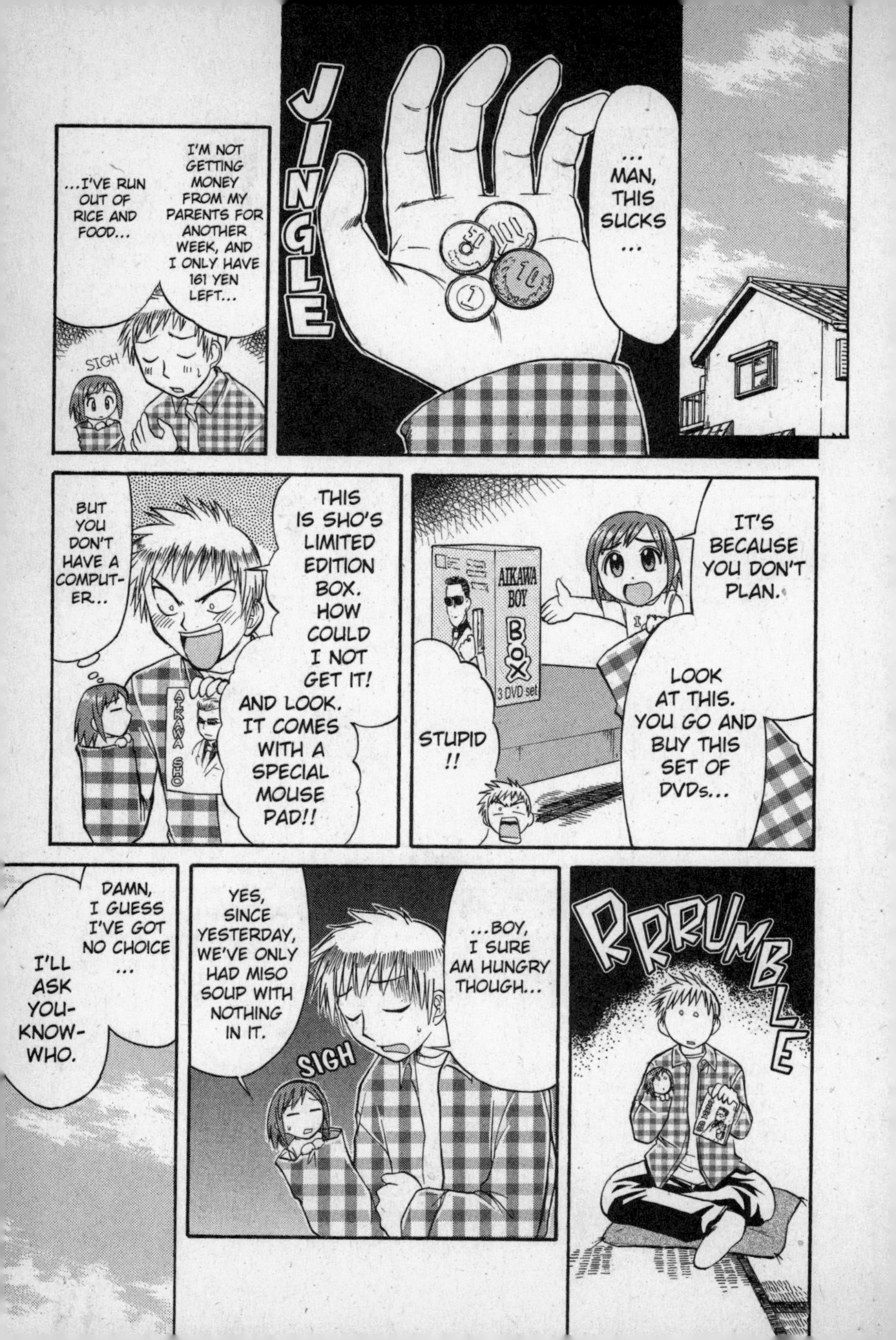
JINGLE
...MAN, THIS SUCKS...
I'M NOT GETTING MONEY FROM MY PARENTS FOR ANOTHER WEEK, AND I ONLY HAVE 161 YEN LEFT...
...I'VE RUN OUT OF RICE AND FOOD...
SIGH
IT'S BECAUSE YOU DON'T PLAN.
AIKAWA BOY BOX 3 DVD set
LOOK AT THIS. YOU GO AND BUY THIS SET OF DVDs...
STUPID !!
THIS IS SHO'S LIMITED EDITION BOX. HOW COULD I NOT GET IT!
AND LOOK. IT COMES WITH A SPECIAL MOUSE PAD!!
AIKAWA SHO
BUT YOU DON'T HAVE A COMPUTER...
RRRUMBLE
...BOY, I SURE AM HUNGRY THOUGH...
YES, SINCE YESTERDAY, WE'VE ONLY HAD MISO SOUP WITH NOTHING IN IT.
SIGH
DAMN, I GUESS I'VE GOT NO CHOICE...
I'LL ASK YOU-KNOW-WHO.

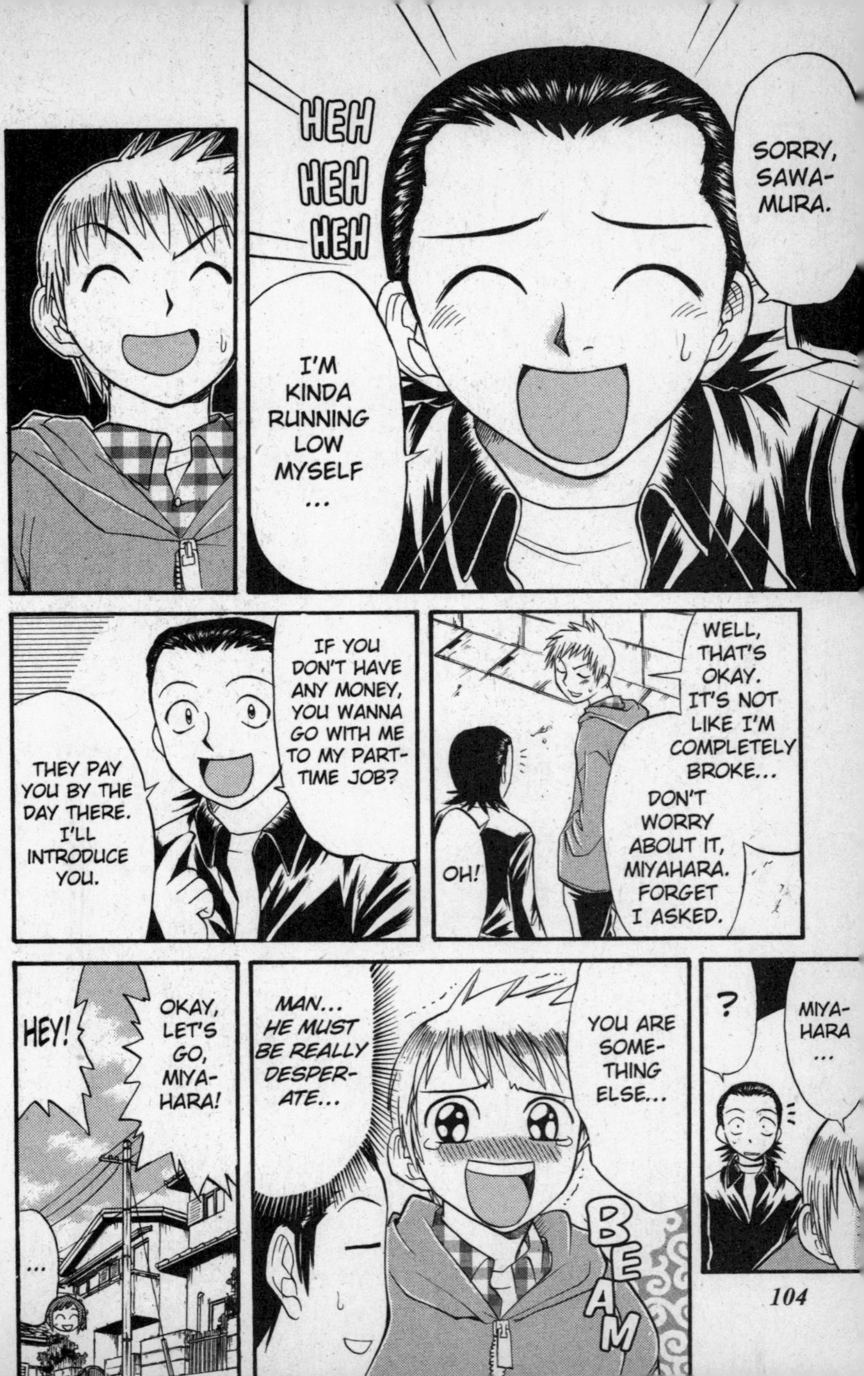
SORRY, SAWAMURA.
HEH HEH HEH
I'M KINDA RUNNING LOW MYSELF ...
WELL, THAT'S OKAY. IT'S NOT LIKE I'M COMPLETELY BROKE...
DON'T WORRY ABOUT IT, MIYAHARA. FORGET I ASKED.
OH!
IF YOU DON'T HAVE ANY MONEY, YOU WANNA GO WITH ME TO MY PART-TIME JOB?
THEY PAY YOU BY THE DAY THERE. I'LL INTRODUCE YOU.
MIYA-HARA ...
?
YOU ARE SOME-THING ELSE...
MAN... HE MUST BE REALLY DESPER-ATE...
BEAM
OKAY, LET'S GO, MIYA-HARA!
HEY!
...

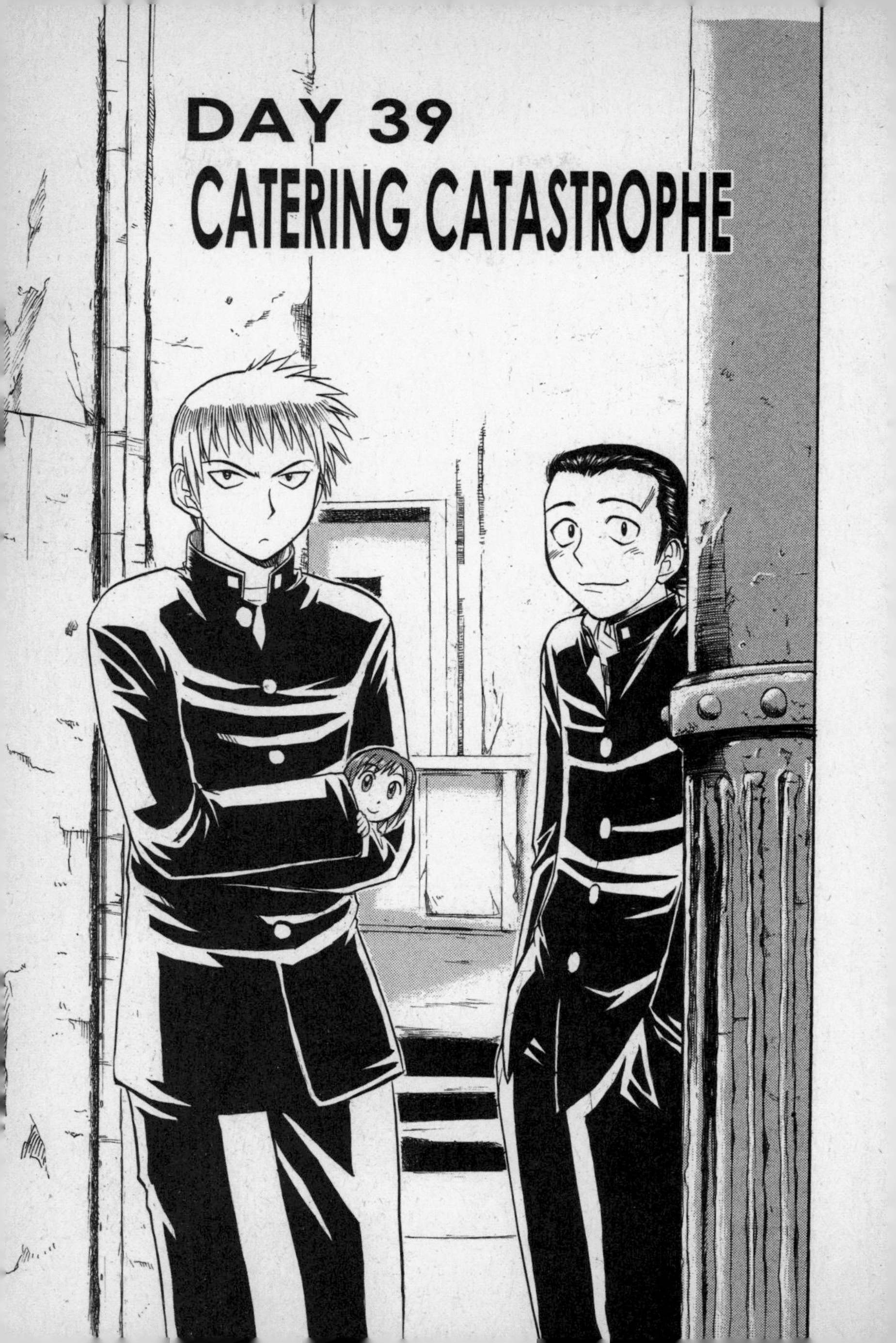
DAY 39
CATERING CATASTROPHE

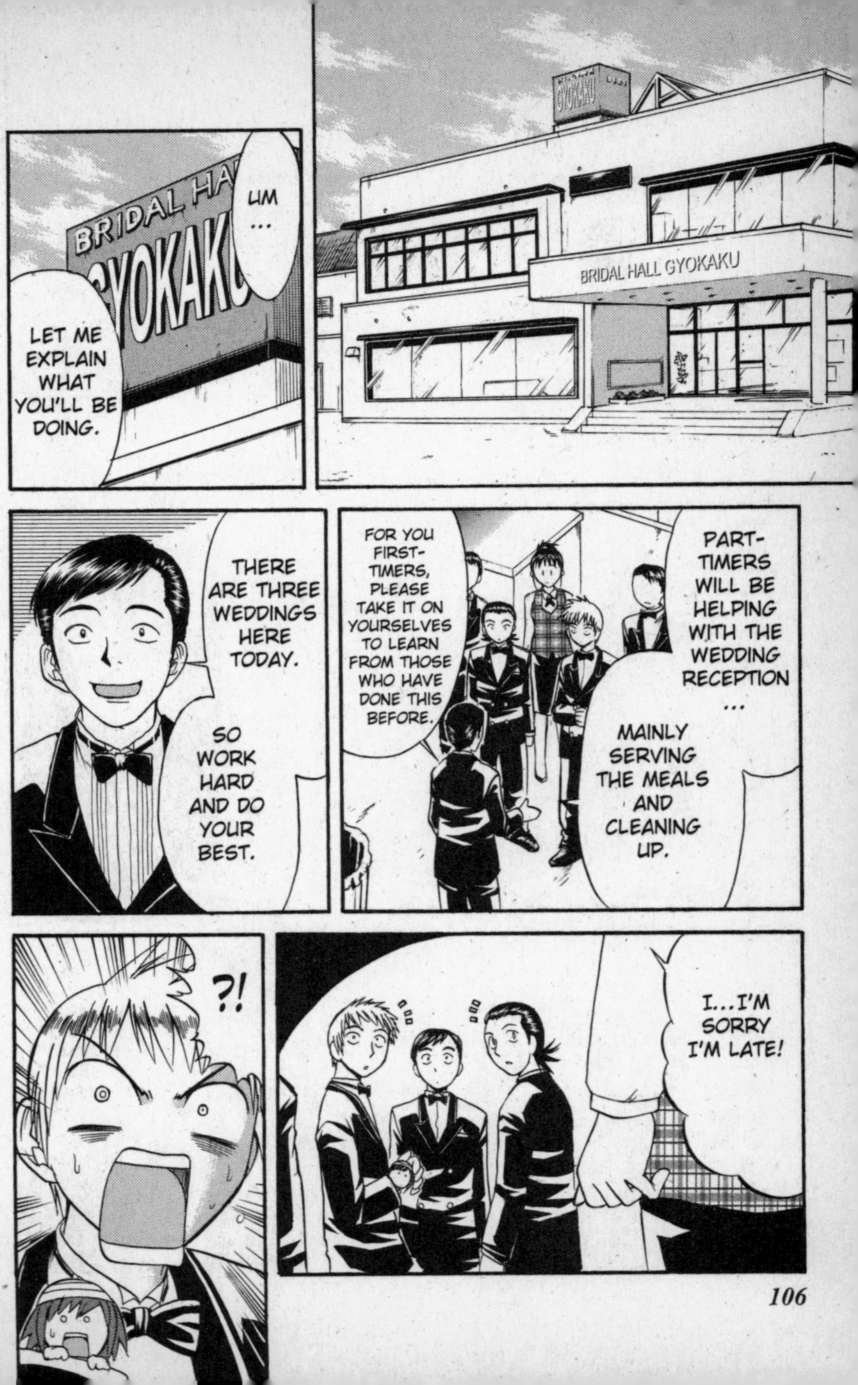
BRIDAL HALL GYOKAKU
UM ...
LET ME EXPLAIN WHAT YOU'LL BE DOING.
PART-TIMERS WILL BE HELPING WITH THE WEDDING RECEPTION ...
MAINLY SERVING THE MEALS AND CLEANING UP.
FOR YOU FIRST-TIMERS, PLEASE TAKE IT ON YOURSELVES TO LEARN FROM THOSE WHO HAVE DONE THIS BEFORE.
THERE ARE THREE WEDDINGS HERE TODAY.
SO WORK HARD AND DO YOUR BEST.
I...I'M SORRY I'M LATE!
?!

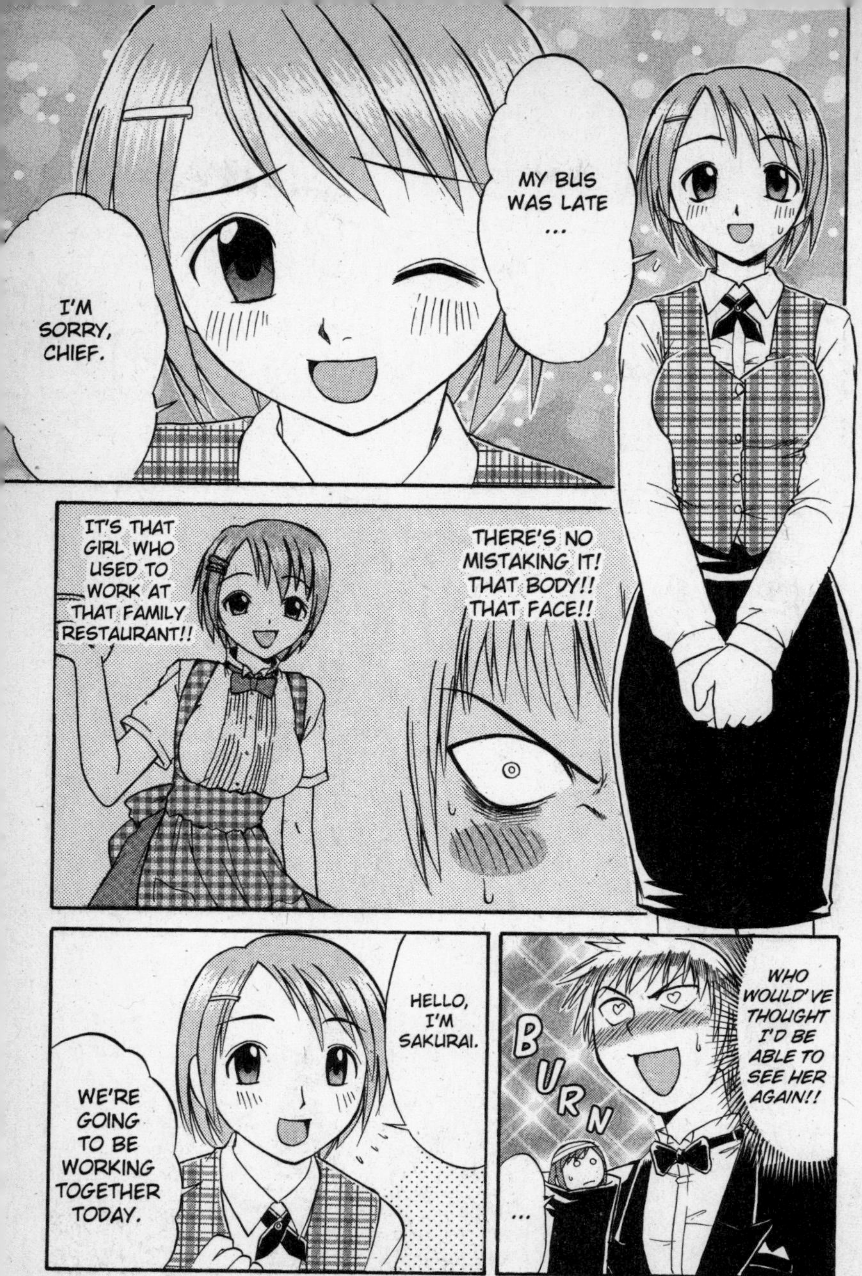
MY BUS WAS LATE ...
I'M SORRY, CHIEF.
THERE'S NO MISTAKING IT! THAT BODY!! THAT FACE!!
IT'S THAT GIRL WHO USED TO WORK AT THAT FAMILY RESTAURANT!!
WHO WOULD'VE THOUGHT I'D BE ABLE TO SEE HER AGAIN!!
BURN
...
HELLO, I'M SAKURAI.
WE'RE GOING TO BE WORKING TOGETHER TODAY.

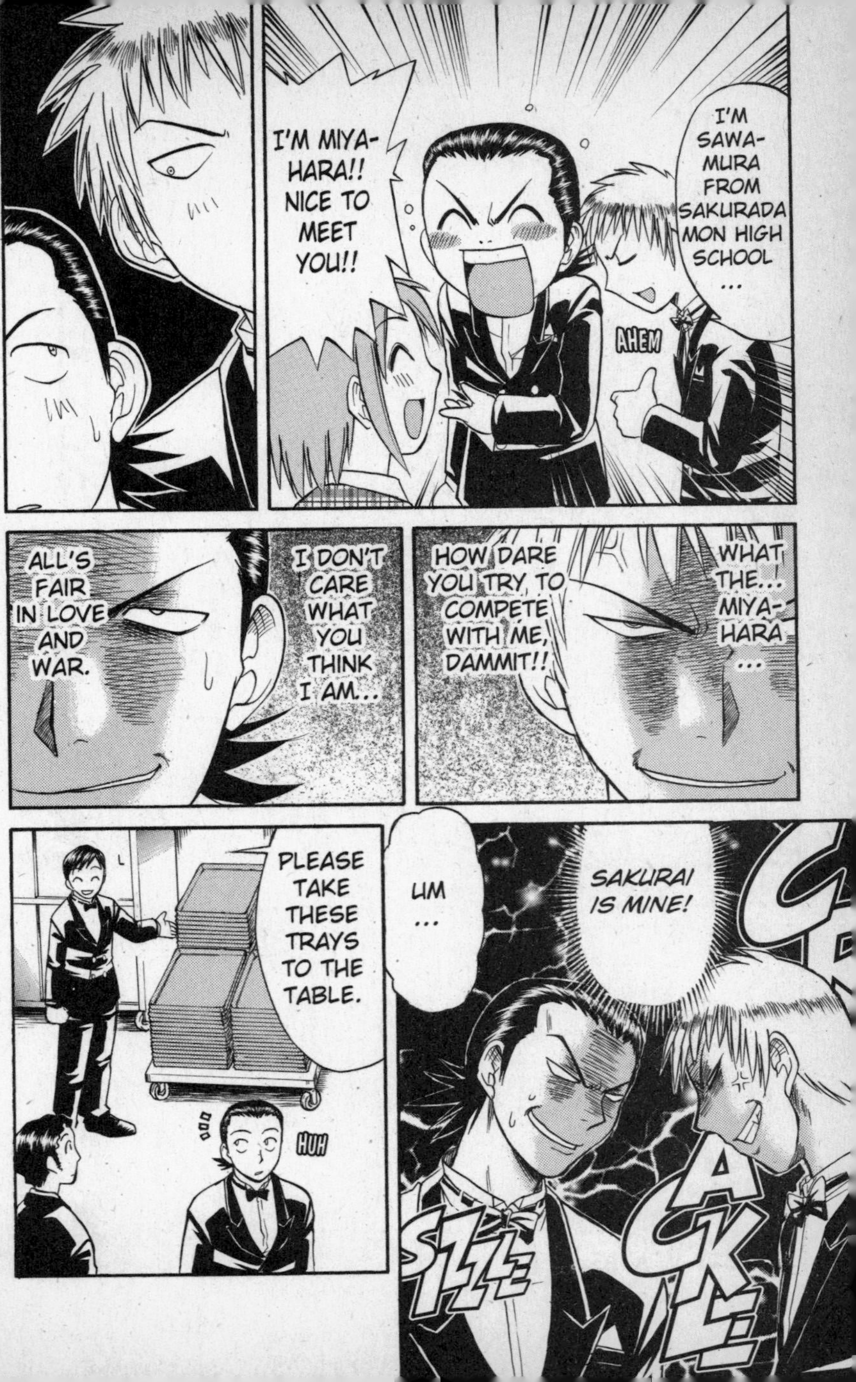
I'M SAWAMURA FROM SAKURADA MON HIGH SCHOOL ...
AHEM
I'M MIYA-HARA!! NICE TO MEET YOU!!
WHAT THE... MIYA-HARA ...
HOW DARE YOU TRY TO COMPETE WITH ME, DAMMIT!!
I DON'T CARE WHAT YOU THINK I AM...
ALL'S FAIR IN LOVE AND WAR.
SAKURAI IS MINE!
SIZZLE
UM ...
PLEASE TAKE THESE TRAYS TO THE TABLE.
HUH

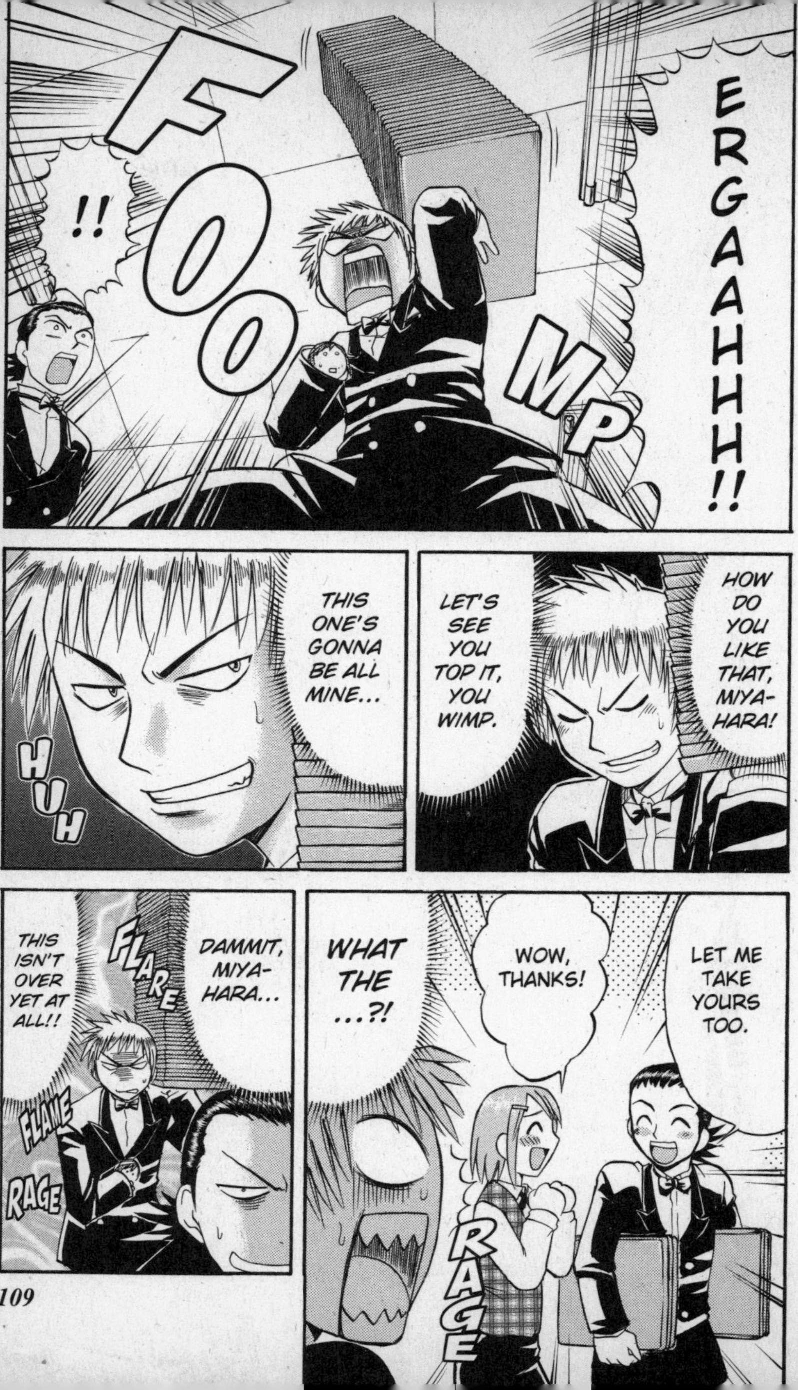
ERGAAHHH!!
FOOMP
!!
HOW DO YOU LIKE THAT, MIYA-HARA!
LET'S SEE YOU TOP IT, YOU WIMP.
THIS ONE'S GONNA BE ALL MINE...
HUH
LET ME TAKE YOURS TOO.
WOW, THANKS!
WHAT THE ...?!
RAGE
DAMMIT, MIYA-HARA...
FLARE
THIS ISN'T OVER YET AT ALL!!
FLAME
RAGE

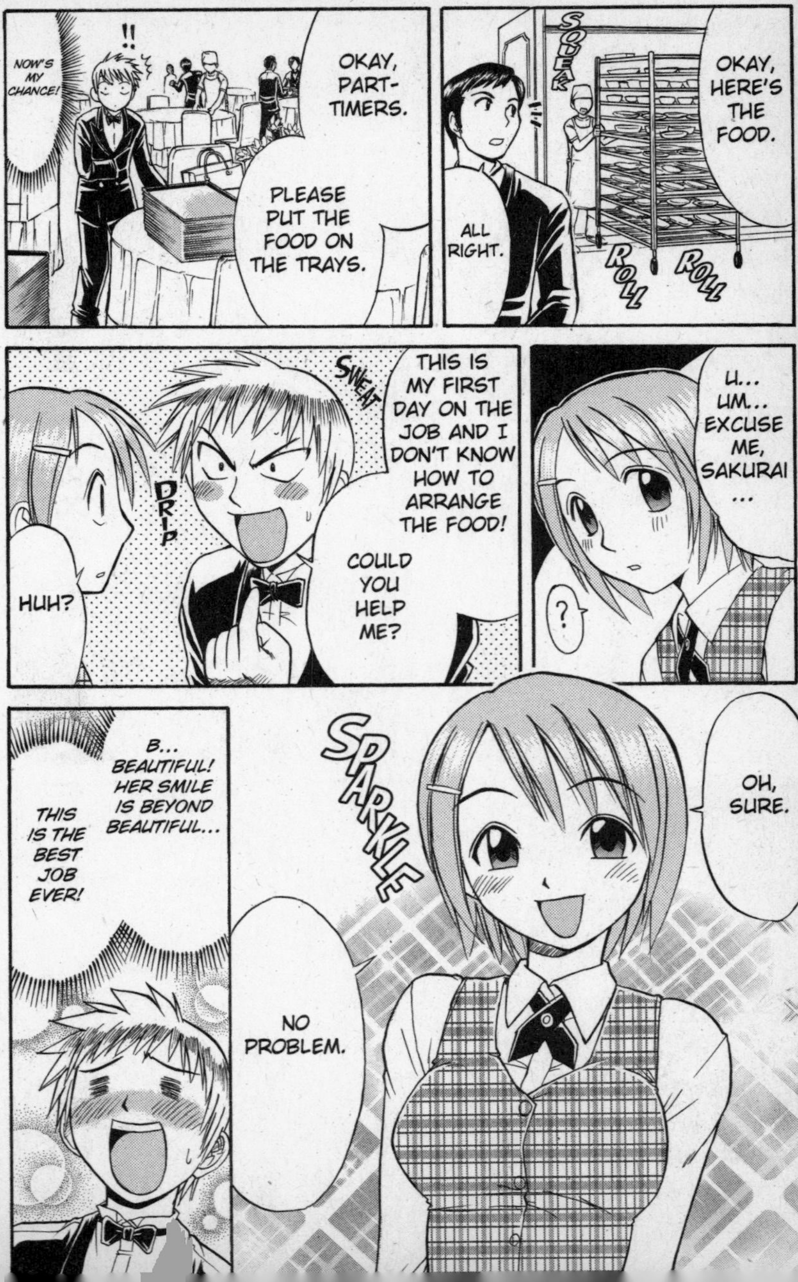
OKAY, HERE'S THE FOOD.
SQUEAK
ALL RIGHT.
ROLL
ROLL
OKAY, PART-TIMERS.
PLEASE PUT THE FOOD ON THE TRAYS.
!!
NOW'S MY CHANCE!
U... UM... EXCUSE ME, SAKURAI...
?
THIS IS MY FIRST DAY ON THE JOB AND I DON'T KNOW HOW TO ARRANGE THE FOOD!
SWEAT
COULD YOU HELP ME?
DRIP
HUH?
OH, SURE.
SPARKLE
NO PROBLEM.
B... BEAUTIFUL! HER SMILE IS BEYOND BEAUTIFUL...
THIS IS THE BEST JOB EVER!

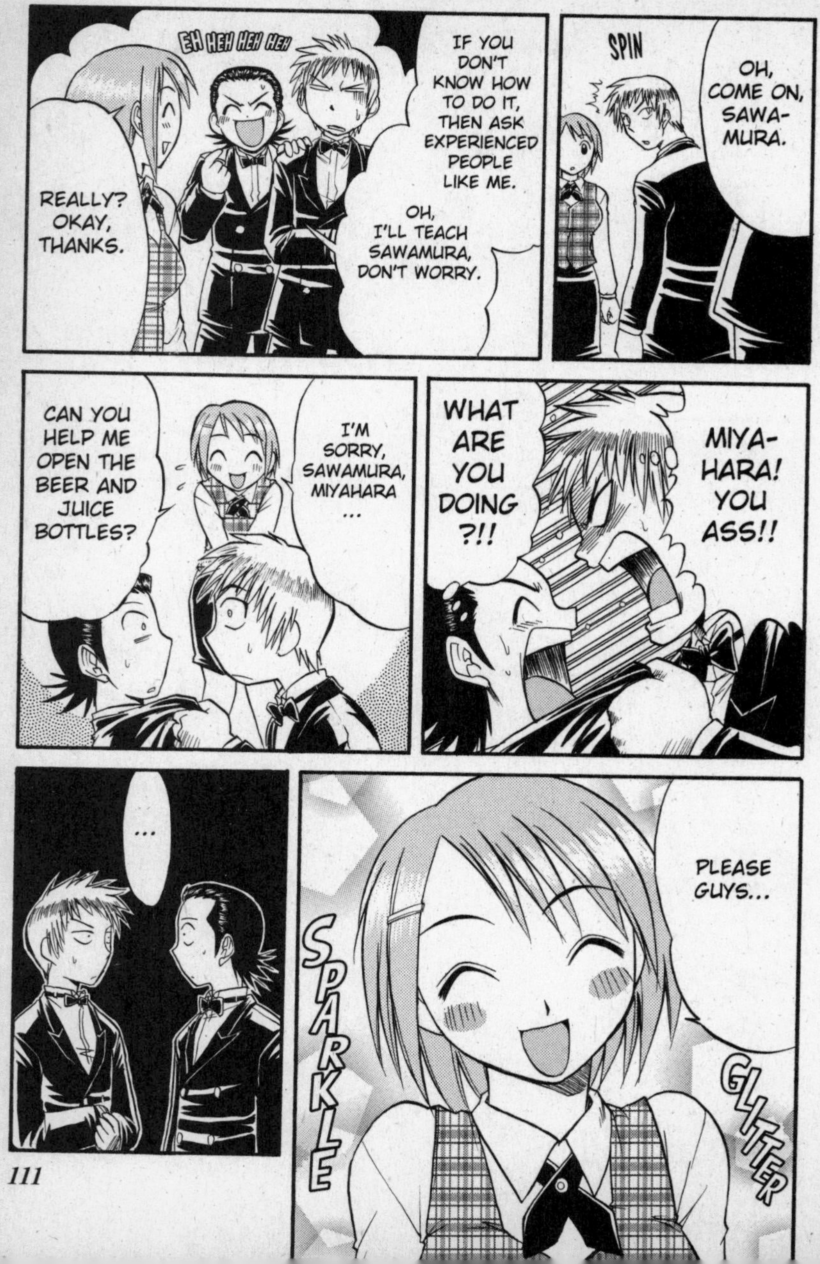
SPIN
OH, COME ON, SAWAMURA.
IF YOU DON'T KNOW HOW TO DO IT, THEN ASK EXPERIENCED PEOPLE LIKE ME.
EH HEH HEH HEH
REALLY? OKAY, THANKS.
OH, I'LL TEACH SAWAMURA, DON'T WORRY.
MIYA-HARA! YOU ASS!!
WHAT ARE YOU DOING ?!!
I'M SORRY, SAWAMURA, MIYAHARA ...
CAN YOU HELP ME OPEN THE BEER AND JUICE BOTTLES?
PLEASE GUYS...
SPARKLE
GLITTER
...

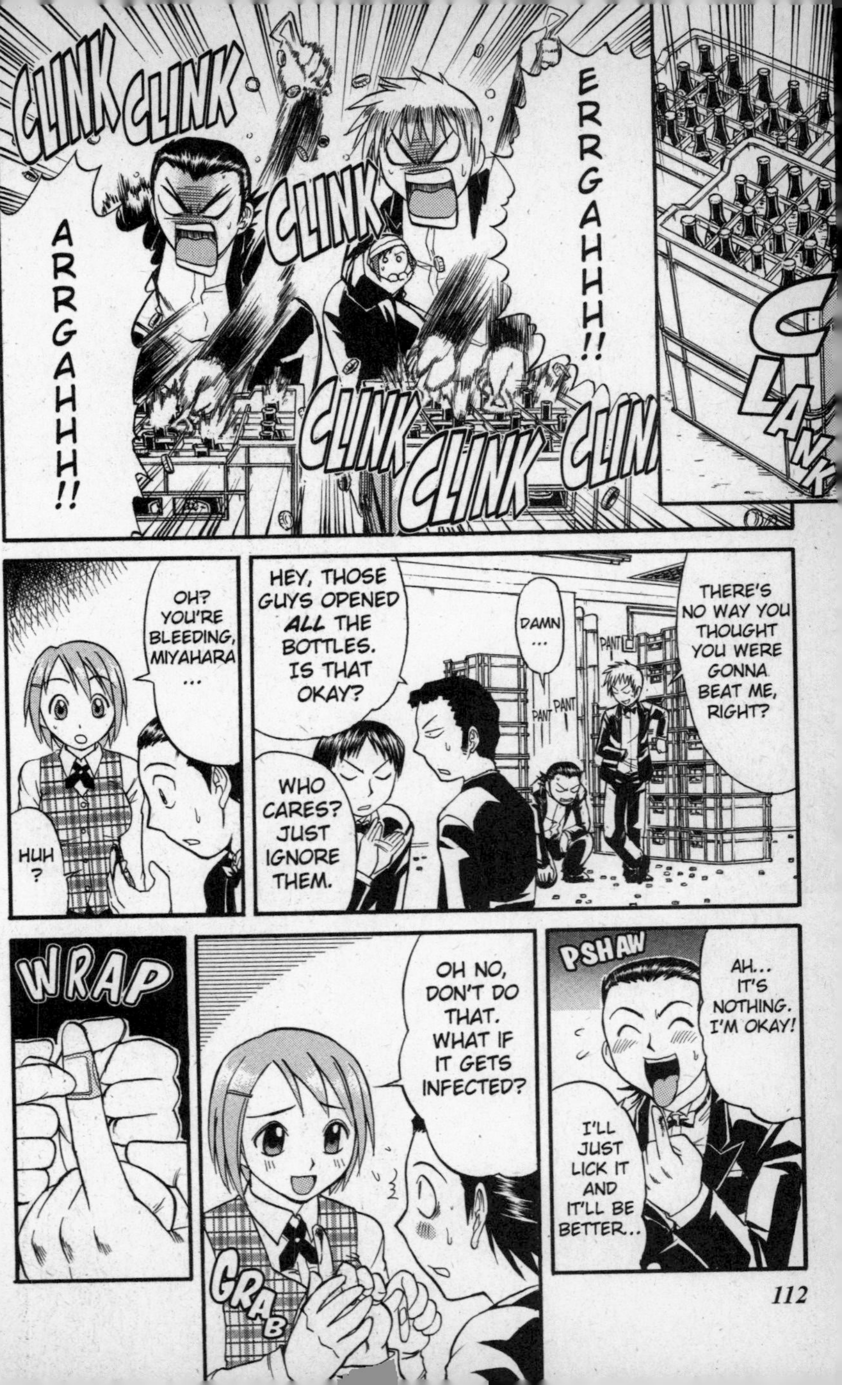
CLANK
ERRGAHHH!!
CLINK CLINK
CLINK
ARRGAHHH!!
CLINK CLINK CLIN
THERE'S NO WAY YOU THOUGHT YOU WERE GONNA BEAT ME, RIGHT?
DAMN...
PANT
PANT PANT
HEY, THOSE GUYS OPENED **ALL** THE BOTTLES. IS THAT OKAY?
WHO CARES? JUST IGNORE THEM.
OH? YOU'RE BLEEDING, MIYAHARA...
HUH?
PSHAW
AH... IT'S NOTHING. I'M OKAY!
I'LL JUST LICK IT AND IT'LL BE BETTER...
OH NO, DON'T DO THAT. WHAT IF IT GETS INFECTED?
GRAB
WRAP

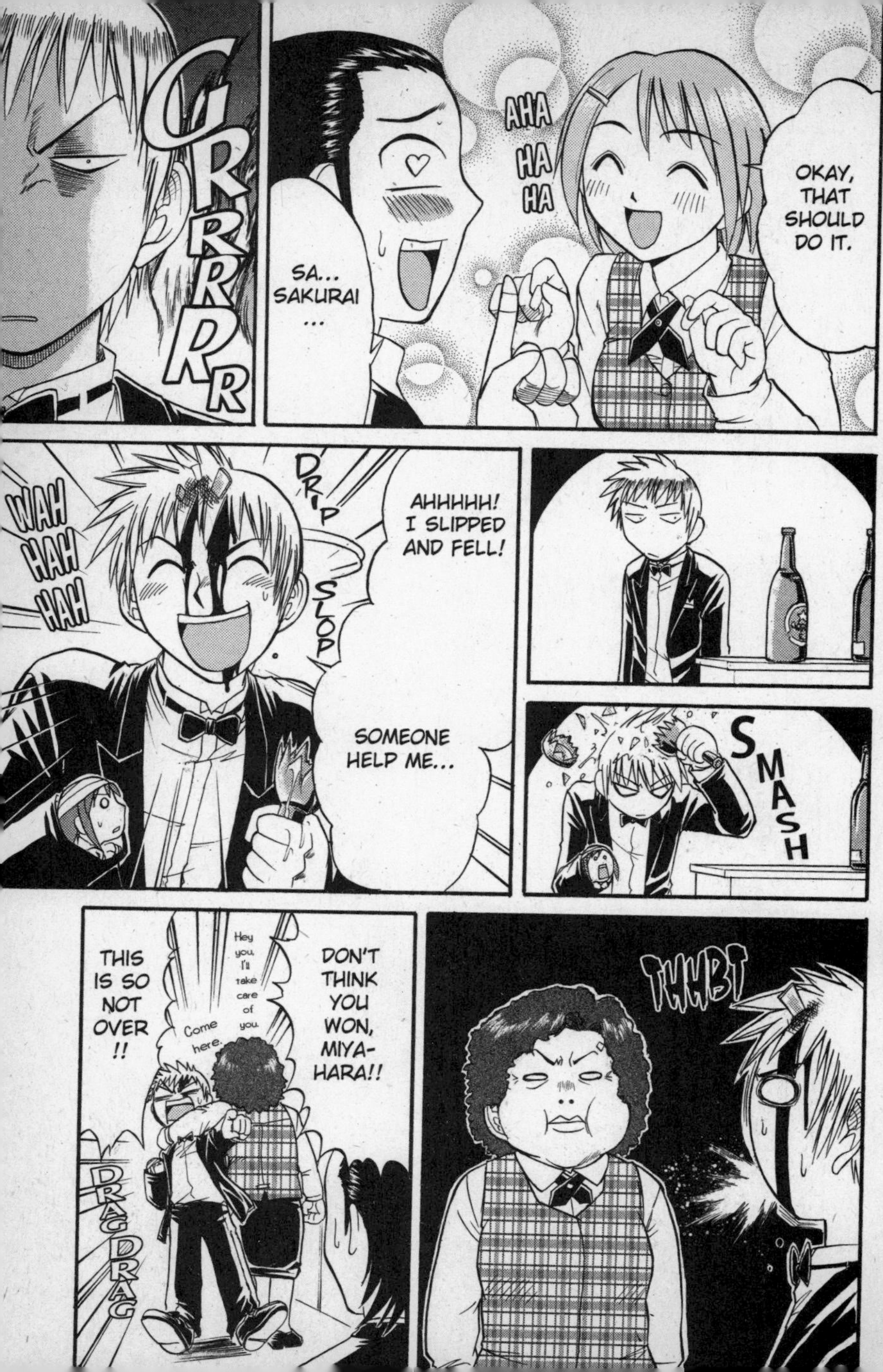
OKAY, THAT SHOULD DO IT.
AHA HA HA
SA... SAKURAI ...
GRRRRR
AHHHHH! I SLIPPED AND FELL!
SOMEONE HELP ME...
DRIP
SLOP
WAH HAH HAH
SMASH
THHBT
DON'T THINK YOU WON, MIYA-HARA!!
Hey you, I'll take care of you.
Come here.
THIS IS SO NOT OVER !!
DRAG DRAG

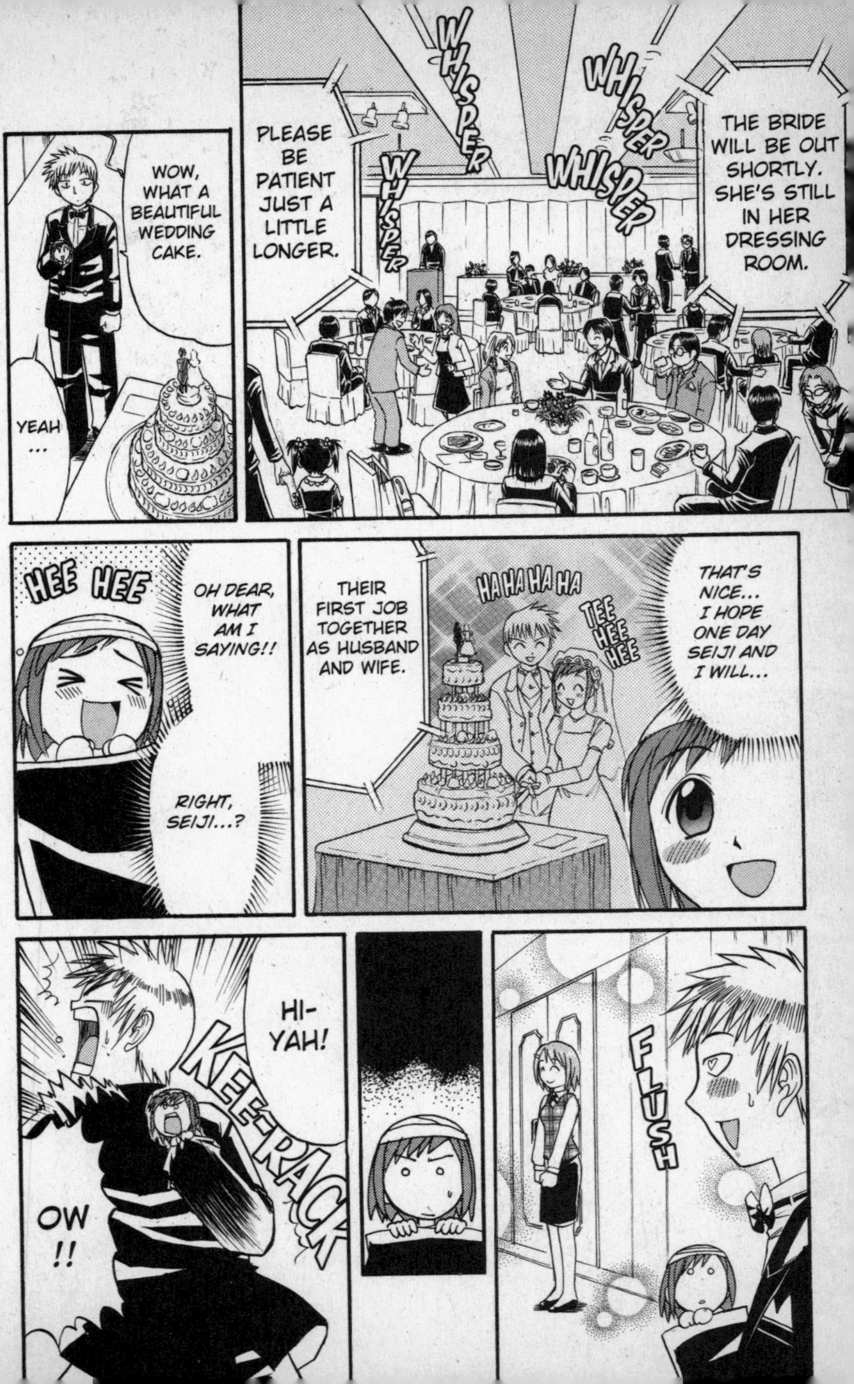
THE BRIDE WILL BE OUT SHORTLY. SHE'S STILL IN HER DRESSING ROOM.
WHISPER
WHISPER
WHISPER
WHISPER
PLEASE BE PATIENT JUST A LITTLE LONGER.
WOW, WHAT A BEAUTIFUL WEDDING CAKE.
YEAH ...
THAT'S NICE... I HOPE ONE DAY SEIJI AND I WILL...
TEE HEE HEE
HA HA HA HA
THEIR FIRST JOB TOGETHER AS HUSBAND AND WIFE.
OH DEAR, WHAT AM I SAYING!!
HEE HEE
RIGHT, SEIJI...?
FLUSH
HI-YAH!
KEE-RACK
OW !!

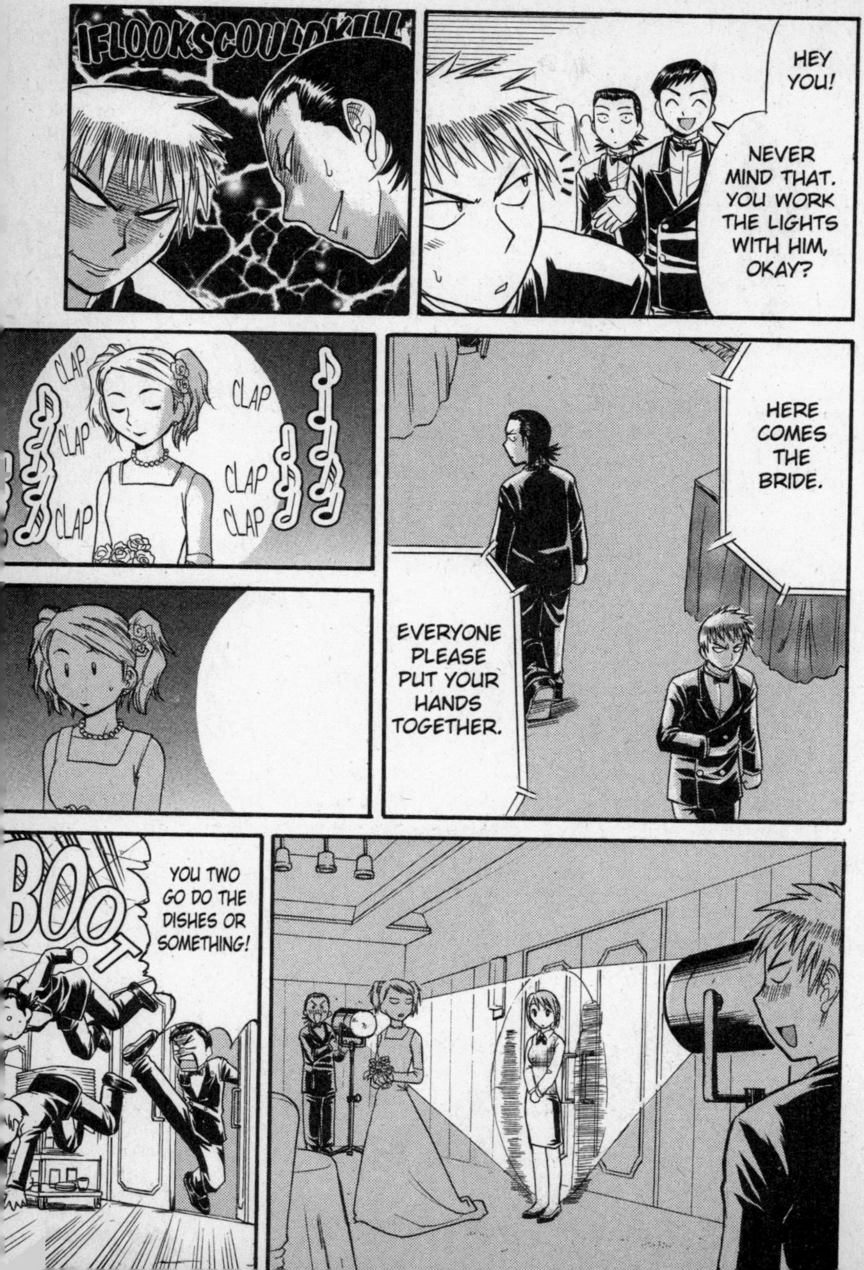
HEY YOU!
NEVER MIND THAT. YOU WORK THE LIGHTS WITH HIM, OKAY?
IFLOOKSCOULDKILL
HERE COMES THE BRIDE.
EVERYONE PLEASE PUT YOUR HANDS TOGETHER.
CLAP
CLAP
CLAP
CLAP
CLAP
CLAP
YOU TWO GO DO THE DISHES OR SOMETHING!
BOOT

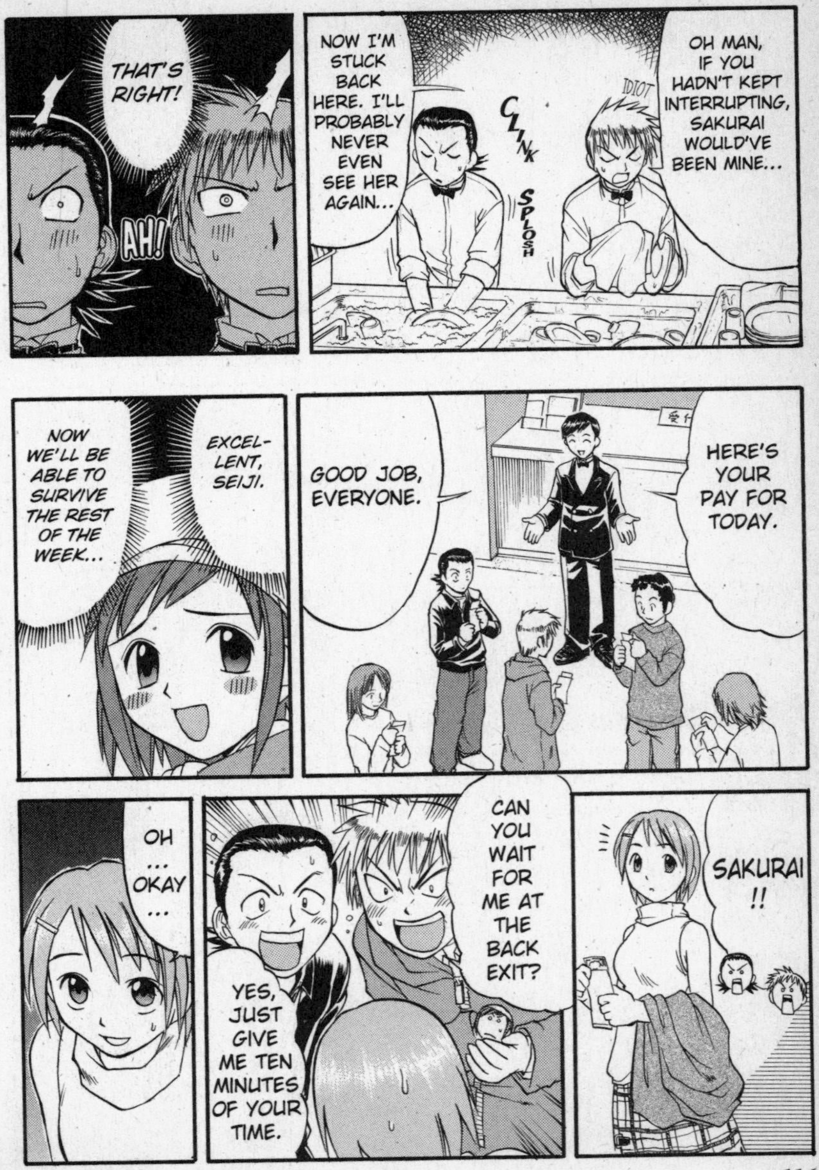
OH MAN, IF YOU HADN'T KEPT INTERRUPTING, SAKURAI WOULD'VE BEEN MINE...
IDIOT
NOW I'M STUCK BACK HERE. I'LL PROBABLY NEVER EVEN SEE HER AGAIN...
CLINK
SPLOSH
THAT'S RIGHT!
AH!
HERE'S YOUR PAY FOR TODAY.
GOOD JOB, EVERYONE.
EXCEL-LENT, SEIJI.
NOW WE'LL BE ABLE TO SURVIVE THE REST OF THE WEEK...
SAKURAI !!
CAN YOU WAIT FOR ME AT THE BACK EXIT?
YES, JUST GIVE ME TEN MINUTES OF YOUR TIME.
OH ... OKAY ...

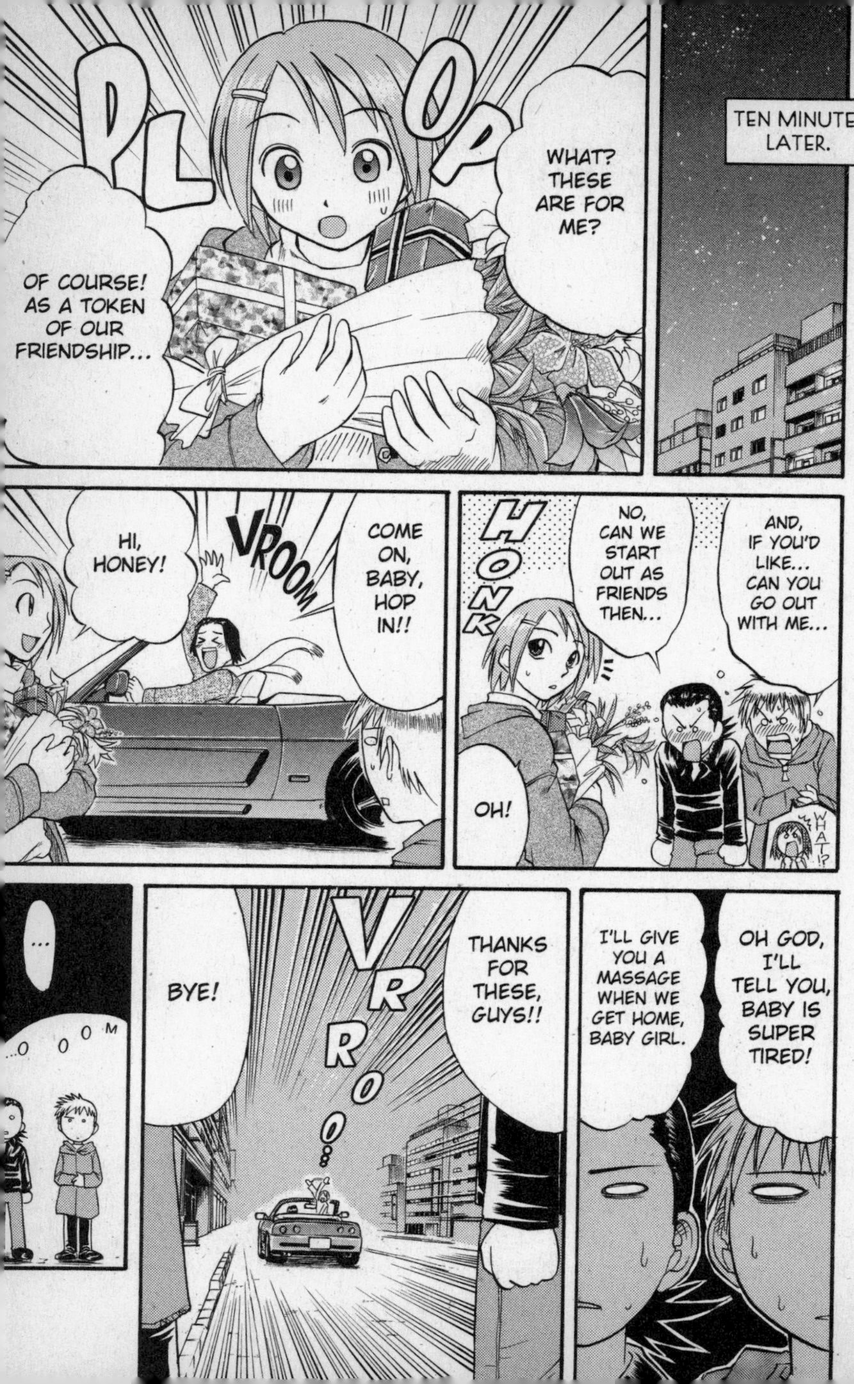
TEN MINUTES LATER.
PLOP
WHAT? THESE ARE FOR ME?
OF COURSE! AS A TOKEN OF OUR FRIENDSHIP...
AND, IF YOU'D LIKE... CAN YOU GO OUT WITH ME...
NO, CAN WE START OUT AS FRIENDS THEN...
HONK
OH!
WHAT!?
COME ON, BABY, HOP IN!!
VROOM
HI, HONEY!
OH GOD, I'LL TELL YOU, BABY IS SUPER TIRED!
I'LL GIVE YOU A MASSAGE WHEN WE GET HOME, BABY GIRL.
THANKS FOR THESE, GUYS!!
VRROOO
BYE!
...
...O O O M

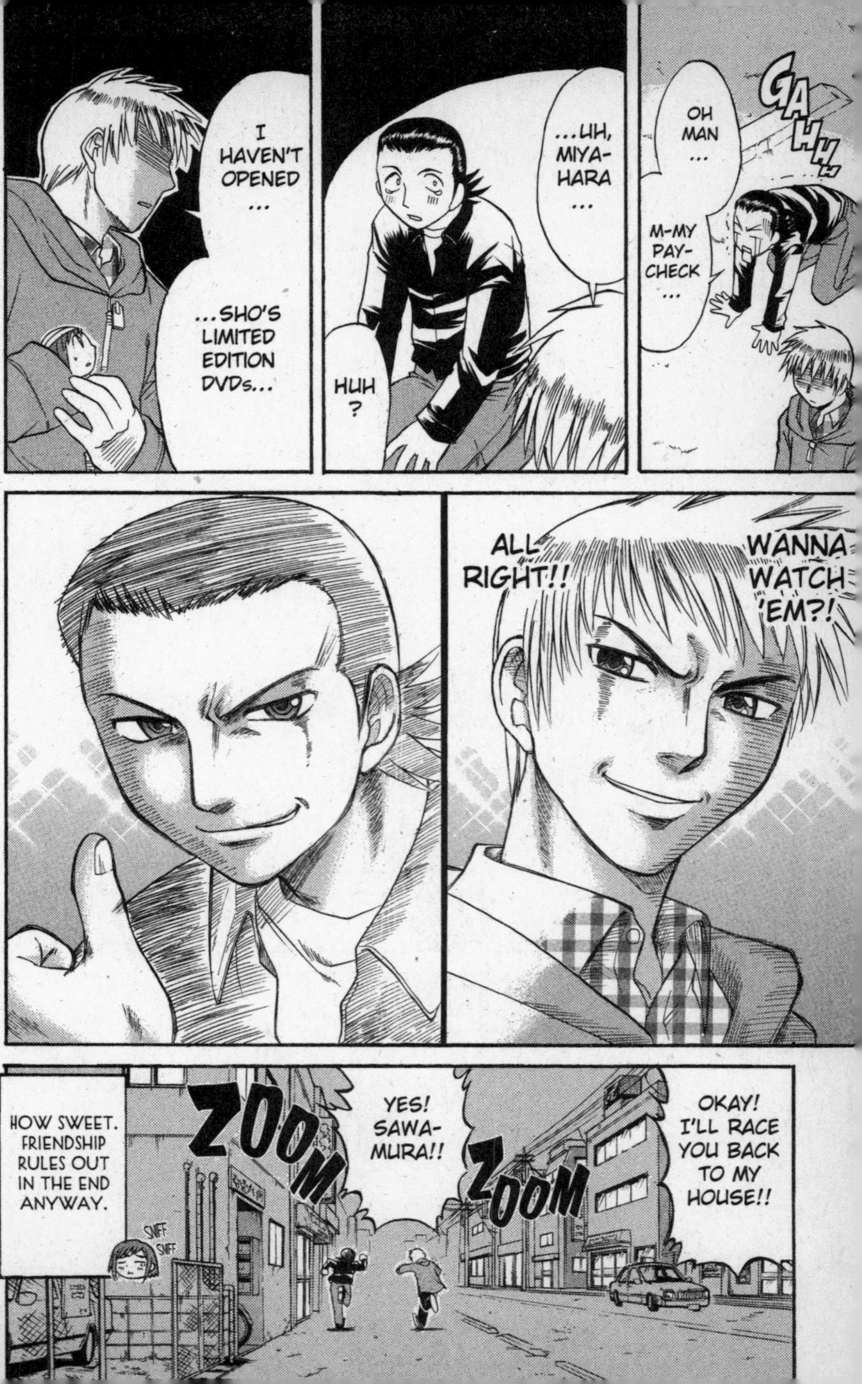
GAHHH
OH MAN ...
M-MY PAY-CHECK ...
...UH, MIYA-HARA ...
HUH ?
I HAVEN'T OPENED ...
...SHO'S LIMITED EDITION DVDs...
WANNA WATCH 'EM?!
ALL RIGHT!!
OKAY! I'LL RACE YOU BACK TO MY HOUSE!!
ZOOM
YES! SAWA-MURA!!
ZOOM
HOW SWEET. FRIENDSHIP RULES OUT IN THE END ANYWAY.
SNIFF SNIFF

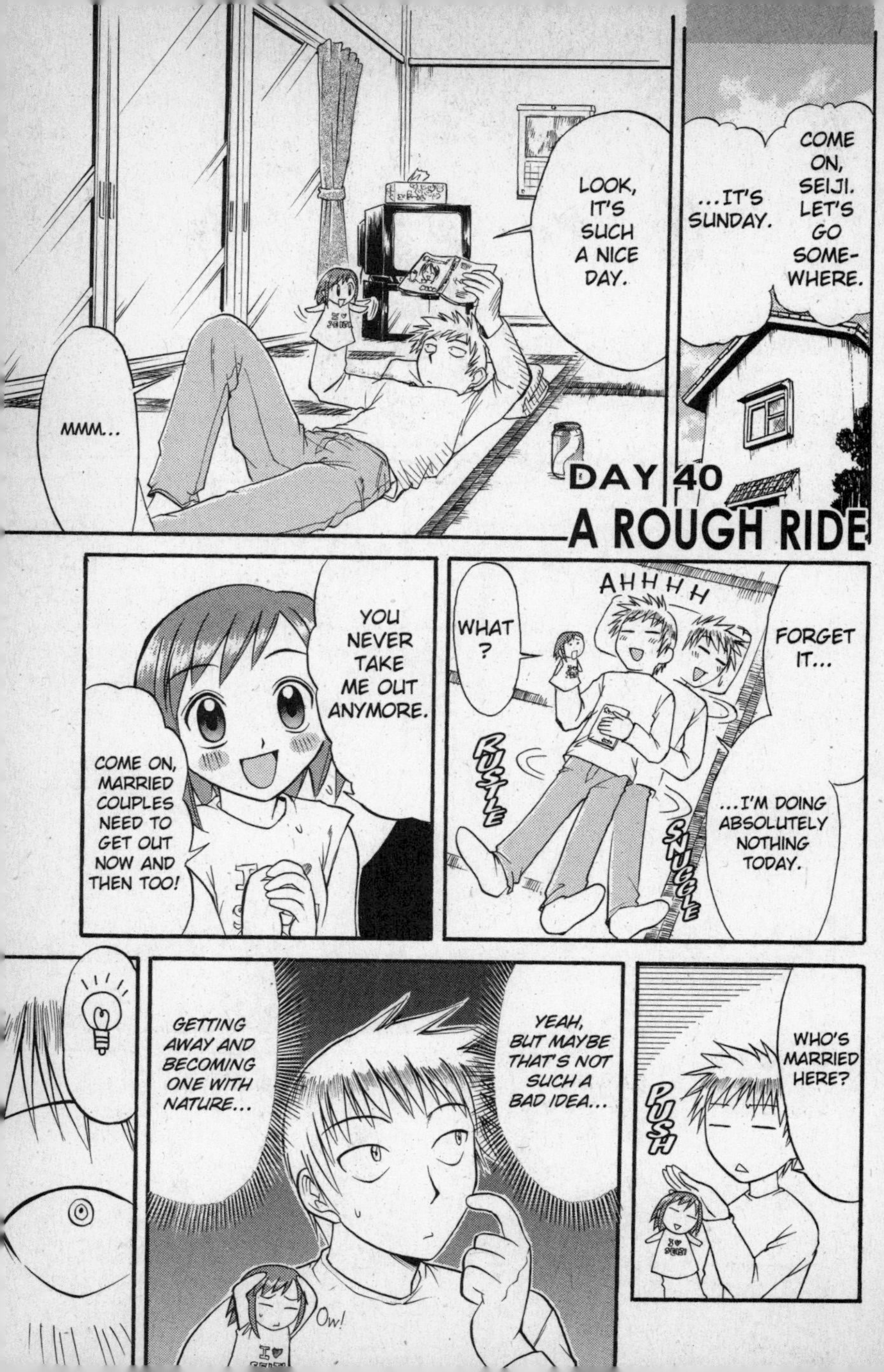
COME ON, SEIJI. LET'S GO SOMEWHERE.
...IT'S SUNDAY.
LOOK, IT'S SUCH A NICE DAY.
MMM...
DAY 40
A ROUGH RIDE
FORGET IT...
AHHHH
WHAT?
...I'M DOING ABSOLUTELY NOTHING TODAY.
RUSTLE
SNUGGLE
YOU NEVER TAKE ME OUT ANYMORE.
COME ON, MARRIED COUPLES NEED TO GET OUT NOW AND THEN TOO!
WHO'S MARRIED HERE?
PUSH
YEAH, BUT MAYBE THAT'S NOT SUCH A BAD IDEA...
GETTING AWAY AND BECOMING ONE WITH NATURE...
OW!

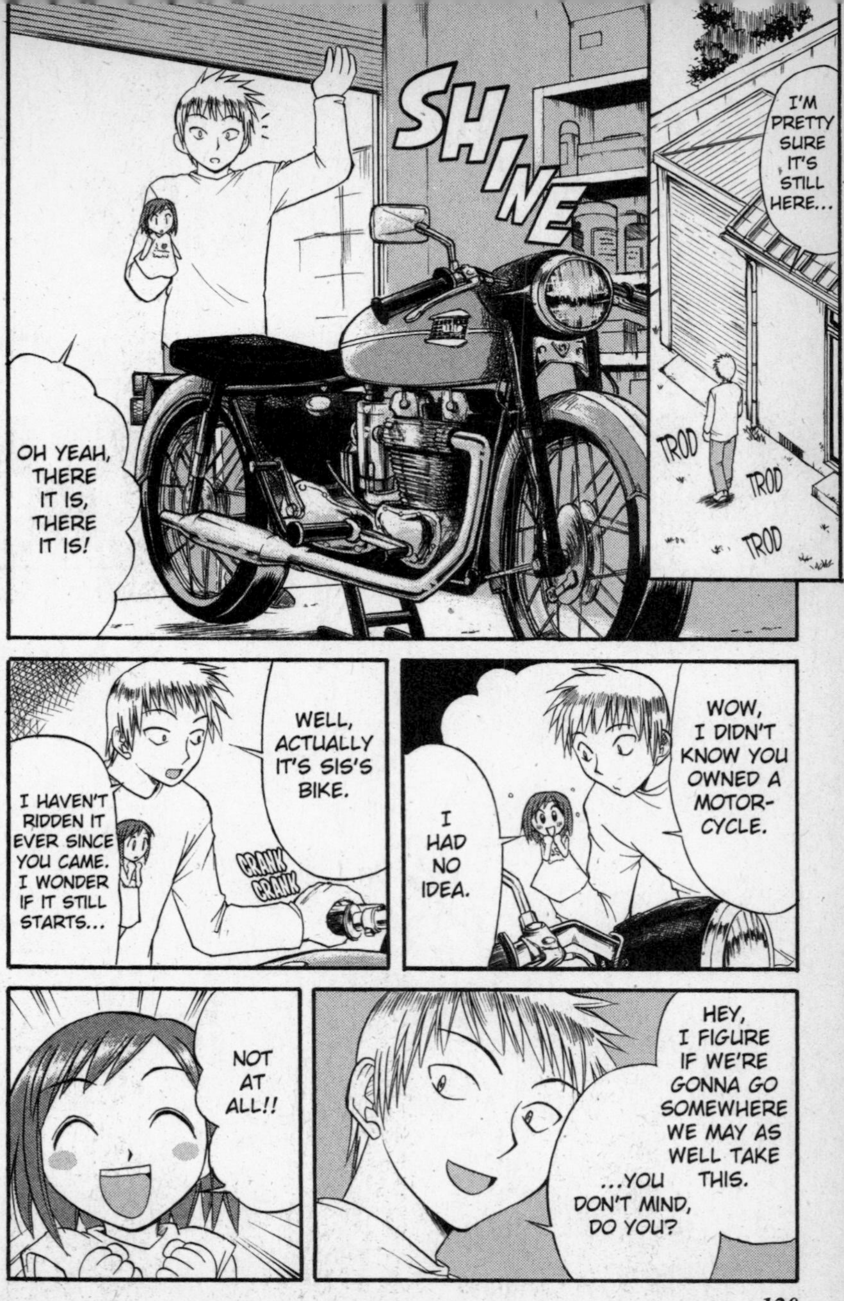
I'M PRETTY SURE IT'S STILL HERE...
TROD
TROD
TROD
SHINE
OH YEAH, THERE IT IS, THERE IT IS!
WOW, I DIDN'T KNOW YOU OWNED A MOTOR-CYCLE.
I HAD NO IDEA.
WELL, ACTUALLY IT'S SIS'S BIKE.
I HAVEN'T RIDDEN IT EVER SINCE YOU CAME. I WONDER IF IT STILL STARTS...
CRANK CRANK
HEY, I FIGURE IF WE'RE GONNA GO SOMEWHERE WE MAY AS WELL TAKE THIS.
...YOU DON'T MIND, DO YOU?
NOT AT ALL!!

DAY 40
A ROUGH RIDE

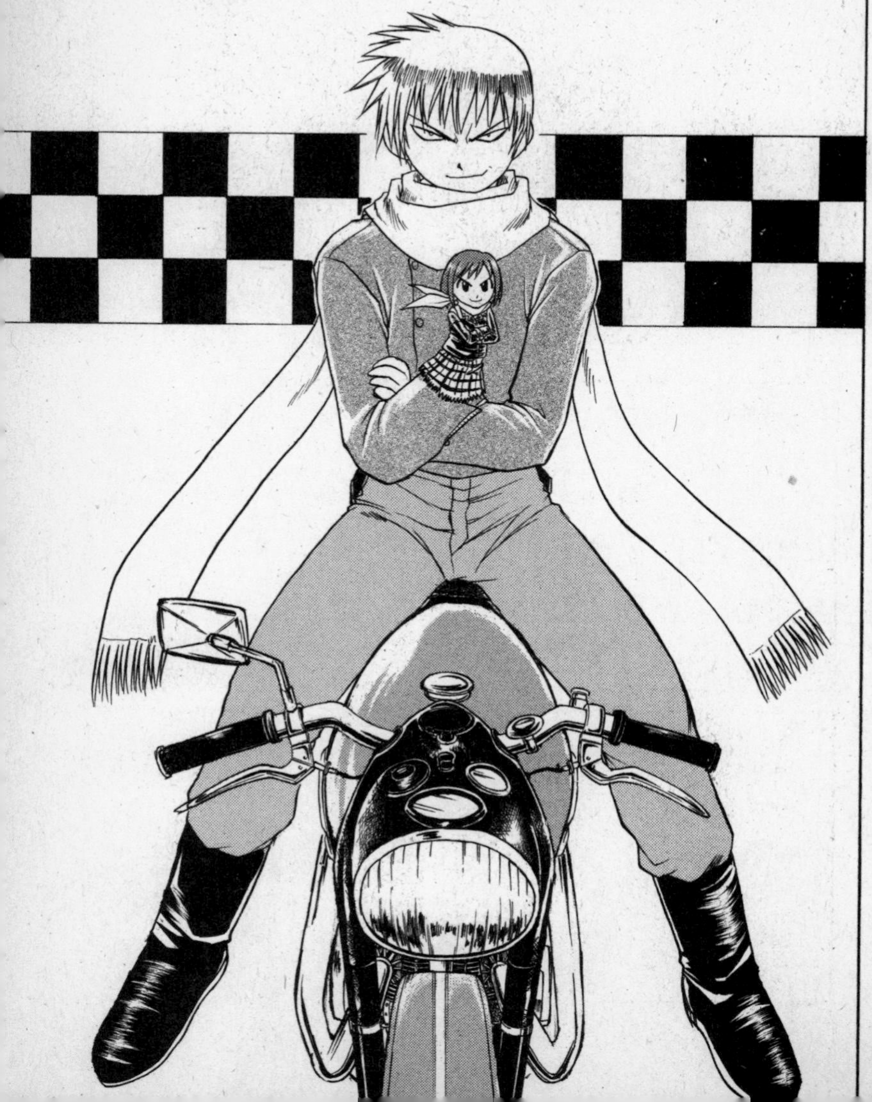

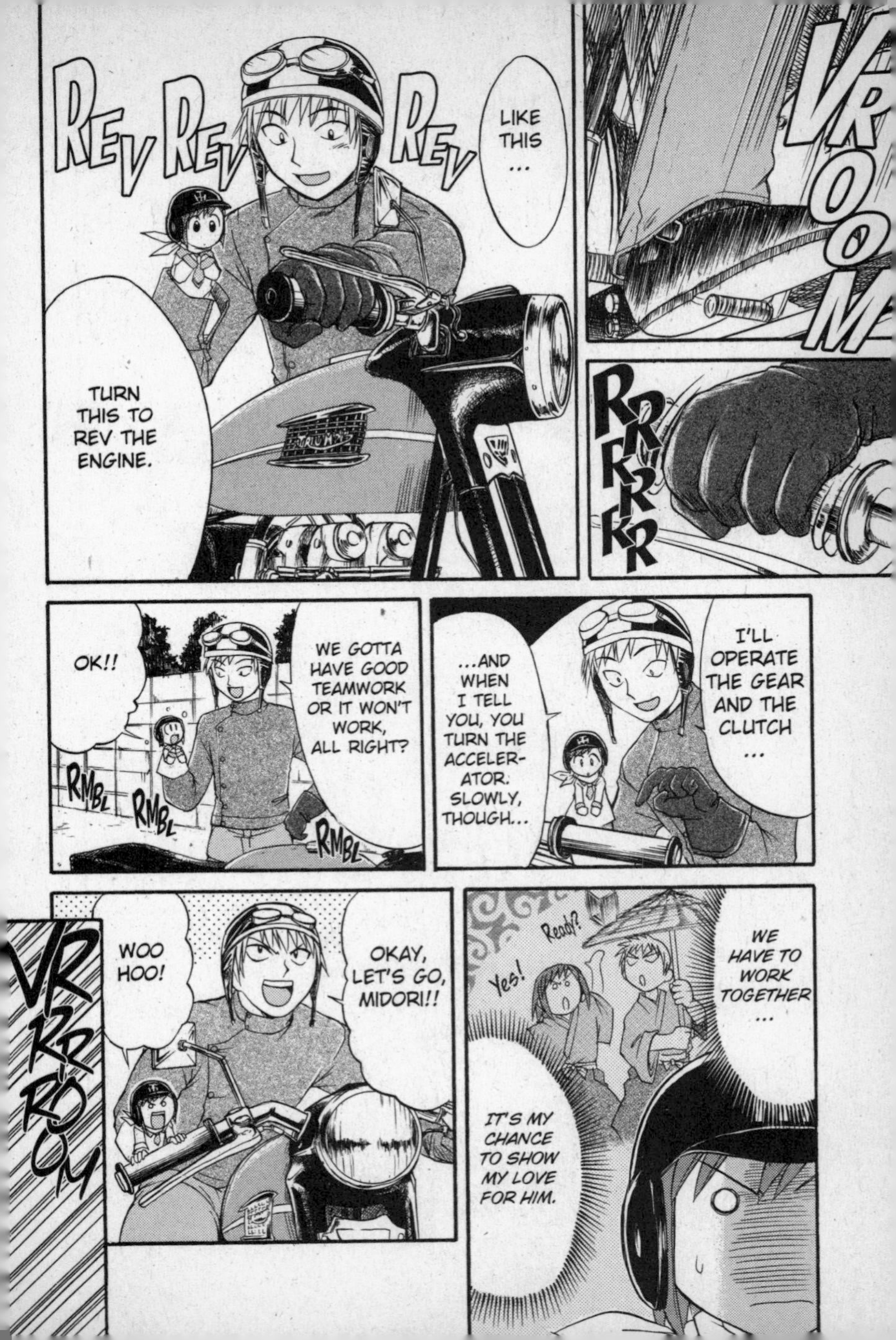
VROOOM
RRRRRRR
LIKE THIS ...
REV REV REV
TURN THIS TO REV THE ENGINE.
I'LL OPERATE THE GEAR AND THE CLUTCH ...
...AND WHEN I TELL YOU, YOU TURN THE ACCELER-ATOR. SLOWLY, THOUGH...
WE GOTTA HAVE GOOD TEAMWORK OR IT WON'T WORK, ALL RIGHT?
OK!!
RMBL RMBL RMBL
WE HAVE TO WORK TOGETHER ...
Ready?
Yes!
IT'S MY CHANCE TO SHOW MY LOVE FOR HIM.
OKAY, LET'S GO, MIDORI!!
WOO HOO!
VRRRROOM

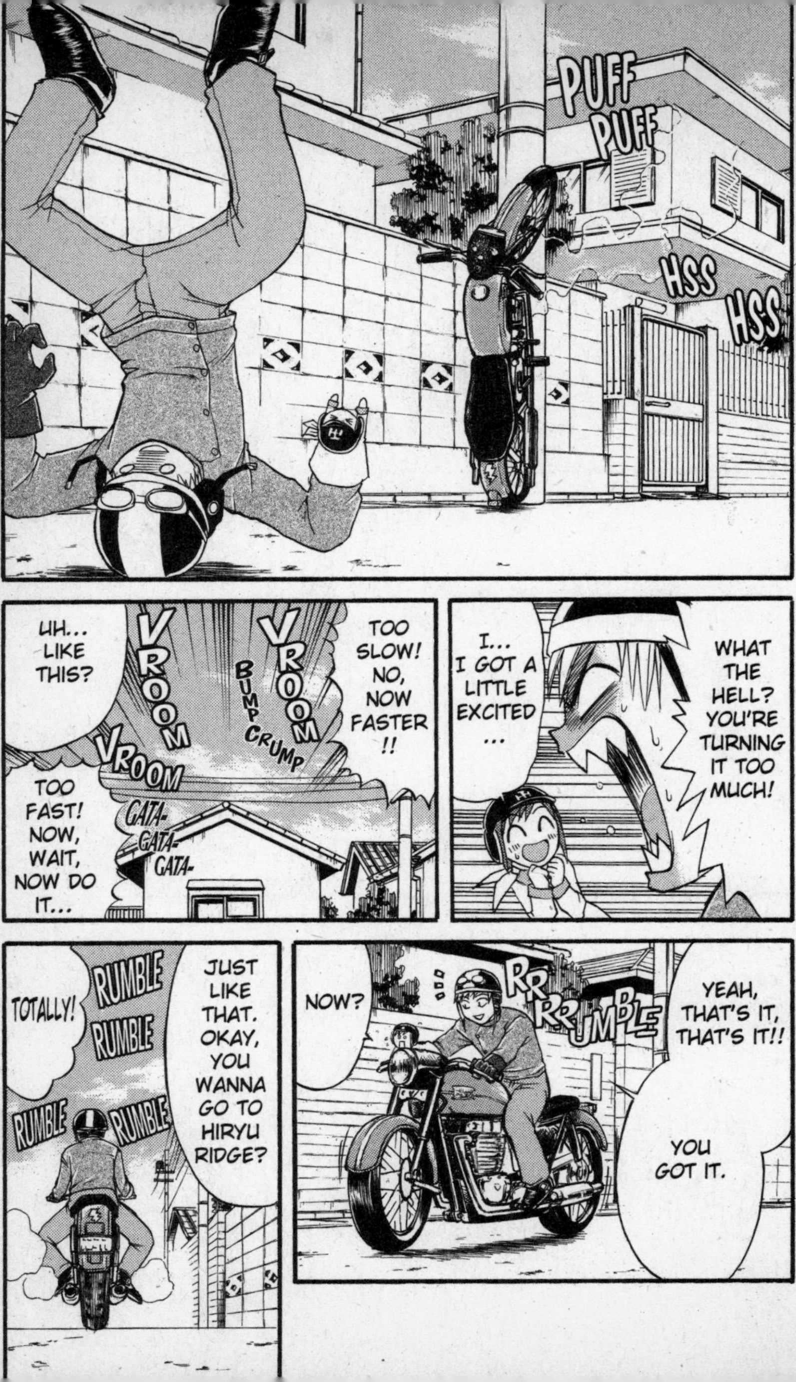
PUFF
PUFF
HSS
HSS
WHAT THE HELL? YOU'RE TURNING IT TOO MUCH!
I... I GOT A LITTLE EXCITED...
TOO SLOW! NO, NOW FASTER!!
VROOM
VROOM
BUMP CRUMP
UH... LIKE THIS?
VROOM
TOO FAST! NOW, WAIT, NOW DO IT...
GATA-GATA-GATA-
YEAH, THAT'S IT, THAT'S IT!!
RRRUMBLE
NOW?
YOU GOT IT.
JUST LIKE THAT. OKAY, YOU WANNA GO TO HIRYU RIDGE?
RUMBLE
RUMBLE
TOTALLY!
RUMBLE
RUMBLE

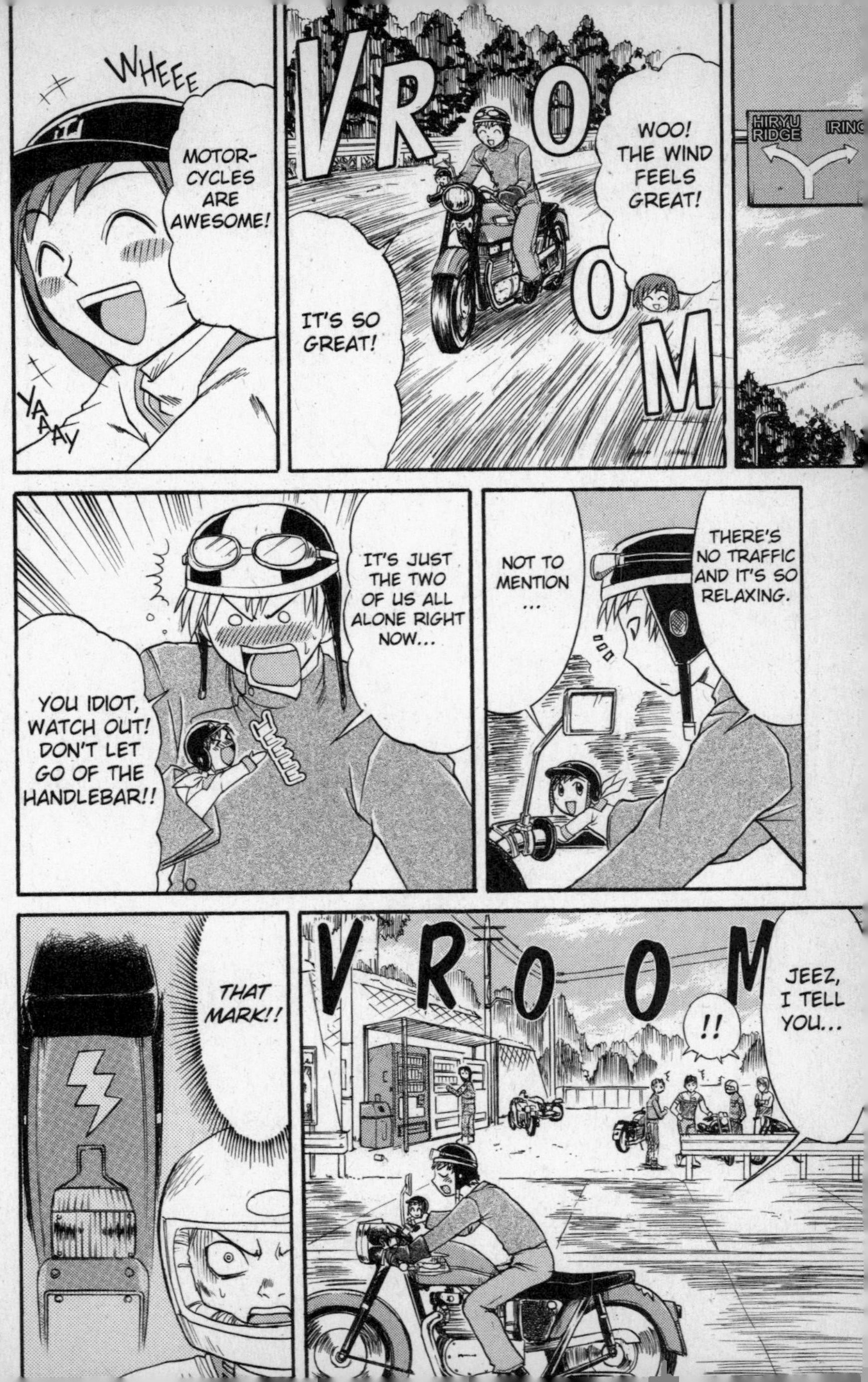
HIRYU RIDGE
VROOM
WOO! THE WIND FEELS GREAT!
IT'S SO GREAT!
WHEEE
MOTOR-CYCLES ARE AWESOME!
YAAAY
THERE'S NO TRAFFIC AND IT'S SO RELAXING.
NOT TO MENTION ...
IT'S JUST THE TWO OF US ALL ALONE RIGHT NOW...
YOU IDIOT, WATCH OUT! DON'T LET GO OF THE HANDLEBAR!!
VROOM
JEEZ, I TELL YOU...
!!
THAT MARK!!

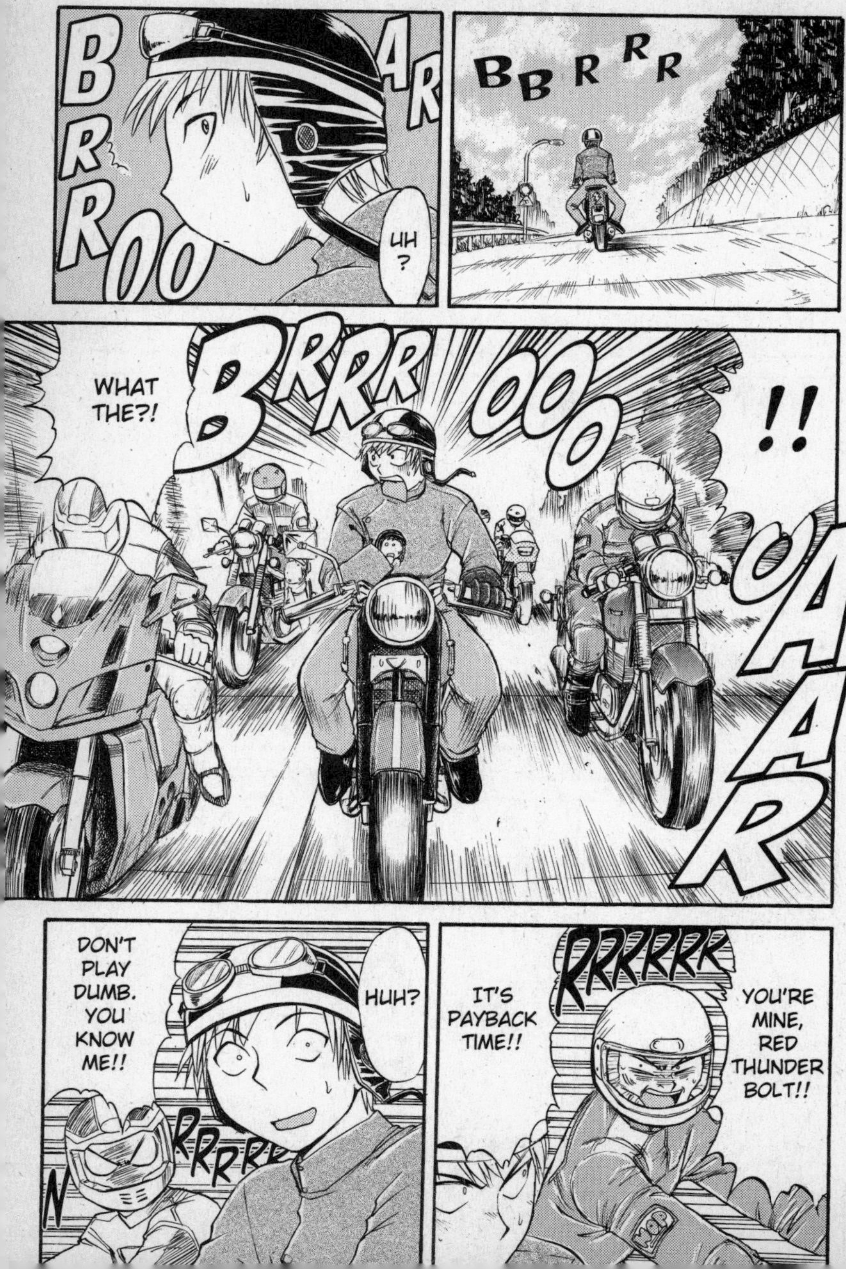
BBRRR
BRROO
AR
UH ?
BRRROOO
!!
OAAR
WHAT THE?!
RRRRRR
YOU'RE MINE, RED THUNDER BOLT!!
IT'S PAYBACK TIME!!
HUH?
DON'T PLAY DUMB. YOU KNOW ME!!
RRRRR
N

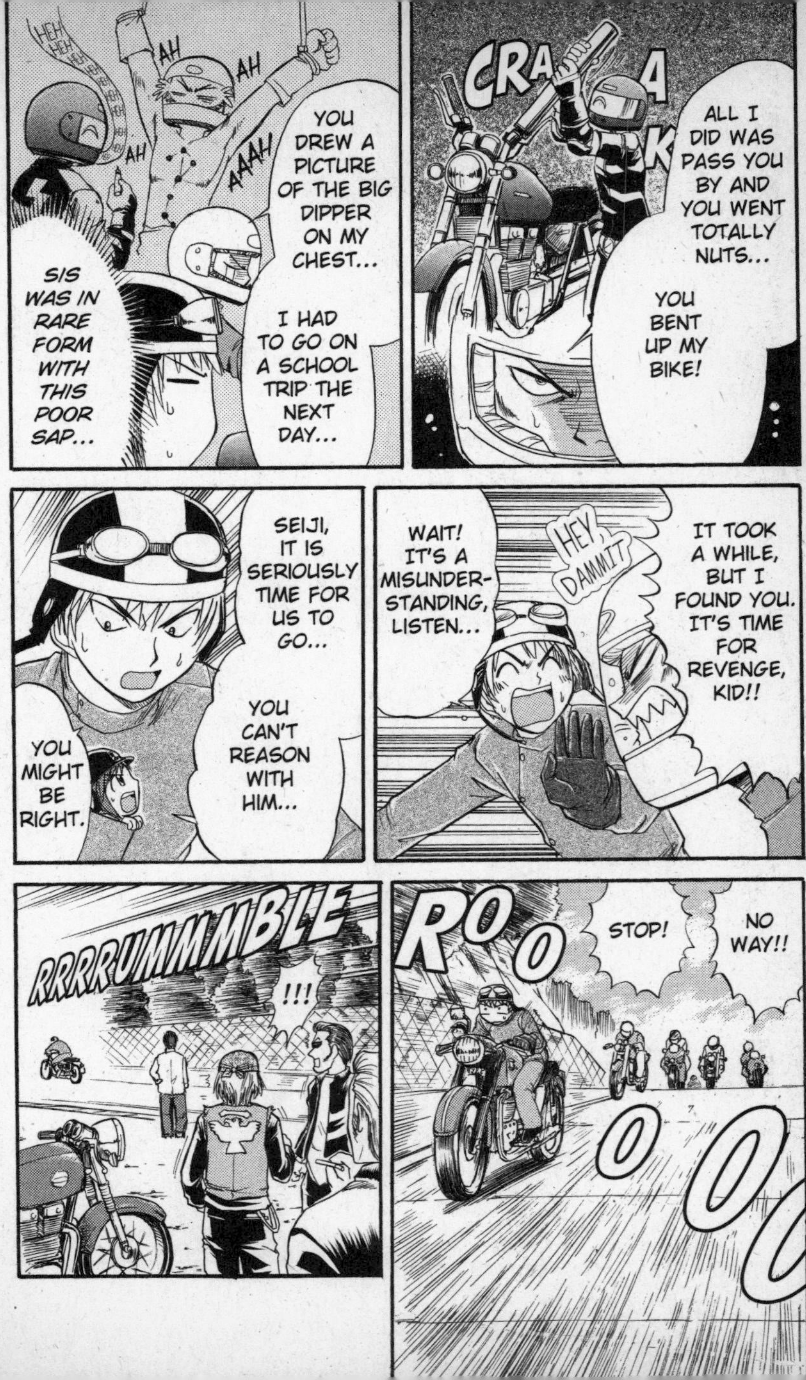
CRAAK
ALL I DID WAS PASS YOU BY AND YOU WENT TOTALLY NUTS...
YOU BENT UP MY BIKE!
HEH HEH
AH AH AH AAAH
YOU DREW A PICTURE OF THE BIG DIPPER ON MY CHEST...
I HAD TO GO ON A SCHOOL TRIP THE NEXT DAY...
SIS WAS IN RARE FORM WITH THIS POOR SAP...
IT TOOK A WHILE, BUT I FOUND YOU. IT'S TIME FOR REVENGE, KID!!
HEY, DAMMIT
WAIT! IT'S A MISUNDERSTANDING, LISTEN...
SEIJI, IT IS SERIOUSLY TIME FOR US TO GO...
YOU CAN'T REASON WITH HIM...
YOU MIGHT BE RIGHT.
ROOOOOO
NO WAY!!
STOP!
RRRRUMMMMBLE
!!!

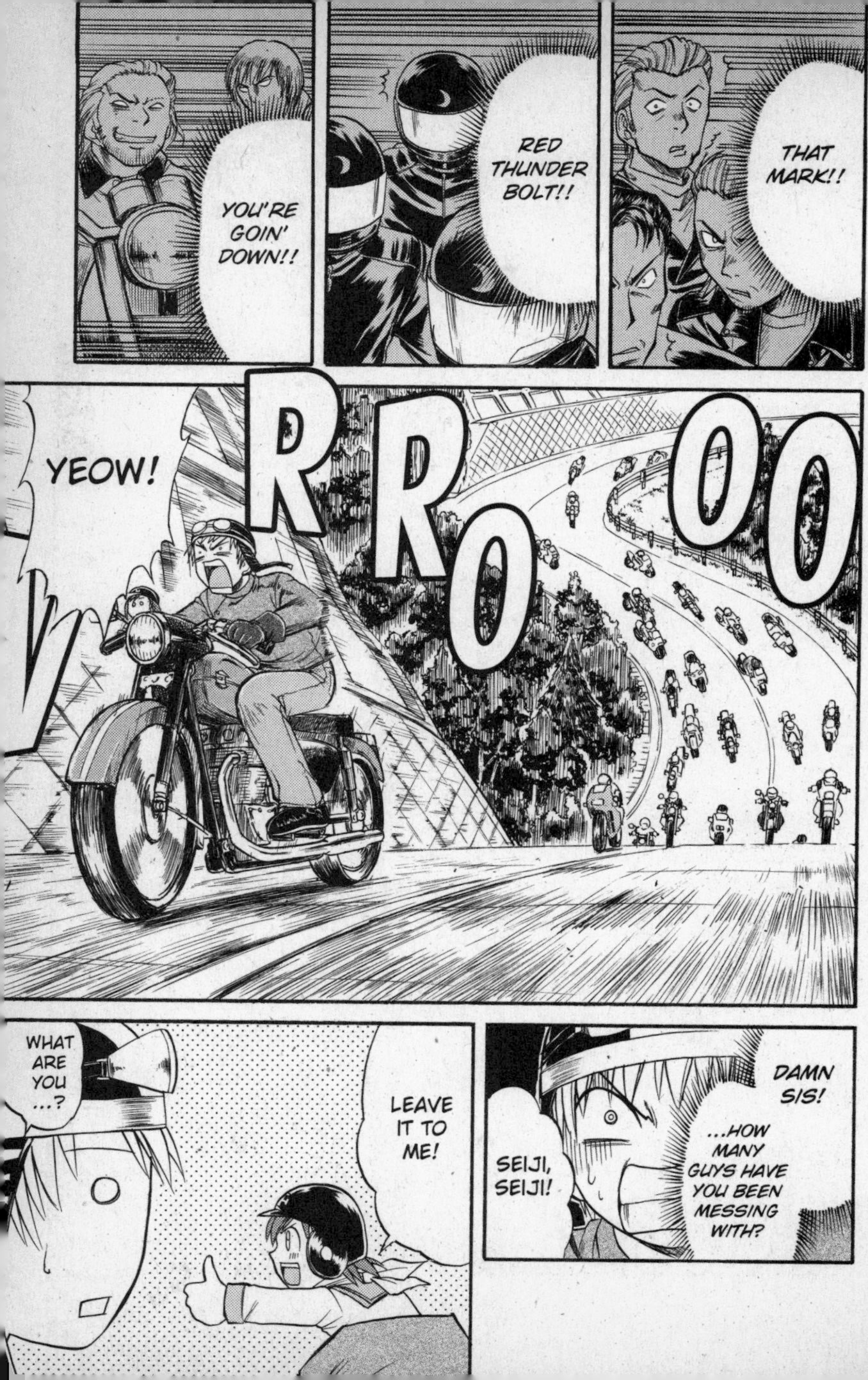
THAT MARK!!
RED THUNDER BOLT!!
YOU'RE GOIN' DOWN!!
RROOO
YEOW!
DAMN SIS!
...HOW MANY GUYS HAVE YOU BEEN MESSING WITH?
SEIJI, SEIJI!
WHAT ARE YOU ...?
LEAVE IT TO ME!

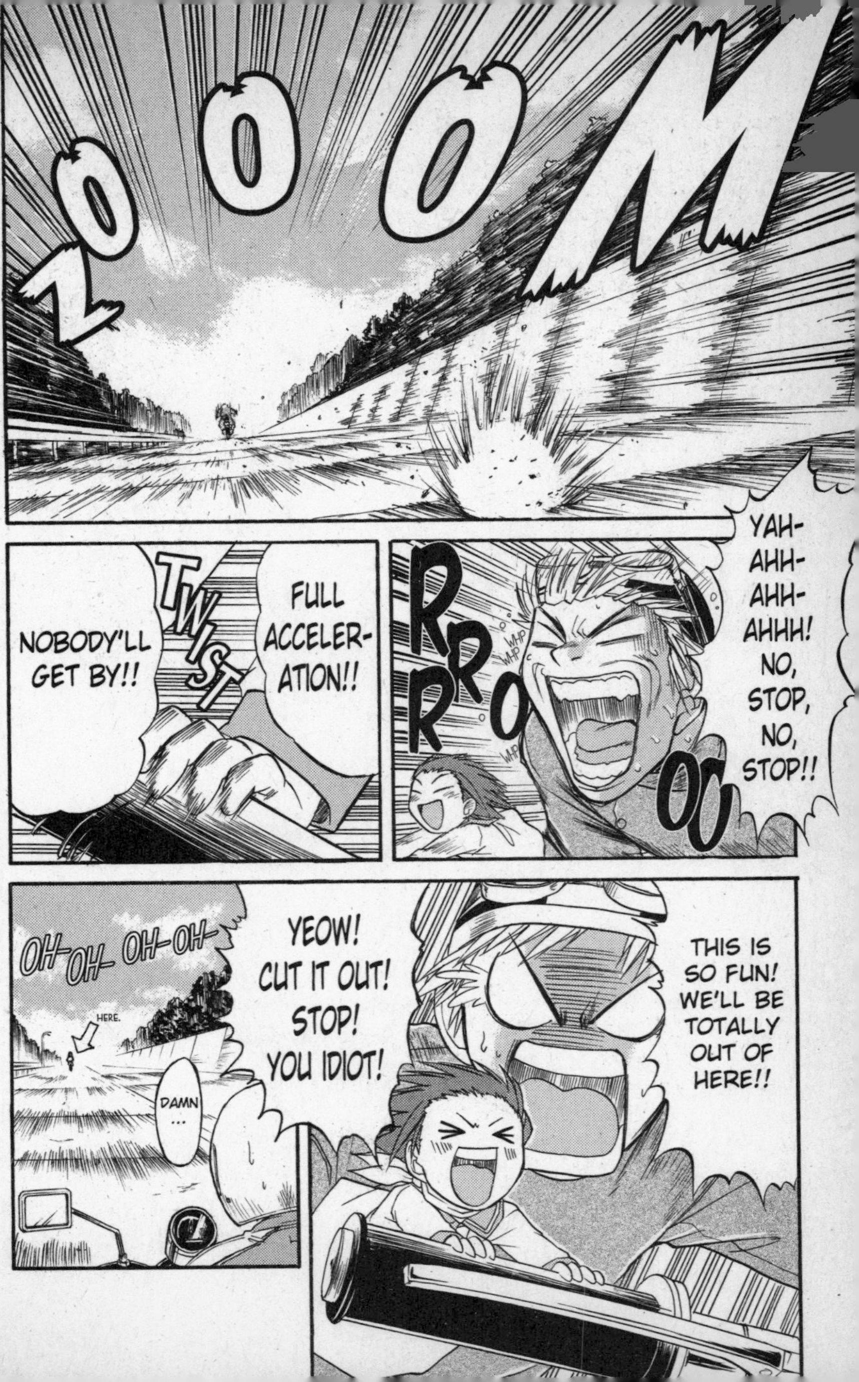
ZOOOOM
RRROOOO
WHP WHP WHP
YAH-AHH-AHH-AHHH! NO, STOP, NO, STOP!!
FULL ACCELER-ATION!!
TWIST
NOBODY'LL GET BY!!
THIS IS SO FUN! WE'LL BE TOTALLY OUT OF HERE!!
YEOW! CUT IT OUT! STOP! YOU IDIOT!
OH-OH-OH-OH-
HERE.
DAMN...

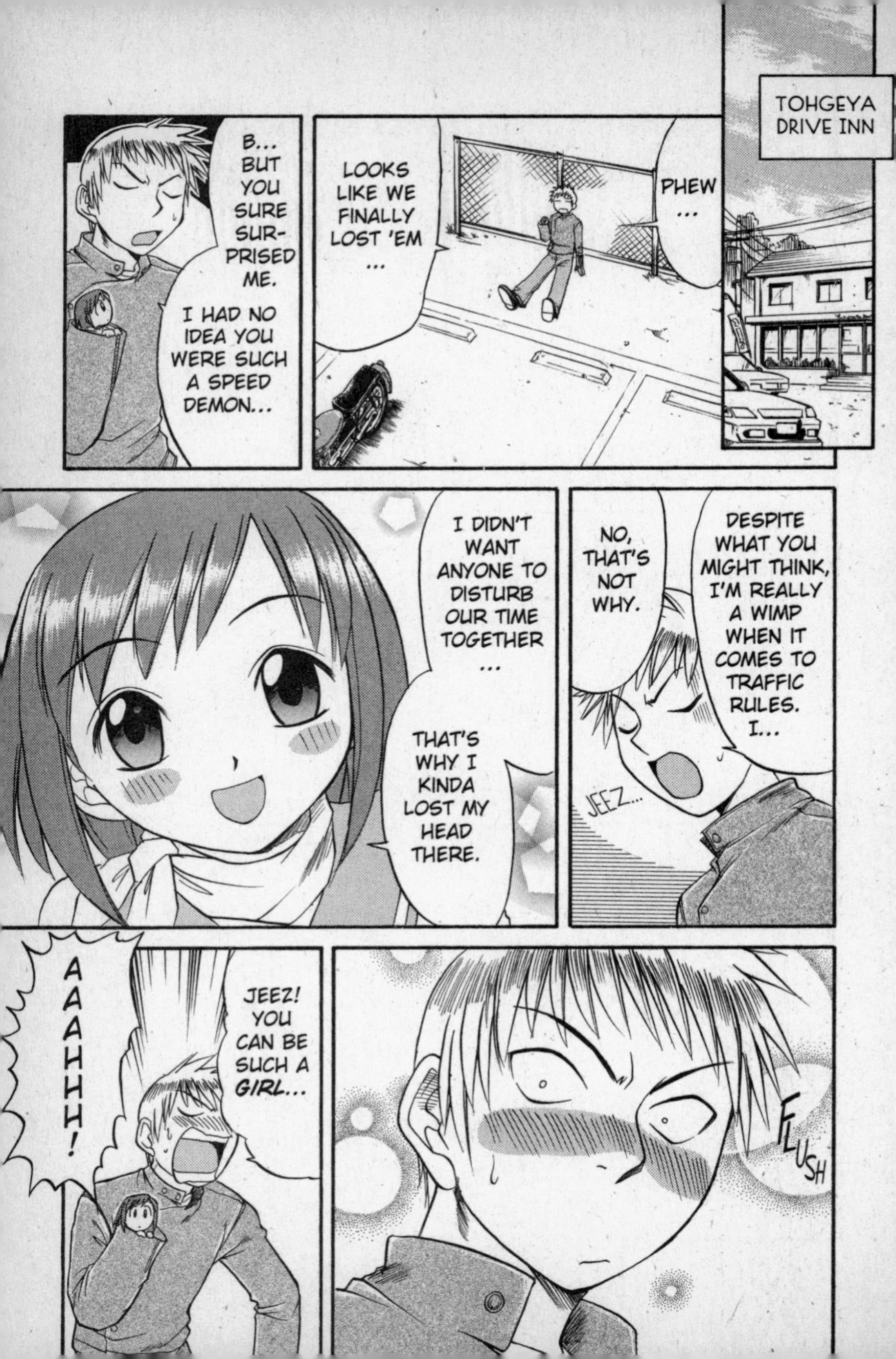
TOHGEYA DRIVE INN
PHEW...
LOOKS LIKE WE FINALLY LOST 'EM...
B... BUT YOU SURE SURPRISED ME.
I HAD NO IDEA YOU WERE SUCH A SPEED DEMON...
DESPITE WHAT YOU MIGHT THINK, I'M REALLY A WIMP WHEN IT COMES TO TRAFFIC RULES. I...
NO, THAT'S NOT WHY.
JEEZ...
I DIDN'T WANT ANYONE TO DISTURB OUR TIME TOGETHER...
THAT'S WHY I KINDA LOST MY HEAD THERE.
FLUSH
JEEZ! YOU CAN BE SUCH A *GIRL*...
AAAHHH!

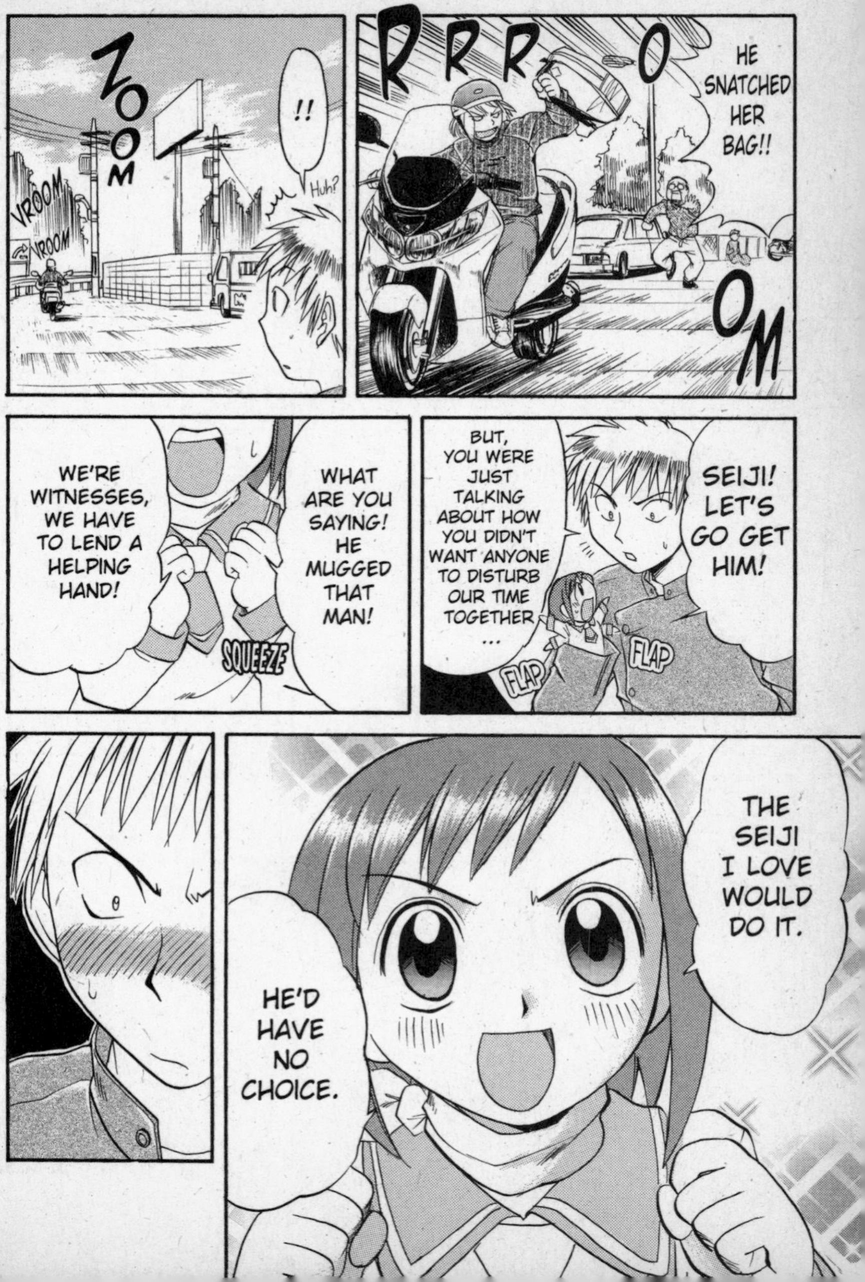

RRRR-O
HE SNATCHED HER BAG!!
OM
ZOOM
VROOM
VROOM
!!
Huh?
SEIJI! LET'S GO GET HIM!
BUT, YOU WERE JUST TALKING ABOUT HOW YOU DIDN'T WANT ANYONE TO DISTURB OUR TIME TOGETHER ...
FLAP
FLAP
WHAT ARE YOU SAYING! HE MUGGED THAT MAN!
WE'RE WITNESSES, WE HAVE TO LEND A HELPING HAND!
SQUEEZE
THE SEIJI I LOVE WOULD DO IT.
HE'D HAVE NO CHOICE.

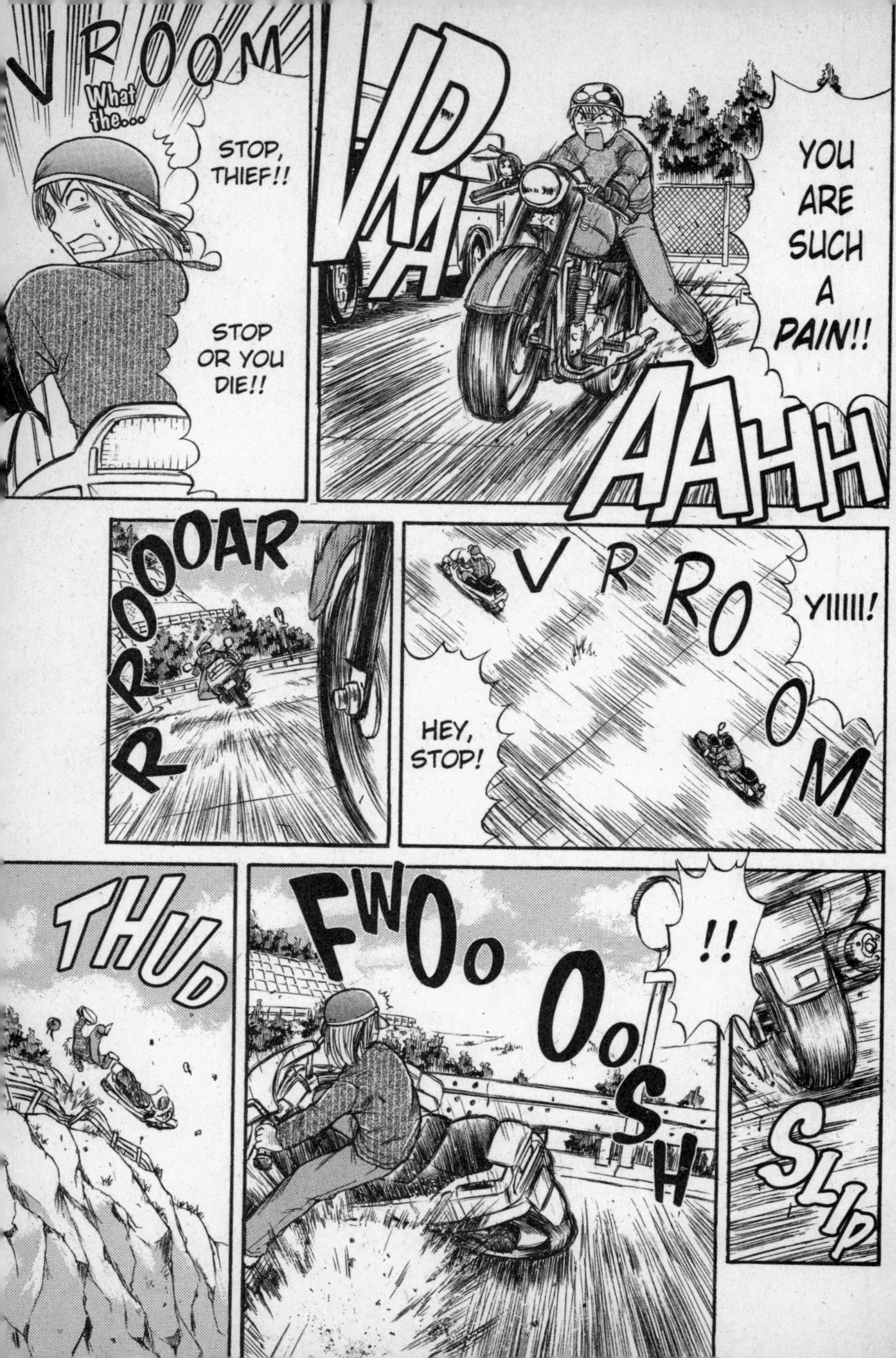
VRA
YOU ARE SUCH A PAIN!!
AAHH
VROOM
What the...
STOP, THIEF!!
STOP OR YOU DIE!!
VRROOM
YIIIII!
HEY, STOP!
ROOOAR
!!
SLIP
FWOOOOSH
THUD

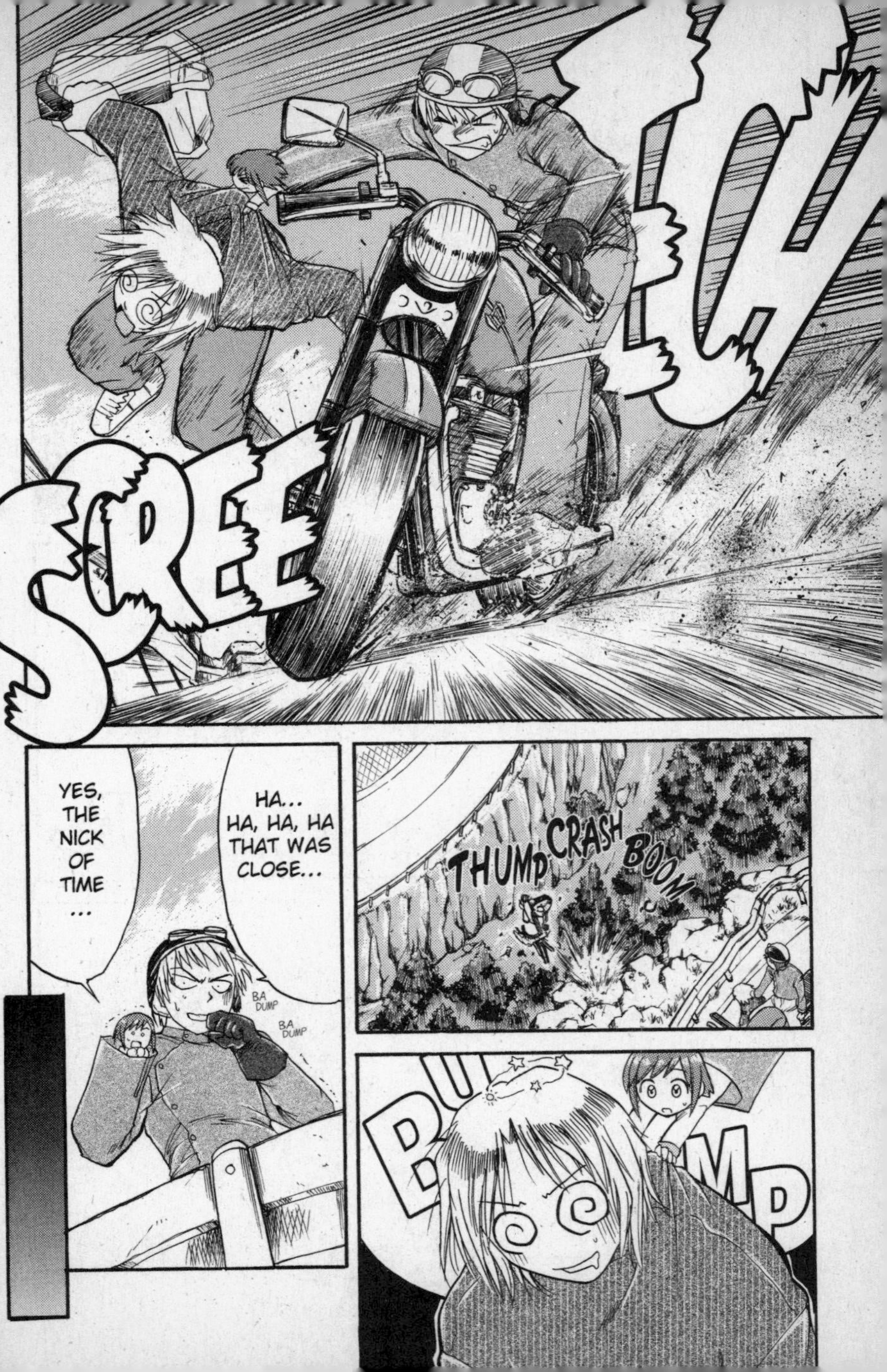
SCREE
CH
THUMP
CRASH
BOOM
BUMP
HA... HA, HA, HA THAT WAS CLOSE...
YES, THE NICK OF TIME ...
BA DUMP
BA DUMP

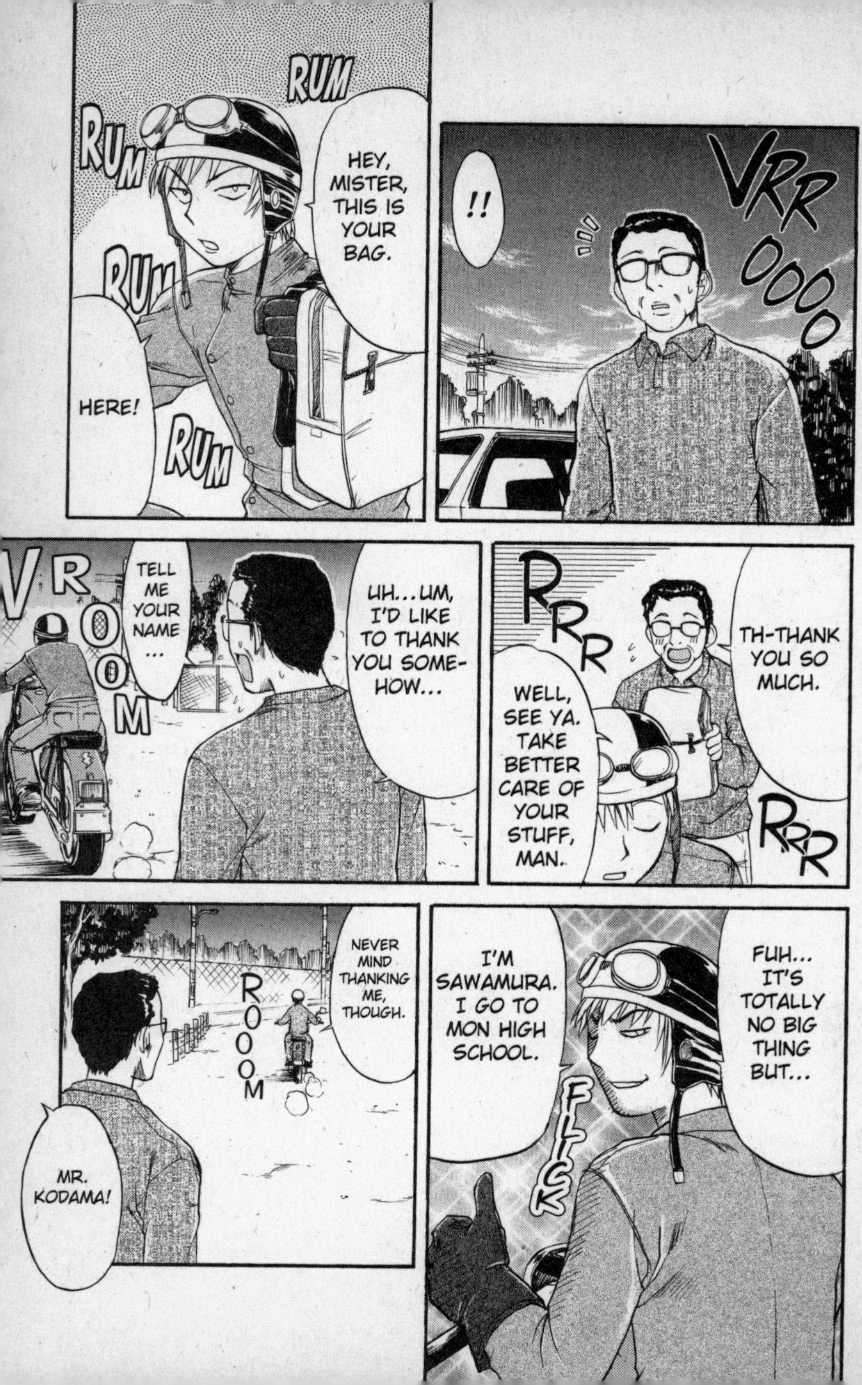
VRRROOOOO
!!
RUM
RUM
HEY, MISTER, THIS IS YOUR BAG.
RUM
HERE!
RUM
RRR
TH-THANK YOU SO MUCH.
WELL, SEE YA. TAKE BETTER CARE OF YOUR STUFF, MAN.
RRR
UH...UM, I'D LIKE TO THANK YOU SOMEHOW...
TELL ME YOUR NAME ...
VROOOM
FUH... IT'S TOTALLY NO BIG THING BUT...
I'M SAWAMURA. I GO TO MON HIGH SCHOOL.
FLICK
NEVER MIND THANKING ME, THOUGH.
ROOOM
MR. KODAMA!

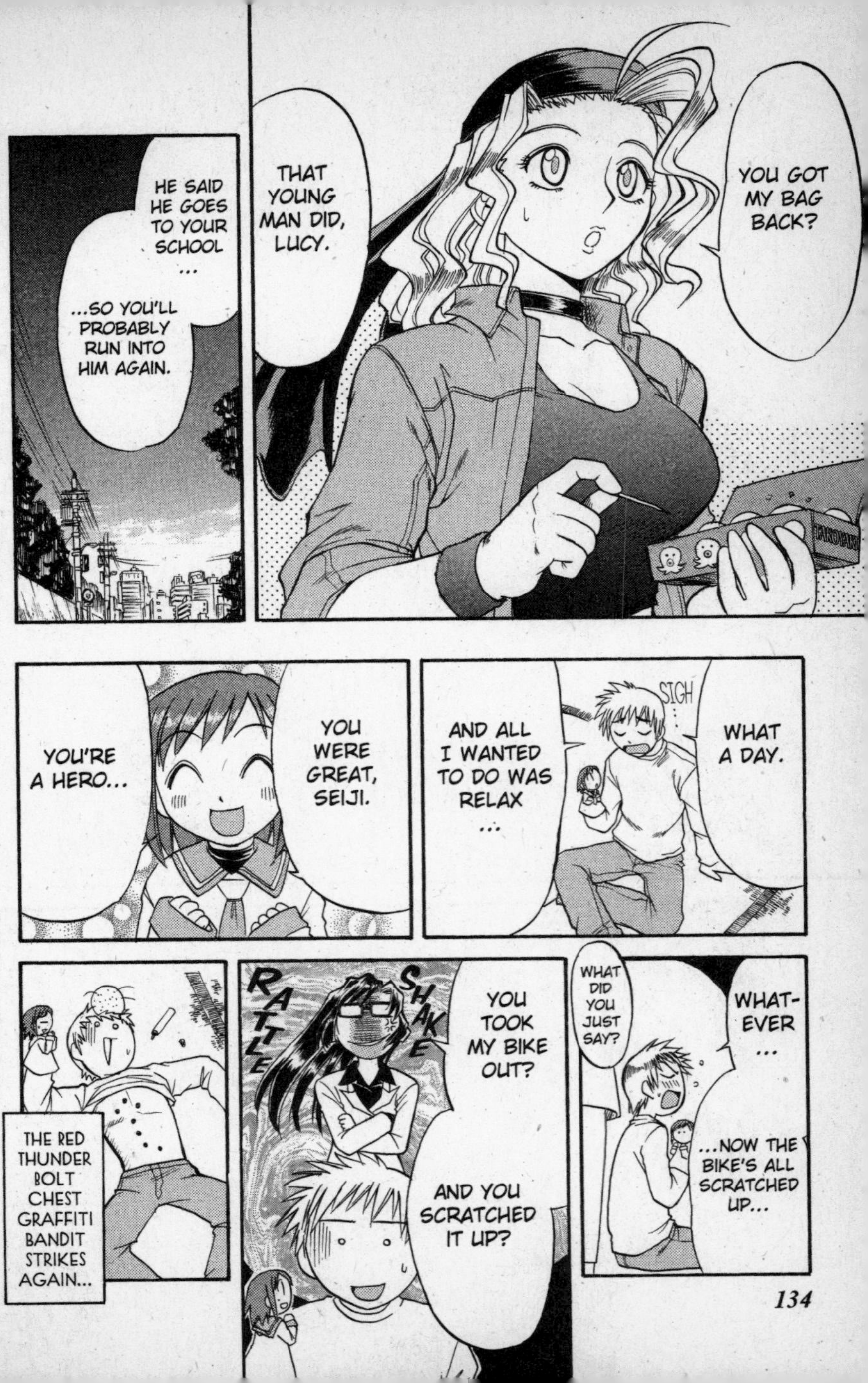
YOU GOT MY BAG BACK?
THAT YOUNG MAN DID, LUCY.
HE SAID HE GOES TO YOUR SCHOOL ...
...SO YOU'LL PROBABLY RUN INTO HIM AGAIN.
WHAT A DAY.
SIGH
AND ALL I WANTED TO DO WAS RELAX ...
YOU WERE GREAT, SEIJI.
YOU'RE A HERO...
WHAT-EVER ...
WHAT DID YOU JUST SAY?
...NOW THE BIKE'S ALL SCRATCHED UP...
RATTLE
SHAKE
YOU TOOK MY BIKE OUT?
AND YOU SCRATCHED IT UP?
THE RED THUNDER BOLT CHEST GRAFFITI BANDIT STRIKES AGAIN...

DAY 41 PROOF OF A "SAMURAI"

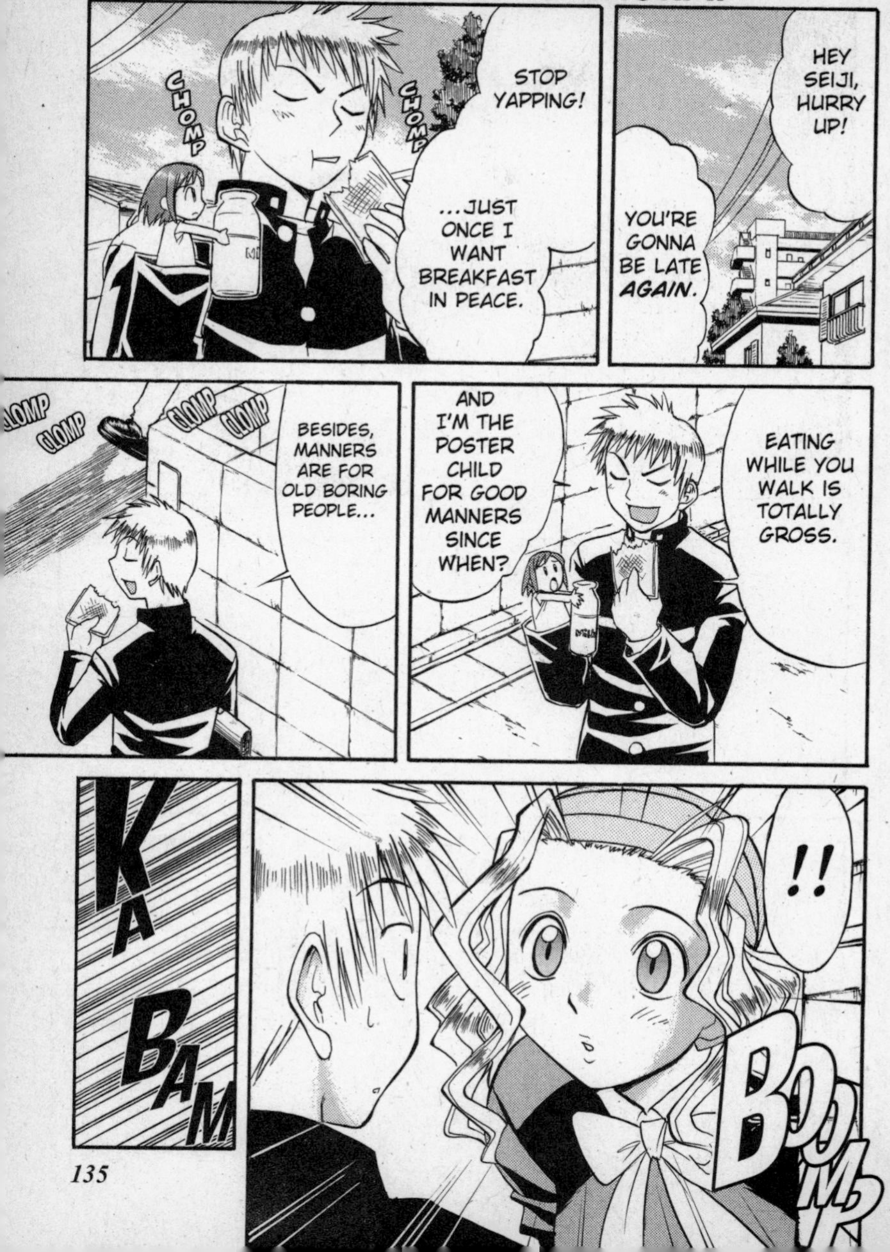
HEY SEIJI, HURRY UP!
YOU'RE GONNA BE LATE *AGAIN*.
CHOMP
CHOMP
STOP YAPPING!
...JUST ONCE I WANT BREAKFAST IN PEACE.
EATING WHILE YOU WALK IS TOTALLY GROSS.
AND I'M THE POSTER CHILD FOR GOOD MANNERS SINCE WHEN?
CLOMP CLOMP
CLOMP
CLOMP
BESIDES, MANNERS ARE FOR OLD BORING PEOPLE...
!!
KABAM

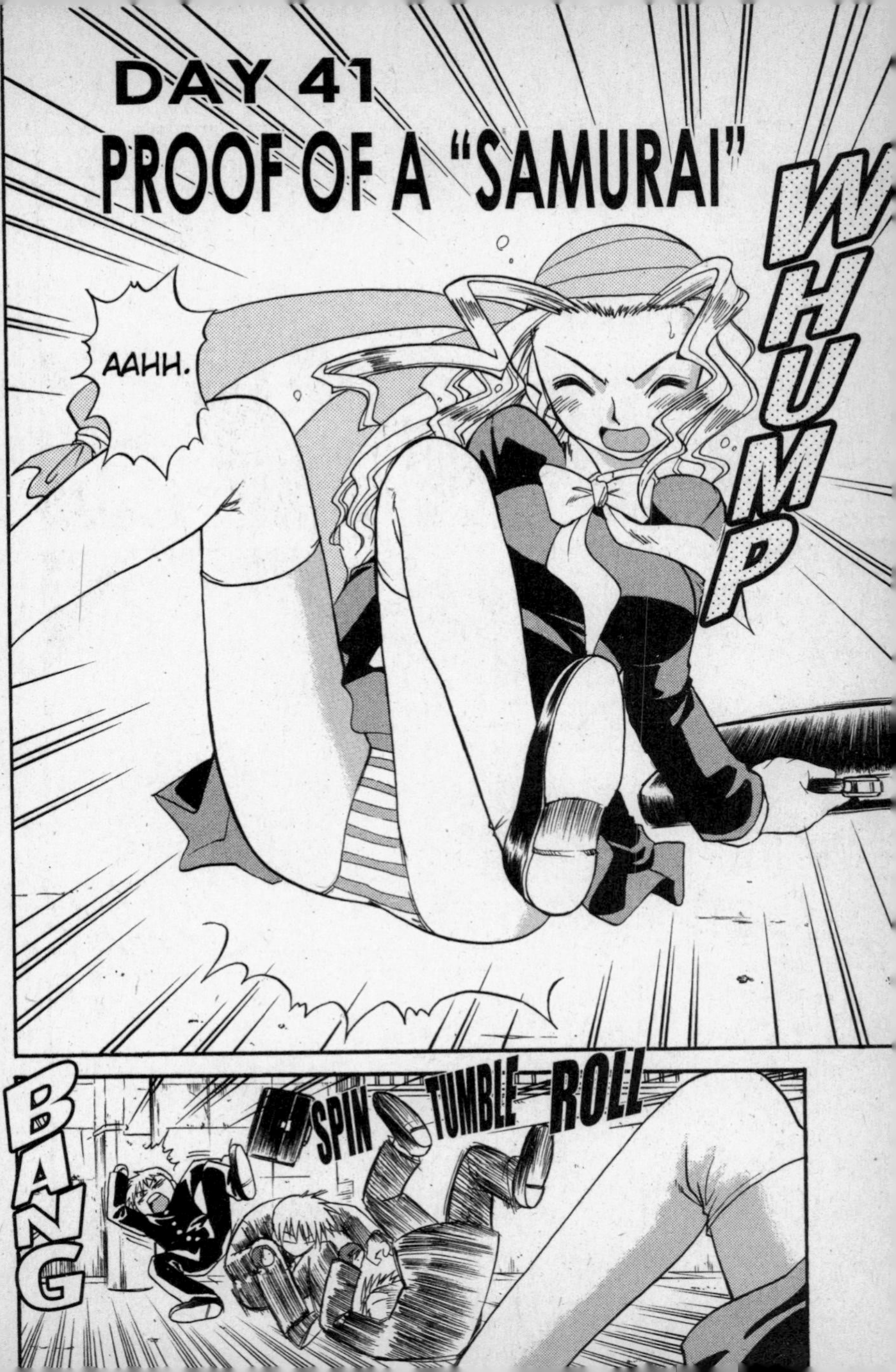
DAY 41
PROOF OF A "SAMURAI"
WHUMP
AAHH.
ROLL
TUMBLE
SPIN
BANG

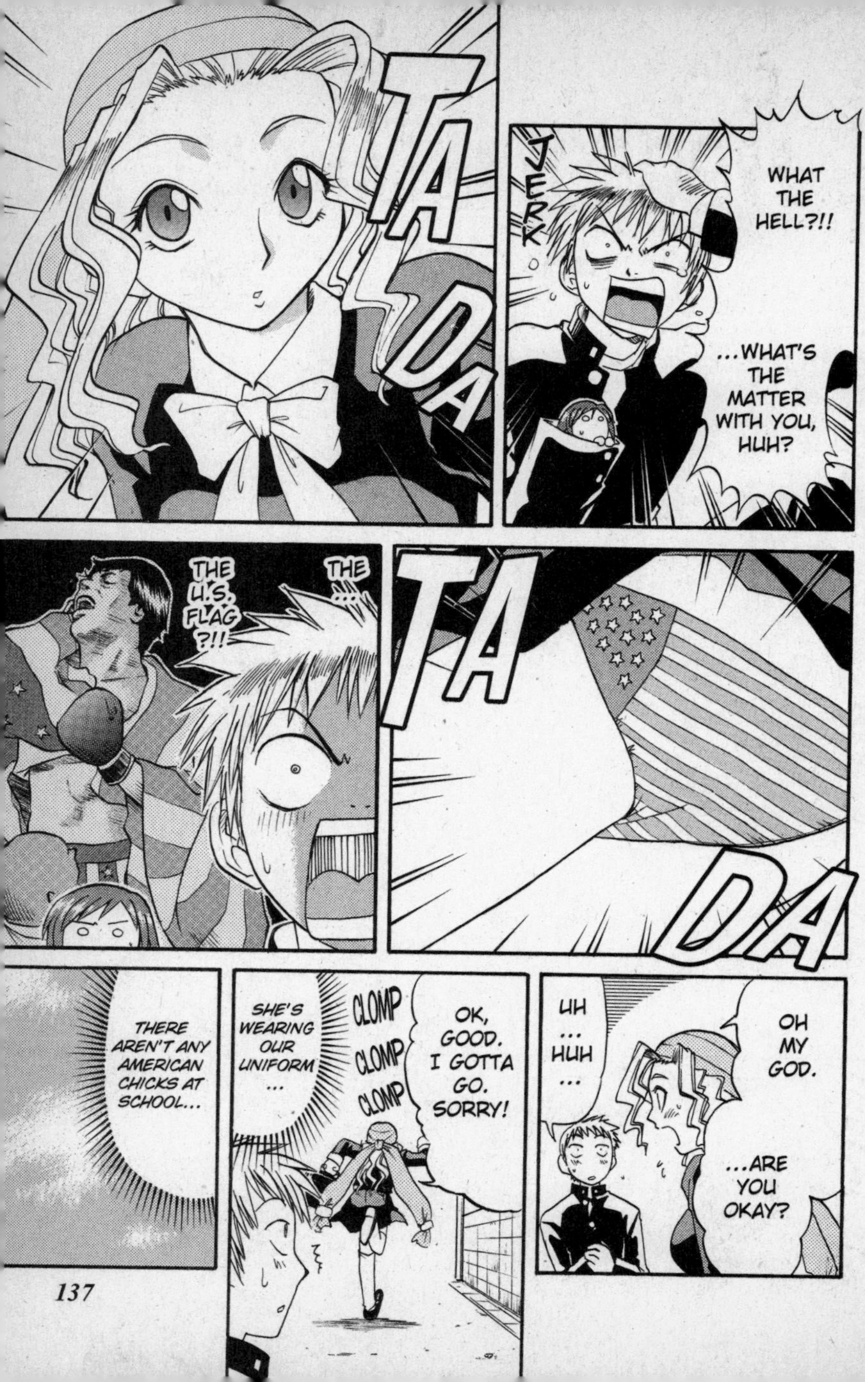
WHAT THE HELL?!!
JERK
...WHAT'S THE MATTER WITH YOU, HUH?
TA DA
TA DA
THE ...
THE U.S. FLAG?!!
OH MY GOD.
UH ... HUH ...
...ARE YOU OKAY?
OK, GOOD. I GOTTA GO. SORRY!
CLOMP CLOMP CLOMP
SHE'S WEARING OUR UNIFORM ...
THERE AREN'T ANY AMERICAN CHICKS AT SCHOOL...

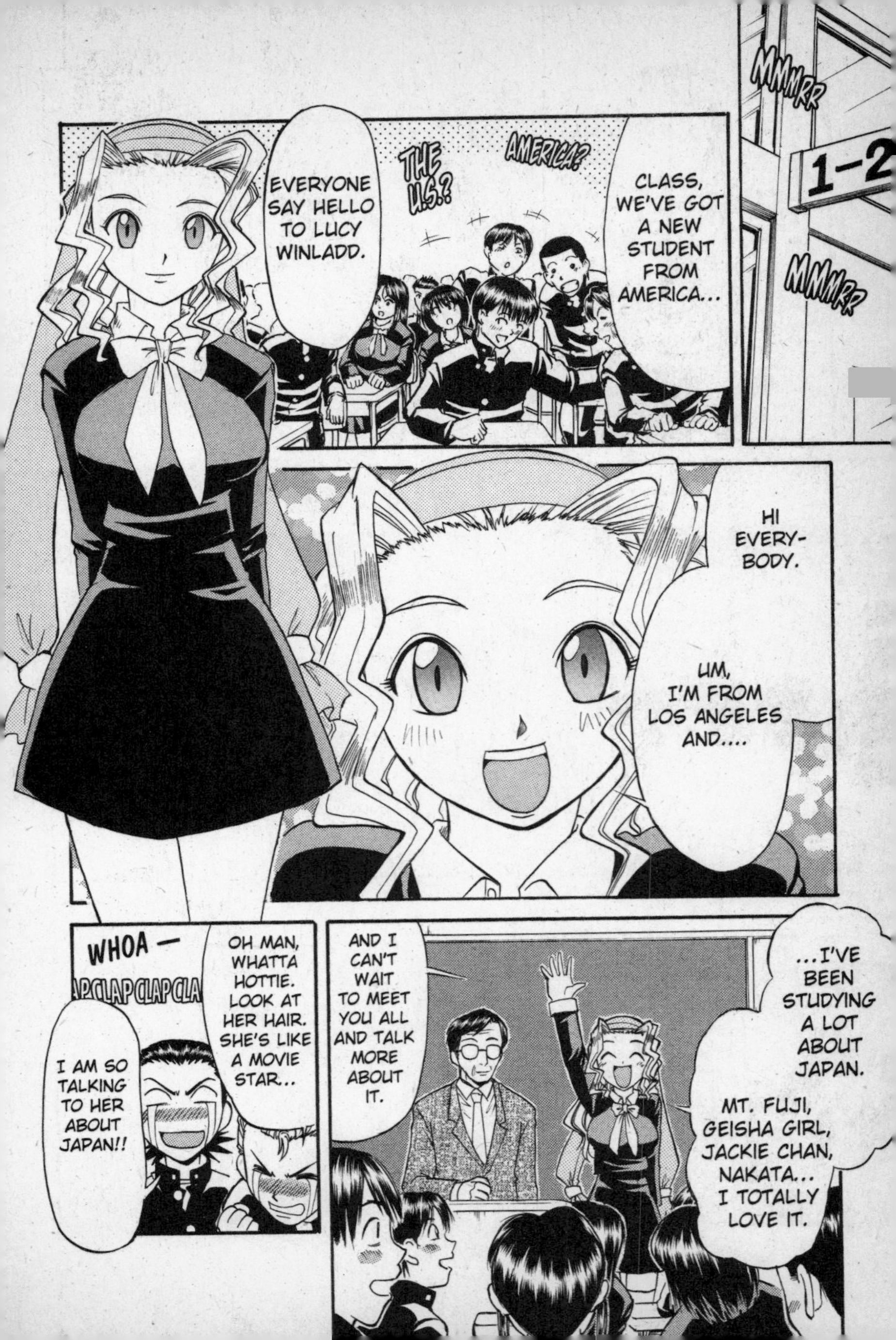

MMMRR
1-2
MMMRR
CLASS, WE'VE GOT A NEW STUDENT FROM AMERICA...
AMERICA?
THE U.S.?
EVERYONE SAY HELLO TO LUCY WINLADD.
HI EVERY-BODY.
UM, I'M FROM LOS ANGELES AND....
...I'VE BEEN STUDYING A LOT ABOUT JAPAN.
MT. FUJI, GEISHA GIRL, JACKIE CHAN, NAKATA... I TOTALLY LOVE IT.
AND I CAN'T WAIT TO MEET YOU ALL AND TALK MORE ABOUT IT.
OH MAN, WHATTA HOTTIE. LOOK AT HER HAIR. SHE'S LIKE A MOVIE STAR...
WHOA —
APCLAP CLAP CLAP CLA
I AM SO TALKING TO HER ABOUT JAPAN!!

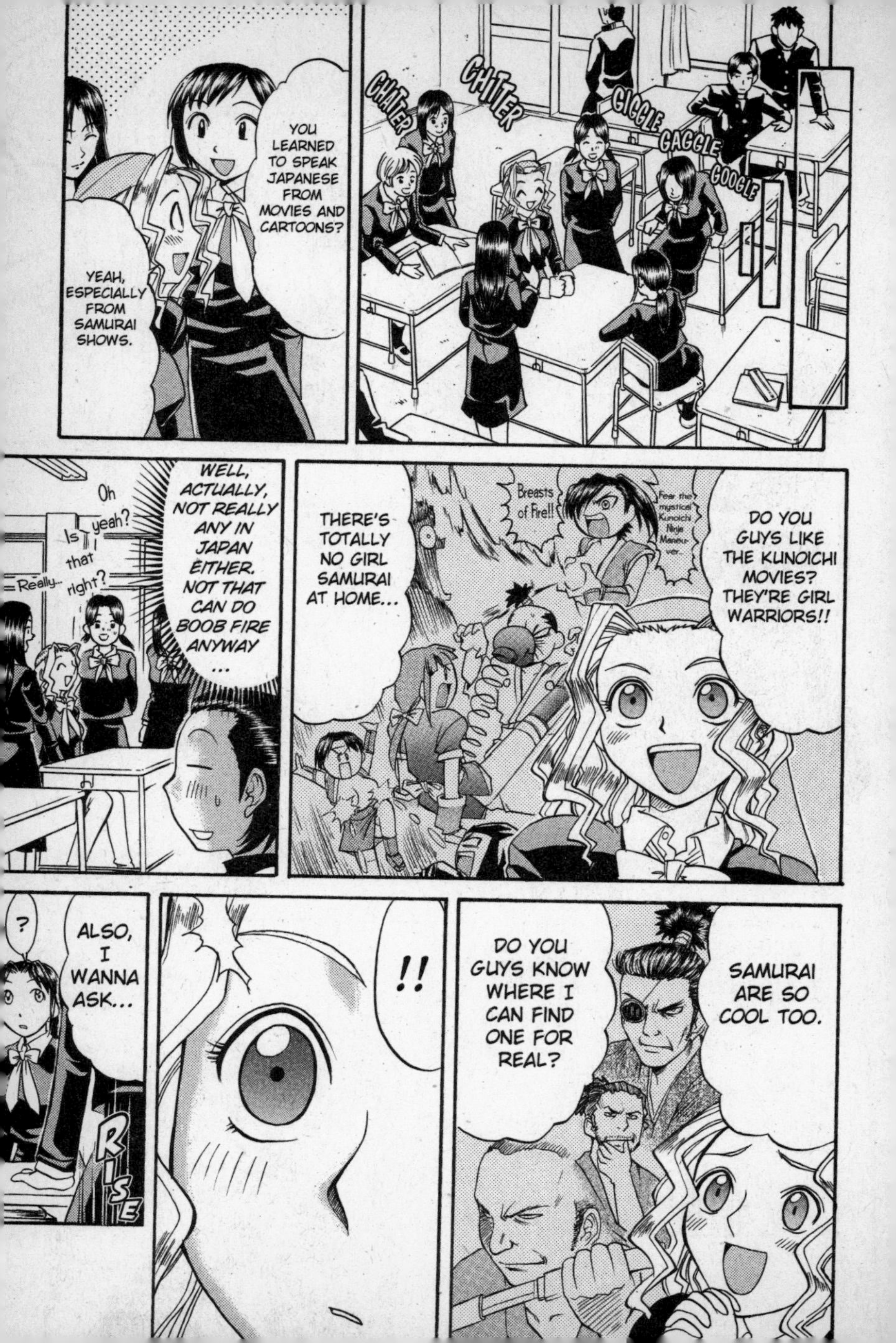
GIGGLE
GAGGLE
GOOGLE
CHITTER
CHATTER
YOU LEARNED TO SPEAK JAPANESE FROM MOVIES AND CARTOONS?
YEAH, ESPECIALLY FROM SAMURAI SHOWS.
DO YOU GUYS LIKE THE KUNOICHI MOVIES? THEY'RE GIRL WARRIORS!!
Fear the mystical Kunoichi Ninja Maneuver...
Breasts of Fire!!
THERE'S TOTALLY NO GIRL SAMURAI AT HOME...
WELL, ACTUALLY, NOT REALLY ANY IN JAPAN EITHER. NOT THAT CAN DO BOOB FIRE ANYWAY ...
Oh yeah?
Is that right?
Really...
SAMURAI ARE SO COOL TOO.
DO YOU GUYS KNOW WHERE I CAN FIND ONE FOR REAL?
!!
ALSO, I WANNA ASK...
?
RISE

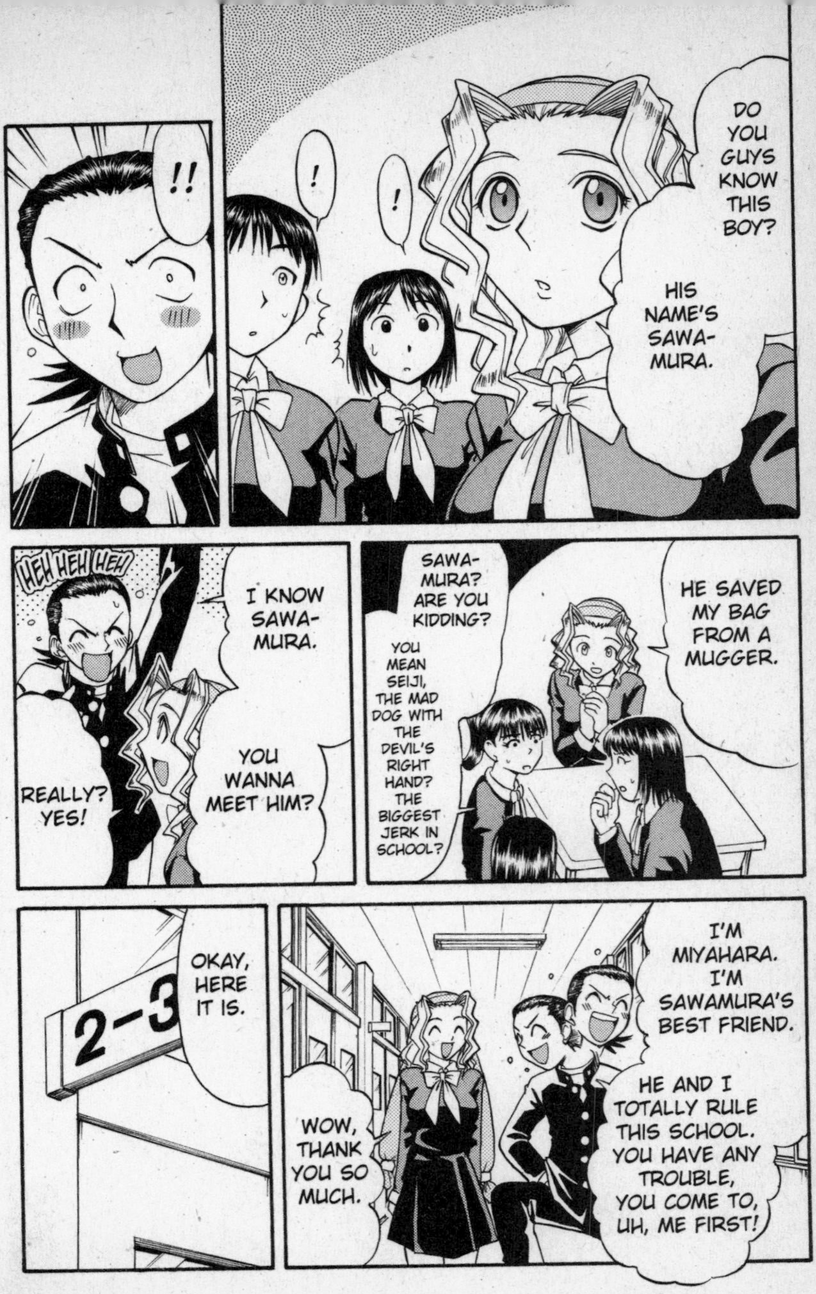
DO YOU GUYS KNOW THIS BOY?
HIS NAME'S SAWA-MURA.
!
!
!!
HE SAVED MY BAG FROM A MUGGER.
SAWA-MURA? ARE YOU KIDDING?
YOU MEAN SEIJI, THE MAD DOG WITH THE DEVIL'S RIGHT HAND? THE BIGGEST JERK IN SCHOOL?
HEH HEH HEH
I KNOW SAWA-MURA.
YOU WANNA MEET HIM?
REALLY? YES!
I'M MIYAHARA. I'M SAWAMURA'S BEST FRIEND.
HE AND I TOTALLY RULE THIS SCHOOL. YOU HAVE ANY TROUBLE, YOU COME TO, UH, ME FIRST!
WOW, THANK YOU SO MUCH.
OKAY, HERE IT IS.
2-3

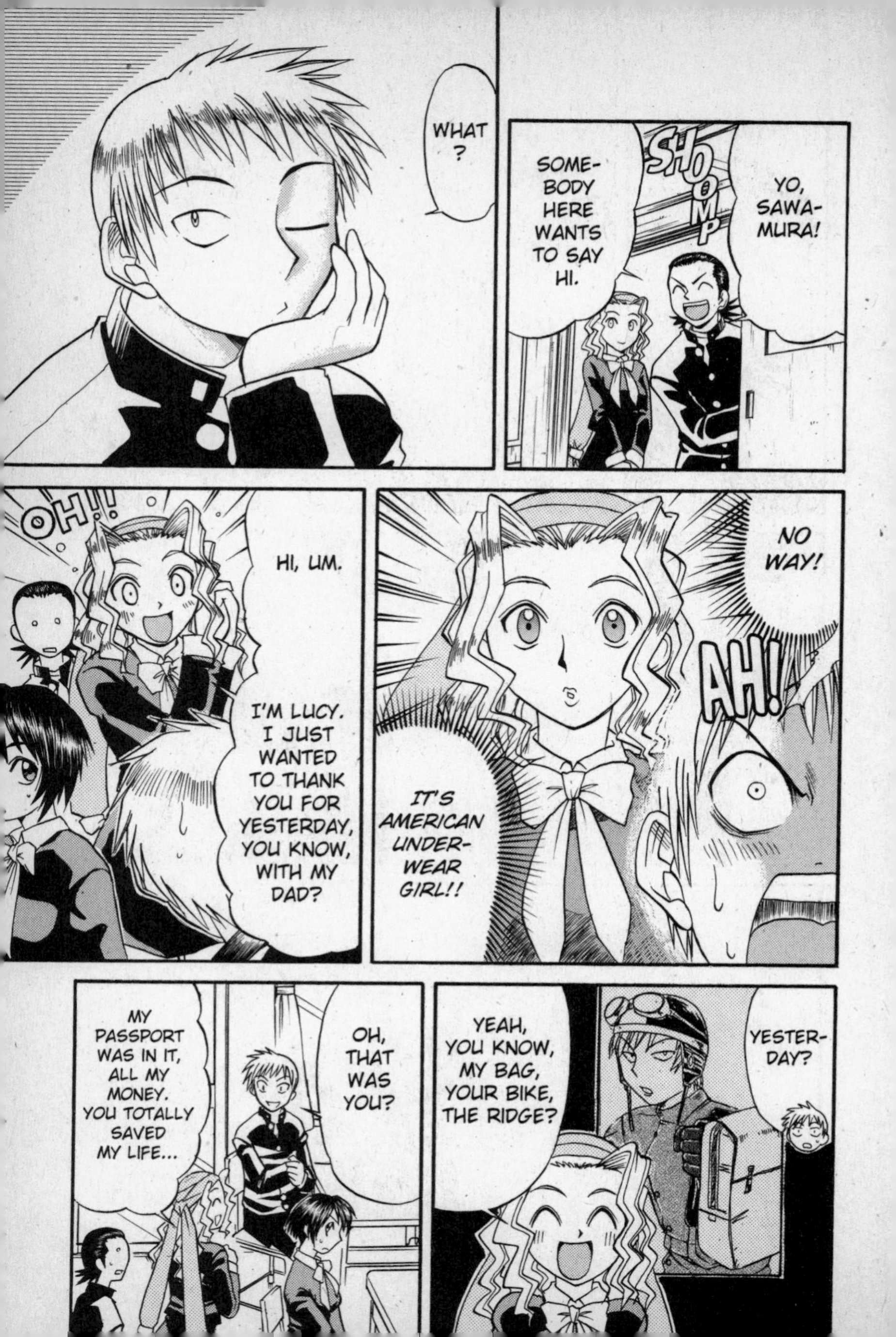
YO, SAWAMURA!
SHOOMP
SOMEBODY HERE WANTS TO SAY HI.
WHAT?
NO WAY!
AH!
IT'S AMERICAN UNDERWEAR GIRL!!
OH!!
HI, UM.
I'M LUCY. I JUST WANTED TO THANK YOU FOR YESTERDAY, YOU KNOW, WITH MY DAD?
YESTERDAY?
YEAH, YOU KNOW, MY BAG, YOUR BIKE, THE RIDGE?
OH, THAT WAS YOU?
MY PASSPORT WAS IN IT, ALL MY MONEY. YOU TOTALLY SAVED MY LIFE...

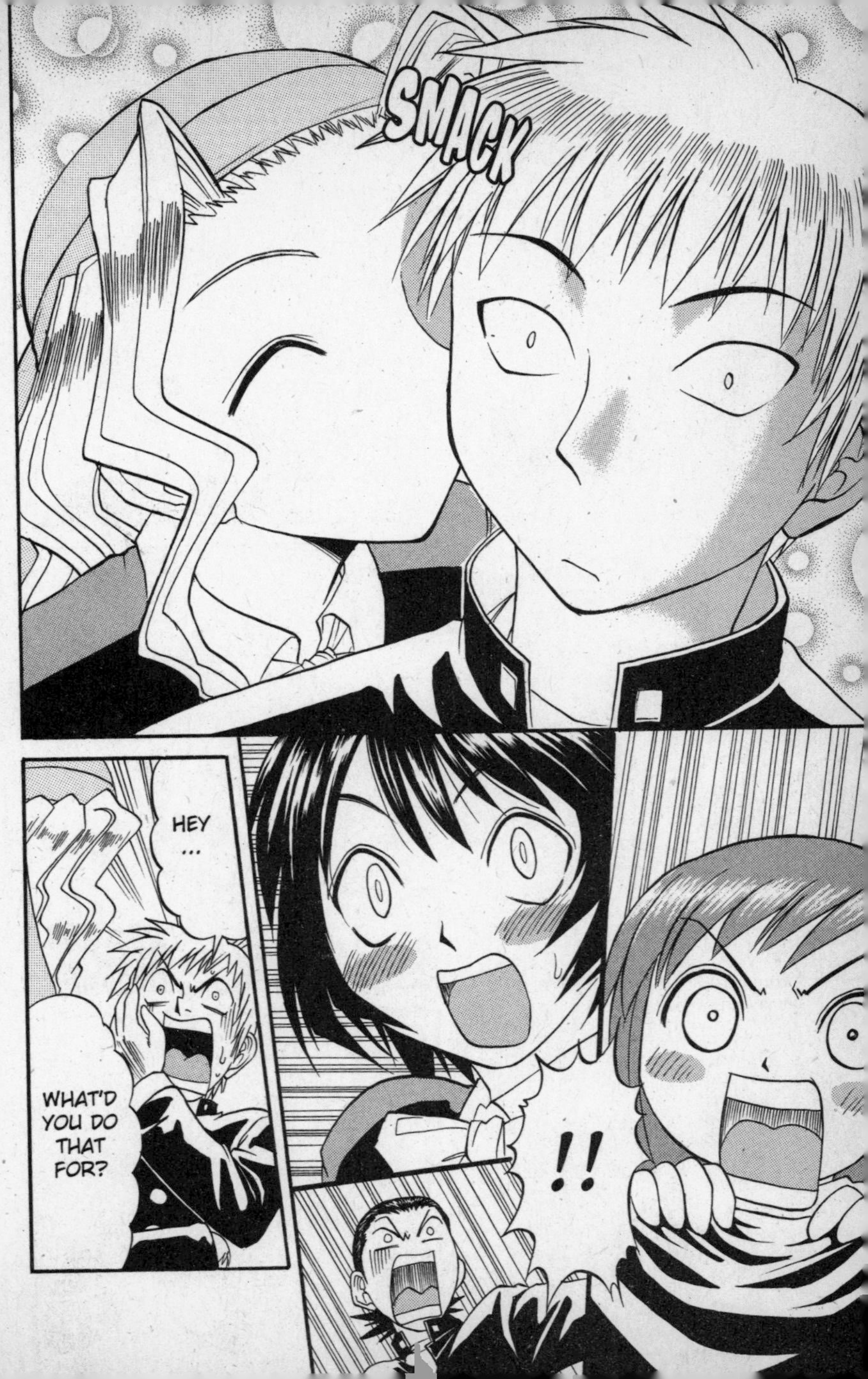
SMACK
!!
HEY
...
WHAT'D YOU DO THAT FOR?

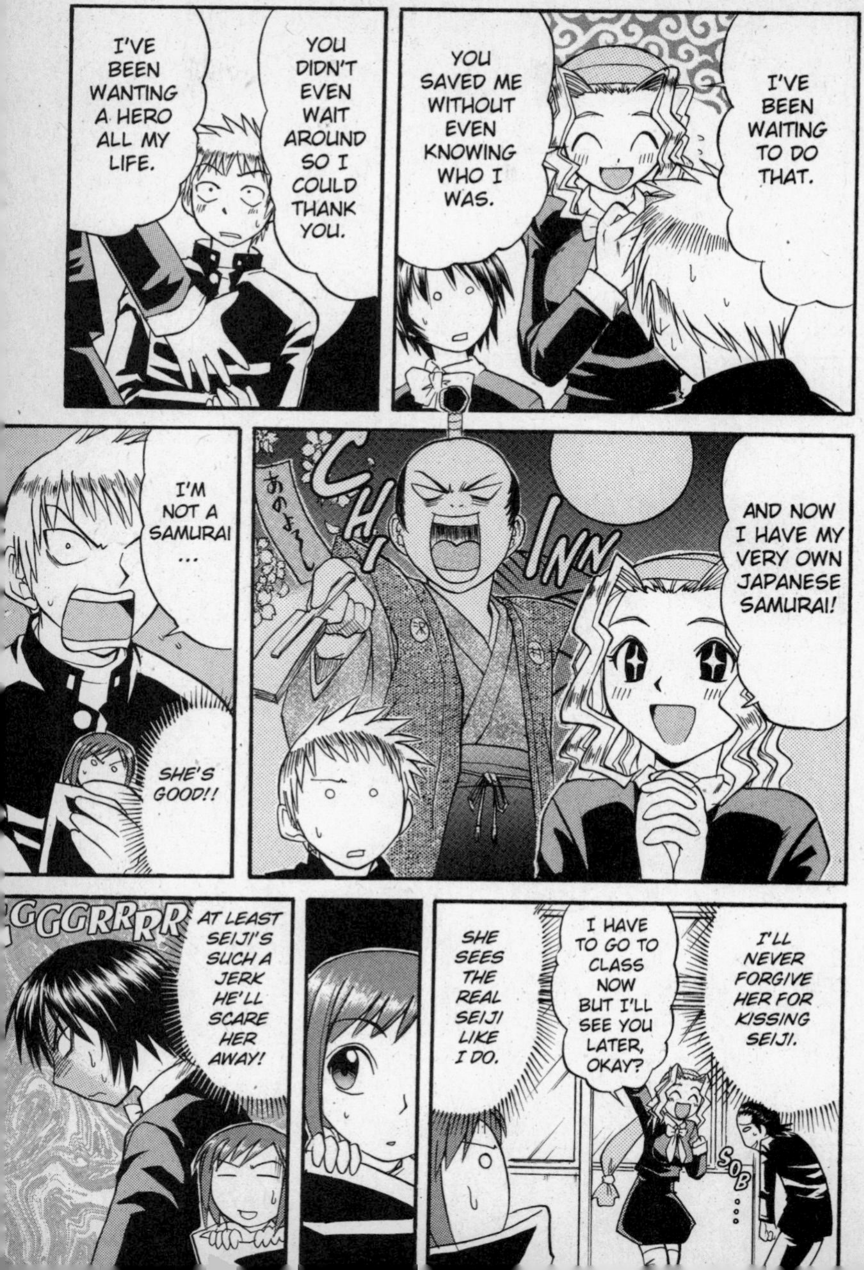
I'VE BEEN WAITING TO DO THAT.
YOU SAVED ME WITHOUT EVEN KNOWING WHO I WAS.
YOU DIDN'T EVEN WAIT AROUND SO I COULD THANK YOU.
I'VE BEEN WANTING A HERO ALL MY LIFE.
AND NOW I HAVE MY VERY OWN JAPANESE SAMURAI!
CHINN
I'M NOT A SAMURAI ...
SHE'S GOOD!!
I'LL NEVER FORGIVE HER FOR KISSING SEIJI.
I HAVE TO GO TO CLASS NOW BUT I'LL SEE YOU LATER, OKAY?
SHE SEES THE REAL SEIJI LIKE I DO.
SOB ...
GGGRRRR
AT LEAST SEIJI'S SUCH A JERK HE'LL SCARE HER AWAY!

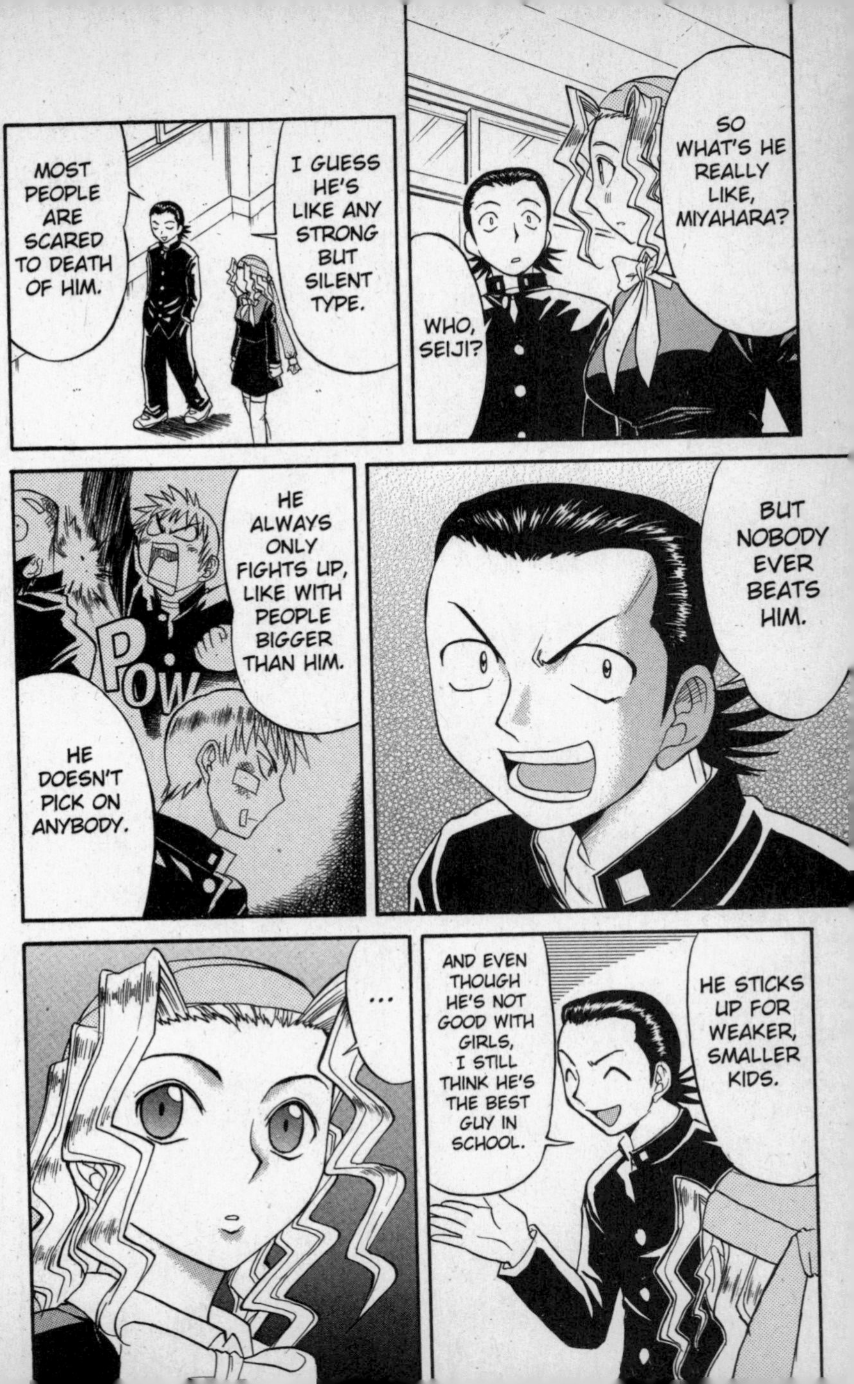
SO WHAT'S HE REALLY LIKE, MIYAHARA?
WHO, SEIJI?
I GUESS HE'S LIKE ANY STRONG BUT SILENT TYPE.
MOST PEOPLE ARE SCARED TO DEATH OF HIM.
BUT NOBODY EVER BEATS HIM.
HE ALWAYS ONLY FIGHTS UP, LIKE WITH PEOPLE BIGGER THAN HIM.
POW
HE DOESN'T PICK ON ANYBODY.
HE STICKS UP FOR WEAKER, SMALLER KIDS.
AND EVEN THOUGH HE'S NOT GOOD WITH GIRLS, I STILL THINK HE'S THE BEST GUY IN SCHOOL.
...

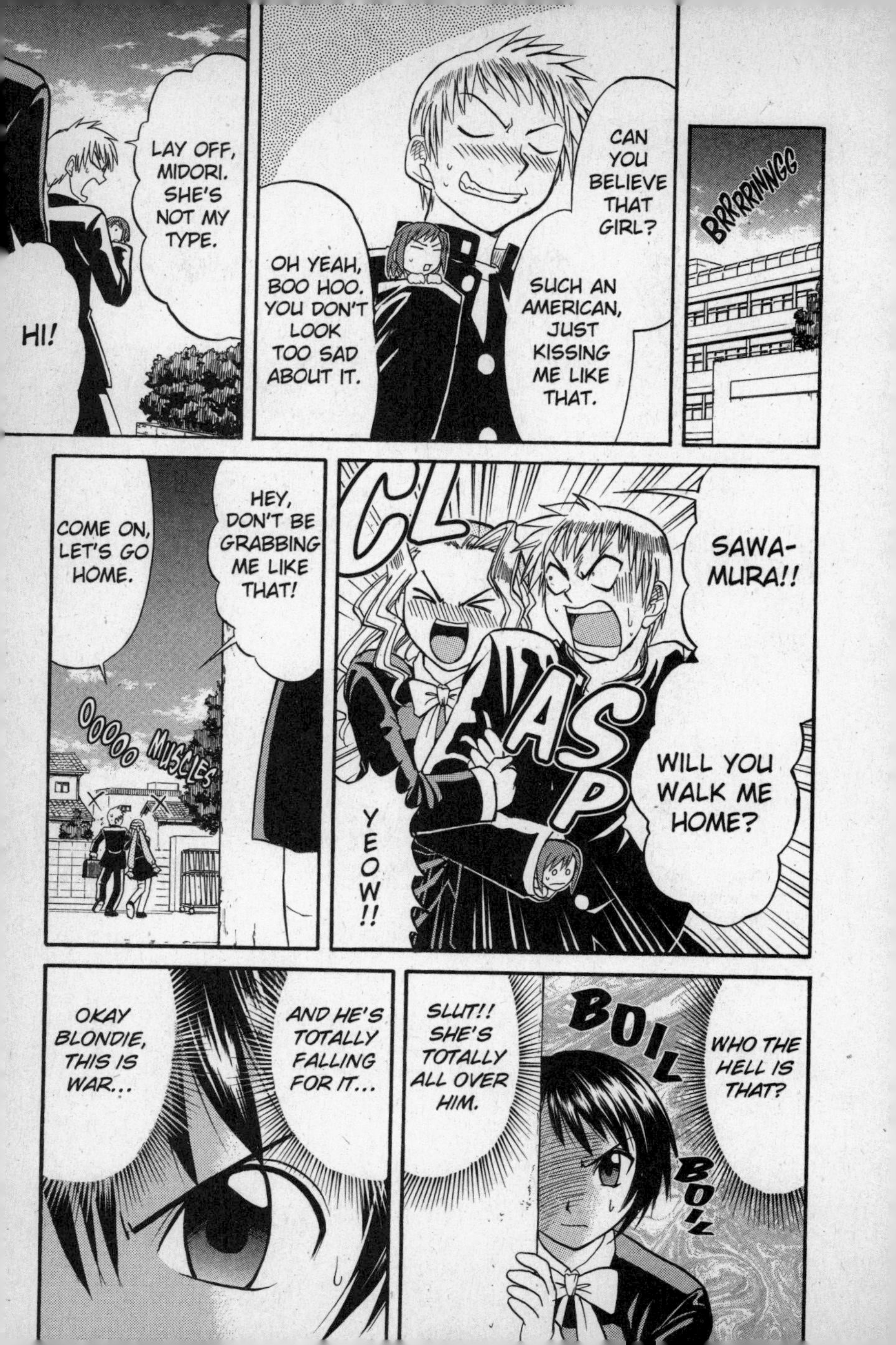
BRRRRINNGG
CAN YOU BELIEVE THAT GIRL?
SUCH AN AMERICAN, JUST KISSING ME LIKE THAT.
OH YEAH, BOO HOO. YOU DON'T LOOK TOO SAD ABOUT IT.
LAY OFF, MIDORI. SHE'S NOT MY TYPE.
HI!
SAWAMURA!!
CLASP
WILL YOU WALK ME HOME?
YEOW!!
HEY, DON'T BE GRABBING ME LIKE THAT!
COME ON, LET'S GO HOME.
OOOOO MUSCLES
WHO THE HELL IS THAT?
BOIL
BOIL
SLUT!! SHE'S TOTALLY ALL OVER HIM.
AND HE'S TOTALLY FALLING FOR IT...
OKAY BLONDIE, THIS IS WAR...

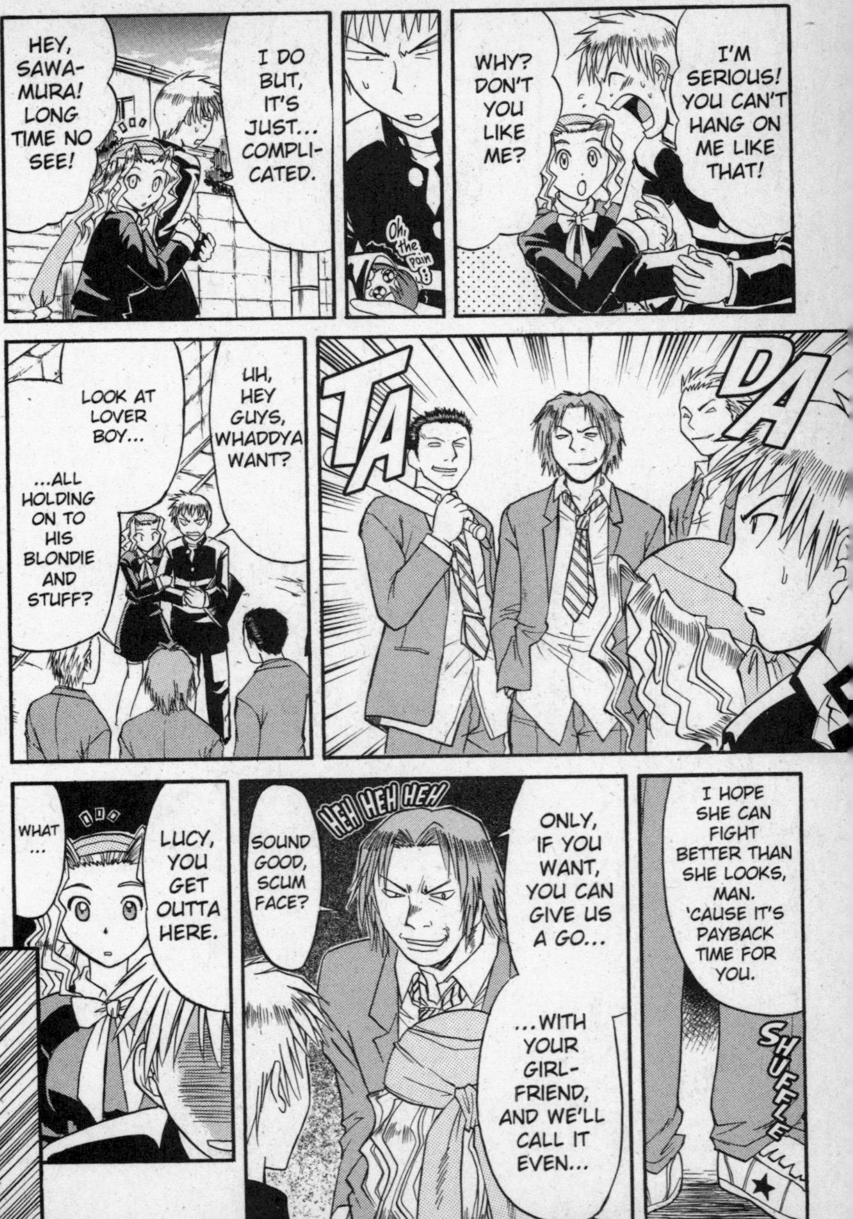
I'M SERIOUS! YOU CAN'T HANG ON ME LIKE THAT!
WHY? DON'T YOU LIKE ME?
Oh, the pain!
I DO BUT, IT'S JUST... COMPLICATED.
HEY, SAWAMURA! LONG TIME NO SEE!
DA
TA
UH, HEY GUYS, WHADDYA WANT?
LOOK AT LOVER BOY...
...ALL HOLDING ON TO HIS BLONDIE AND STUFF?
I HOPE SHE CAN FIGHT BETTER THAN SHE LOOKS, MAN. 'CAUSE IT'S PAYBACK TIME FOR YOU.
SHUFFLE
ONLY, IF YOU WANT, YOU CAN GIVE US A GO...
...WITH YOUR GIRL-FRIEND, AND WE'LL CALL IT EVEN...
HEH HEH HEH
SOUND GOOD, SCUM FACE?
LUCY, YOU GET OUTTA HERE.
WHAT ...

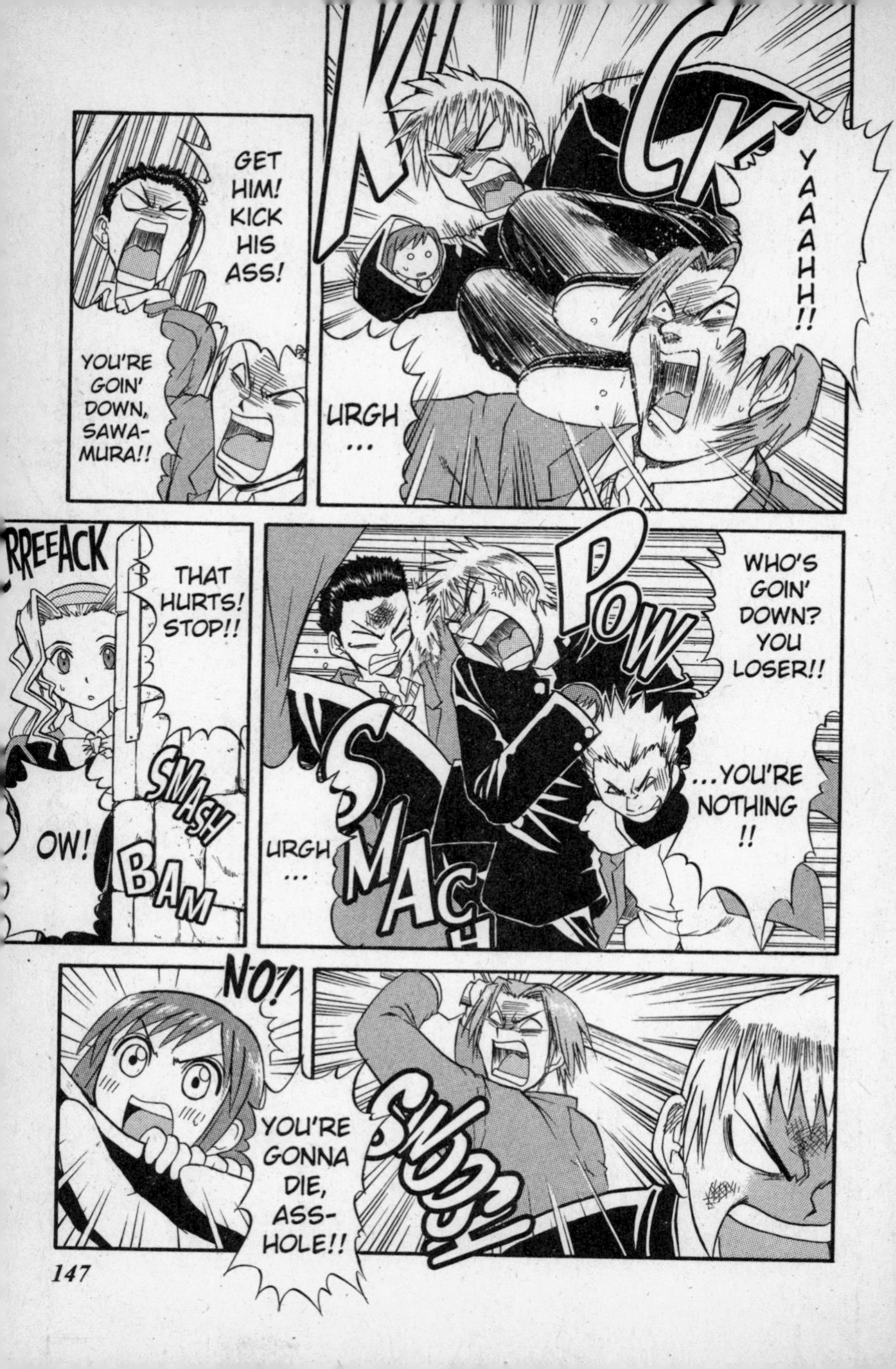
KICK
YAAAAHH!!
URGH...
GET HIM! KICK HIS ASS!
YOU'RE GOIN' DOWN, SAWAMURA!!
POW
WHO'S GOIN' DOWN? YOU LOSER!!
...YOU'RE NOTHING!!
SMAC
URGH...
RREEACK
THAT HURTS! STOP!!
SMASH
BAM
OW!
SWOOSH
YOU'RE GONNA DIE, ASS-HOLE!!
NO!

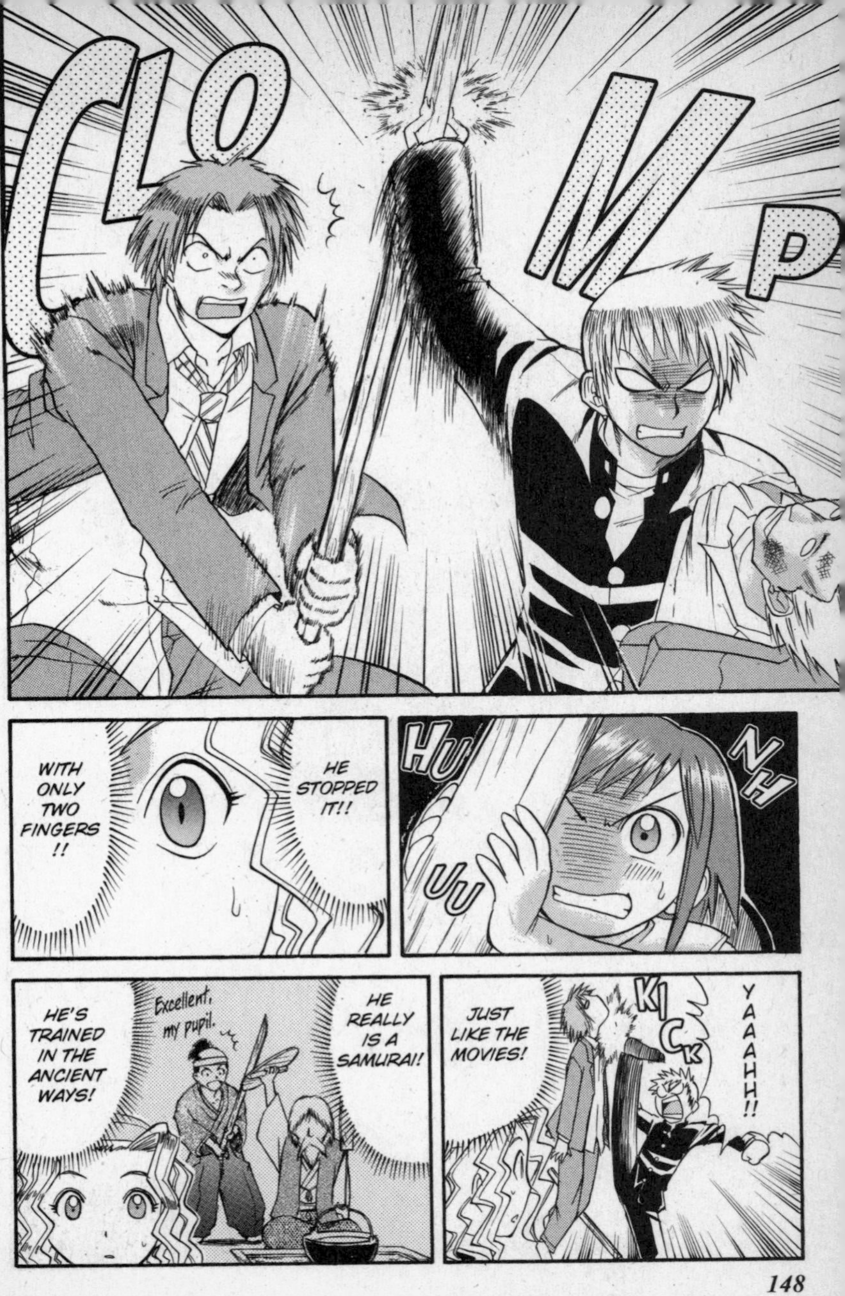
CLOMP
HU
NH
UU
HE STOPPED IT!!
WITH ONLY TWO FINGERS !!
YAAAHH!!
KICK
JUST LIKE THE MOVIES!
HE REALLY IS A SAMURAI!
Excellent, my pupil.
HE'S TRAINED IN THE ANCIENT WAYS!

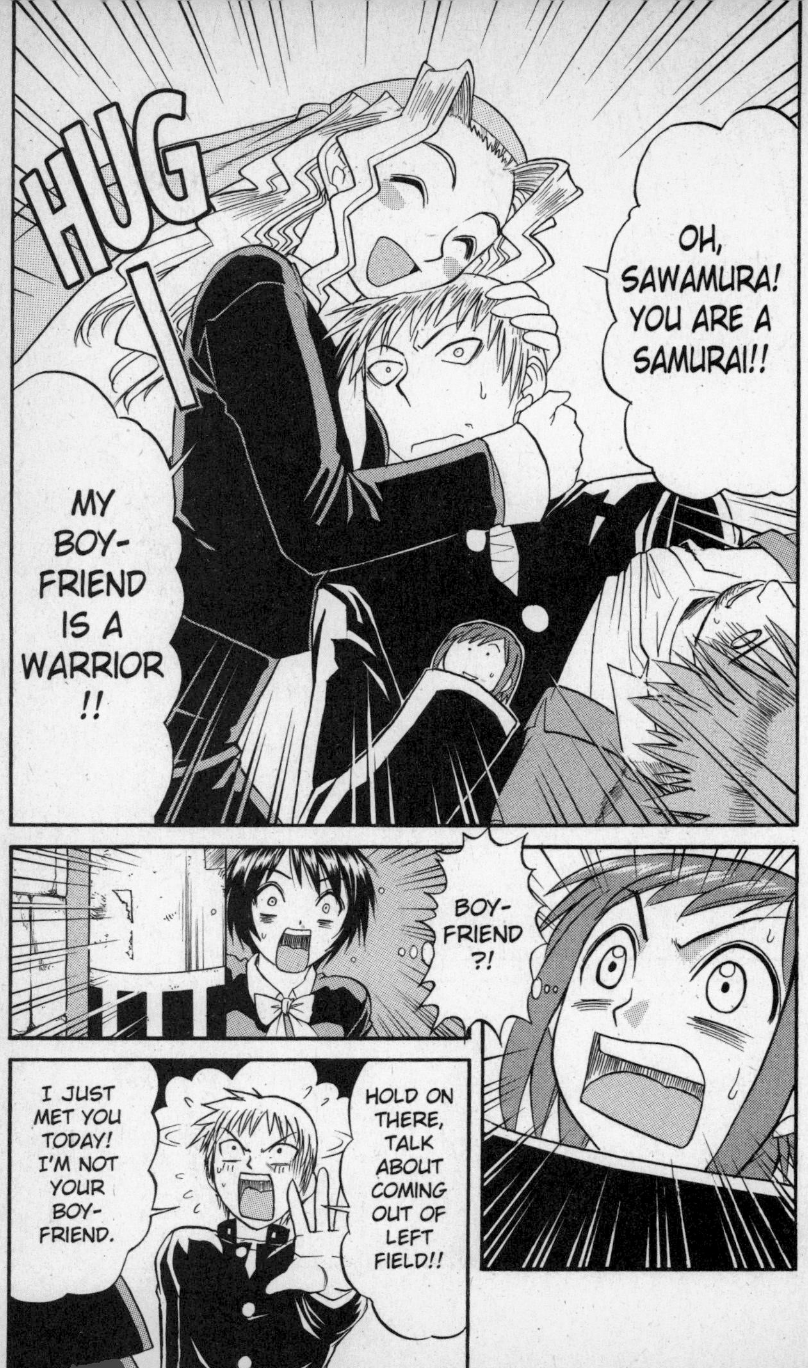
OH, SAWAMURA! YOU ARE A SAMURAI!!
HUG
MY BOY-FRIEND IS A WARRIOR!!
BOY-FRIEND ?!
HOLD ON THERE, TALK ABOUT COMING OUT OF LEFT FIELD!!
I JUST MET YOU TODAY! I'M NOT YOUR BOY-FRIEND.

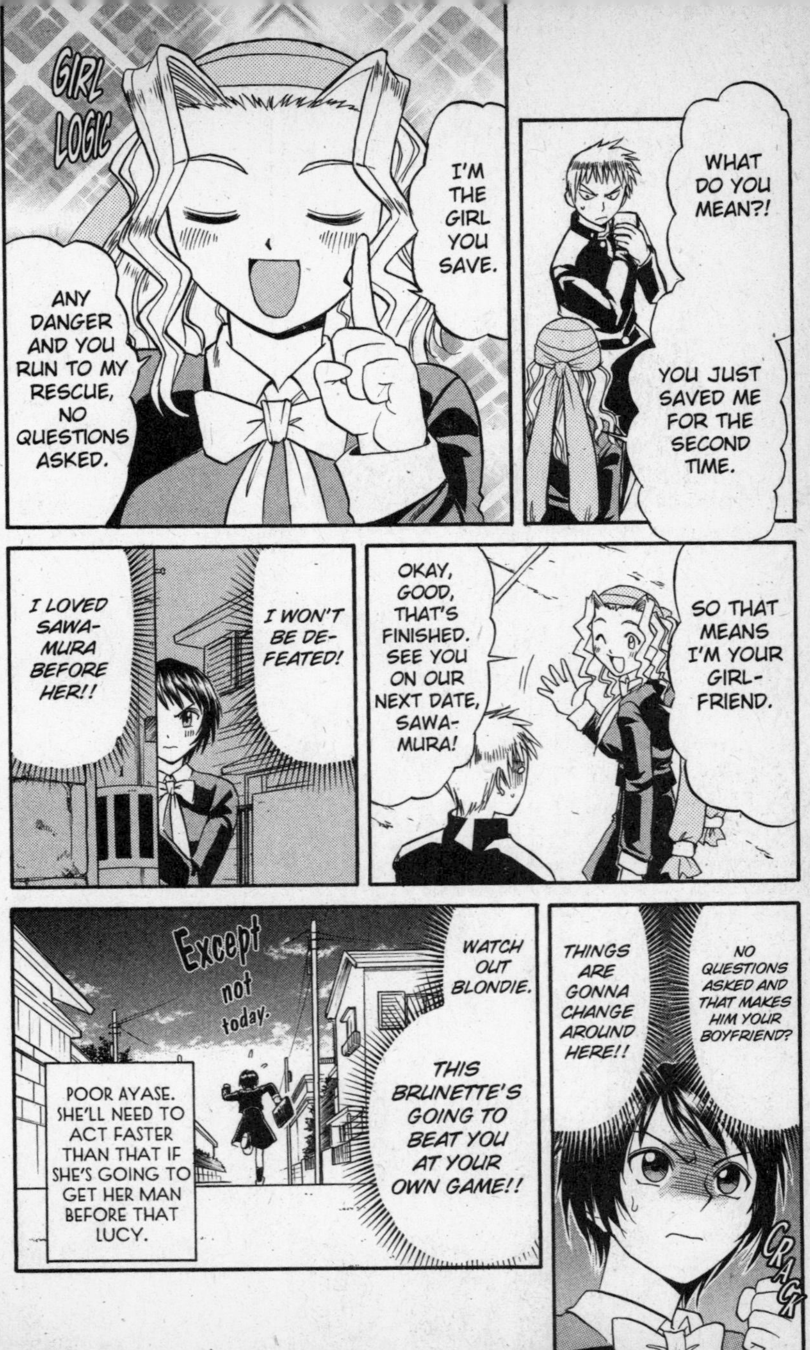
WHAT DO YOU MEAN?!
YOU JUST SAVED ME FOR THE SECOND TIME.
GIRL LOGIC
I'M THE GIRL YOU SAVE.
ANY DANGER AND YOU RUN TO MY RESCUE, NO QUESTIONS ASKED.
SO THAT MEANS I'M YOUR GIRL-FRIEND.
OKAY, GOOD, THAT'S FINISHED. SEE YOU ON OUR NEXT DATE, SAWA-MURA!
I WON'T BE DE-FEATED!
I LOVED SAWA-MURA BEFORE HER!!
NO QUESTIONS ASKED AND THAT MAKES HIM YOUR BOYFRIEND?
THINGS ARE GONNA CHANGE AROUND HERE!!
CRACK
WATCH OUT BLONDIE.
THIS BRUNETTE'S GOING TO BEAT YOU AT YOUR OWN GAME!!
Except not today.
POOR AYASE. SHE'LL NEED TO ACT FASTER THAN THAT IF SHE'S GOING TO GET HER MAN BEFORE THAT LUCY.

DAY 42
A WORLD OF THEIR OWN

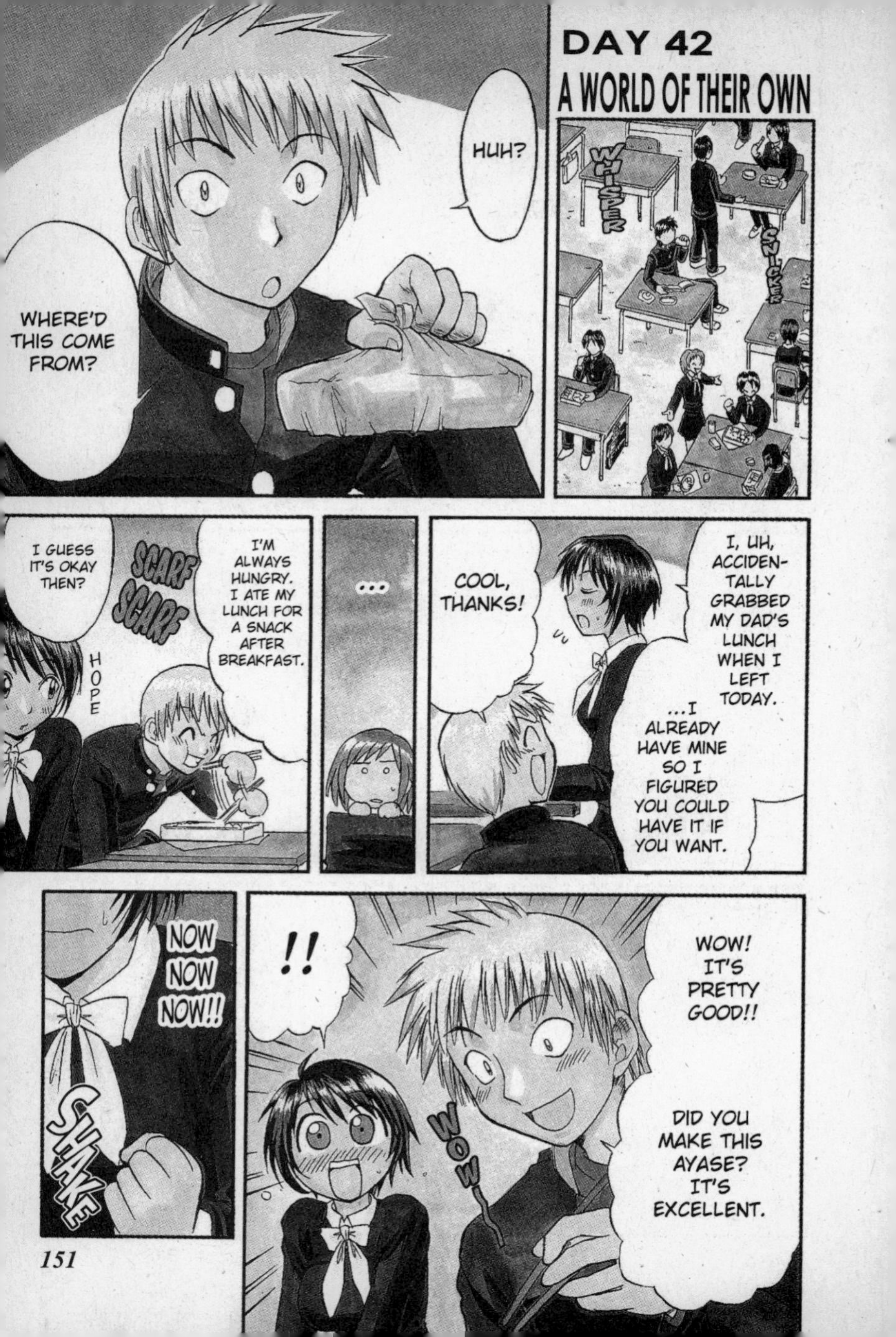
WHISPER
SNICKER
HUH?
WHERE'D THIS COME FROM?
I, UH, ACCIDENTALLY GRABBED MY DAD'S LUNCH WHEN I LEFT TODAY.
...I ALREADY HAVE MINE SO I FIGURED YOU COULD HAVE IT IF YOU WANT.
COOL, THANKS!
...
I'M ALWAYS HUNGRY. I ATE MY LUNCH FOR A SNACK AFTER BREAKFAST.
SCARF SCARF
I GUESS IT'S OKAY THEN?
HOPE
WOW! IT'S PRETTY GOOD!!
DID YOU MAKE THIS AYASE? IT'S EXCELLENT.
!!
WOW
NOW NOW NOW!!
SHAKE

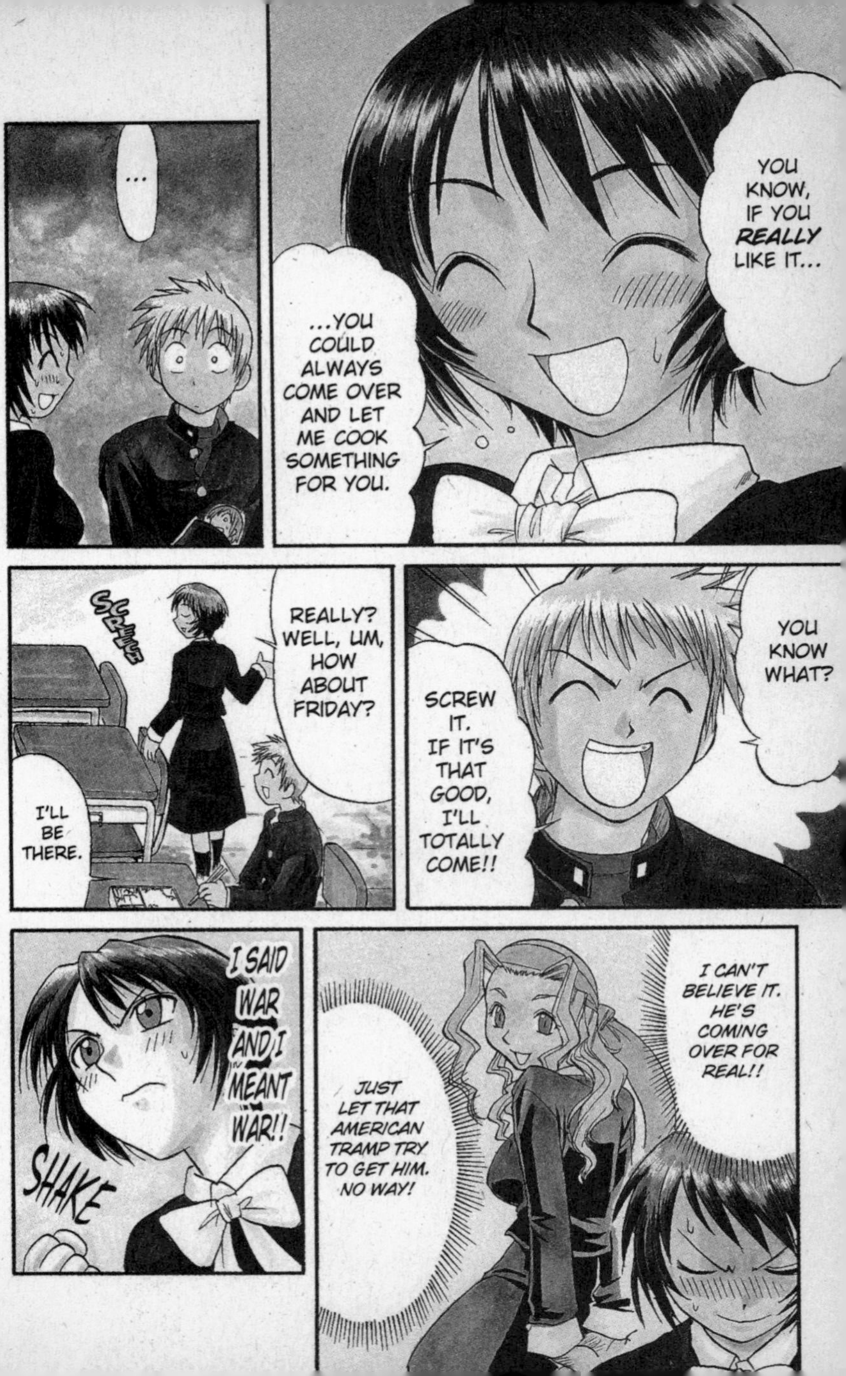
YOU KNOW, IF YOU *REALLY* LIKE IT...
...YOU COULD ALWAYS COME OVER AND LET ME COOK SOMETHING FOR YOU.
...
YOU KNOW WHAT?
SCREW IT. IF IT'S THAT GOOD, I'LL TOTALLY COME!!
SCREECH
REALLY? WELL, UM, HOW ABOUT FRIDAY?
I'LL BE THERE.
I CAN'T BELIEVE IT. HE'S COMING OVER FOR REAL!!
JUST LET THAT AMERICAN TRAMP TRY TO GET HIM. NO WAY!
I SAID WAR AND I MEANT WAR!!
SHAKE

DAY 42
A WORLD OF THEIR OWN

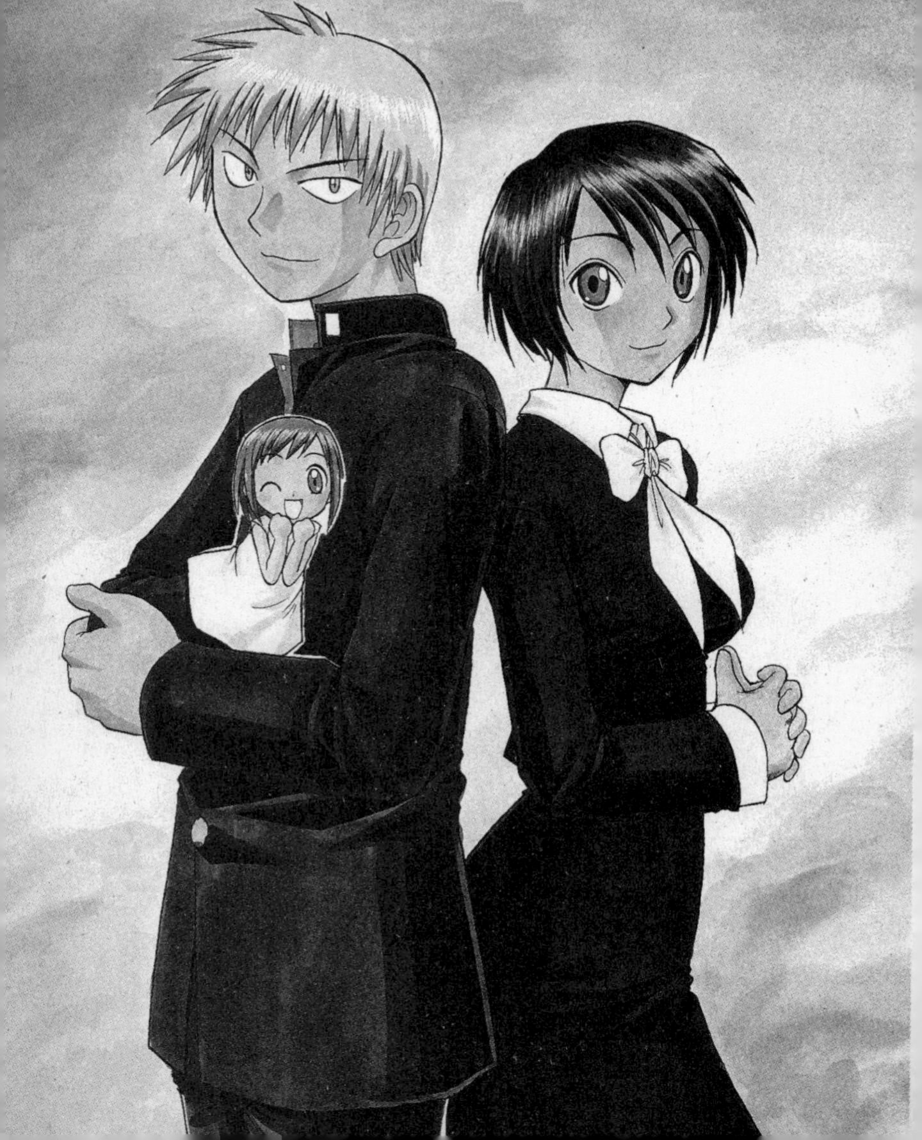

MIDORI DAYS

美鳥の日々

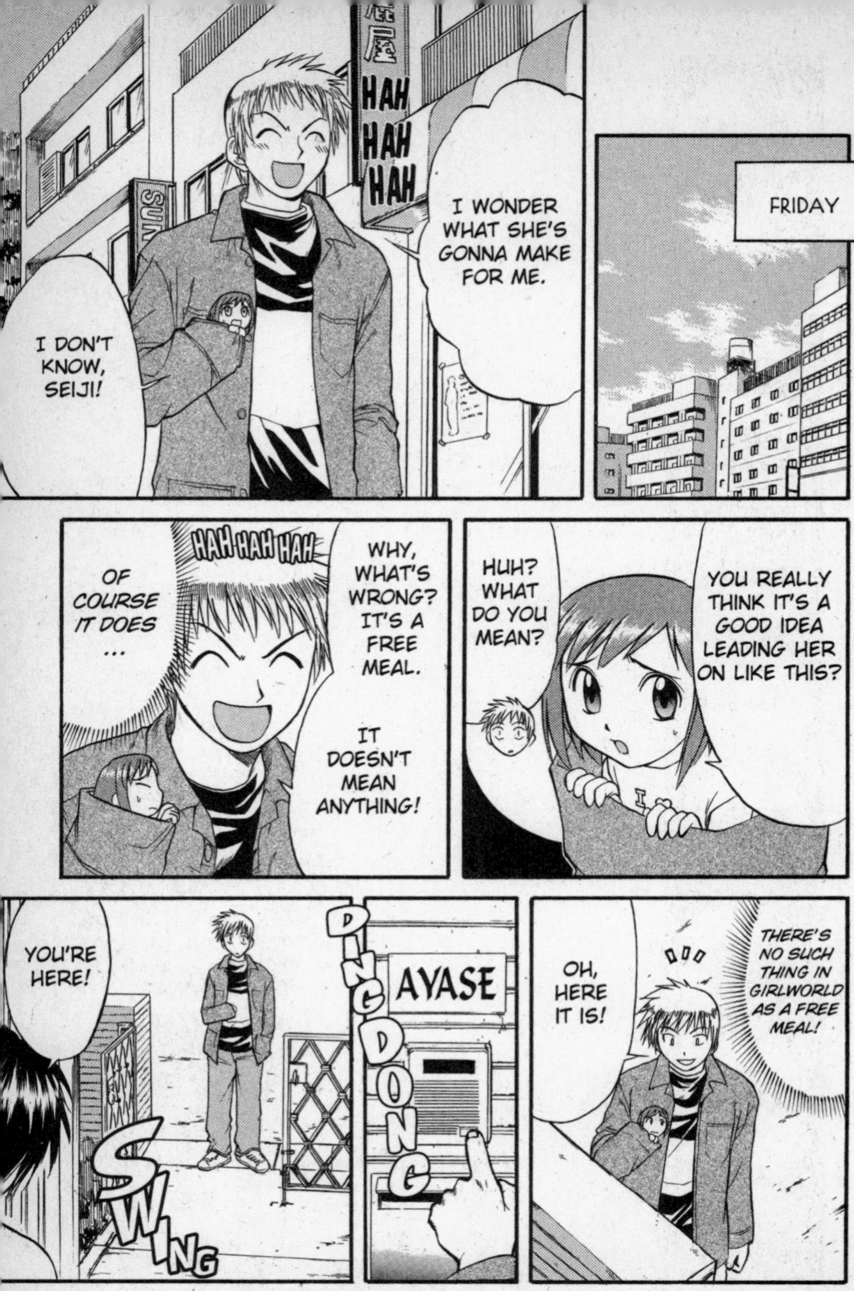
FRIDAY
HAH HAH HAH
I WONDER WHAT SHE'S GONNA MAKE FOR ME.
I DON'T KNOW, SEIJI!
YOU REALLY THINK IT'S A GOOD IDEA LEADING HER ON LIKE THIS?
HUH? WHAT DO YOU MEAN?
WHY, WHAT'S WRONG? IT'S A FREE MEAL.
HAH HAH HAH
IT DOESN'T MEAN ANYTHING!
OF COURSE IT DOES ...
THERE'S NO SUCH THING IN GIRLWORLD AS A FREE MEAL!
OH, HERE IT IS!
AYASE
DING DONG
YOU'RE HERE!
SWING

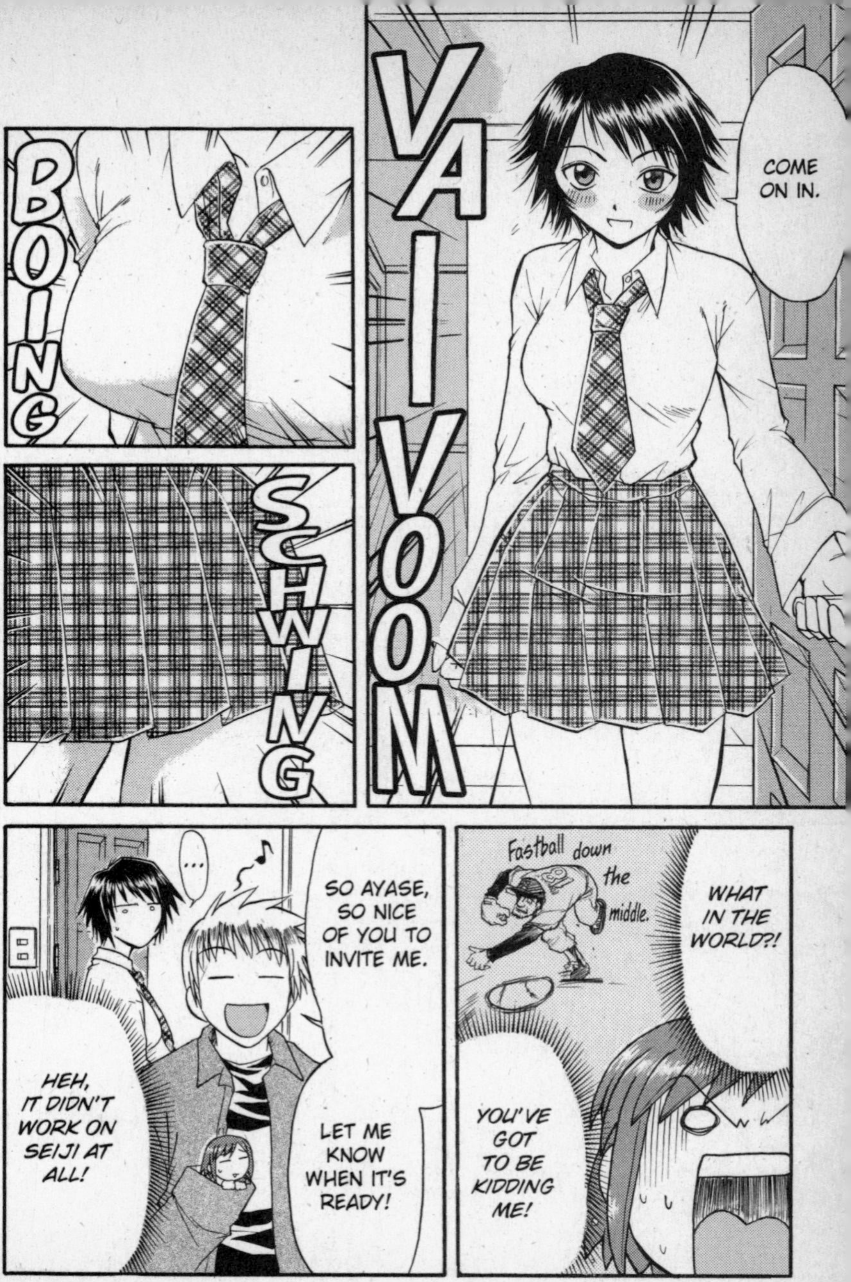
COME ON IN.
VAVOOM
BOING
SCHWING
WHAT IN THE WORLD?!
Fastball down the middle.
YOU'VE GOT TO BE KIDDING ME!
SO AYASE, SO NICE OF YOU TO INVITE ME.
...
LET ME KNOW WHEN IT'S READY!
HEH, IT DIDN'T WORK ON SEIJI AT ALL!

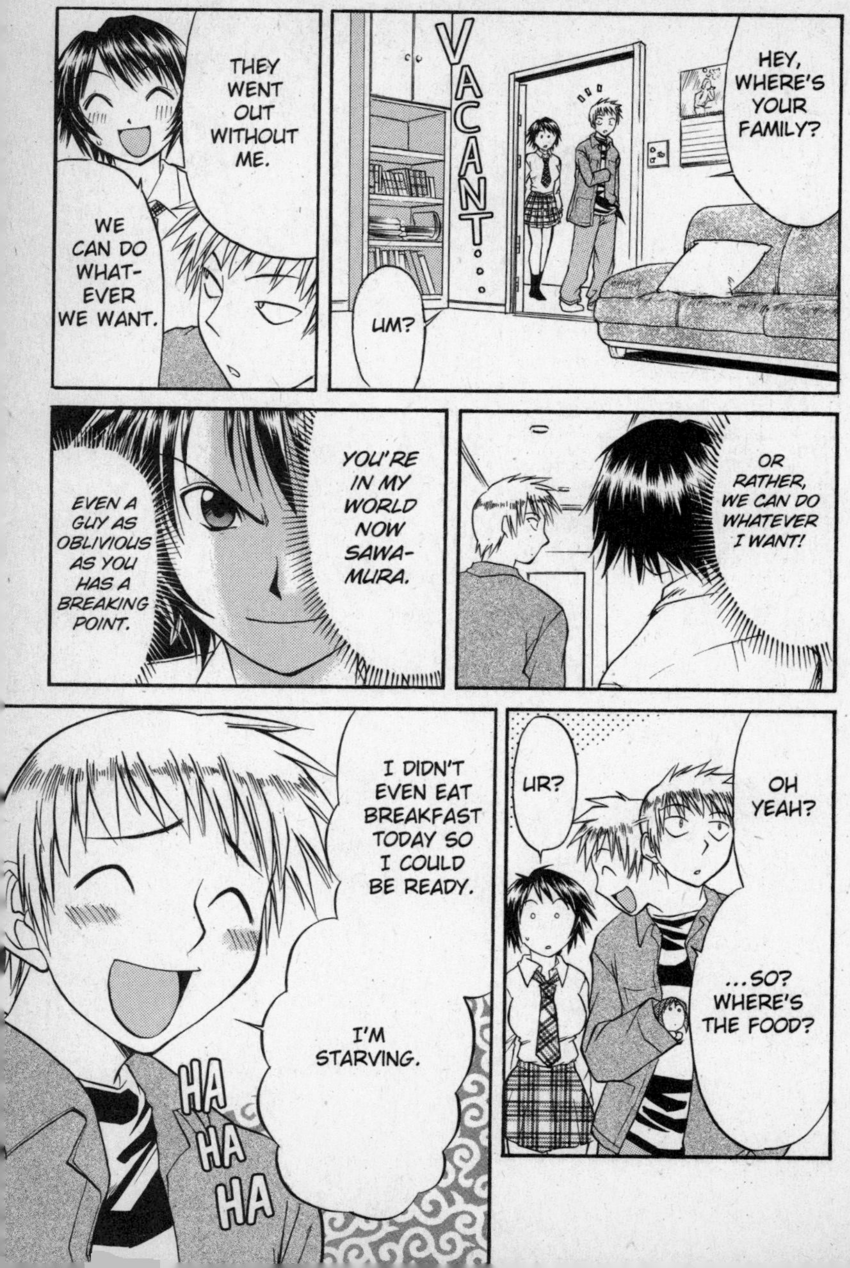
HEY, WHERE'S YOUR FAMILY?
VACANT...
UM?
THEY WENT OUT WITHOUT ME.
WE CAN DO WHAT-EVER WE WANT.
OR RATHER, WE CAN DO WHATEVER I WANT!
YOU'RE IN MY WORLD NOW SAWA-MURA.
EVEN A GUY AS OBLIVIOUS AS YOU HAS A BREAKING POINT.
OH YEAH?
UR?
...SO? WHERE'S THE FOOD?
I DIDN'T EVEN EAT BREAKFAST TODAY SO I COULD BE READY.
I'M STARVING.
HA HA HA

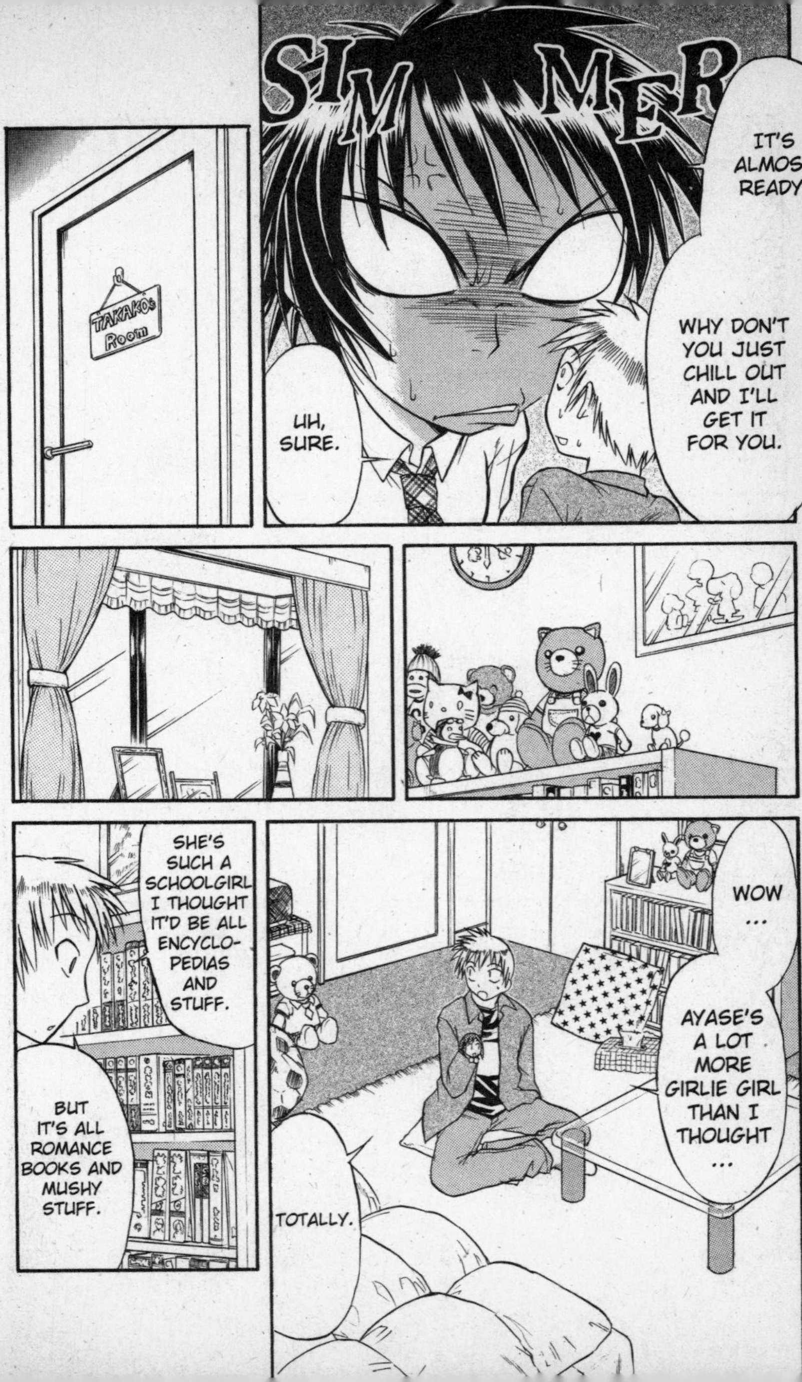
SIMMER
IT'S ALMOST READY.
WHY DON'T YOU JUST CHILL OUT AND I'LL GET IT FOR YOU.
UH, SURE.
TAKAKO's Room
WOW ...
AYASE'S A LOT MORE GIRLIE GIRL THAN I THOUGHT ...
TOTALLY.
SHE'S SUCH A SCHOOLGIRL I THOUGHT IT'D BE ALL ENCYCLO-PEDIAS AND STUFF.
BUT IT'S ALL ROMANCE BOOKS AND MUSHY STUFF.

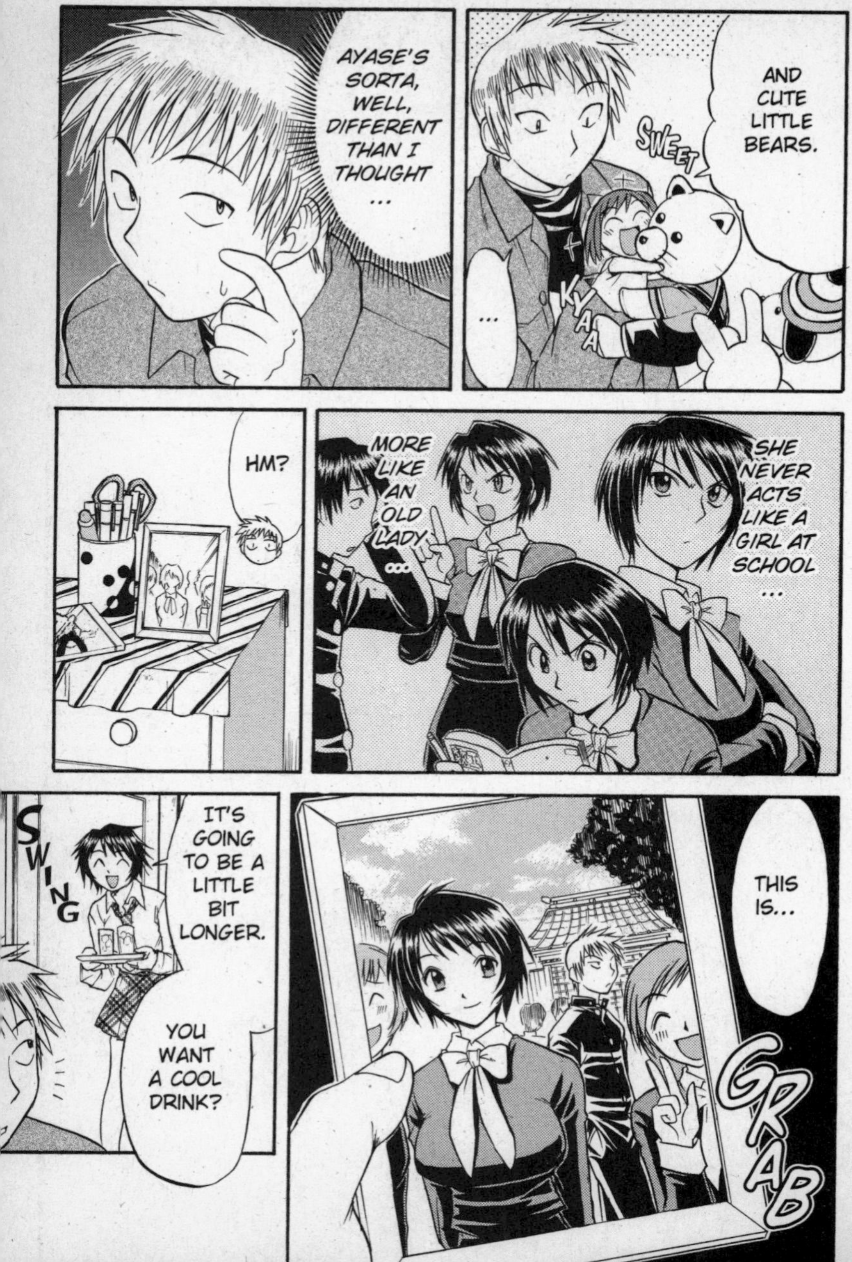
AND CUTE LITTLE BEARS.
SWEET
KYAA
...
AYASE'S SORTA, WELL, DIFFERENT THAN I THOUGHT ...
SHE NEVER ACTS LIKE A GIRL AT SCHOOL ...
MORE LIKE AN OLD LADY
...
HM?
THIS IS...
GRAB
IT'S GOING TO BE A LITTLE BIT LONGER.
SWING
YOU WANT A COOL DRINK?

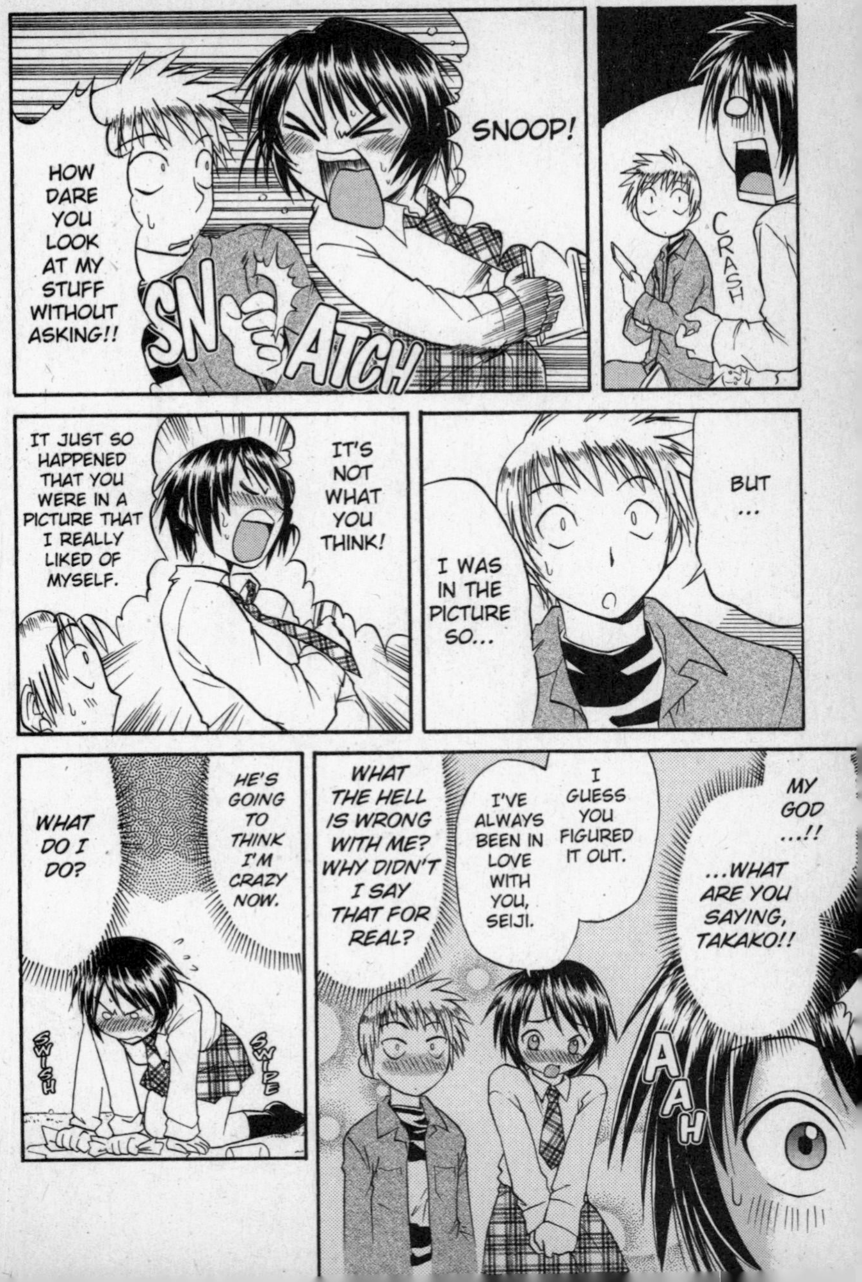
CRASH
SNOOP!
HOW DARE YOU LOOK AT MY STUFF WITHOUT ASKING!!
SNATCH
BUT ...
I WAS IN THE PICTURE SO...
IT'S NOT WHAT YOU THINK!
IT JUST SO HAPPENED THAT YOU WERE IN A PICTURE THAT I REALLY LIKED OF MYSELF.
MY GOD ...!!
...WHAT ARE YOU SAYING, TAKAKO!!
AAAH
I GUESS YOU FIGURED IT OUT.
I'VE ALWAYS BEEN IN LOVE WITH YOU, SEIJI.
WHAT THE HELL IS WRONG WITH ME? WHY DIDN'T I SAY THAT FOR REAL?
HE'S GOING TO THINK I'M CRAZY NOW.
WHAT DO I DO?
SWIPE
SWISH

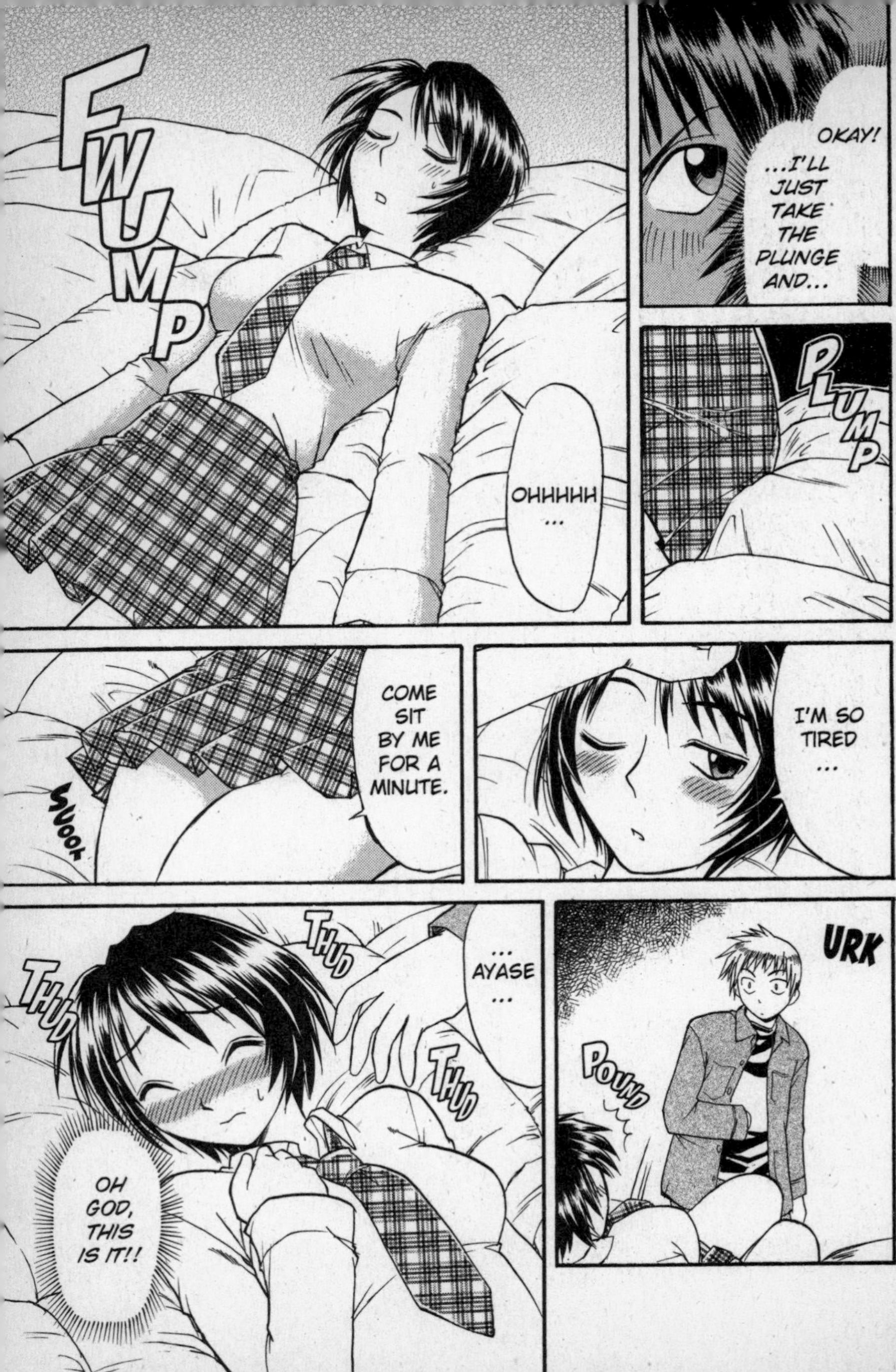
OKAY! ...I'LL JUST TAKE THE PLUNGE AND...
PLUMP
OHHHHH ...
FWUMP
I'M SO TIRED ...
COME SIT BY ME FOR A MINUTE.
SWOOF
URK
POUND
... AYASE ...
THUD
THUD
THUD
OH GOD, THIS IS IT!!

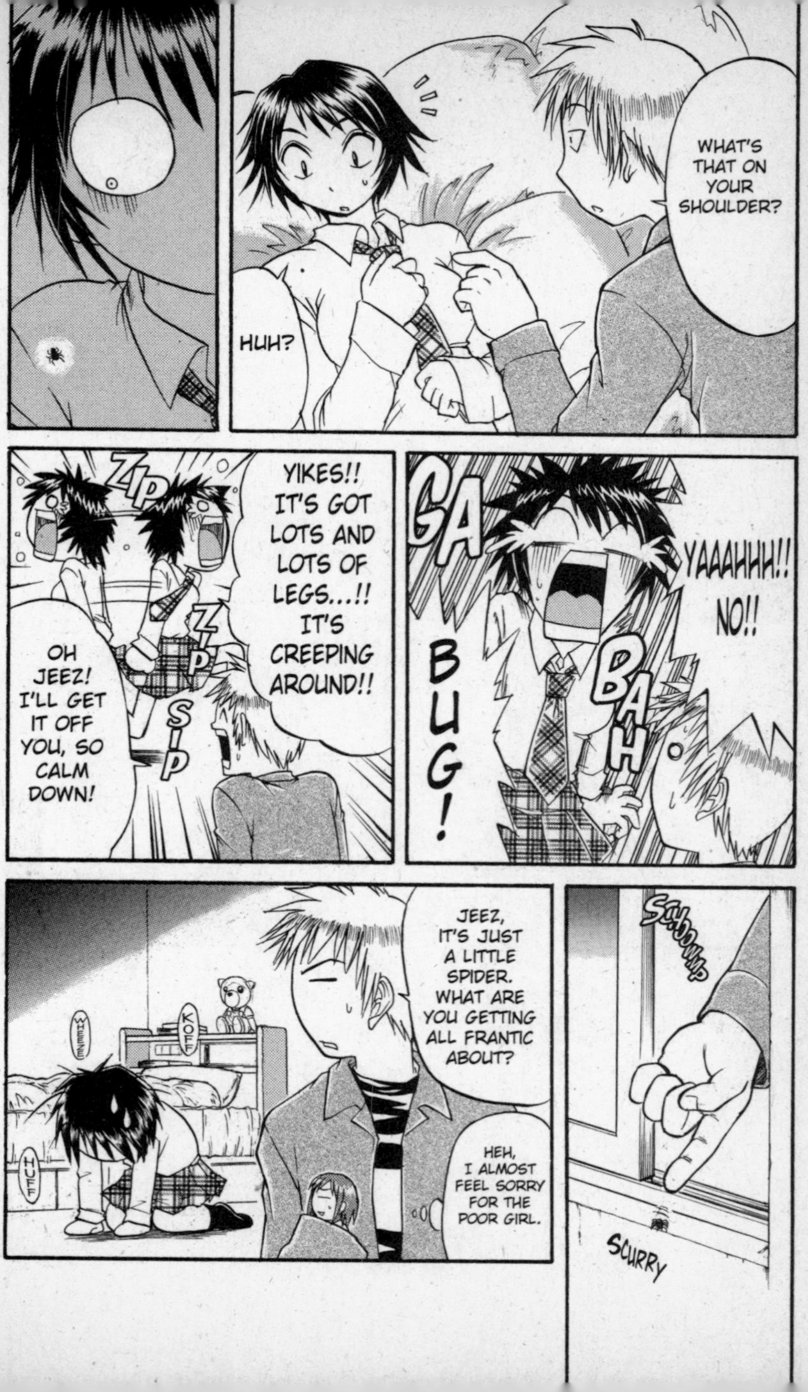
WHAT'S THAT ON YOUR SHOULDER?
HUH?
YAAAHHH!! NO!!
GA
BAH
BUG!
YIKES!! IT'S GOT LOTS AND LOTS OF LEGS...!! IT'S CREEPING AROUND!!
ZIP
ZIP
SIP
OH JEEZ! I'LL GET IT OFF YOU, SO CALM DOWN!
SCHOMP
SCURRY
JEEZ, IT'S JUST A LITTLE SPIDER. WHAT ARE YOU GETTING ALL FRANTIC ABOUT?
KOFF
WHEEE
HEH, I ALMOST FEEL SORRY FOR THE POOR GIRL.
HUFF

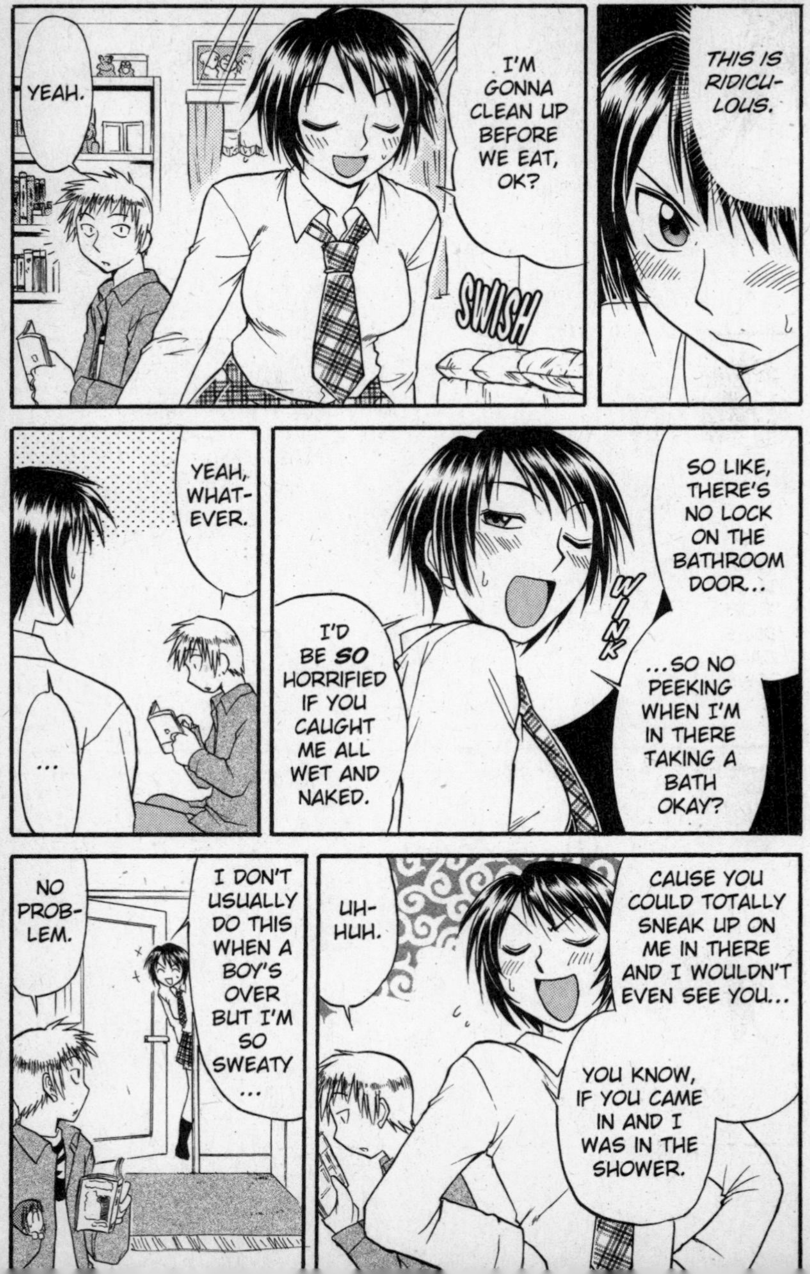
THIS IS RIDICULOUS.
I'M GONNA CLEAN UP BEFORE WE EAT, OK?
SWISH
YEAH.
SO LIKE, THERE'S NO LOCK ON THE BATHROOM DOOR...
WINK
...SO NO PEEKING WHEN I'M IN THERE TAKING A BATH OKAY?
I'D BE **SO** HORRIFIED IF YOU CAUGHT ME ALL WET AND NAKED.
YEAH, WHATEVER.
...
CAUSE YOU COULD TOTALLY SNEAK UP ON ME IN THERE AND I WOULDN'T EVEN SEE YOU...
UH-HUH.
YOU KNOW, IF YOU CAME IN AND I WAS IN THE SHOWER.
I DON'T USUALLY DO THIS WHEN A BOY'S OVER BUT I'M SO SWEATY ...
NO PROBLEM.

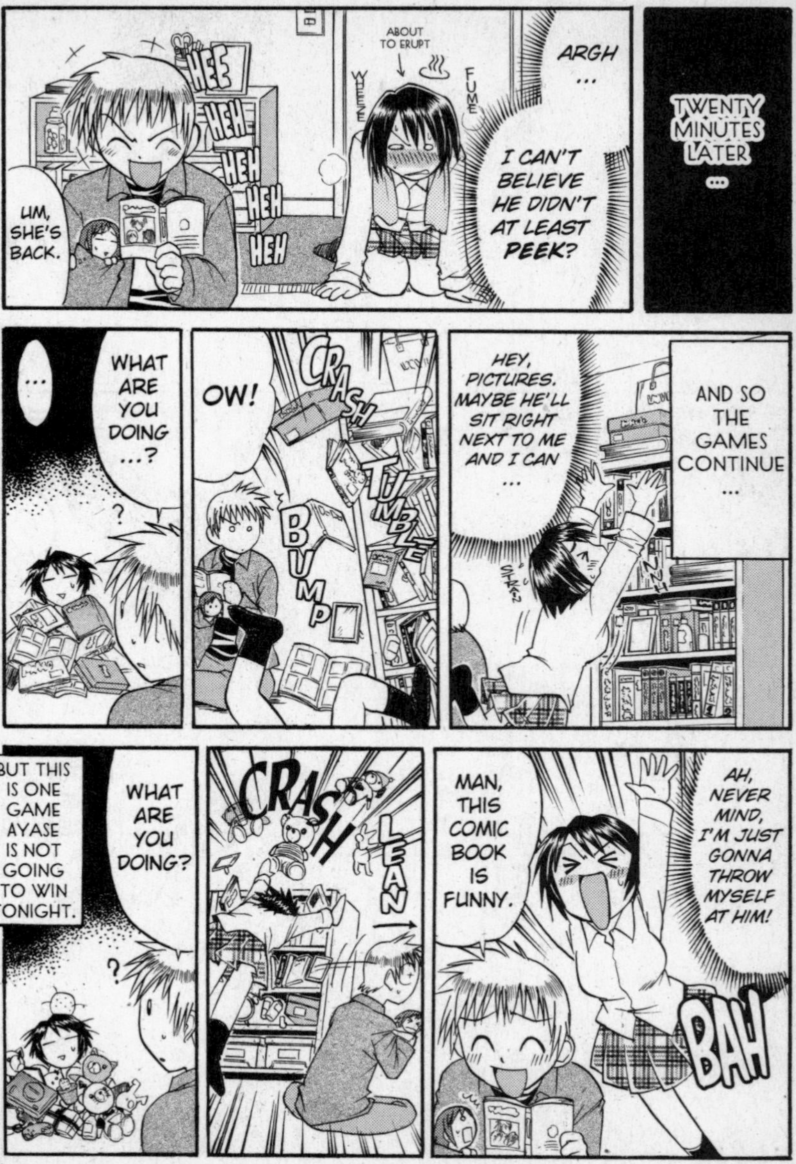
TWENTY MINUTES LATER ...
ARGH ...
I CAN'T BELIEVE HE DIDN'T AT LEAST PEEK?
ABOUT TO ERUPT
FUME
WHEEZE
HEE HEH HEH HEH HEH
UM, SHE'S BACK.
AND SO THE GAMES CONTINUE ...
HEY, PICTURES. MAYBE HE'LL SIT RIGHT NEXT TO ME AND I CAN ...
STRAIN
NNH
CRASH
TUMBLE
BUMP
OW!
WHAT ARE YOU DOING ...?
...
AH, NEVER MIND, I'M JUST GONNA THROW MYSELF AT HIM!
BAH
MAN, THIS COMIC BOOK IS FUNNY.
CRASH
LEAN
WHAT ARE YOU DOING?
BUT THIS IS ONE GAME AYASE IS NOT GOING TO WIN TONIGHT.

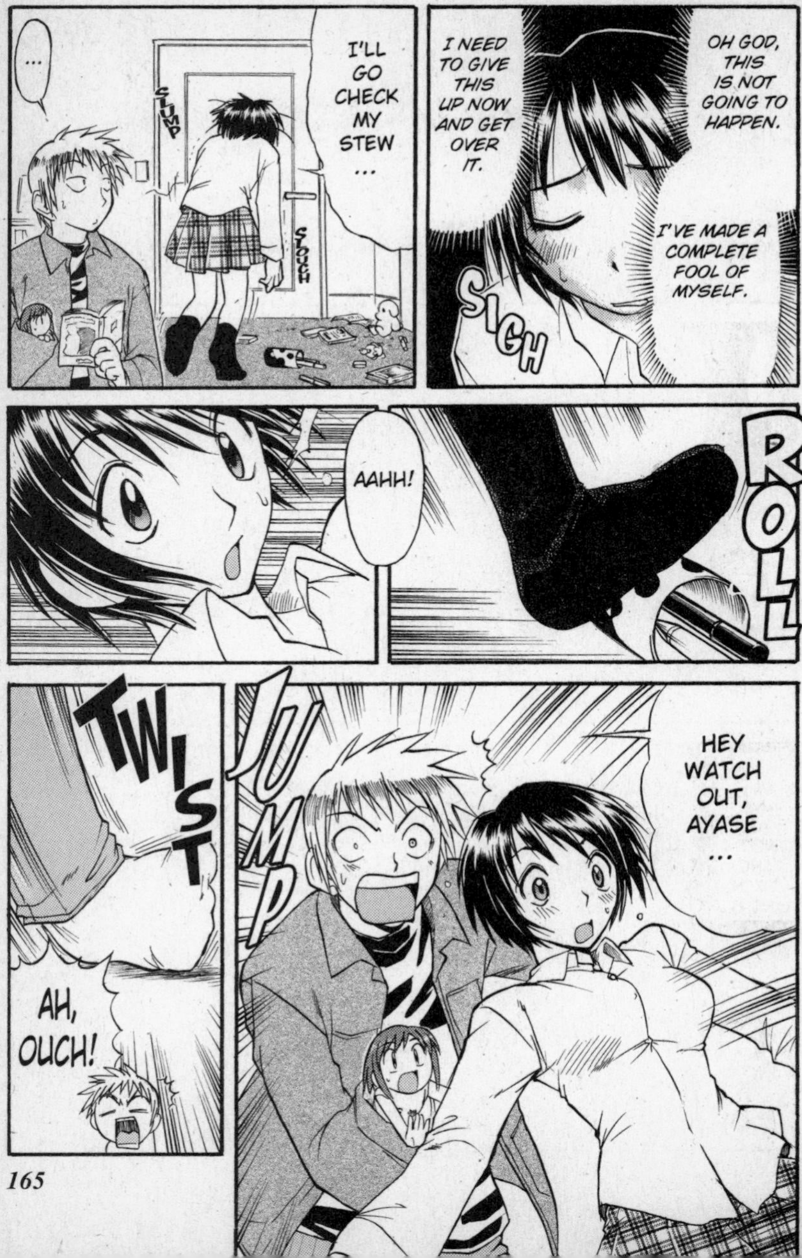
OH GOD, THIS IS NOT GOING TO HAPPEN.
I NEED TO GIVE THIS UP NOW AND GET OVER IT.
I'VE MADE A COMPLETE FOOL OF MYSELF.
SIGH
I'LL GO CHECK MY STEW ...
SLUMP
SLOUCH
...
ROLL
AAHH!
HEY WATCH OUT, AYASE ...
JUMP
TWIST
AH, OUCH!

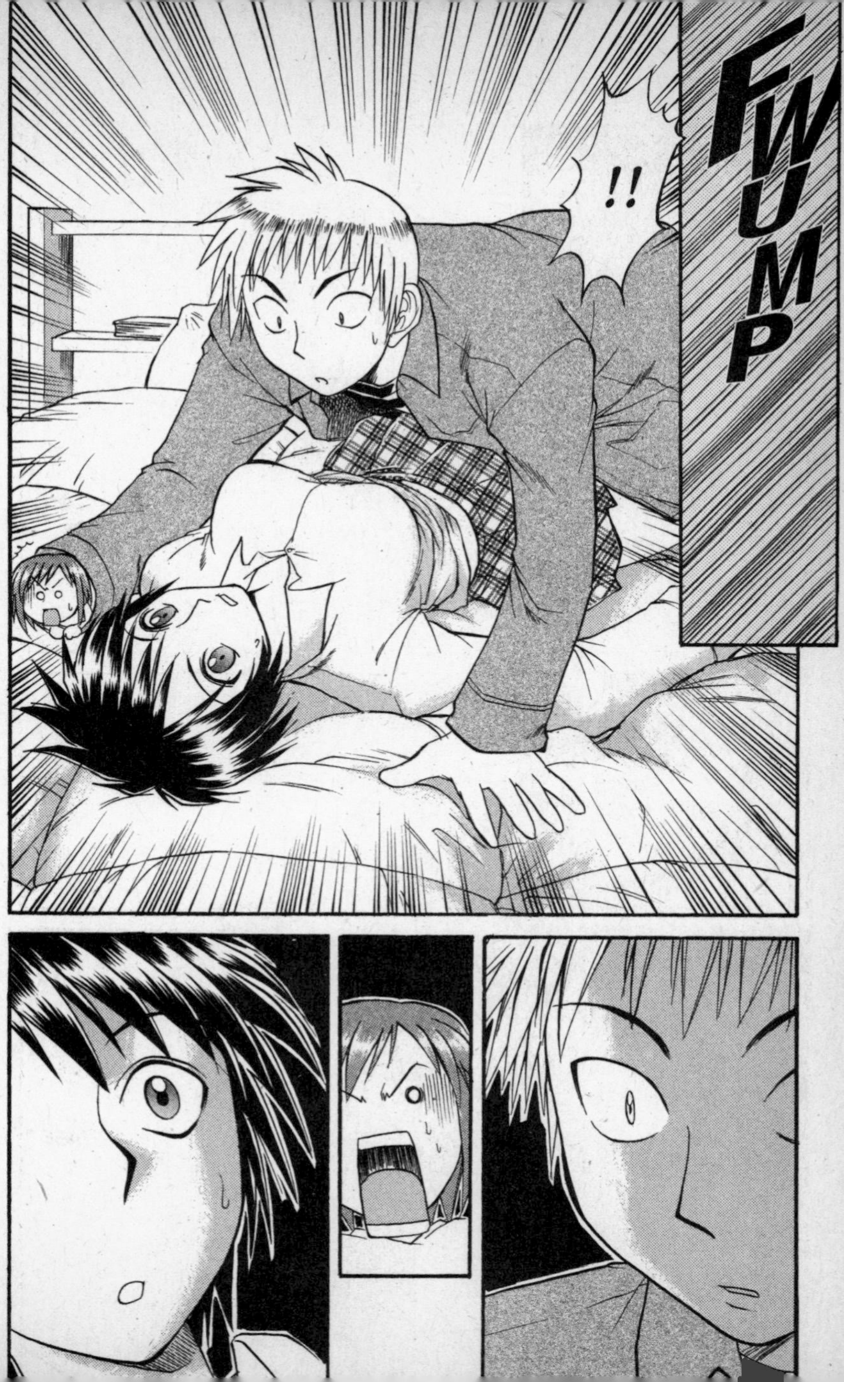
FWUMP
!!

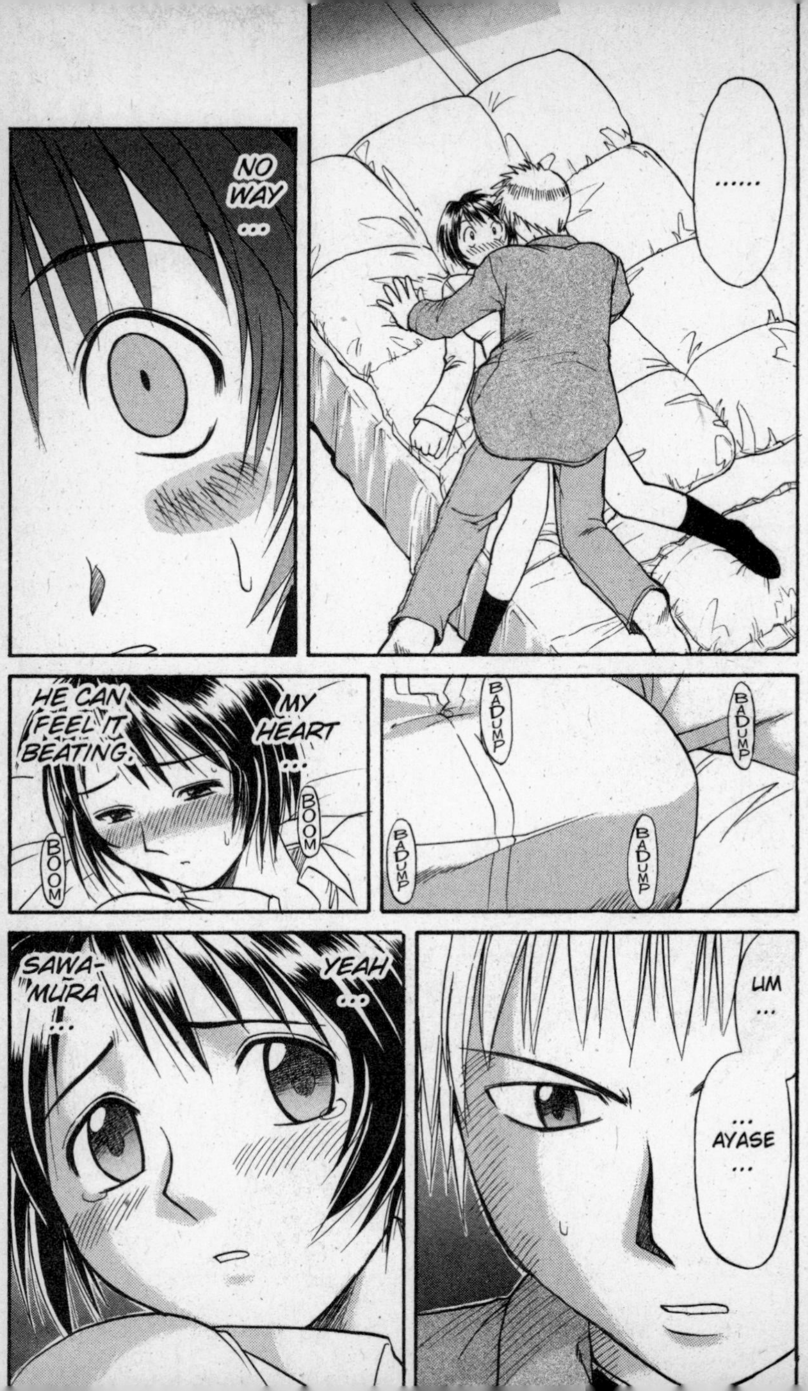
......
NO WAY ...
BADUMP
BADUMP
BADUMP
BADUMP
MY HEART ...
HE CAN FEEL IT BEATING.
BOOM
BOOM
UM ...
... AYASE ...
YEAH ...
SAWAMŪRA ...

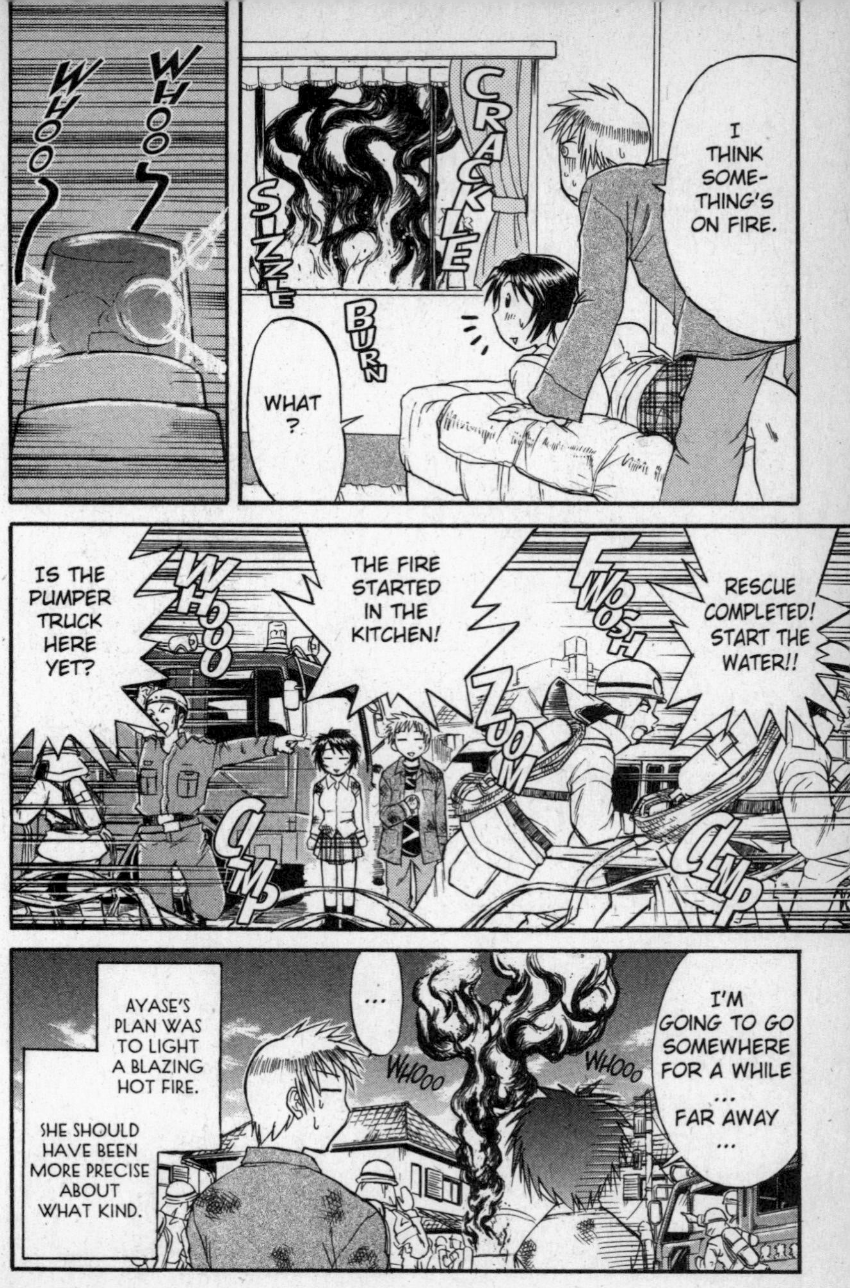
I THINK SOME-THING'S ON FIRE.
CRACKLE
SIZZLE
BURN
WHAT?
WHOOO~
WHOOO~
RESCUE COMPLETED! START THE WATER!!
FWOSH
ZOOM
CLMP
THE FIRE STARTED IN THE KITCHEN!
WHOOO
IS THE PUMPER TRUCK HERE YET?
CLMP
I'M GOING TO GO SOMEWHERE FOR A WHILE ... FAR AWAY ...
WHOOo
...
WHOOo
AYASE'S PLAN WAS TO LIGHT A BLAZING HOT FIRE.
SHE SHOULD HAVE BEEN MORE PRECISE ABOUT WHAT KIND.

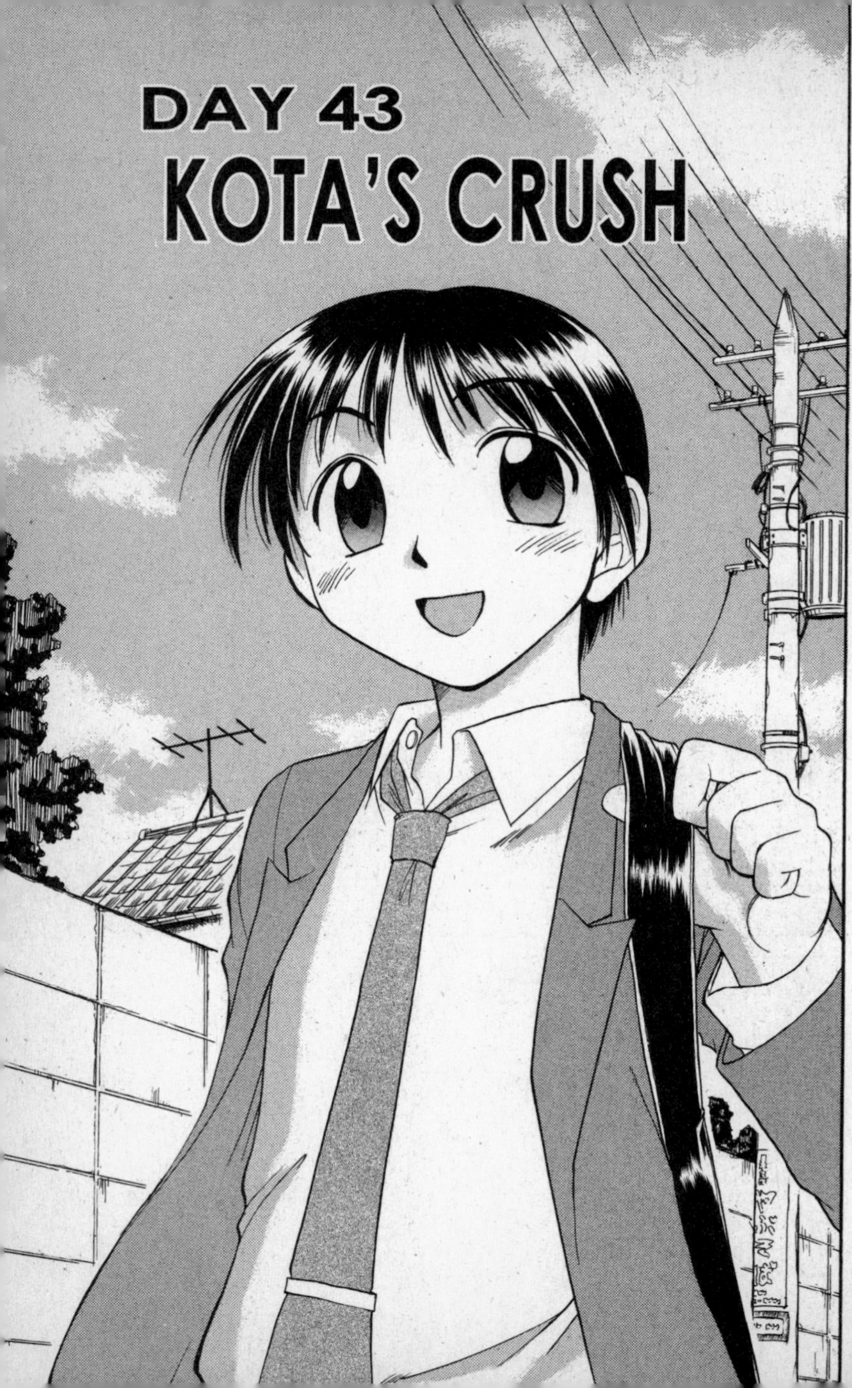
DAY 43
KOTA'S CRUSH

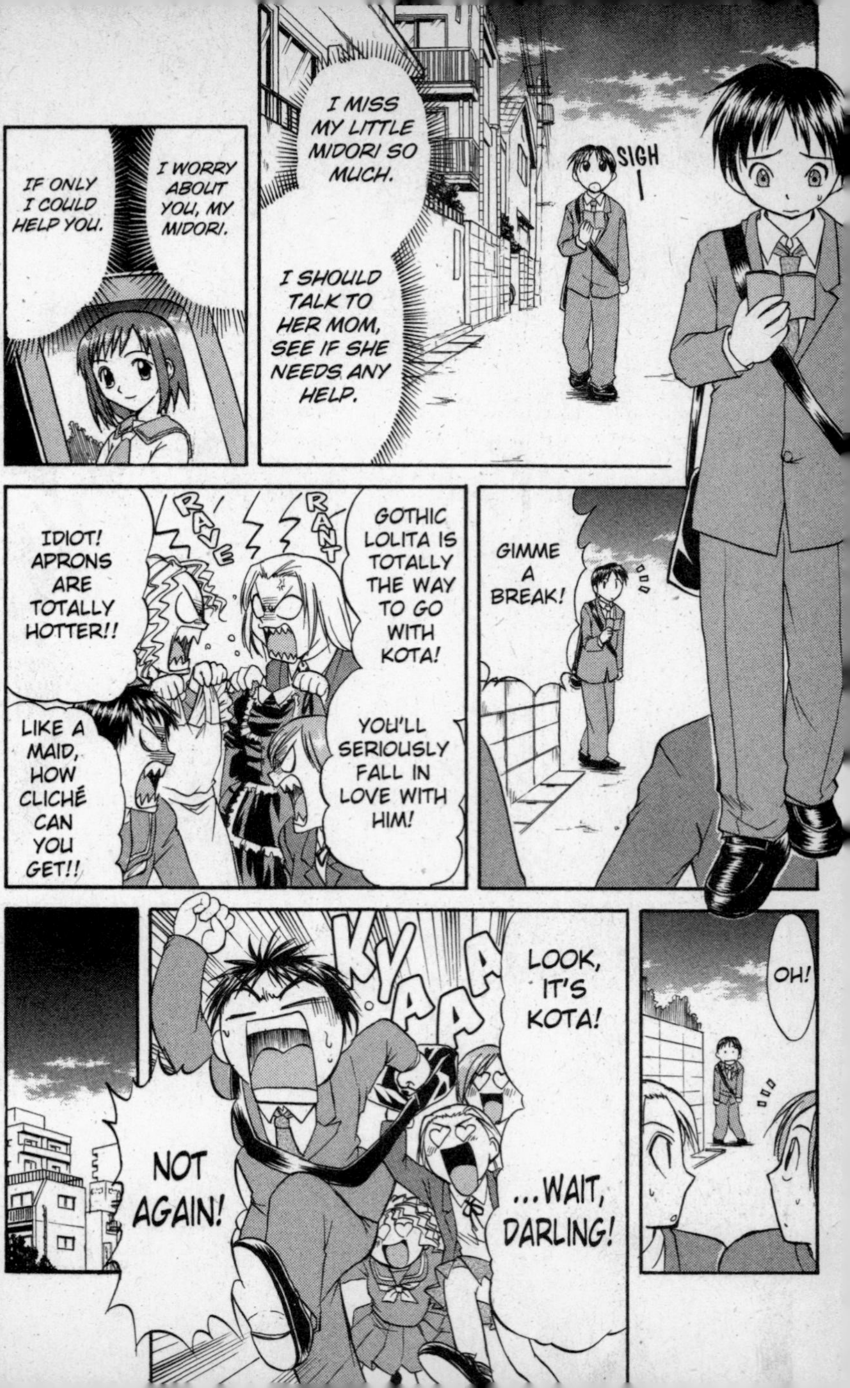
SIGH
I MISS MY LITTLE MIDORI SO MUCH.
I SHOULD TALK TO HER MOM, SEE IF SHE NEEDS ANY HELP.
I WORRY ABOUT YOU, MY MIDORI.
IF ONLY I COULD HELP YOU.
GIMME A BREAK!
RANT
GOTHIC LOLITA IS TOTALLY THE WAY TO GO WITH KOTA!
YOU'LL SERIOUSLY FALL IN LOVE WITH HIM!
RAVE
IDIOT! APRONS ARE TOTALLY HOTTER!!
LIKE A MAID, HOW CLICHÉ CAN YOU GET!!
OH!
LOOK, IT'S KOTA!
KYAAA
...WAIT, DARLING!
NOT AGAIN!

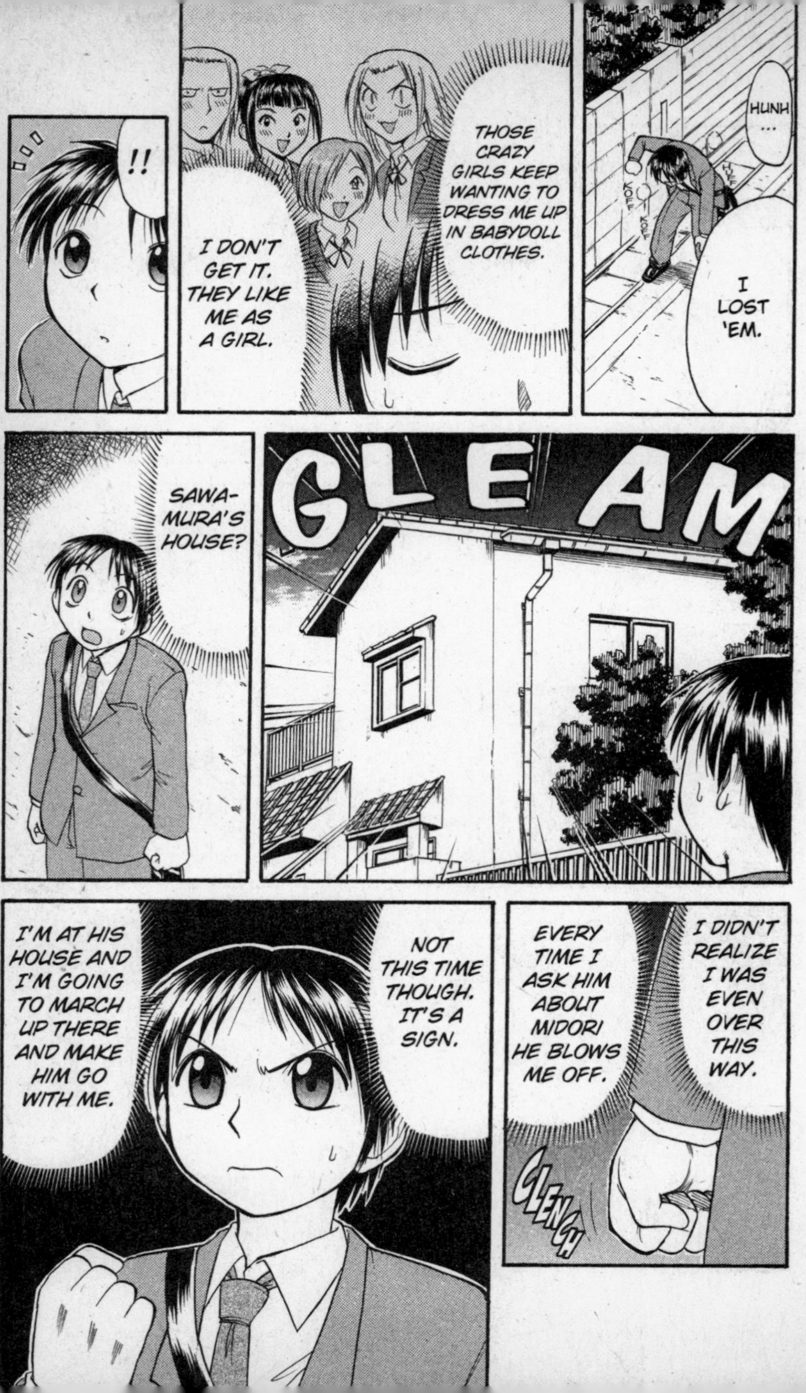
HUNH ...
I LOST 'EM.
THOSE CRAZY GIRLS KEEP WANTING TO DRESS ME UP IN BABYDOLL CLOTHES.
I DON'T GET IT. THEY LIKE ME AS A GIRL.
!!
GLEAM
SAWA-MURA'S HOUSE?
I DIDN'T REALIZE I WAS EVEN OVER THIS WAY.
EVERY TIME I ASK HIM ABOUT MIDORI HE BLOWS ME OFF.
CLENCH
NOT THIS TIME THOUGH. IT'S A SIGN.
I'M AT HIS HOUSE AND I'M GOING TO MARCH UP THERE AND MAKE HIM GO WITH ME.

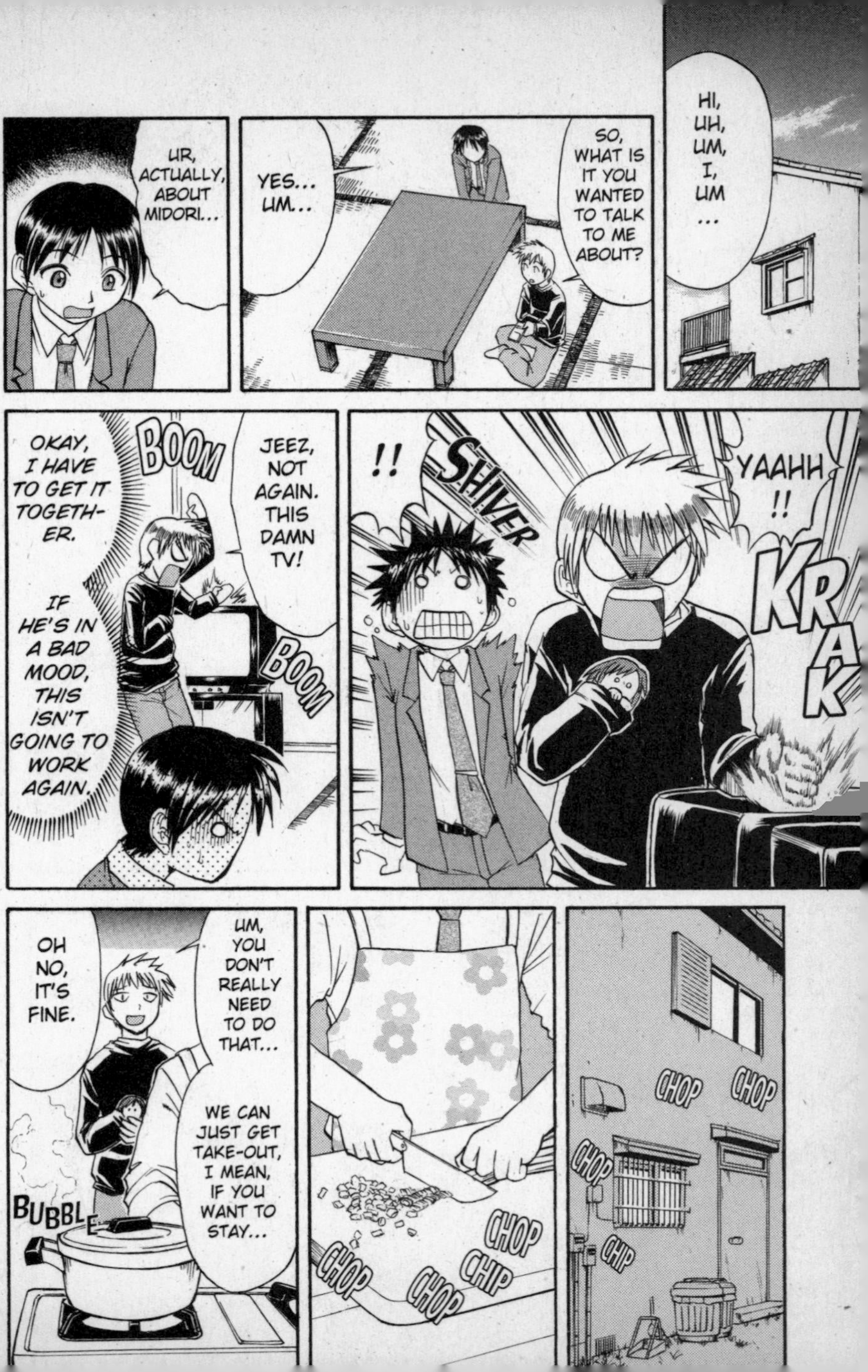
HI, UH, UM, I, UM ...
SO, WHAT IS IT YOU WANTED TO TALK TO ME ABOUT?
YES... UM...
UR, ACTUALLY, ABOUT MIDORI...
YAAHH!!
KRAK
SHIVER
!!
JEEZ, NOT AGAIN. THIS DAMN TV!
BOOM
BOOM
OKAY, I HAVE TO GET IT TOGETHER.
IF HE'S IN A BAD MOOD, THIS ISN'T GOING TO WORK AGAIN.
CHOP
CHOP
CHOP
CHIP
CHOP
CHIP
CHOP
CHOP
UM, YOU DON'T REALLY NEED TO DO THAT...
WE CAN JUST GET TAKE-OUT, I MEAN, IF YOU WANT TO STAY...
OH NO, IT'S FINE.
BUBBLE

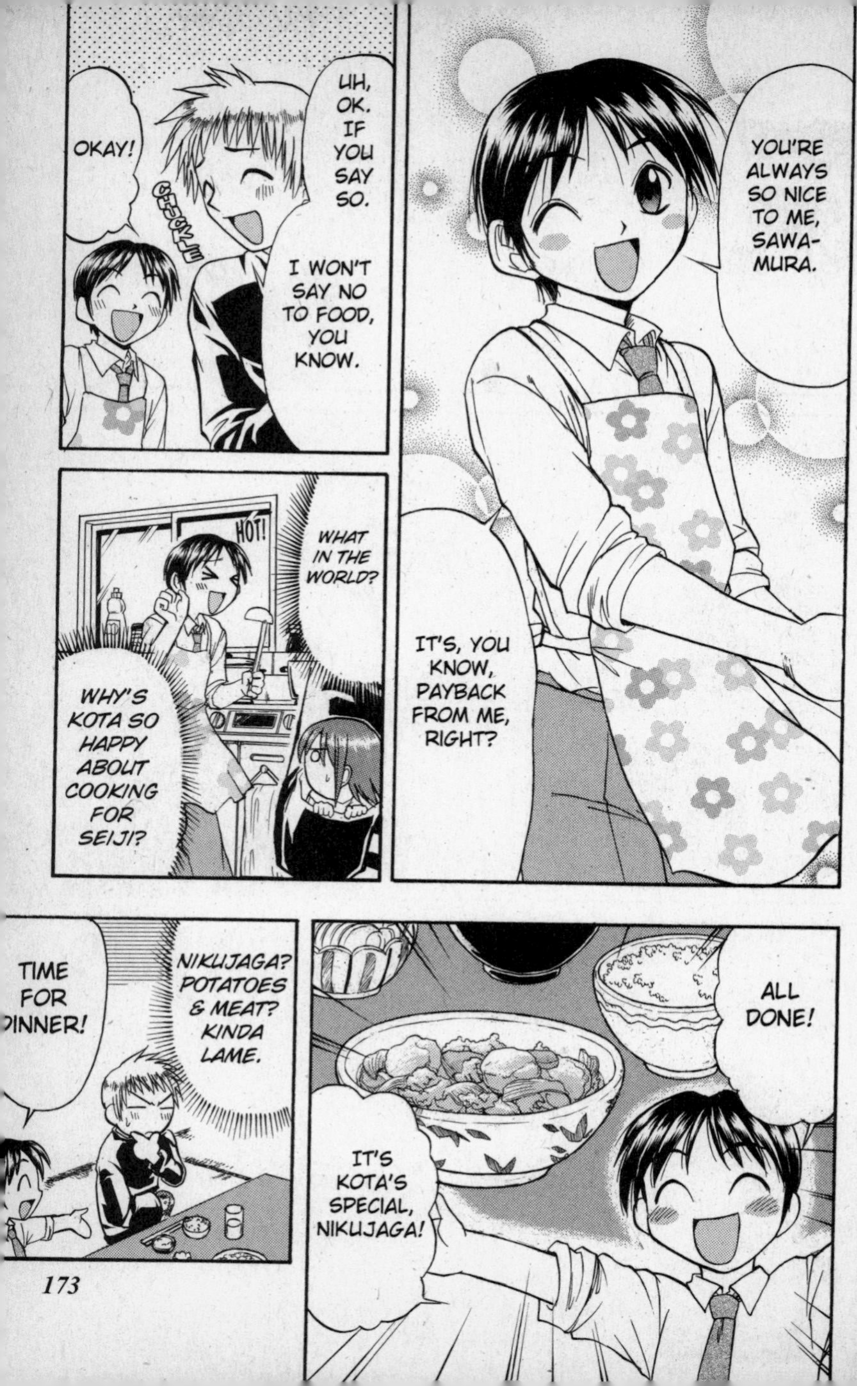
YOU'RE ALWAYS SO NICE TO ME, SAWAMURA.
IT'S, YOU KNOW, PAYBACK FROM ME, RIGHT?
UH, OK. IF YOU SAY SO.
I WON'T SAY NO TO FOOD, YOU KNOW.
CHUCKLE
OKAY!
WHAT IN THE WORLD?
HOT!
WHY'S KOTA SO HAPPY ABOUT COOKING FOR SEIJI?
ALL DONE!
IT'S KOTA'S SPECIAL, NIKUJAGA!
NIKUJAGA? POTATOES & MEAT? KINDA LAME.
TIME FOR DINNER!

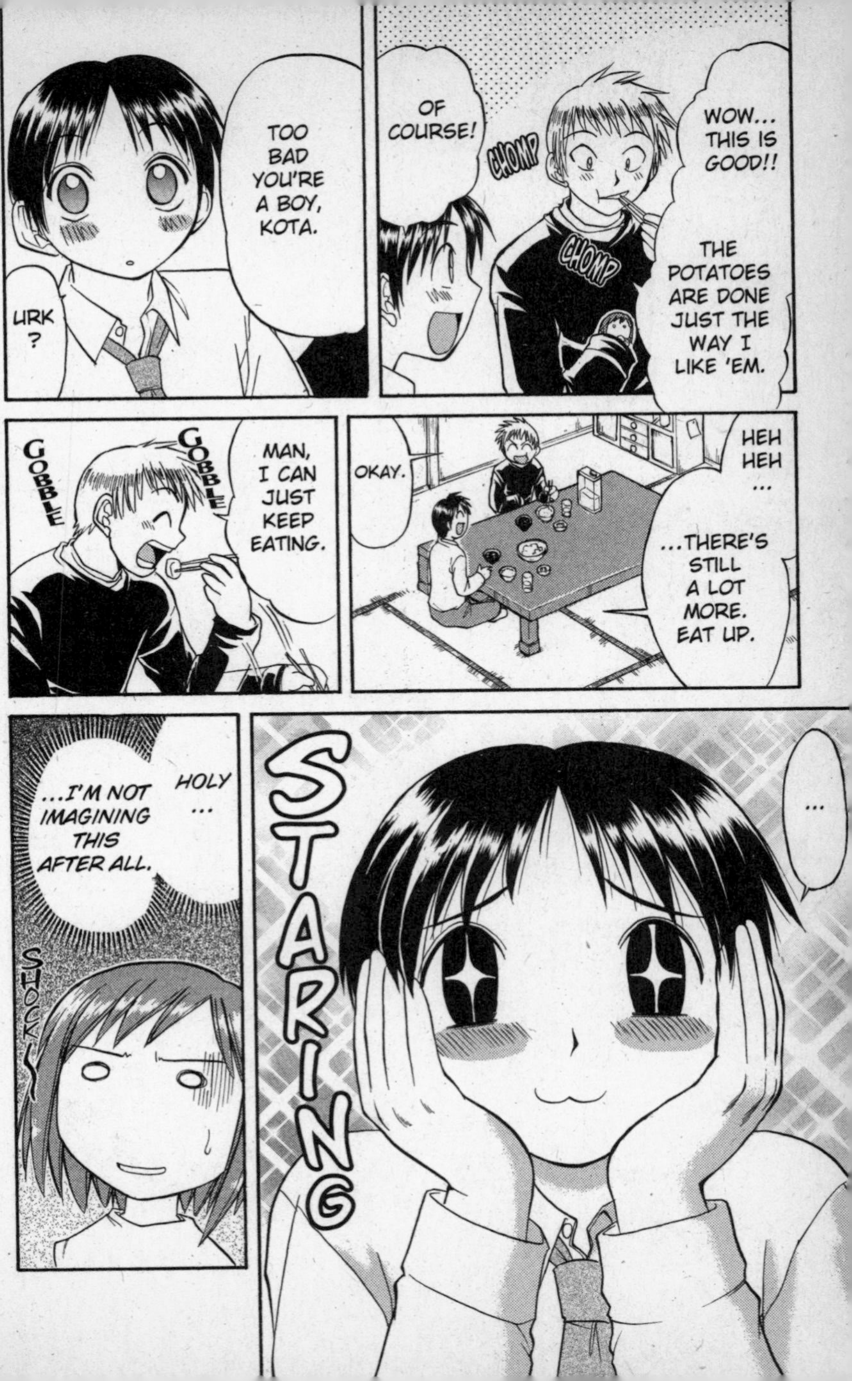
WOW... THIS IS GOOD!!
CHOMP
CHOMP
THE POTATOES ARE DONE JUST THE WAY I LIKE 'EM.
OF COURSE!
TOO BAD YOU'RE A BOY, KOTA.
URK ?
HEH HEH ...
...THERE'S STILL A LOT MORE. EAT UP.
OKAY.
MAN, I CAN JUST KEEP EATING.
GOBBLE
GOBBLE
...
STARING
HOLY ...
...I'M NOT IMAGINING THIS AFTER ALL.
SHOCK

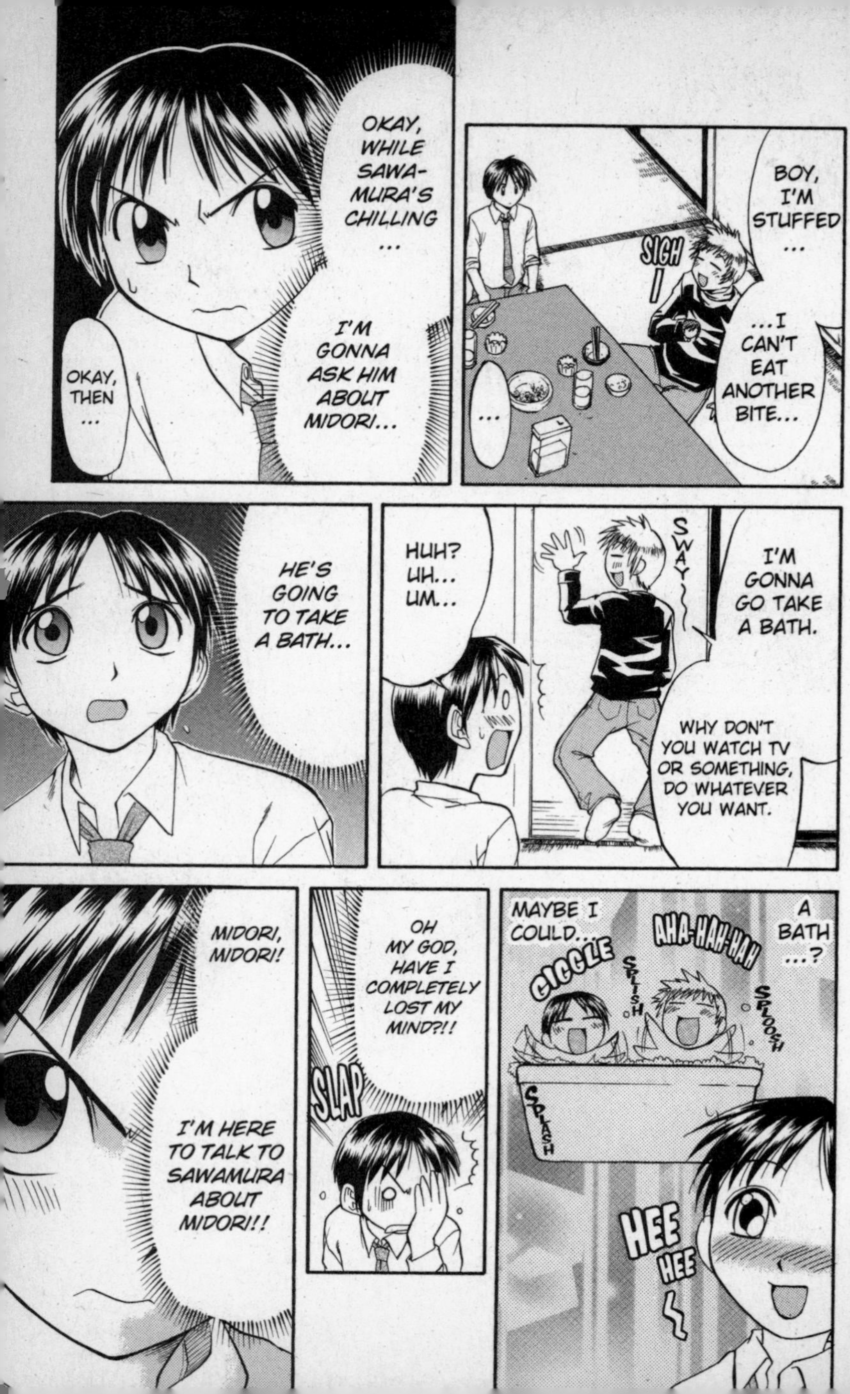
BOY, I'M STUFFED...
SIGH
...I CAN'T EAT ANOTHER BITE...
...
OKAY, WHILE SAWA-MURA'S CHILLING...
I'M GONNA ASK HIM ABOUT MIDORI...
OKAY, THEN...
I'M GONNA GO TAKE A BATH.
SWAY
WHY DON'T YOU WATCH TV OR SOMETHING, DO WHATEVER YOU WANT.
HUH? UH... UM...
HE'S GOING TO TAKE A BATH...
A BATH...?
AHA-HAH-HAH
MAYBE I COULD...
GIGGLE
SPLISH
SPLOOSH
SPLASH
HEE HEE
OH MY GOD, HAVE I COMPLETELY LOST MY MIND?!!
SLAP
MIDORI, MIDORI!
I'M HERE TO TALK TO SAWAMURA ABOUT MIDORI!!

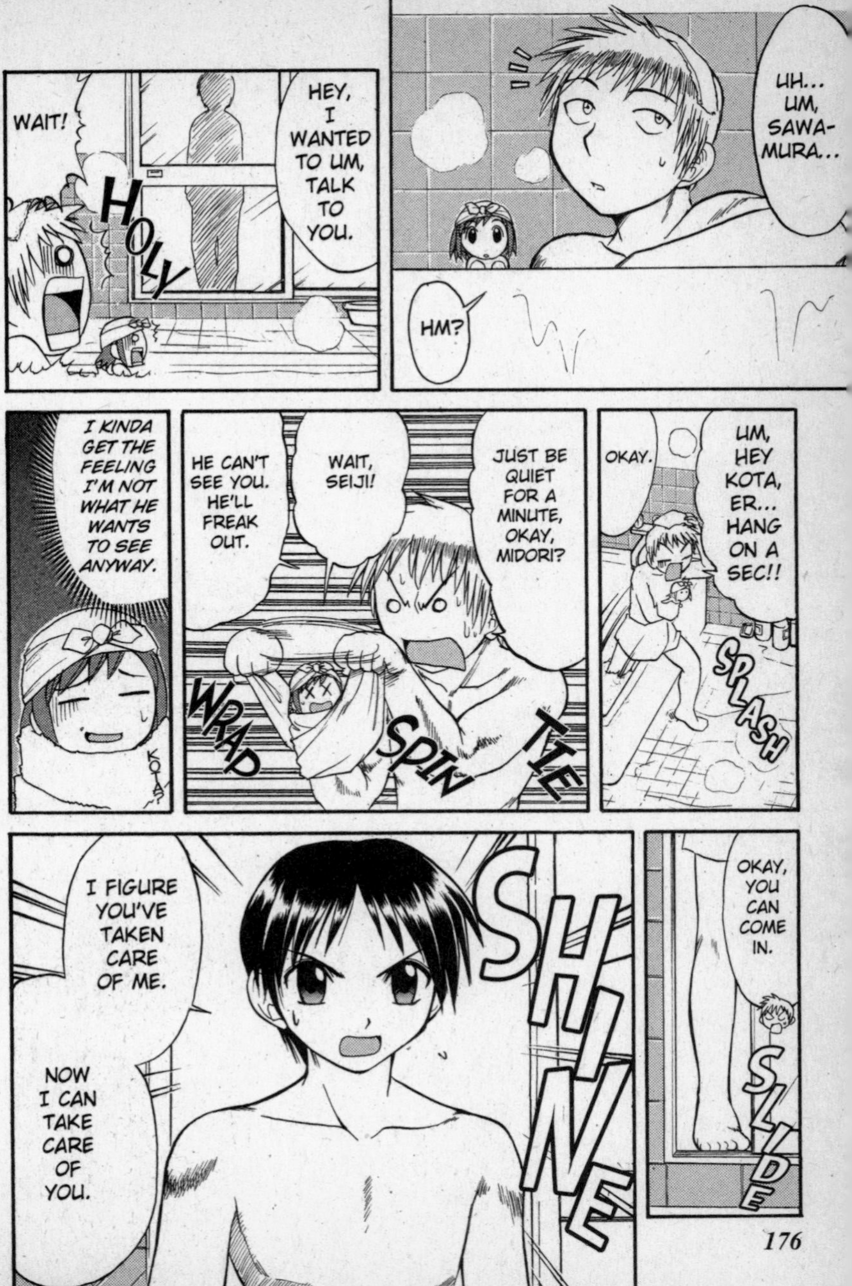
UH... UM, SAWAMURA...
HM?
HEY, I WANTED TO UM, TALK TO YOU.
WAIT!
HOLY
UM, HEY KOTA, ER... HANG ON A SEC!!
OKAY.
SPLASH
JUST BE QUIET FOR A MINUTE, OKAY, MIDORI?
WAIT, SEIJI!
HE CAN'T SEE YOU. HE'LL FREAK OUT.
TIE
SPIN
WRAP
I KINDA GET THE FEELING I'M NOT WHAT HE WANTS TO SEE ANYWAY.
KOTA!
OKAY, YOU CAN COME IN.
SLIDE
SHINE
I FIGURE YOU'VE TAKEN CARE OF ME.
NOW I CAN TAKE CARE OF YOU.

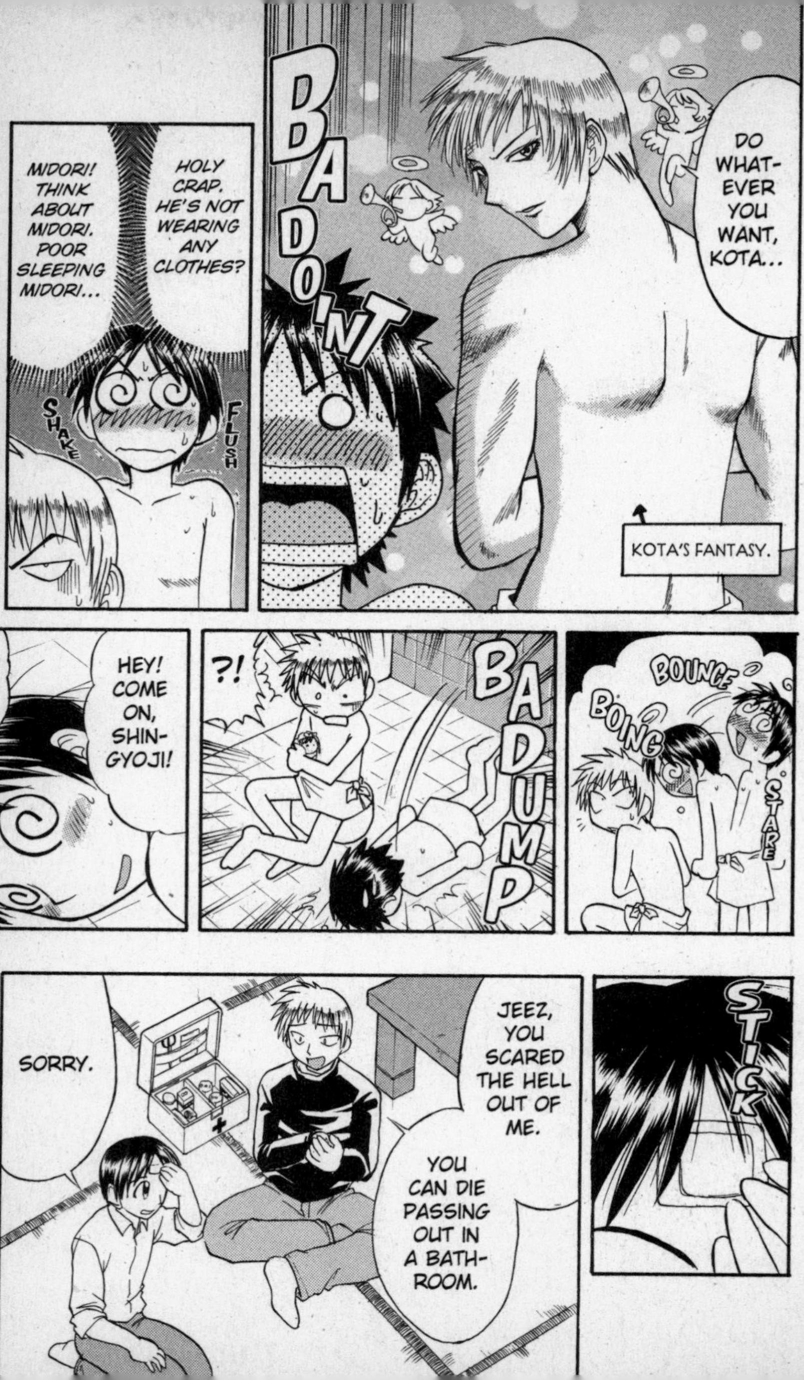
DO WHATEVER YOU WANT, KOTA...
BADOINT
KOTA'S FANTASY.
HOLY CRAP. HE'S NOT WEARING ANY CLOTHES?
MIDORI! THINK ABOUT MIDORI. POOR SLEEPING MIDORI...
FLUSH
SHAKE
BOUNCE
BOING
STARE
BADUMP
?!
HEY! COME ON, SHIN-GYOJI!
GET UP!
STICK
JEEZ, YOU SCARED THE HELL OUT OF ME.
YOU CAN DIE PASSING OUT IN A BATHROOM.
SORRY.

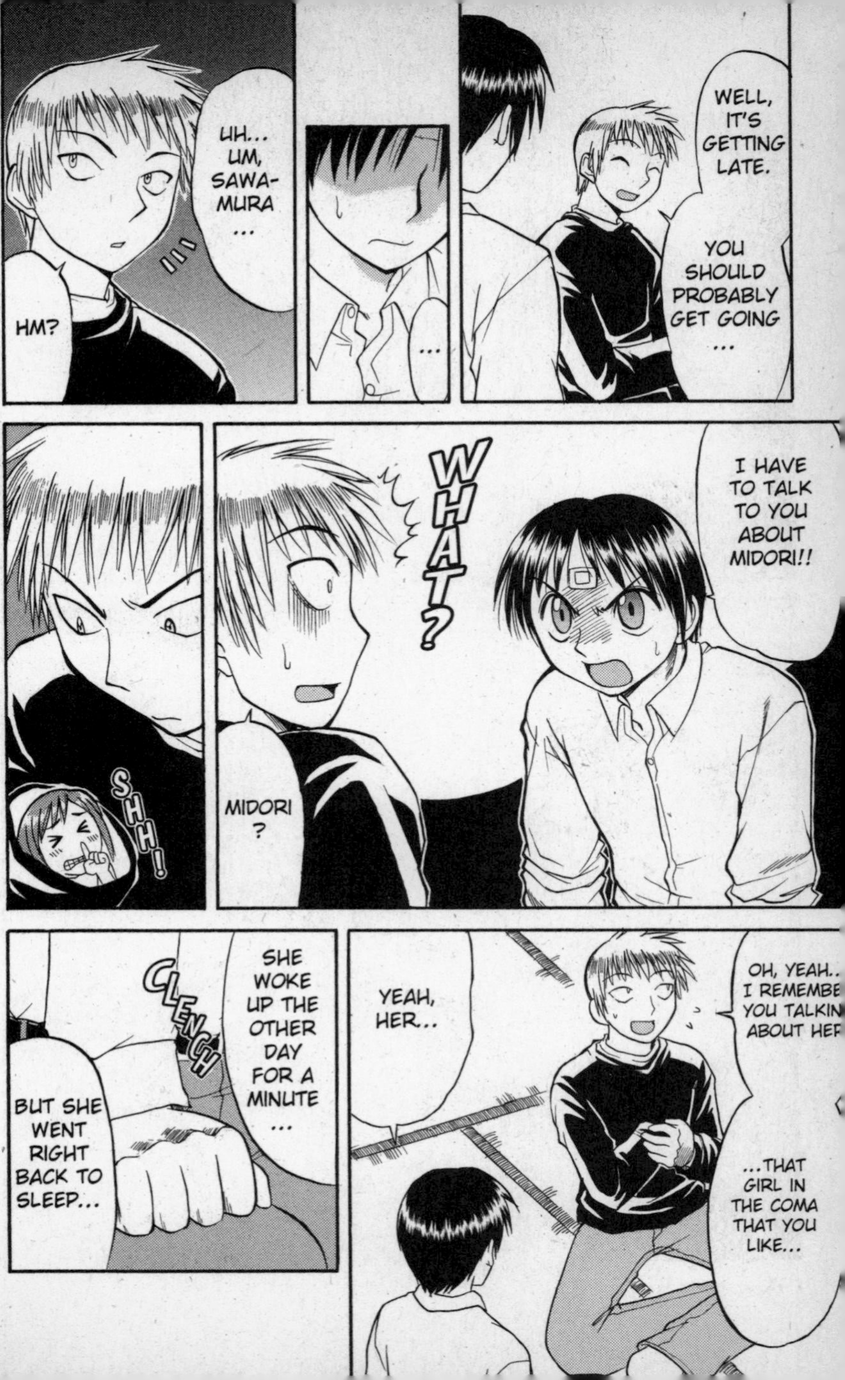
WELL, IT'S GETTING LATE.
YOU SHOULD PROBABLY GET GOING...
...
UH... UM, SAWAMURA...
HM?
I HAVE TO TALK TO YOU ABOUT MIDORI!!
WHAT?
MIDORI?
SHHH!
OH, YEAH.. I REMEMBE YOU TALKIN ABOUT HEF
...THAT GIRL IN THE COMA THAT YOU LIKE...
YEAH, HER...
SHE WOKE UP THE OTHER DAY FOR A MINUTE...
CLENCH
BUT SHE WENT RIGHT BACK TO SLEEP...

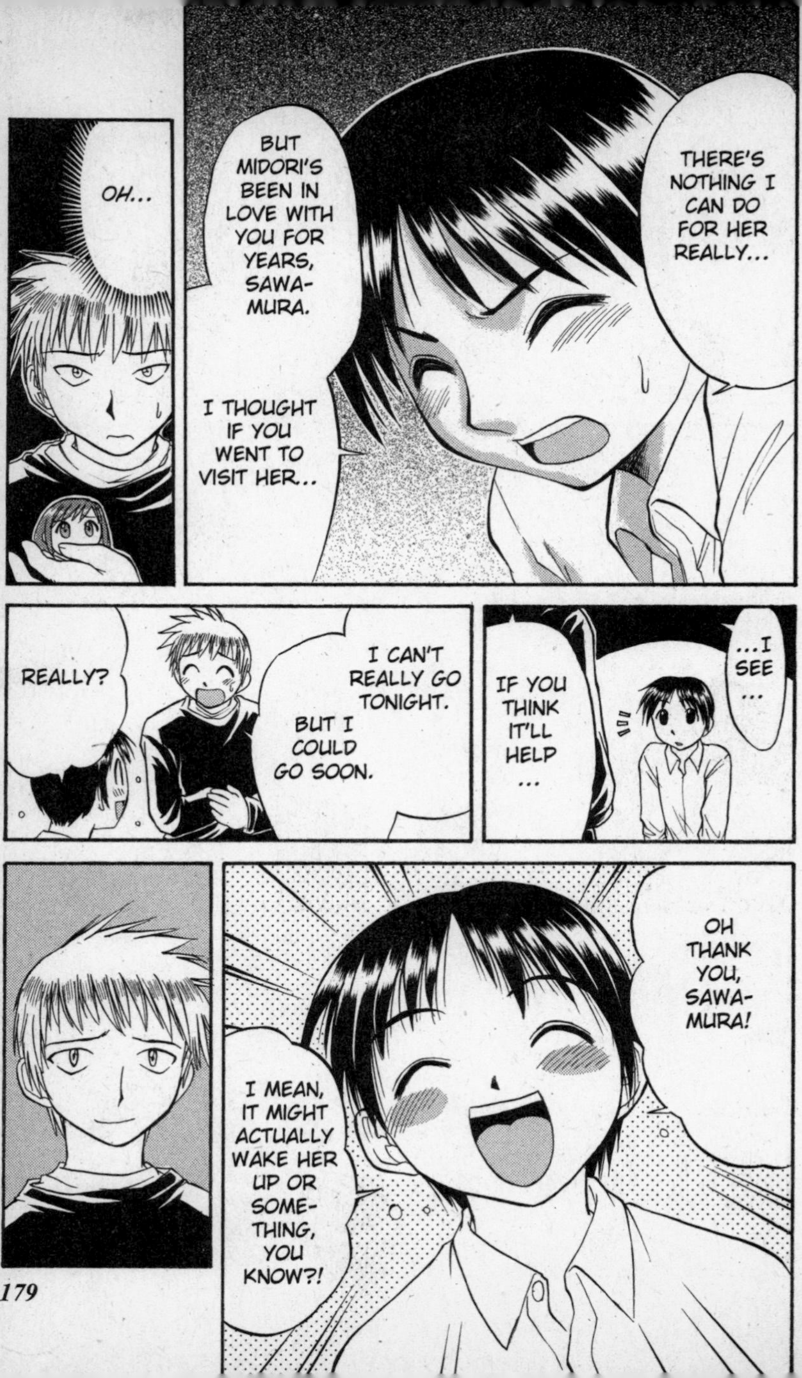
THERE'S NOTHING I CAN DO FOR HER REALLY...
BUT MIDORI'S BEEN IN LOVE WITH YOU FOR YEARS, SAWAMURA.
I THOUGHT IF YOU WENT TO VISIT HER...
OH...
...I SEE...
IF YOU THINK IT'LL HELP...
I CAN'T REALLY GO TONIGHT.
BUT I COULD GO SOON.
REALLY?
OH THANK YOU, SAWAMURA!
I MEAN, IT MIGHT ACTUALLY WAKE HER UP OR SOMETHING, YOU KNOW?!

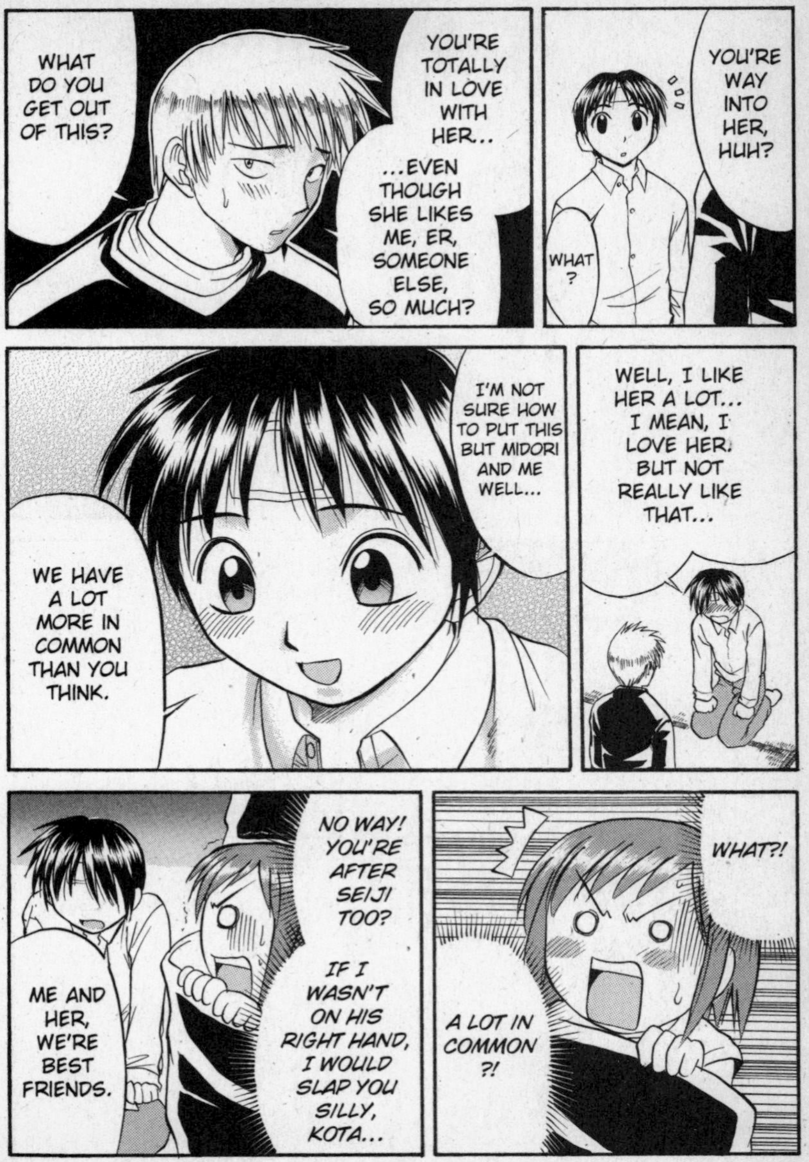
YOU'RE WAY INTO HER, HUH?
WHAT?
YOU'RE TOTALLY IN LOVE WITH HER...
...EVEN THOUGH SHE LIKES ME, ER, SOMEONE ELSE, SO MUCH?
WHAT DO YOU GET OUT OF THIS?
WELL, I LIKE HER A LOT... I MEAN, I LOVE HER. BUT NOT REALLY LIKE THAT...
I'M NOT SURE HOW TO PUT THIS BUT MIDORI AND ME WELL...
WE HAVE A LOT MORE IN COMMON THAN YOU THINK.
WHAT?!
A LOT IN COMMON?!
NO WAY! YOU'RE AFTER SEIJI TOO?
IF I WASN'T ON HIS RIGHT HAND, I WOULD SLAP YOU SILLY, KOTA...
ME AND HER, WE'RE BEST FRIENDS.

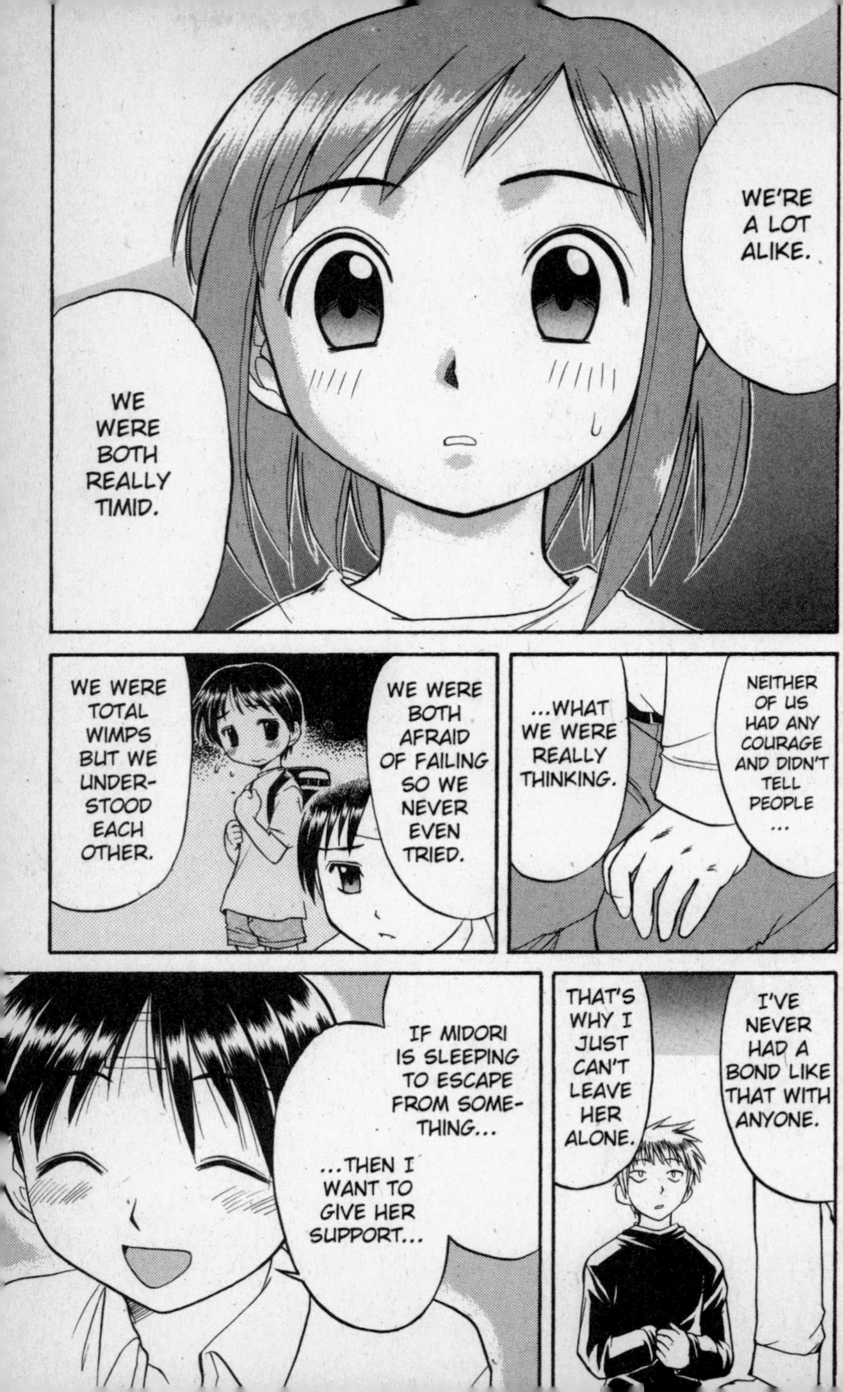
WE'RE A LOT ALIKE.
WE WERE BOTH REALLY TIMID.
NEITHER OF US HAD ANY COURAGE AND DIDN'T TELL PEOPLE ...
...WHAT WE WERE REALLY THINKING.
WE WERE BOTH AFRAID OF FAILING SO WE NEVER EVEN TRIED.
WE WERE TOTAL WIMPS BUT WE UNDER-STOOD EACH OTHER.
I'VE NEVER HAD A BOND LIKE THAT WITH ANYONE.
THAT'S WHY I JUST CAN'T LEAVE HER ALONE.
IF MIDORI IS SLEEPING TO ESCAPE FROM SOME-THING...
...THEN I WANT TO GIVE HER SUPPORT...

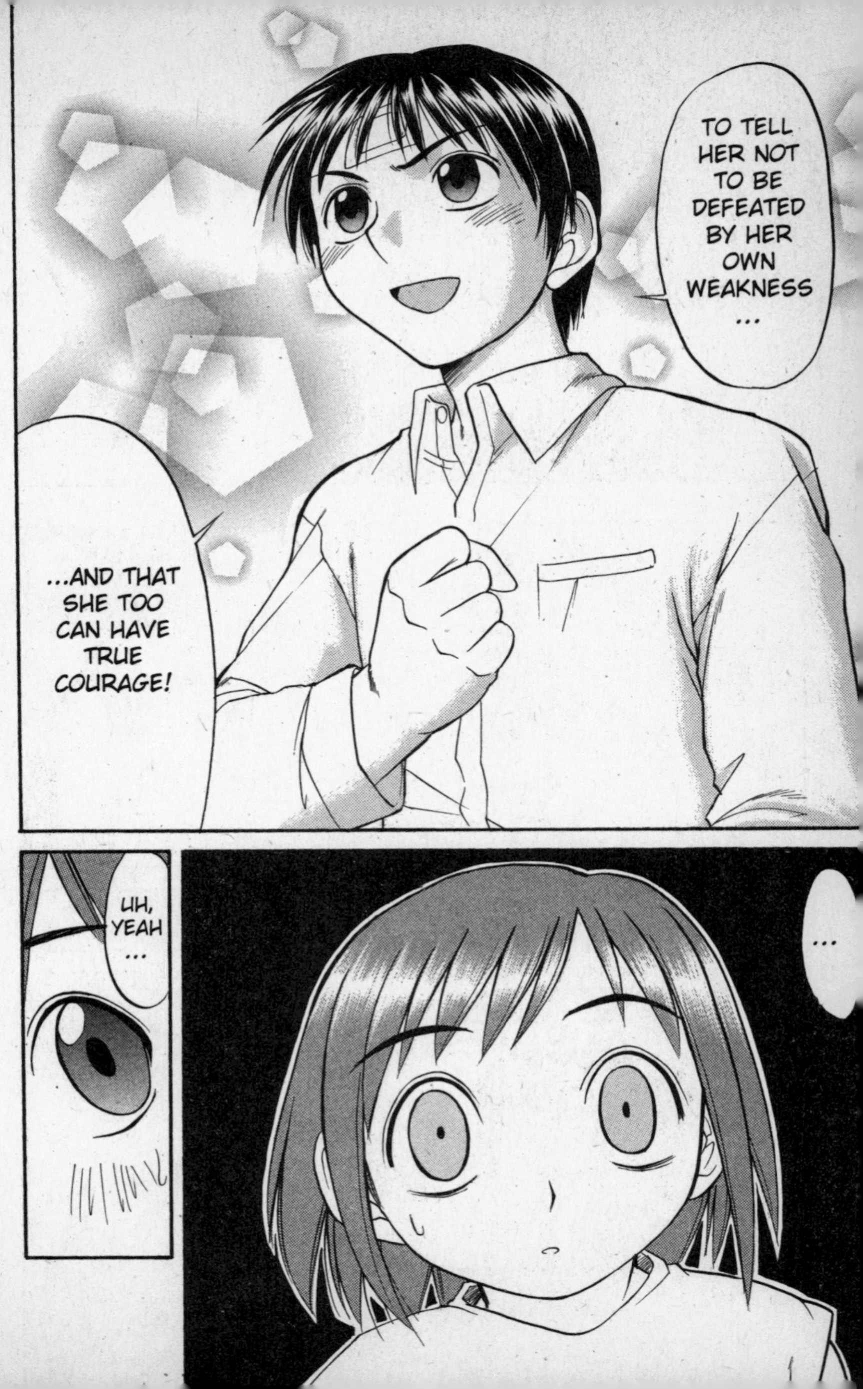
TO TELL HER NOT TO BE DEFEATED BY HER OWN WEAKNESS ...
...AND THAT SHE TOO CAN HAVE TRUE COURAGE!
...
UH, YEAH ...

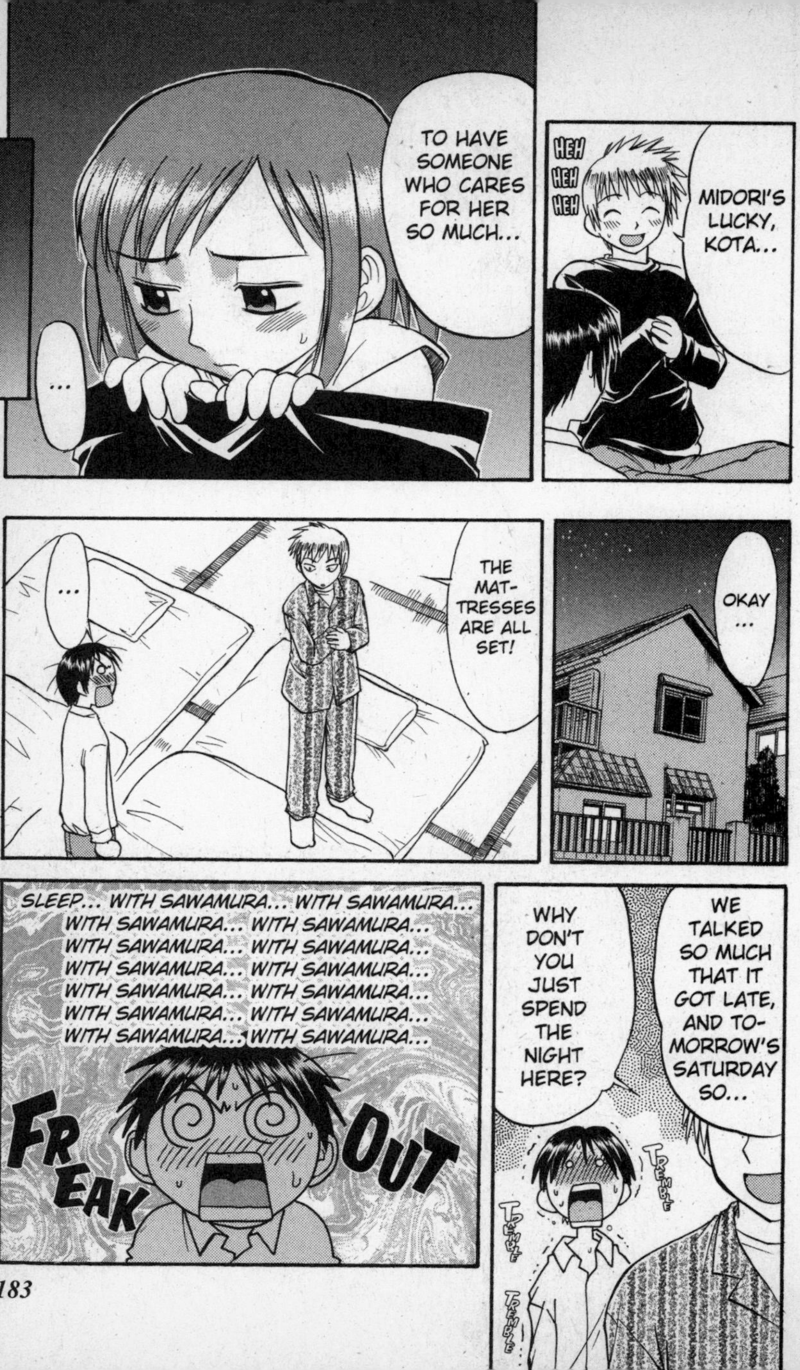
HEH HEH HEH
MIDORI'S LUCKY, KOTA...
TO HAVE SOMEONE WHO CARES FOR HER SO MUCH...
...
OKAY ...
THE MAT-TRESSES ARE ALL SET!
...
WE TALKED SO MUCH THAT IT GOT LATE, AND TO-MORROW'S SATURDAY SO...
WHY DON'T YOU JUST SPEND THE NIGHT HERE?
TREMBLE TREMBLE TREMBLE
SLEEP... WITH SAWAMURA... WITH SAWAMURA... WITH SAWAMURA... WITH SAWAMURA... WITH SAWAMURA... WITH SAWAMURA... WITH SAWAMURA... WITH SAWAMURA... WITH SAWAMURA... WITH SAWAMURA... WITH SAWAMURA... WITH SAWAMURA... WITH SAWAMURA... WITH SAWAMURA...
FREAK OUT

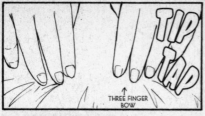

DUDE, I GOTTA SLEEP.
TIP TAP
THREE FINGER BOW
IT'S MY FIRST TIME. BE GENTLE OKAY?
FLUSH
...
URR
OHMIGOD, YOU HAD ME GOING FOR A SEC...
HA HA HA
CHUCKLE, CHUCKLE, GIGGLE...
HA HA
A JOKE? POOR KOTA, HE WASN'T JOKING AT ALL.
SNORE
SNORE

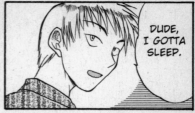

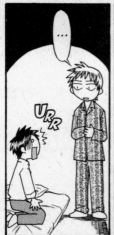

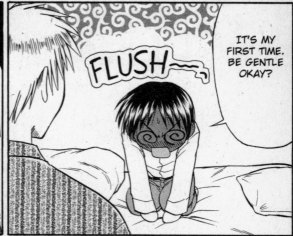

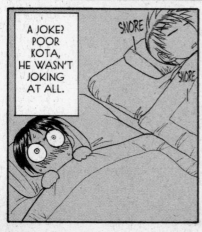

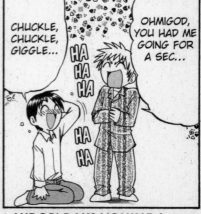

MIDORI DAYS VOLUME 4 THE END

A DISCONTINUOUS DELUSIONAL SUPPLEMENTARY COMIC STRIP

The days before "MIDORI DAYS"

BY KAZUROU INOUE

The story so far: Kazurou, a young aspiring cartoonist is in a rut, having his works rejected by the editors. One day, the comic God appears in front of him and tells him that his work lacks impact and eroticism...

Cast

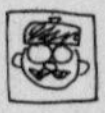

God
...
The God of Manga
Mighty guy.

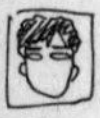

Kazurou
...
Loves zombies and worships Bronson.

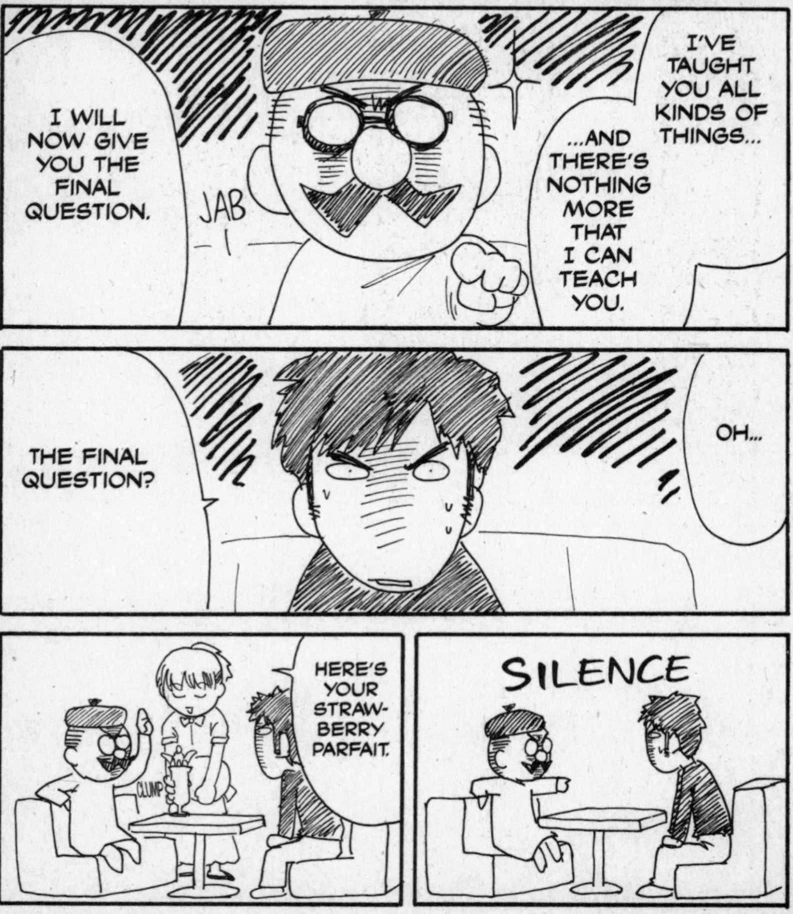
I'VE TAUGHT YOU ALL KINDS OF THINGS...
...AND THERE'S NOTHING MORE THAT I CAN TEACH YOU.
JAB
I WILL NOW GIVE YOU THE FINAL QUESTION.
OH...
THE FINAL QUESTION?
SILENCE
HERE'S YOUR STRAWBERRY PARFAIT.
CLUMP

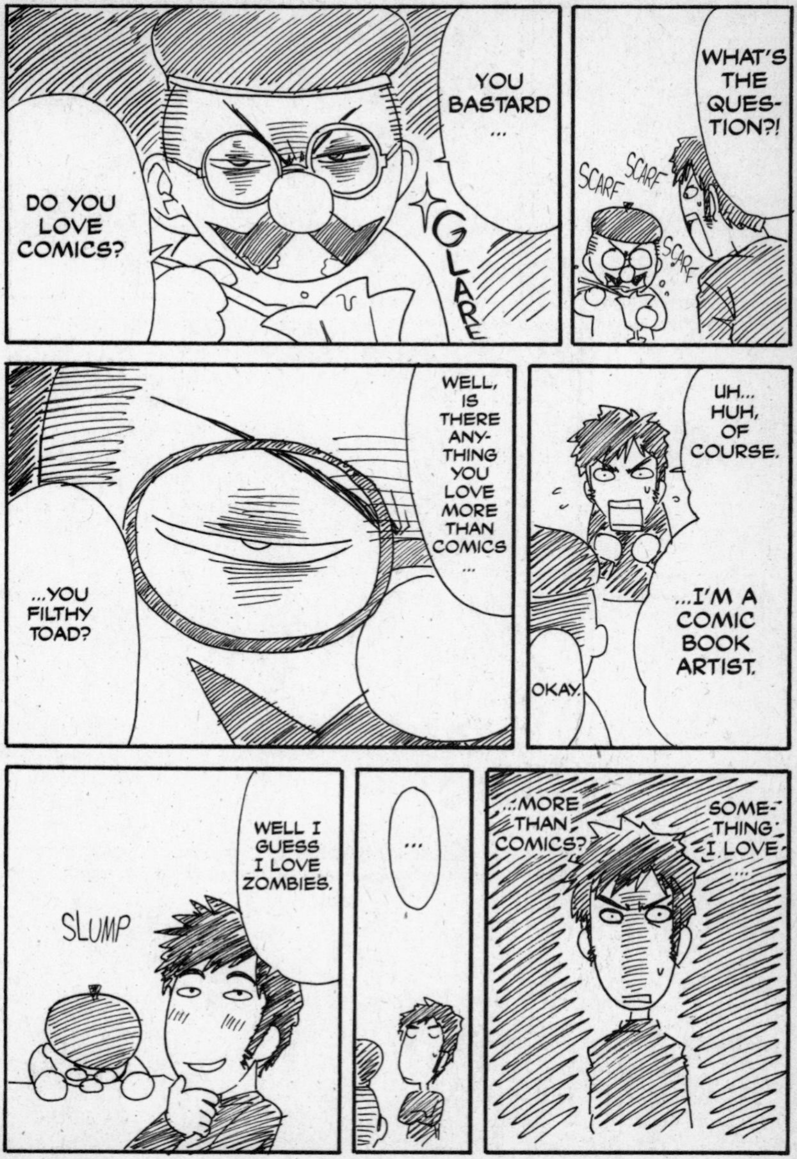
WHAT'S THE QUES-TION?!
SCARF
SCARF
SCARF
YOU BASTARD ...
GLARE
DO YOU LOVE COMICS?
UH... HUH, OF COURSE.
...I'M A COMIC BOOK ARTIST.
OKAY.
WELL, IS THERE ANY-THING YOU LOVE MORE THAN COMICS ...
...YOU FILTHY TOAD?
SOME-THING I LOVE ...
...MORE THAN COMICS?
...
WELL I GUESS I LOVE ZOMBIES.
SLUMP

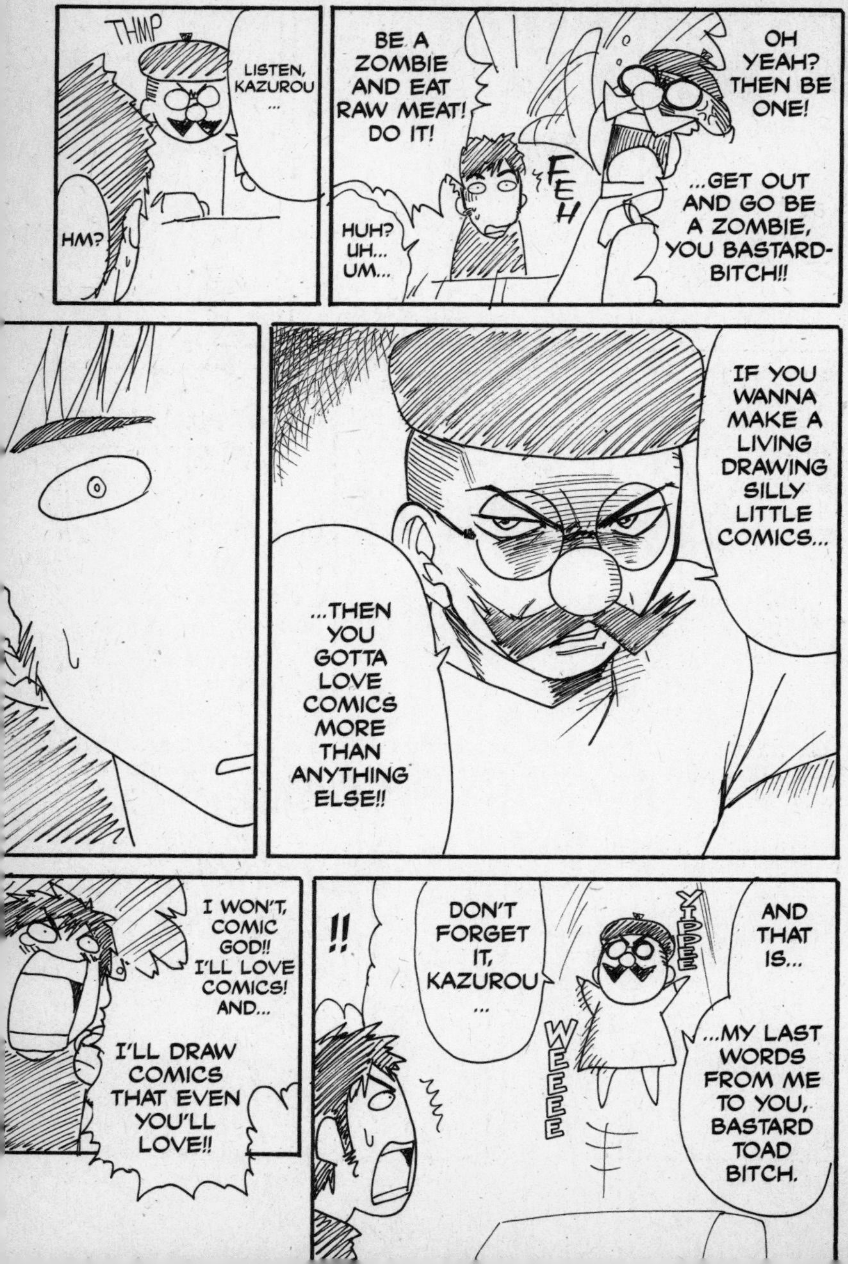
OH YEAH? THEN BE ONE!
BE A ZOMBIE AND EAT RAW MEAT! DO IT!
FEH
...GET OUT AND GO BE A ZOMBIE, YOU BASTARD-BITCH!!
HUH? UH... UM...
THMP
LISTEN, KAZUROU ...
HM?
IF YOU WANNA MAKE A LIVING DRAWING SILLY LITTLE COMICS...
...THEN YOU GOTTA LOVE COMICS MORE THAN ANYTHING ELSE!!
AND THAT IS...
YIPPEE
DON'T FORGET IT, KAZUROU ...
!!
...MY LAST WORDS FROM ME TO YOU, BASTARD TOAD BITCH.
WEEEE
I WON'T, COMIC GOD!! I'LL LOVE COMICS! AND...
I'LL DRAW COMICS THAT EVEN YOU'LL LOVE!!

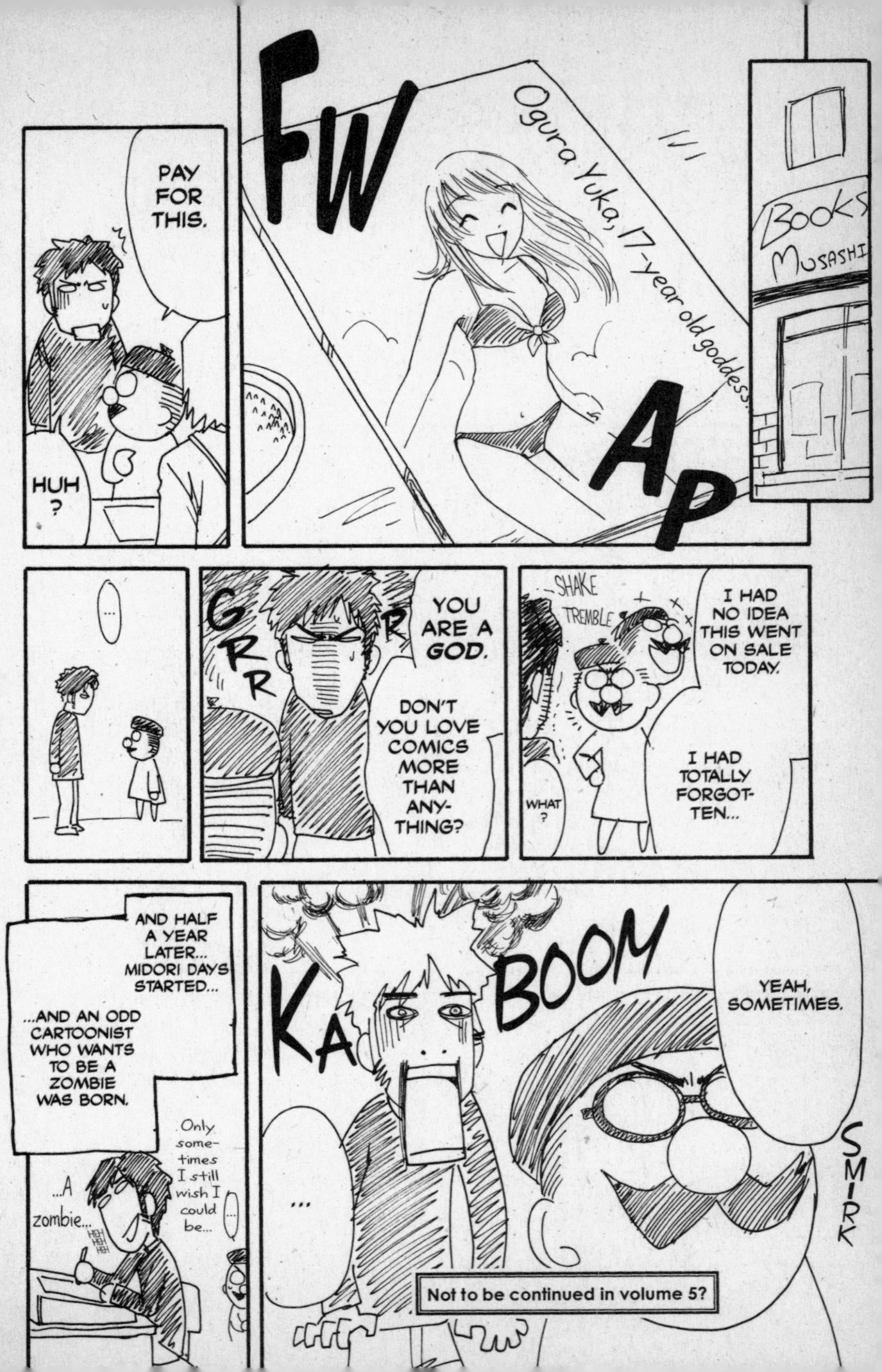
BOOKS
MUSASHI
Ogura Yuka, 17-year old goddess.
FWAP
PAY FOR THIS.
HUH?
SHAKE
TREMBLE
I HAD NO IDEA THIS WENT ON SALE TODAY.
I HAD TOTALLY FORGOT-TEN...
WHAT?
GRRR
YOU ARE A *GOD.*
DON'T YOU LOVE COMICS MORE THAN ANY-THING?
...
YEAH, SOMETIMES.
SMIRK
KABOOM
...
AND HALF A YEAR LATER... MIDORI DAYS STARTED...
...AND AN ODD CARTOONIST WHO WANTS TO BE A ZOMBIE WAS BORN.
Only sometimes I still wish I could be...
...A zombie...
HEH HEH HEH
...
Not to be continued in volume 5?

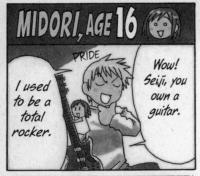

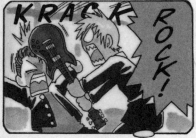

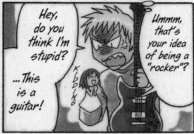

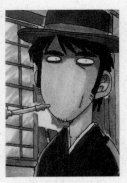

KAZUROU INOUE

Oh, my... Before I even realized it, I reached volume 4. When I spend my days having such fun with Seiji, Midori and the others, I tend to lose track of time and everything else. Not good...

...But I'm really enjoying this festival-like atmosphere. I hope all of you are having just as much fun with it as I am.

MIDORI, AGE 16
Wow! Seiji, you own a guitar.
PRIDE
I used to be a total rocker.
ROCK!
KRACK
Ummm, that's your idea of being a "rocker"?
Hey, do you think I'm stupid?
KIDDING
...This is a guitar!
You have to take advantage of its width.
BUWAHHN
Oh well... whatever...
...just play me a song.

Editor's Note:

I gotta admit, taking on *Midori Days* was a little intimidating. The original team did such a bang-up job. Plus the plot is NOT your typical tale of a high school romance.

Boy is lonely. Girl has crush on boy. Girl literally becomes boy's right HAND? How could anyone suspend enough disbelief to actually get into this story? But I read the first two volumes. And now I'm a fan as well as the new editor. Seiji & Midori and their supporting cast have sucked me into their bizarre little world. Traditional? Nah. Awesome? Totally.

Kazurou Inoue's imagination shines so bright it makes this one of the most original mangas I've come across in a while. His writing, his art: he makes this universe work.

You just believe.

And that's okay.

Isn't that really what good manga is all about? If you haven't done it yet, check out the first three volumes of the series. And keep reading… there's much more to this unusual little tale than you've seen so far. And if you need something to tide you over until volume 5, pick up *Tuxedo Gin* — it isn't a conventional love story either. And it has penguins.

Thanks for reading —

Joel Enos
Editor
Midori Days

LOVE MANGA? LET US KNOW!

☐ Please do NOT send me information about VIZ Media products, news and events, special offers, or other information.

☐ Please do NOT send me information from VIZ Media's trusted business partners.

Name: _____

Address: _____

City: _____ State: _____ Zip: _____

E-mail: _____

☐ Male ☐ Female Date of Birth (mm/dd/yyyy): ___ / ___ / ___ (Under 13? Parental consent required)

What race/ethnicity do you consider yourself? (check all that apply)

☐ White/Caucasian ☐ Black/African American ☐ Hispanic/Latino

☐ Asian/Pacific Islander ☐ Native American/Alaskan Native ☐ Other: _____

What VIZ Media title(s) did you purchase? (indicate title(s) purchased) _____

_____

What other VIZ Media titles do you own? _____

_____

Reason for purchase: (check all that apply)

☐ Special offer ☐ Favorite title / author / artist / genre

☐ Gift ☐ Recommendation ☐ Collection

☐ Read excerpt in VIZ Media manga sampler ☐ Other _____

Where did you make your purchase? (please check one)

☐ Comic store ☐ Bookstore ☐ Grocery Store

☐ Convention ☐ Newsstand ☐ Video Game Store

☐ Online (site:_____) ☐ Other _____

How many manga titles have you purchased in the last year? How many were VIZ Media titles?
(please check one from each column)

MANGA	VIZ Media
☐ None	☐ None
☐ 1 – 4	☐ 1 – 4
☐ 5 – 10	☐ 5 – 10
☐ 11+	☐ 11+

How much influence do special promotions and gifts-with-purchase have on the titles you buy?
(please circle, with 5 being great influence and 1 being none)

1 2 3 4 5

Do you purchase every volume of your favorite series?

☐ Yes! Gotta have 'em as my own ☐ No. Please explain: ______________________

What kind of manga storylines do you most enjoy? (check all that apply)

☐ Action / Adventure
☐ Comedy
☐ Fighting
☐ Artistic / Alternative
☐ Science Fiction
☐ Romance (shojo)
☐ Sports
☐ Other ______________________
☐ Horror
☐ Fantasy (shojo)
☐ Historical

If you watch the anime or play a video or TCG game from a series, how likely are you to buy the manga? (please circle, with 5 being very likely and 1 being unlikely)

1 2 3 4 5

If unlikely, please explain: ______________________

Who are your favorite authors / artists? ______________________

____

What titles would like you translated and sold in English? ______________________

____

THANK YOU! Please send the completed form to:

VIZ media™

NJW Research
42 Catharine Street
Poughkeepsie, NY 12601

Your privacy is very important to us. All information provided will be used for internal purposes only and will not be sold or otherwise divulged.